W9-CJR-103

"*Octopus Pie* is the perfect mix of plot and punch lines."
—HOPE LARSON, author of *Mercury* and *Chiggers*

"The wit is sharp, the pace fresh, and the art as inventive and rewarding as in any classic pulp series." —NICK DOUGLAS, editor of *Twitter Wit*

"Gran is proving to be one of the brightest new voices in comics."
—KAZU KIBUISHI, co-creator of *Flight*

"*Octopus Pie* is made from two cups of Brooklyn, half an ounce of strawberry cough, a dram of grim desperation, all of your most embarrassing childhood memories, a splash of genius, and a teaspoon of love. Plus one seriously pissed-off octopus, I would imagine. It is my favorite comic entity."
—JONATHAN ROSENBERG, author of Goats: The Infinite Pendergast Cycle

Octopus Pie

There Are No Stars in Brooklyn

Meredith Gran

Villard Trade Paperbacks • New York

Octopus Pie: There Are No Stars in Brooklyn is a work of fiction. Names, characters, places, and incidents are the products of the author's imagination or are used fictitiously. Any resemblance to actual events, locales, or persons, living or dead, is entirely coincidental.

A Villard Books Trade Paperback Original

Copyright © 2010 by Meredith Gran

All rights reserved.

Published in the United States by Villard Books, an imprint of The Random House Publishing Group, a division of Random House, Inc., New York.

VILLARD BOOKS and VILLARD & "V" CIRCLED Design are registered trademarks of Random House, Inc.

"Effnocka" character by Ian Jones-Quartey appears here by permission of the creator, copyright © 2007 by Ian Jones-Quartey.

Printed in China

ISBN 978-0-345-52043-2

www.octopuspie.com
www.delreybooks.com

9 8 7 6 5 4 3 2 1

Designed by Meredith Gran and Richard Stevens

To Jackie & Joe

Thank-yous are in order to Rich Stevens, Jon Rosenberg, Judy Hansen,
and the countless friends, colleagues, and fans who've offered their support
from day one. It's good to have you.

Octopus Pie

introductions

UNCOMFORTABLE, OVERCROWDED, OVER-PRICED, OVER-MARKETED.

OLLY'S ORGANIX

PUSHY, OBNOXIOUS, INCOMPETENT PEOPLE RUSHING AROUND IN CRAMPED TIN CANS.

TRASH. NEW YORK IS UTTER *TRASH*.

WELL, WHY DO YOU LIVE HERE, THEN?

ARE YOU KIDDING?

HAVE YOU SEEN THE *REST* OF THE COUNTRY?

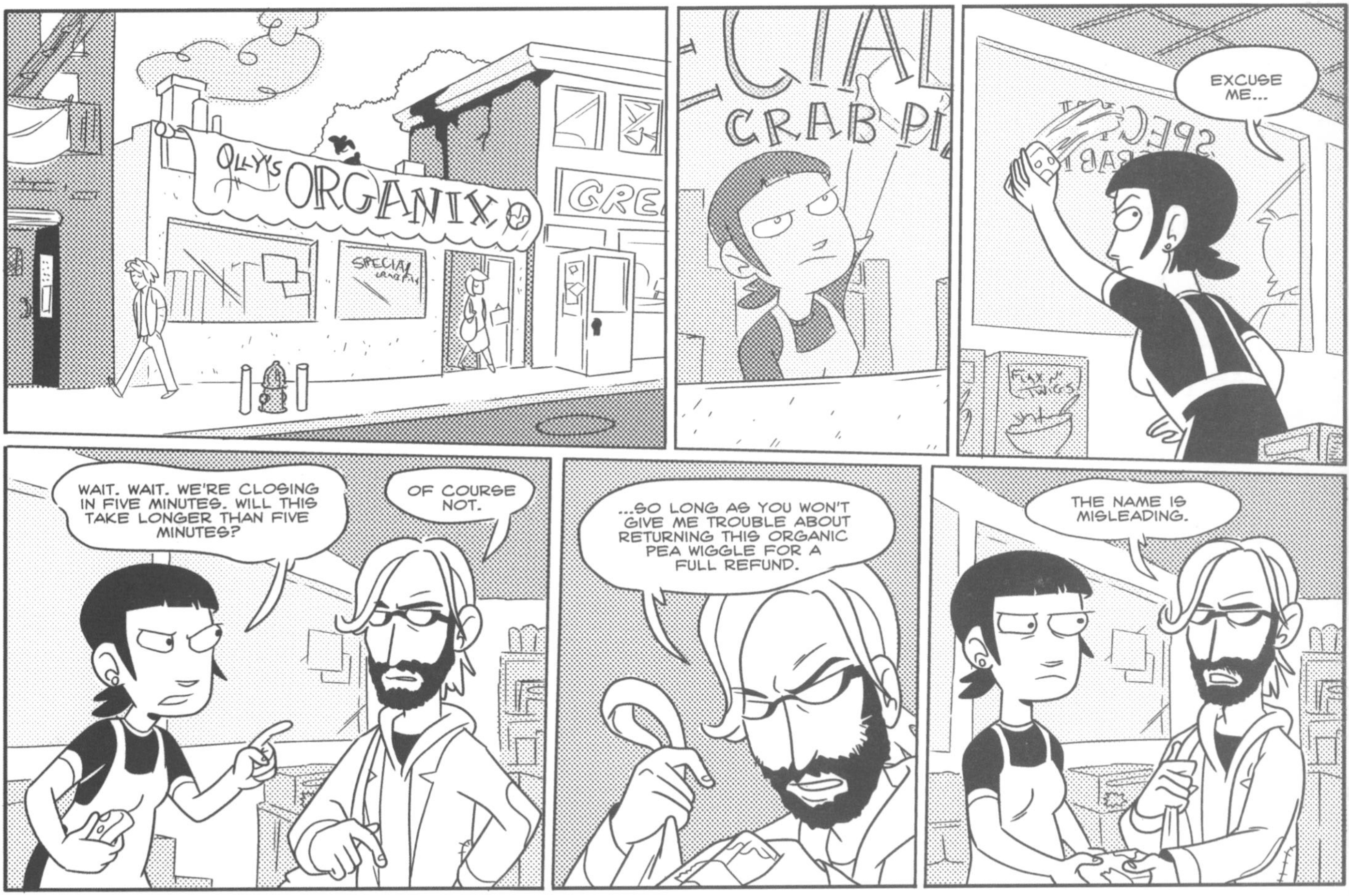
OLLY'S ORGANIX
SPECIAL
CRAB PI
EXCUSE ME...
WAIT. WAIT. WE'RE CLOSING IN FIVE MINUTES. WILL THIS TAKE LONGER THAN FIVE MINUTES?
OF COURSE NOT.
...SO LONG AS YOU WON'T GIVE ME TROUBLE ABOUT RETURNING THIS ORGANIC PEA WIGGLE FOR A FULL REFUND.
THE NAME IS MISLEADING.

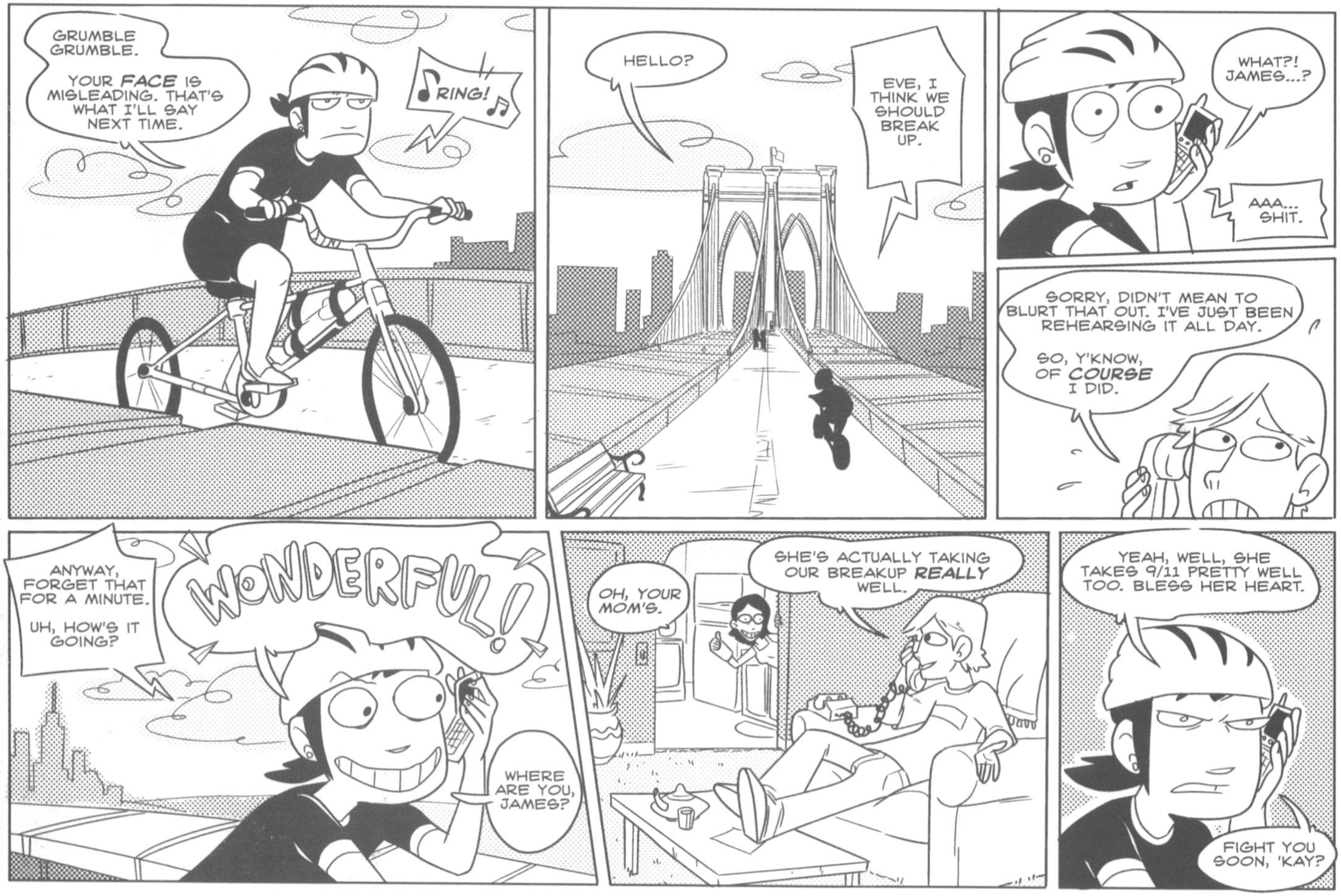
GRUMBLE GRUMBLE.
YOUR FACE IS MISLEADING. THAT'S WHAT I'LL SAY NEXT TIME.
RING!
HELLO?
EVE, I THINK WE SHOULD BREAK UP.
WHAT?! JAMES...?
AAA... SHIT.
SORRY, DIDN'T MEAN TO BLURT THAT OUT. I'VE JUST BEEN REHEARSING IT ALL DAY.
SO, Y'KNOW, OF COURSE I DID.
ANYWAY, FORGET THAT FOR A MINUTE.
UH, HOW'S IT GOING?
WONDERFUL!
WHERE ARE YOU, JAMES?
OH, YOUR MOM'S.
SHE'S ACTUALLY TAKING OUR BREAKUP REALLY WELL.
YEAH, WELL, SHE TAKES 9/11 PRETTY WELL TOO. BLESS HER HEART.
FIGHT YOU SOON, 'KAY?

AND I MEAN, THE FACT IS THAT BILLIONS OF UNIVERSES EXIST WHERE EVE AND I *AREN'T* DATING. WE MAINLY EXIST TO BE BROKEN UP FOREVER, Y'KNOW?

AND LIKE, YOU CAN TOTALLY APPLY THAT TO LIFE AND DEATH. EVERYTHING'S JUST A BLIP ON THE RADAR. SOMETIMES I'LL JUST SIT FOR HOURS WONDERING IF ANYTHING I DO MAKES ANY DIFFERENCE AT ALL.

MAN, LIKE GUYS ARGUIN INTERNET FORUMS? Y SCRABBLE OR S OU'RE JUST THROW HUMAN-DERIVED VO & ONE MOTHERFUC TELL ME I WAS LA SEE THE REALITY O COULD GO ON AND TERALLY FOR DAYS

MEAN THIS TEA IS OUS BUT IT'S ALMO N WORTH NOTING, S A BIG MUG OF WAT HINGS WE CAN HAR MORE THAN DUST ENSE UNIVERSE WE DED BY. WHO'S TO TS BEYON MIGHT HAVE

ALL RIGHT, STEVEN SCHPIELBERG. OUT WE GO.

BUT I'M NOT DONE SCHPIELING!

DON'T BE SILLY. YOU'VE ALREADY SHOWN ME THE LIGHT!

I HAVE? REALLY?

HELL YES. *NO MORE EXISTENTIAL BOYFRIENDS!!*

SLAM!

NOT EVEN IN THE MULTIVERSE?

NEVER!

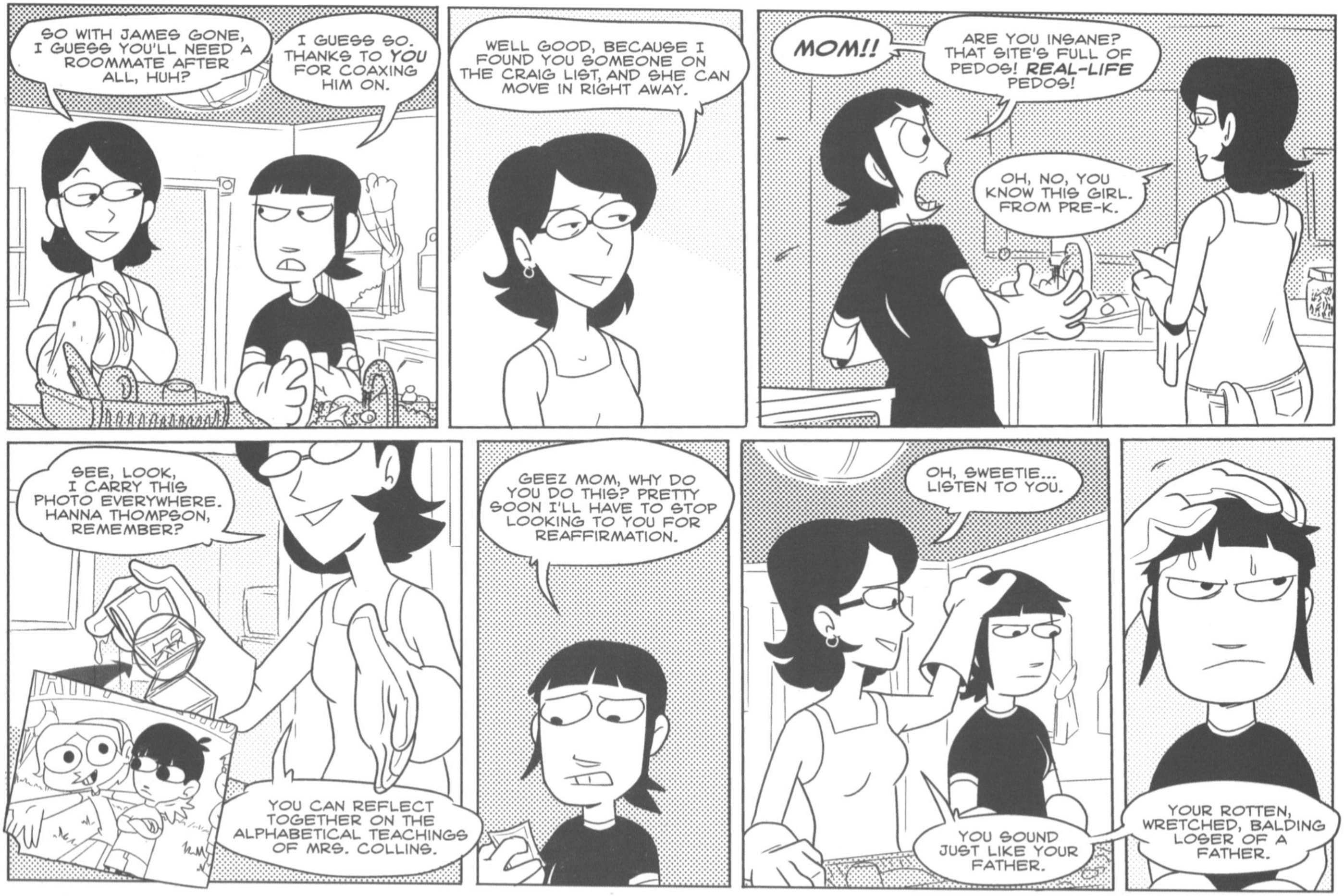
SO WITH JAMES GONE, I GUESS YOU'LL NEED A ROOMMATE AFTER ALL, HUH?
I GUESS SO. THANKS TO YOU FOR COAXING HIM ON.
WELL GOOD, BECAUSE I FOUND YOU SOMEONE ON THE CRAIG LIST, AND SHE CAN MOVE IN RIGHT AWAY.
MOM!!
ARE YOU INSANE? THAT SITE'S FULL OF PEDOS! REAL-LIFE PEDOS!
OH, NO, YOU KNOW THIS GIRL. FROM PRE-K.
SEE, LOOK, I CARRY THIS PHOTO EVERYWHERE. HANNA THOMPSON, REMEMBER?
YOU CAN REFLECT TOGETHER ON THE ALPHABETICAL TEACHINGS OF MRS. COLLINS.
GEEZ MOM, WHY DO YOU DO THIS? PRETTY SOON I'LL HAVE TO STOP LOOKING TO YOU FOR REAFFIRMATION.
OH, SWEETIE... LISTEN TO YOU.
YOU SOUND JUST LIKE YOUR FATHER.
YOUR ROTTEN, WRETCHED, BALDING LOSER OF A FATHER.

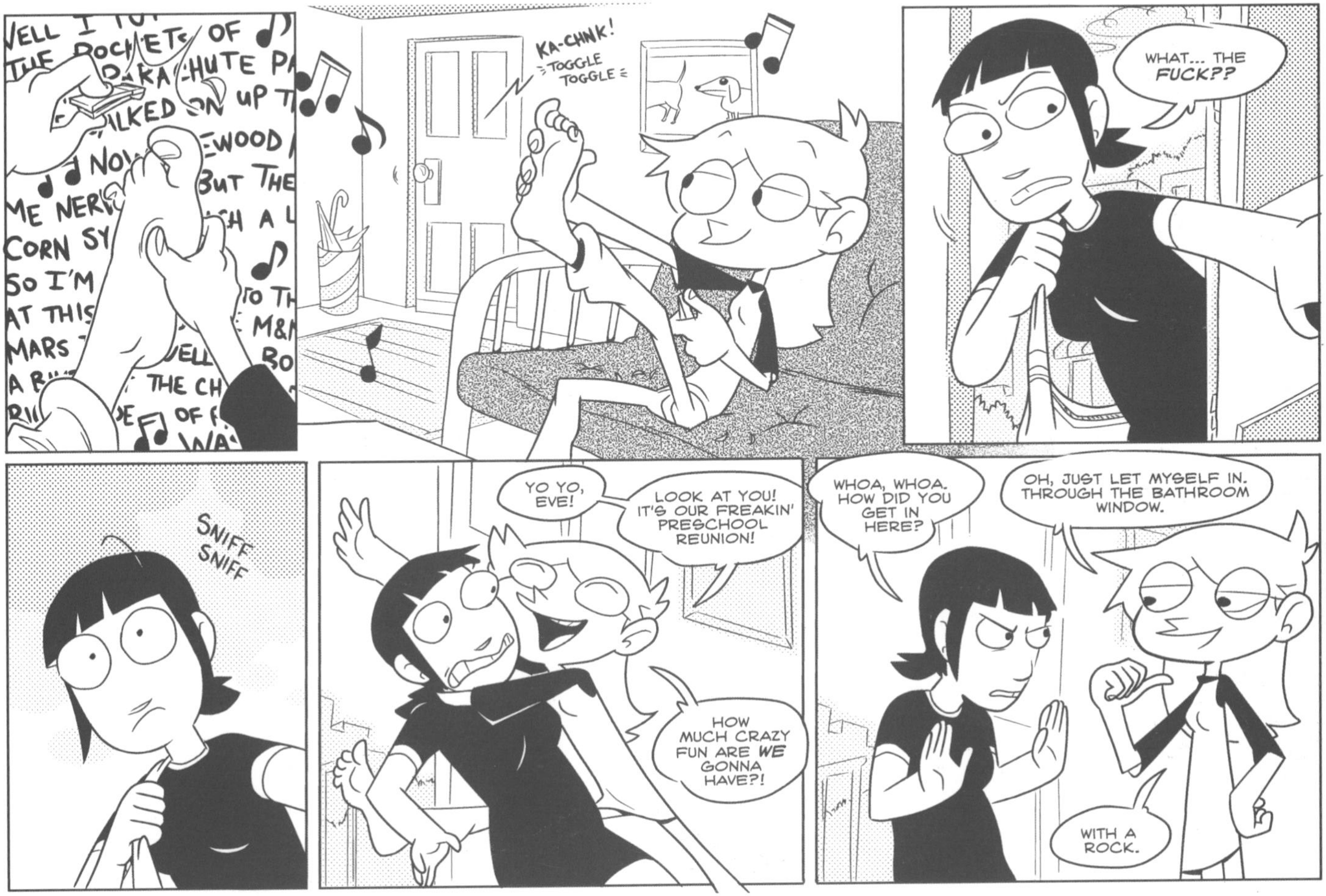
KA-CHINK!
TOGGLE TOGGLE
WHAT... THE FUCK??
SNIFF SNIFF
YO YO, EVE!
LOOK AT YOU! IT'S OUR FREAKIN' PRESCHOOL REUNION!
HOW MUCH CRAZY FUN ARE WE GONNA HAVE?!
WHOA, WHOA. HOW DID YOU GET IN HERE?
OH, JUST LET MYSELF IN. THROUGH THE BATHROOM WINDOW.
WITH A ROCK.

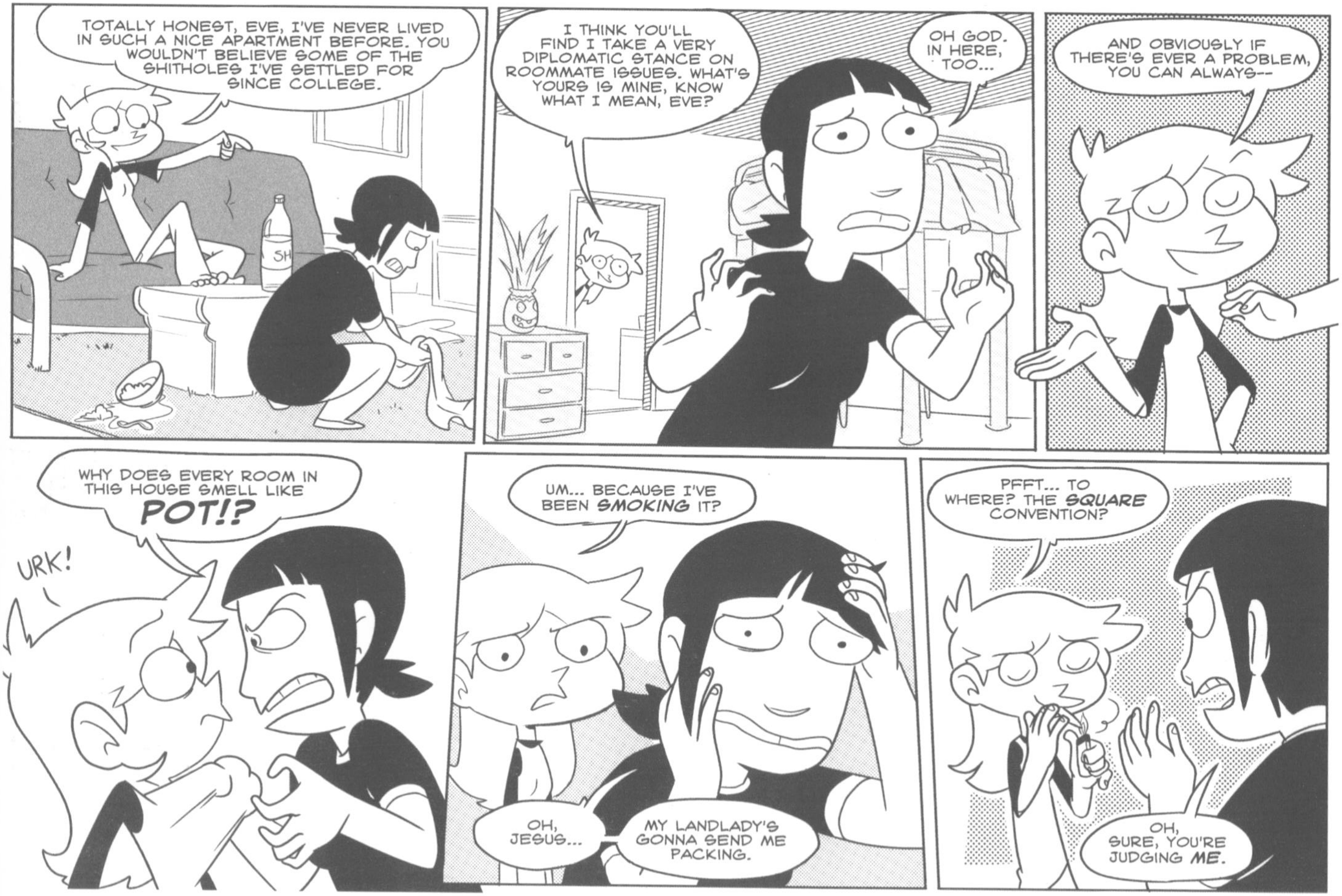
TOTALLY HONEST, EVE, I'VE NEVER LIVED IN SUCH A NICE APARTMENT BEFORE. YOU WOULDN'T BELIEVE SOME OF THE SHITHOLES I'VE SETTLED FOR SINCE COLLEGE.
SH
I THINK YOU'LL FIND I TAKE A VERY DIPLOMATIC STANCE ON ROOMMATE ISSUES. WHAT'S YOURS IS MINE, KNOW WHAT I MEAN, EVE?
OH GOD. IN HERE, TOO...
AND OBVIOUSLY IF THERE'S EVER A PROBLEM, YOU CAN ALWAYS--
WHY DOES EVERY ROOM IN THIS HOUSE SMELL LIKE POT!?
URK!
UM... BECAUSE I'VE BEEN SMOKING IT?
OH, JESUS...
MY LANDLADY'S GONNA SEND ME PACKING.
PFFT... TO WHERE? THE SQUARE CONVENTION?
OH, SURE, YOU'RE JUDGING ME.

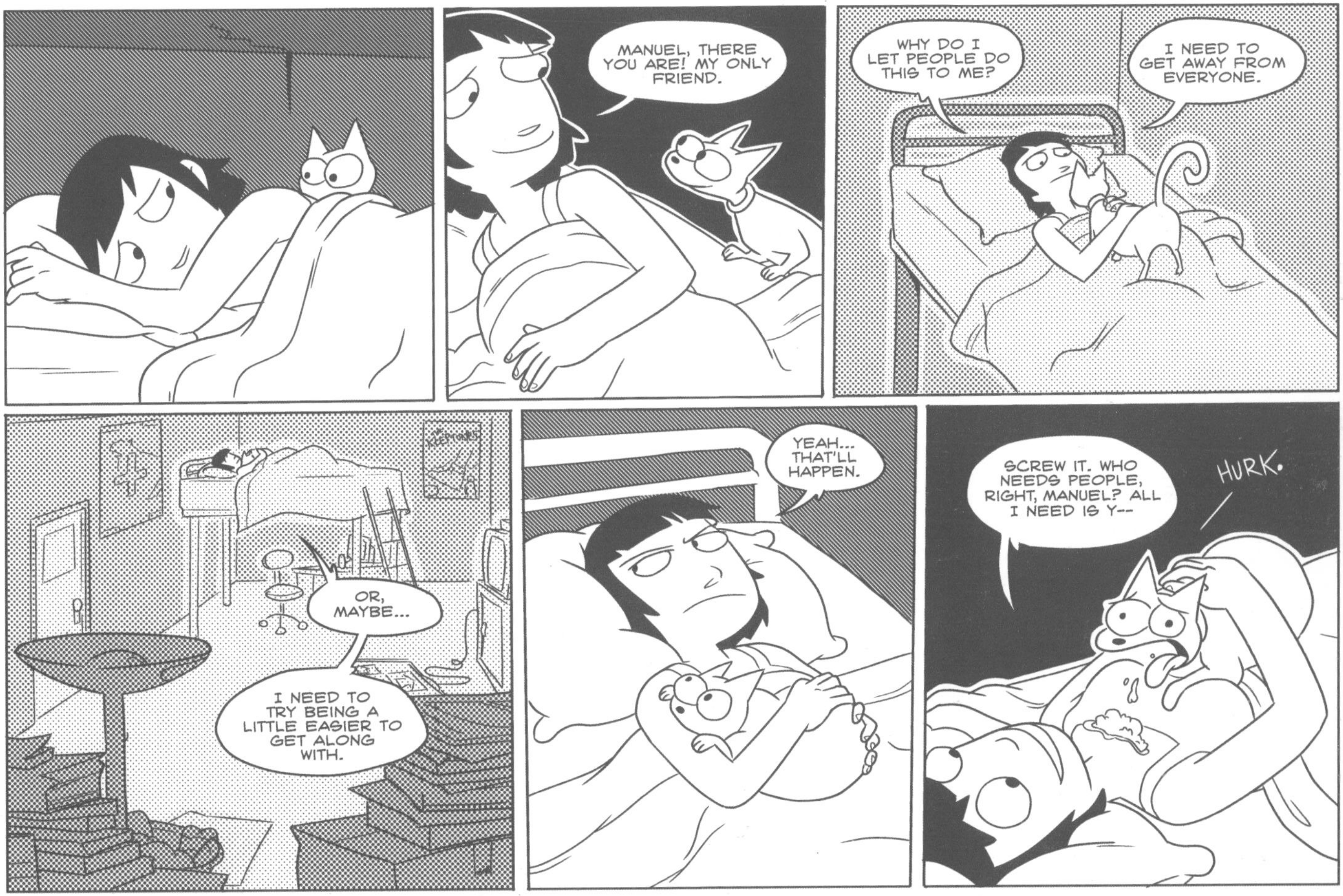
MANUEL, THERE YOU ARE! MY ONLY FRIEND.
WHY DO I LET PEOPLE DO THIS TO ME?
I NEED TO GET AWAY FROM EVERYONE.
OR, MAYBE...
I NEED TO TRY BEING A LITTLE EASIER TO GET ALONG WITH.
YEAH... THAT'LL HAPPEN.
SCREW IT. WHO NEEDS PEOPLE, RIGHT, MANUEL? ALL I NEED IS Y--
HURK.

bicycle rights

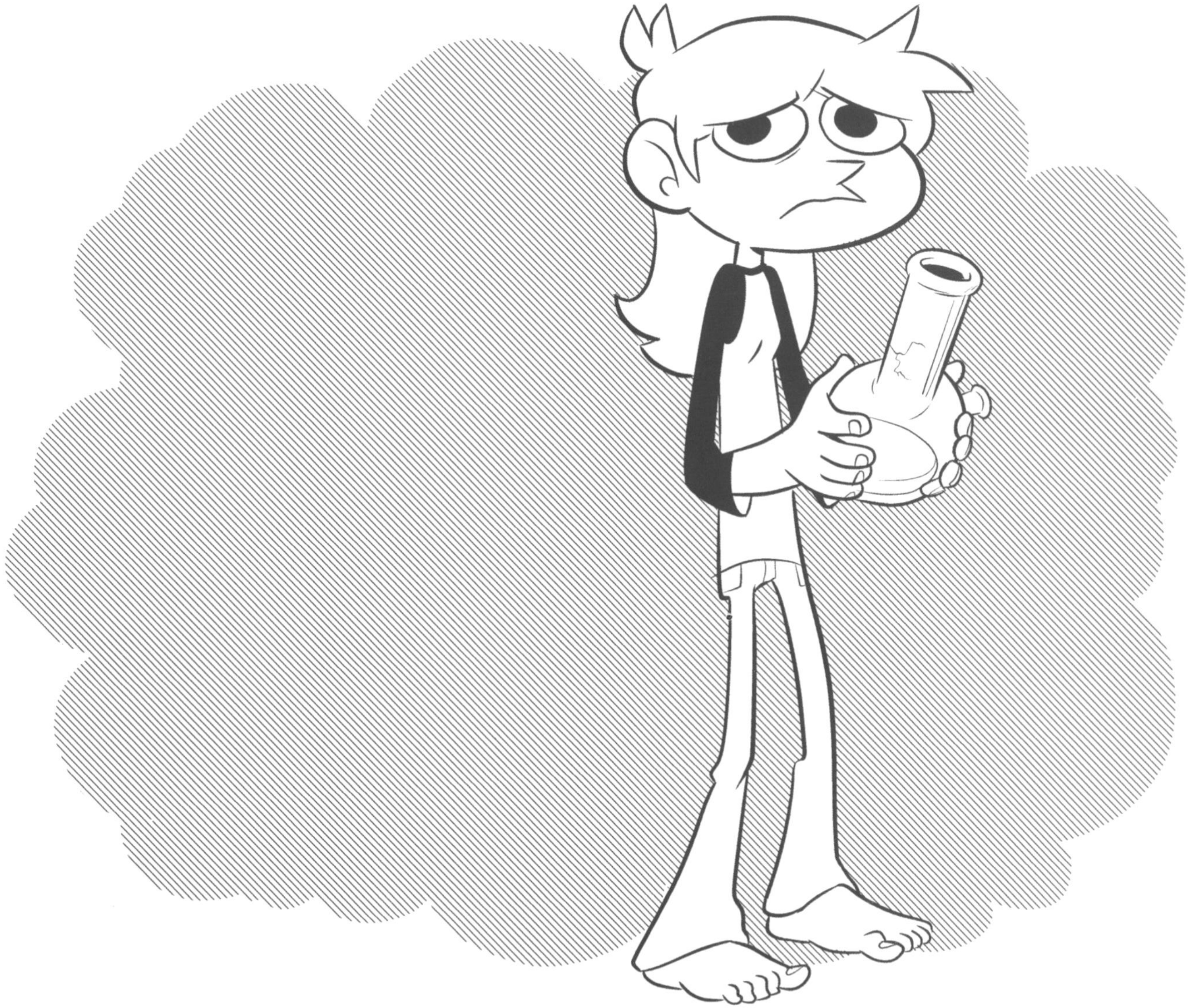

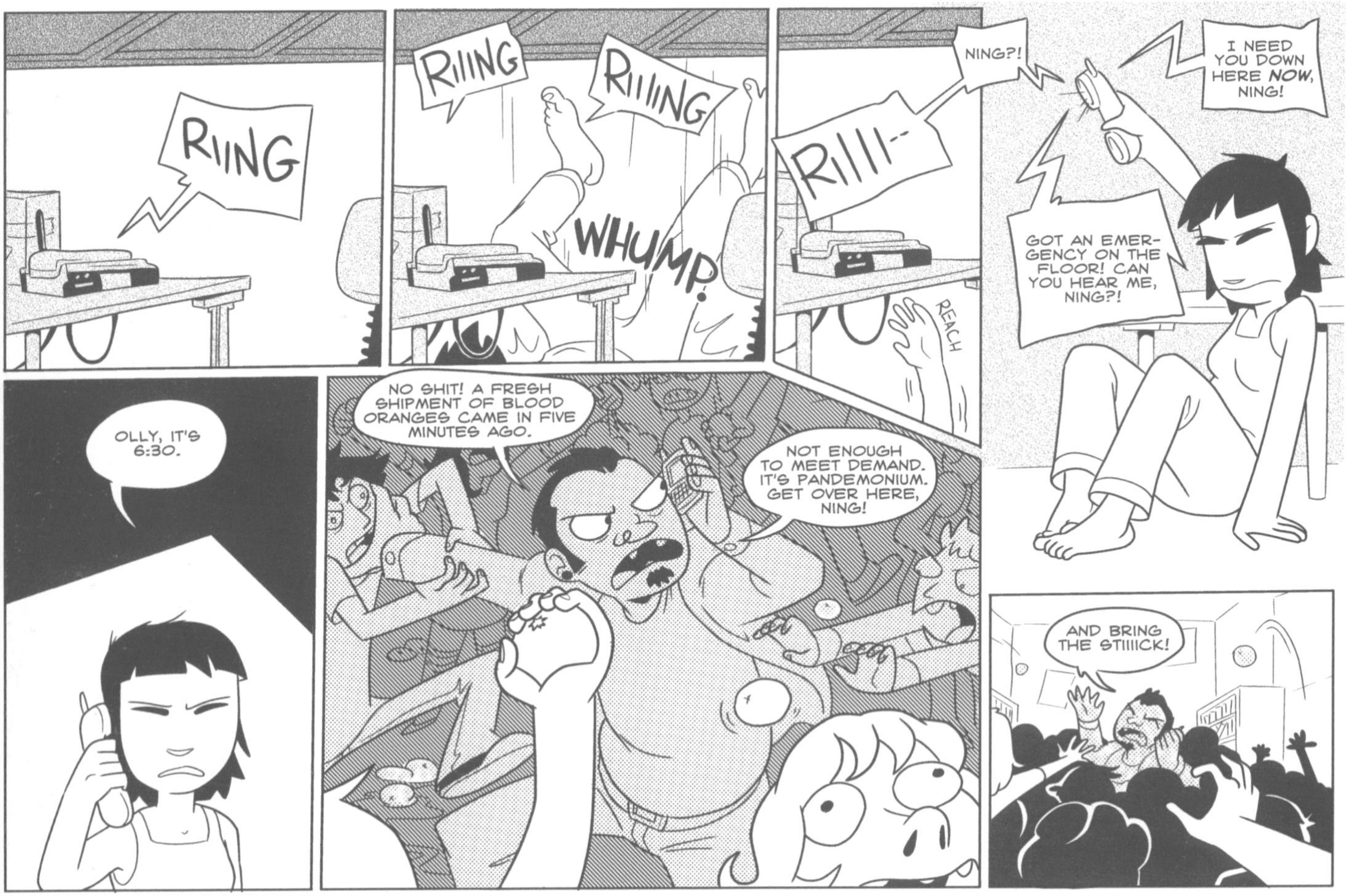
RIING
RIIING
RIIIING
WHUMP!
RIIII--
REACH
NING?!
I NEED YOU DOWN HERE NOW, NING!
GOT AN EMERGENCY ON THE FLOOR! CAN YOU HEAR ME, NING?!
OLLY, IT'S 6:30.
NO SHIT! A FRESH SHIPMENT OF BLOOD ORANGES CAME IN FIVE MINUTES AGO.
NOT ENOUGH TO MEET DEMAND. IT'S PANDEMONIUM. GET OVER HERE, NING!
AND BRING THE STIIIICK!

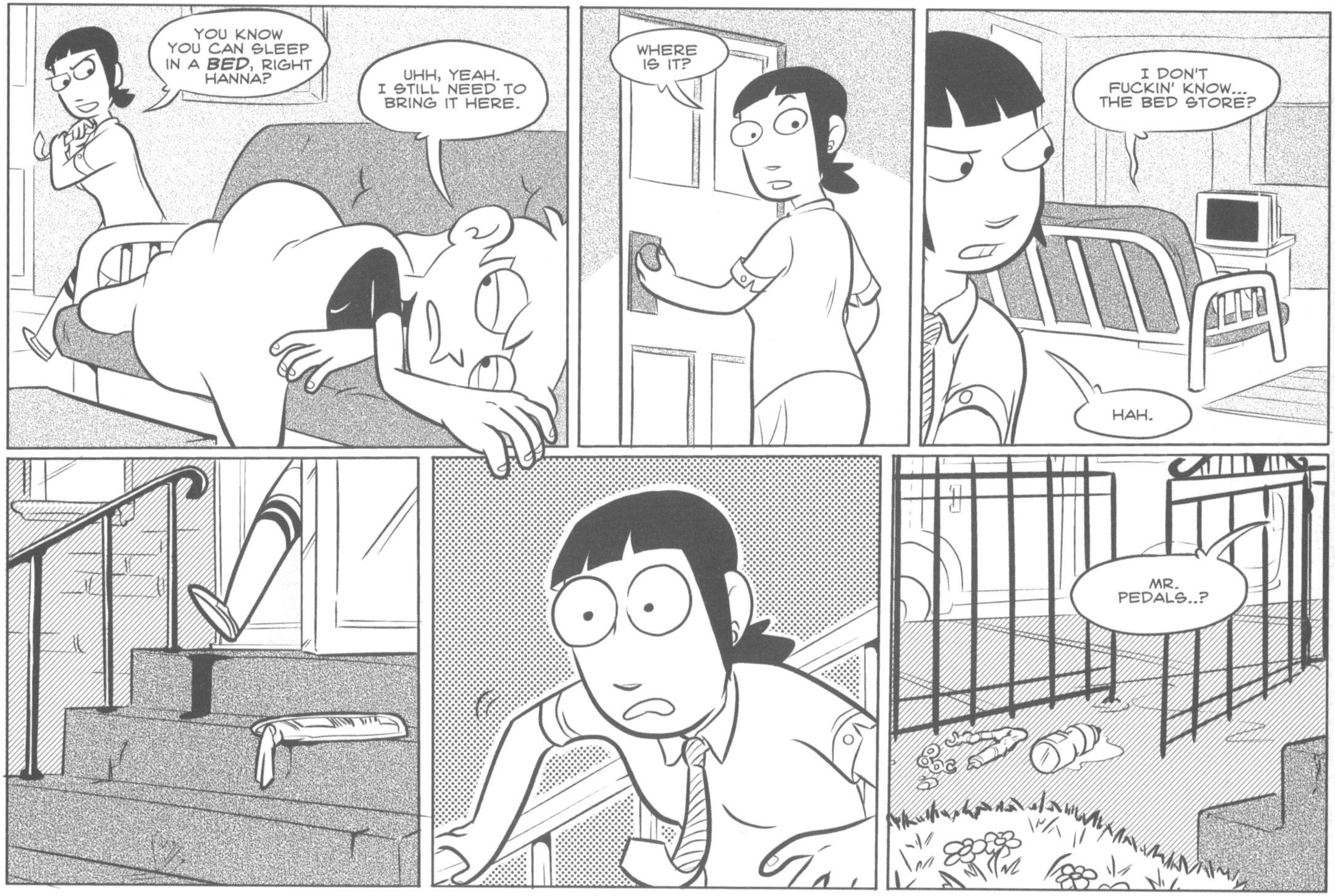
YOU KNOW YOU CAN SLEEP IN A BED, RIGHT HANNA?
UHH, YEAH. I STILL NEED TO BRING IT HERE.
WHERE IS IT?
I DON'T FUCKIN' KNOW... THE BED STORE?
HAH.
MR. PEDALS..?

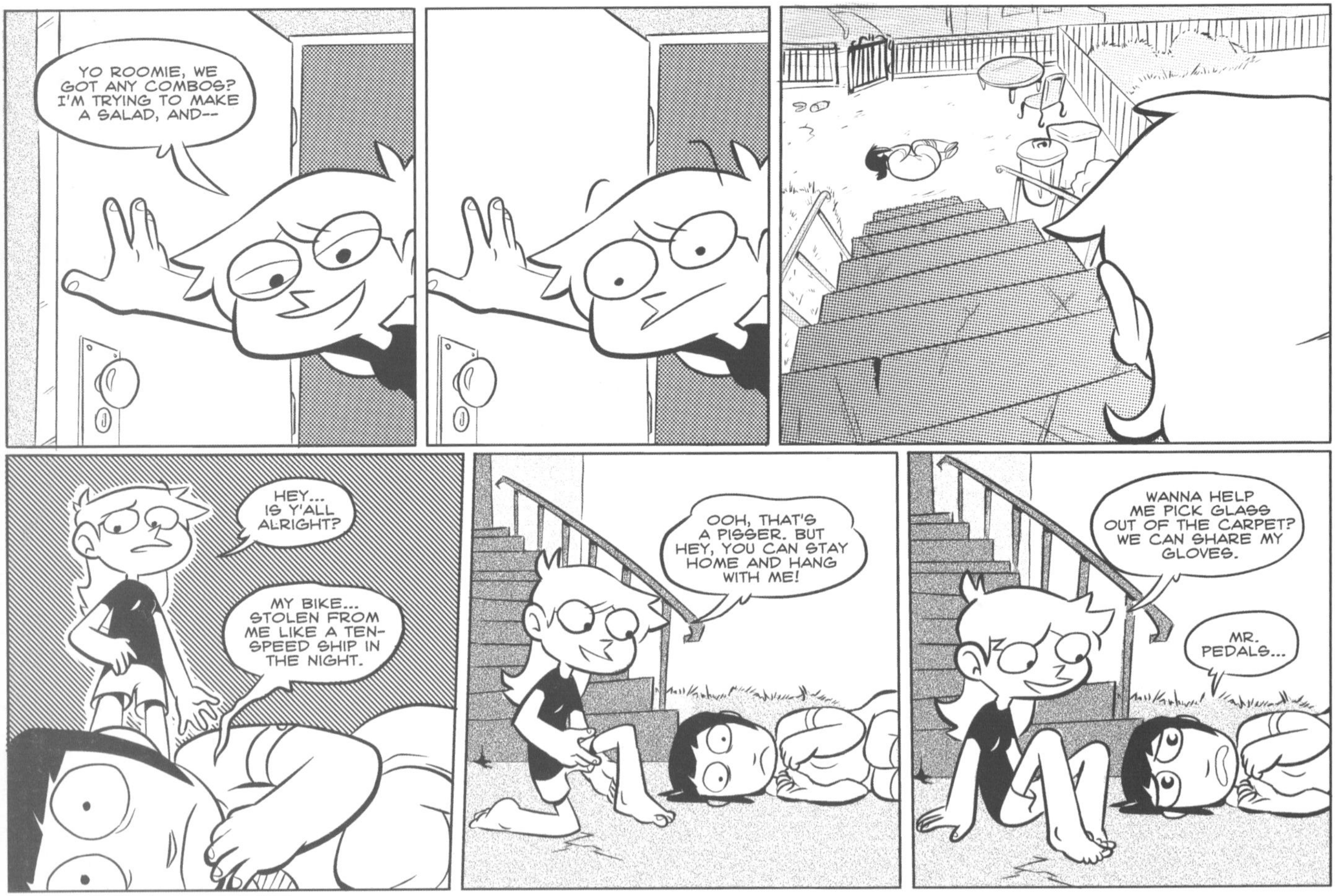
YO ROOMIE, WE GOT ANY COMBOS? I'M TRYING TO MAKE A SALAD, AND--
HEY... IS Y'ALL ALRIGHT?
MY BIKE... STOLEN FROM ME LIKE A TEN-SPEED SHIP IN THE NIGHT.
OOH, THAT'S A PISSER. BUT HEY, YOU CAN STAY HOME AND HANG WITH ME!
WANNA HELP ME PICK GLASS OUT OF THE CARPET? WE CAN SHARE MY GLOVES.
MR. PEDALS...

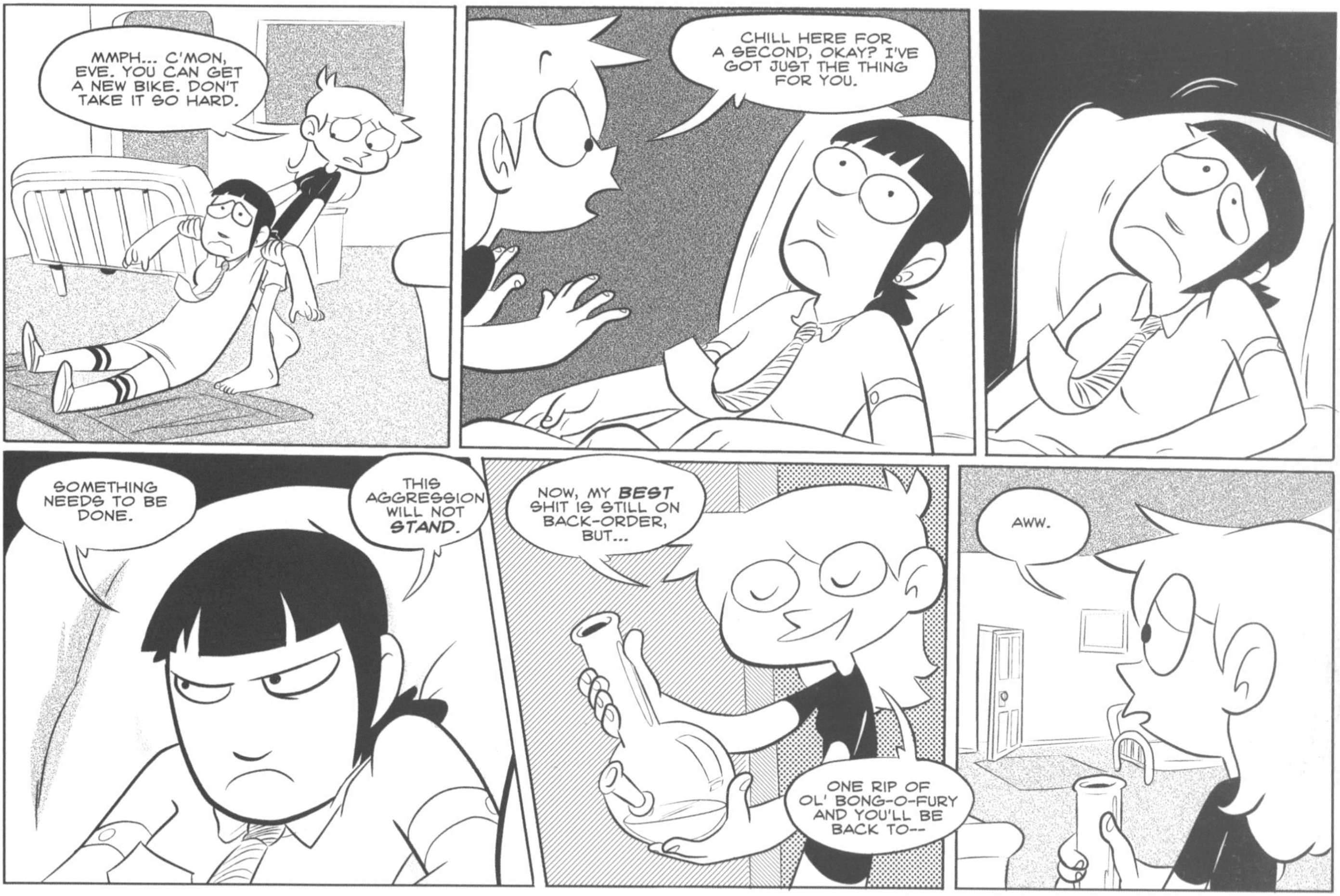
MMPH... C'MON, EVE. YOU CAN GET A NEW BIKE. DON'T TAKE IT SO HARD.
CHILL HERE FOR A SECOND, OKAY? I'VE GOT JUST THE THING FOR YOU.
SOMETHING NEEDS TO BE DONE.
THIS AGGRESSION WILL NOT ***STAND.***
NOW, MY ***BEST*** SHIT IS STILL ON BACK-ORDER, BUT...
ONE RIP OF OL' BONG-O-FURY AND YOU'LL BE BACK TO--
AWW.

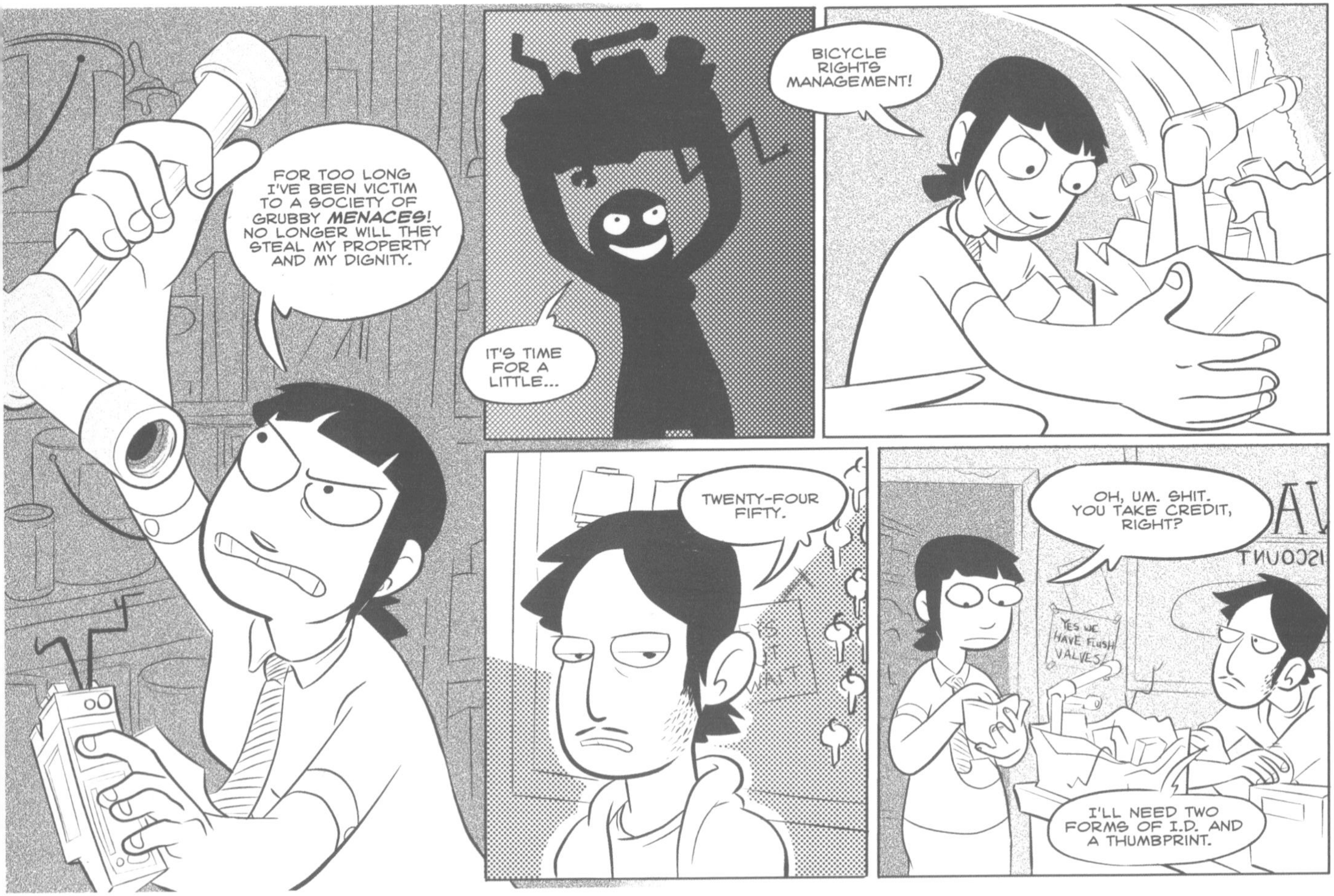
FOR TOO LONG I'VE BEEN VICTIM TO A SOCIETY OF GRUBBY MENACES! NO LONGER WILL THEY STEAL MY PROPERTY AND MY DIGNITY.
IT'S TIME FOR A LITTLE...
BICYCLE RIGHTS MANAGEMENT!
TWENTY-FOUR FIFTY.
OH, UM. SHIT. YOU TAKE CREDIT, RIGHT?
YES WE HAVE FLUSH VALVES!
I'LL NEED TWO FORMS OF I.D. AND A THUMBPRINT.

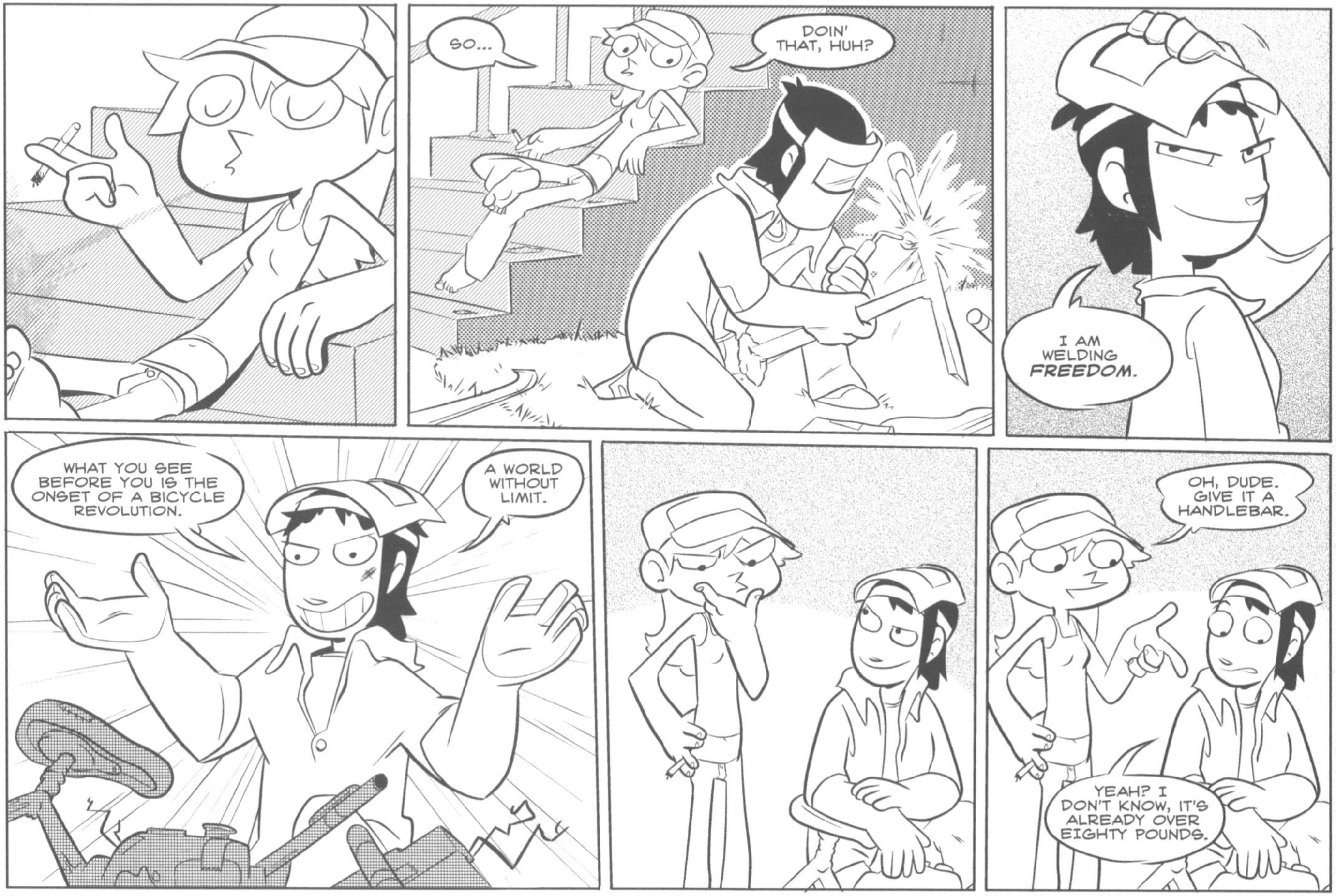
SO...
DOIN' THAT, HUH?
I AM WELDING FREEDOM.
WHAT YOU SEE BEFORE YOU IS THE ONSET OF A BICYCLE REVOLUTION.
A WORLD WITHOUT LIMIT.
OH, DUDE. GIVE IT A HANDLEBAR.
YEAH? I DON'T KNOW, IT'S ALREADY OVER EIGHTY POUNDS.

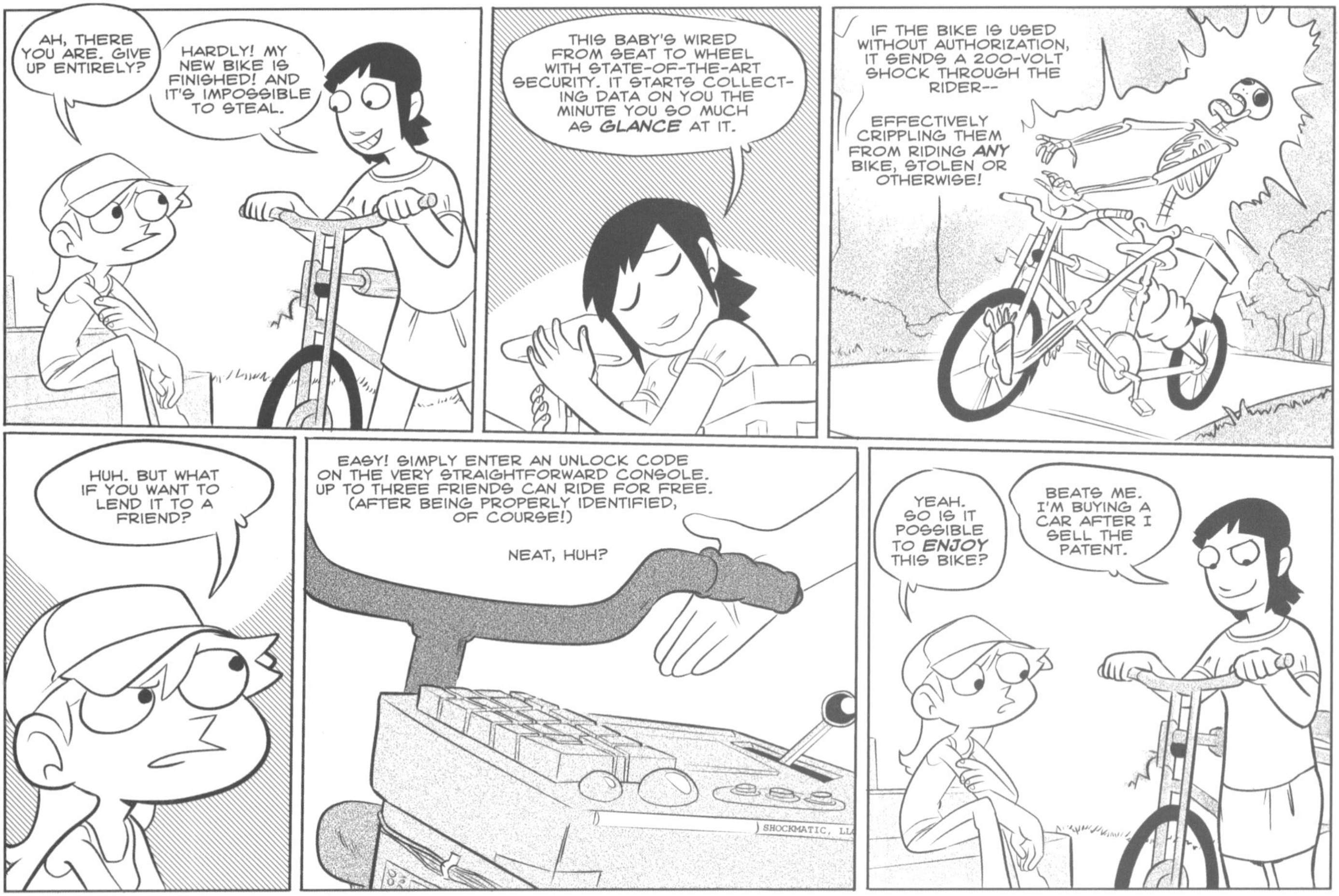
AH, THERE YOU ARE. GIVE UP ENTIRELY?
HARDLY! MY NEW BIKE IS FINISHED! AND IT'S IMPOSSIBLE TO STEAL.
THIS BABY'S WIRED FROM SEAT TO WHEEL WITH STATE-OF-THE-ART SECURITY. IT STARTS COLLECTING DATA ON YOU THE MINUTE YOU SO MUCH AS *GLANCE* AT IT.
IF THE BIKE IS USED WITHOUT AUTHORIZATION, IT SENDS A 200-VOLT SHOCK THROUGH THE RIDER--
EFFECTIVELY CRIPPLING THEM FROM RIDING *ANY* BIKE, STOLEN OR OTHERWISE!
HUH. BUT WHAT IF YOU WANT TO LEND IT TO A FRIEND?
EASY! SIMPLY ENTER AN UNLOCK CODE ON THE VERY STRAIGHTFORWARD CONSOLE. UP TO THREE FRIENDS CAN RIDE FOR FREE. (AFTER BEING PROPERLY IDENTIFIED, OF COURSE!)
NEAT, HUH?
SHOCKMATIC, LL
YEAH. SO IS IT POSSIBLE TO *ENJOY* THIS BIKE?
BEATS ME. I'M BUYING A CAR AFTER I SELL THE PATENT.

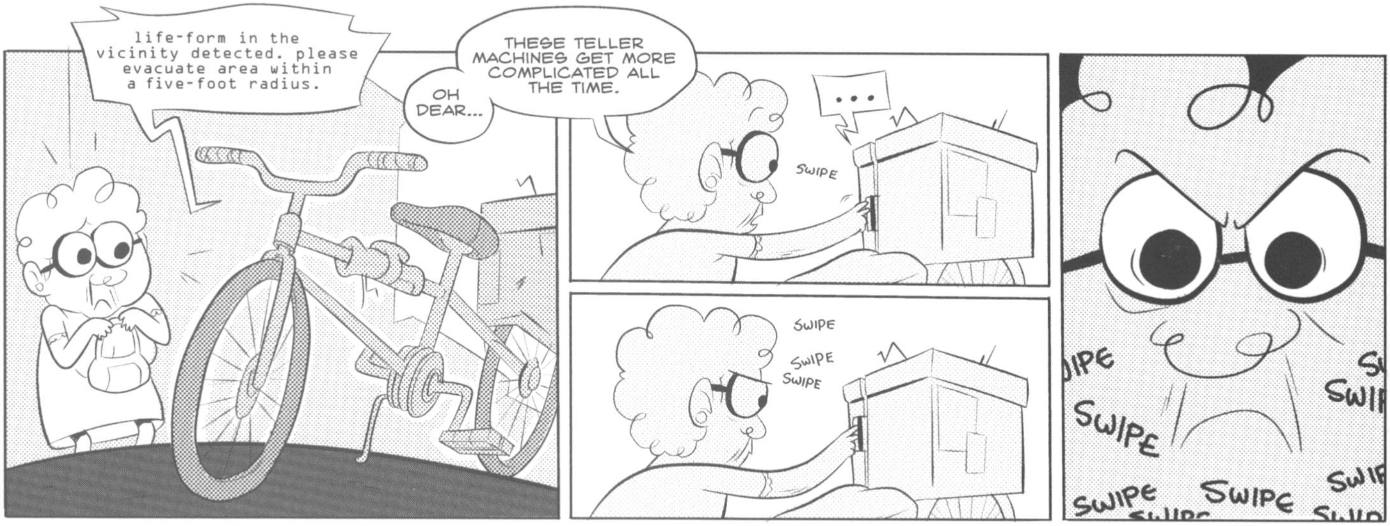
life-form in the vicinity detected. please evacuate area within a five-foot radius.
OH DEAR...
THESE TELLER MACHINES GET MORE COMPLICATED ALL THE TIME.
...
SWIPE
SWIPE
SWIPE
SWIPE
SWIPE
SWIPE
SWIPE

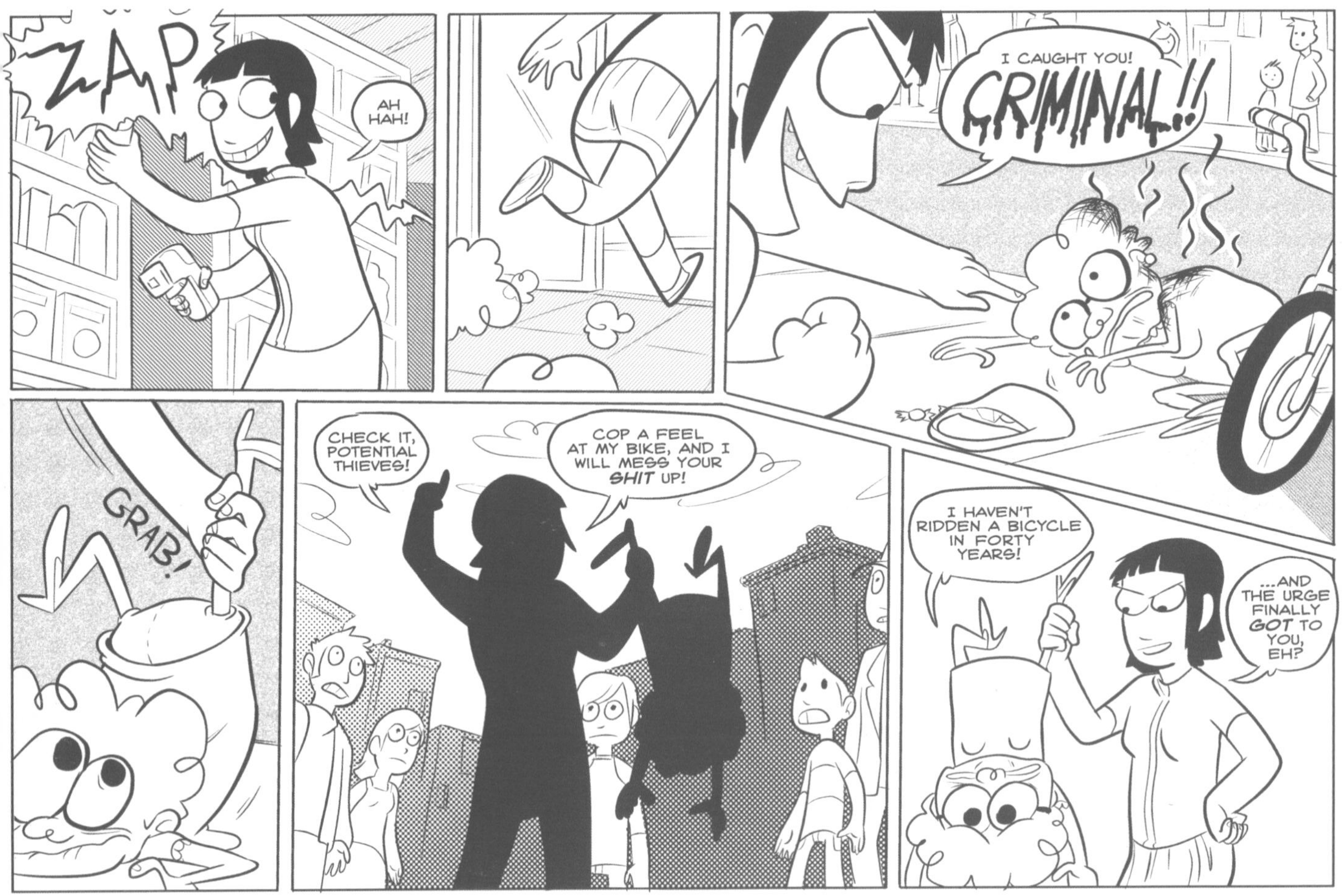
ZAP
AH HAH!
I CAUGHT YOU! CRIMINAL!!
GRAB!
CHECK IT, POTENTIAL THIEVES!
COP A FEEL AT MY BIKE, AND I WILL MESS YOUR SHIT UP!
I HAVEN'T RIDDEN A BICYCLE IN FORTY YEARS!
...AND THE URGE FINALLY GOT TO YOU, EH?

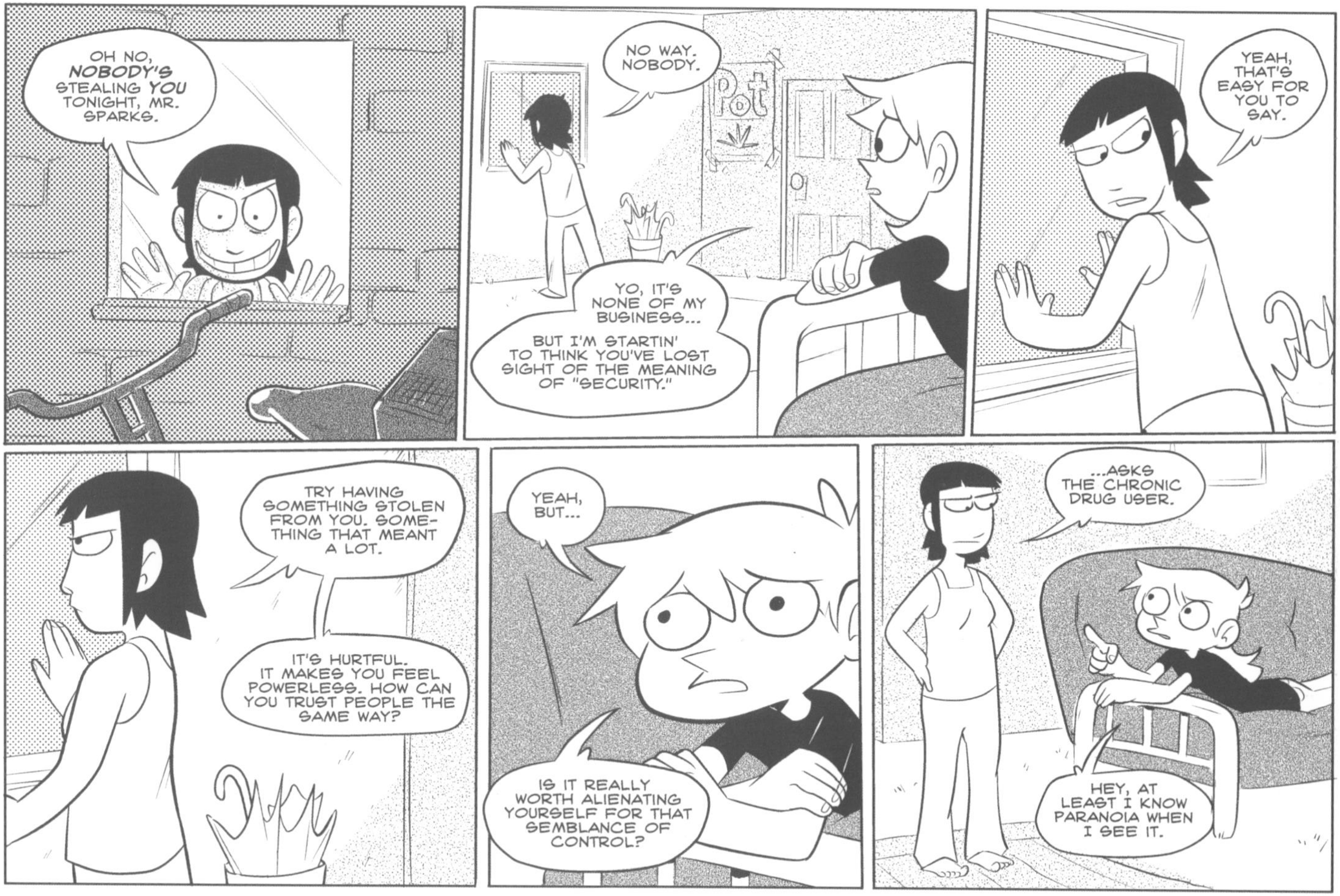
OH NO, NOBODY'S STEALING YOU TONIGHT, MR. SPARKS.
NO WAY. NOBODY.
Pot
YO, IT'S NONE OF MY BUSINESS...
BUT I'M STARTIN' TO THINK YOU'VE LOST SIGHT OF THE MEANING OF "SECURITY."
YEAH, THAT'S EASY FOR YOU TO SAY.
TRY HAVING SOMETHING STOLEN FROM YOU. SOME-THING THAT MEANT A LOT.
IT'S HURTFUL. IT MAKES YOU FEEL POWERLESS. HOW CAN YOU TRUST PEOPLE THE SAME WAY?
YEAH, BUT...
IS IT REALLY WORTH ALIENATING YOURSELF FOR THAT SEMBLANCE OF CONTROL?
...ASKS THE CHRONIC DRUG USER.
HEY, AT LEAST I KNOW PARANOIA WHEN I SEE IT.

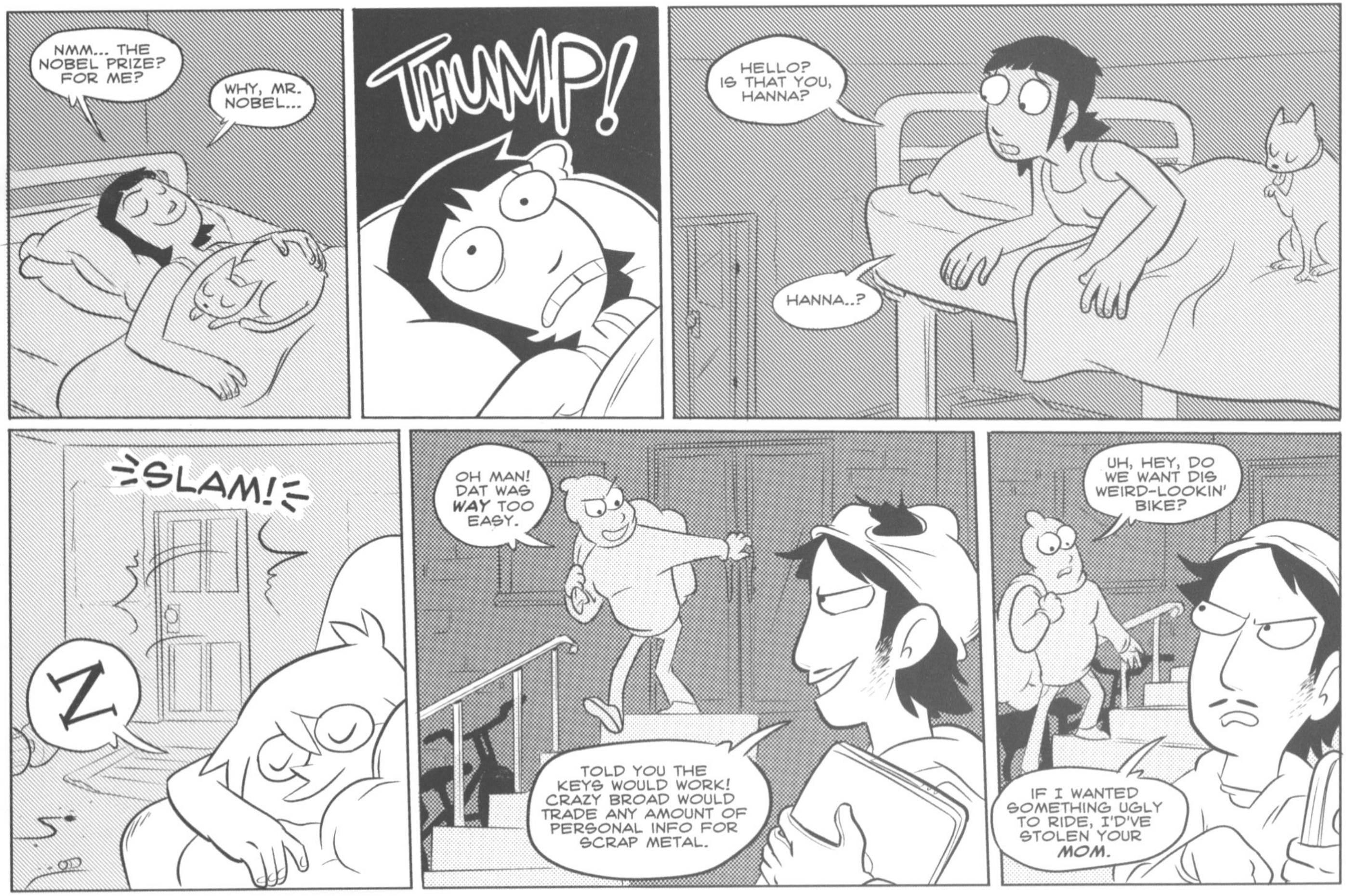
NMM... THE NOBEL PRIZE? FOR ME?
WHY, MR. NOBEL...
THUMP!
HELLO? IS THAT YOU, HANNA?
HANNA..?
SLAM!
Z
OH MAN! DAT WAS WAY TOO EASY.
TOLD YOU THE KEYS WOULD WORK! CRAZY BROAD WOULD TRADE ANY AMOUNT OF PERSONAL INFO FOR SCRAP METAL.
UH, HEY, DO WE WANT DIS WEIRD-LOOKIN' BIKE?
IF I WANTED SOMETHING UGLY TO RIDE, I'D'VE STOLEN YOUR MOM.

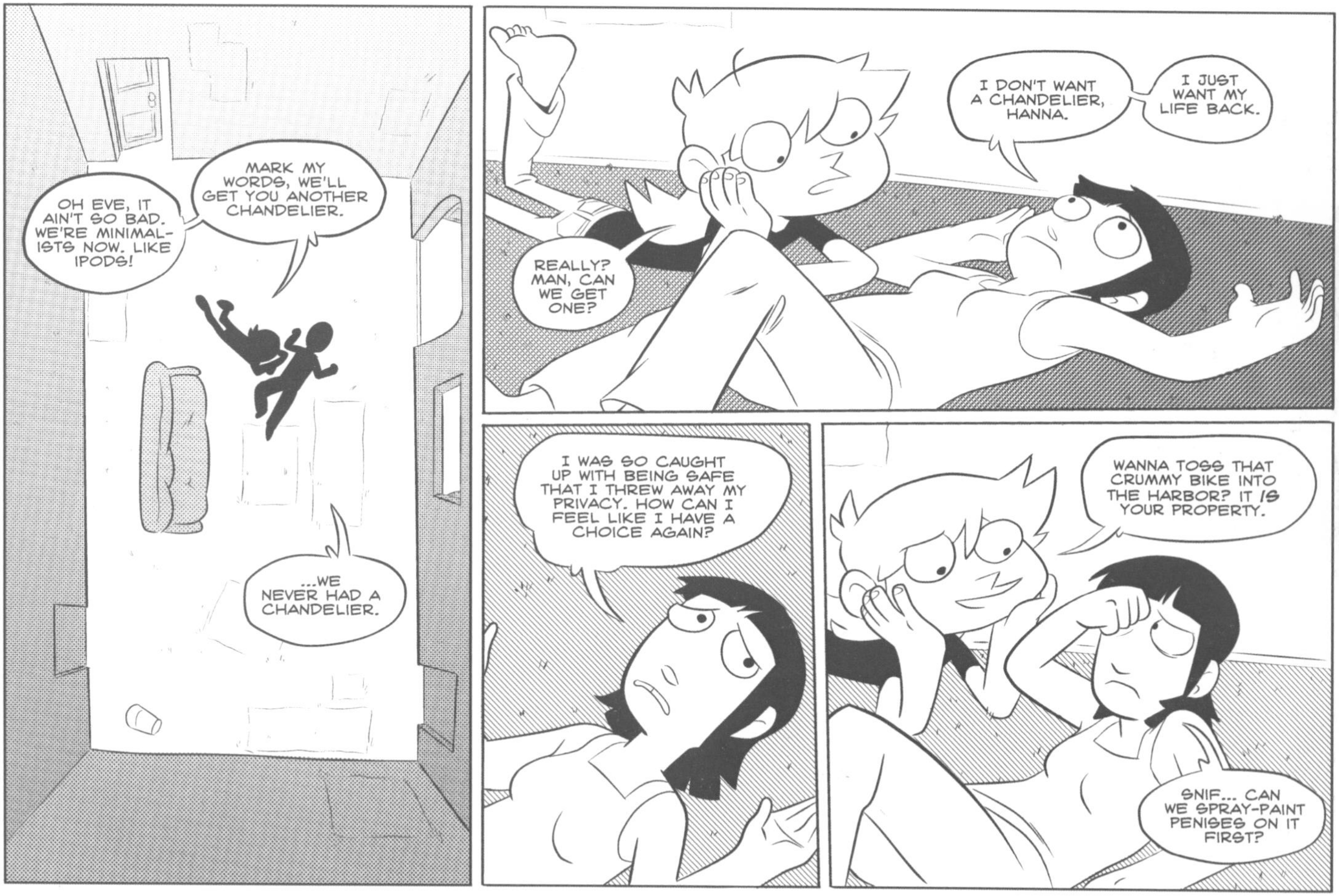
MARK MY WORDS, WE'LL GET YOU ANOTHER CHANDELIER.
OH EVE, IT AIN'T SO BAD. WE'RE MINIMAL-ISTS NOW. LIKE IPODS!
...WE NEVER HAD A CHANDELIER.
REALLY? MAN, CAN WE GET ONE?
I DON'T WANT A CHANDELIER, HANNA.
I JUST WANT MY LIFE BACK.
I WAS SO CAUGHT UP WITH BEING SAFE THAT I THREW AWAY MY PRIVACY. HOW CAN I FEEL LIKE I HAVE A CHOICE AGAIN?
WANNA TOSS THAT CRUMMY BIKE INTO THE HARBOR? IT IS YOUR PROPERTY.
SNIF... CAN WE SPRAY-PAINT PENISES ON IT FIRST?

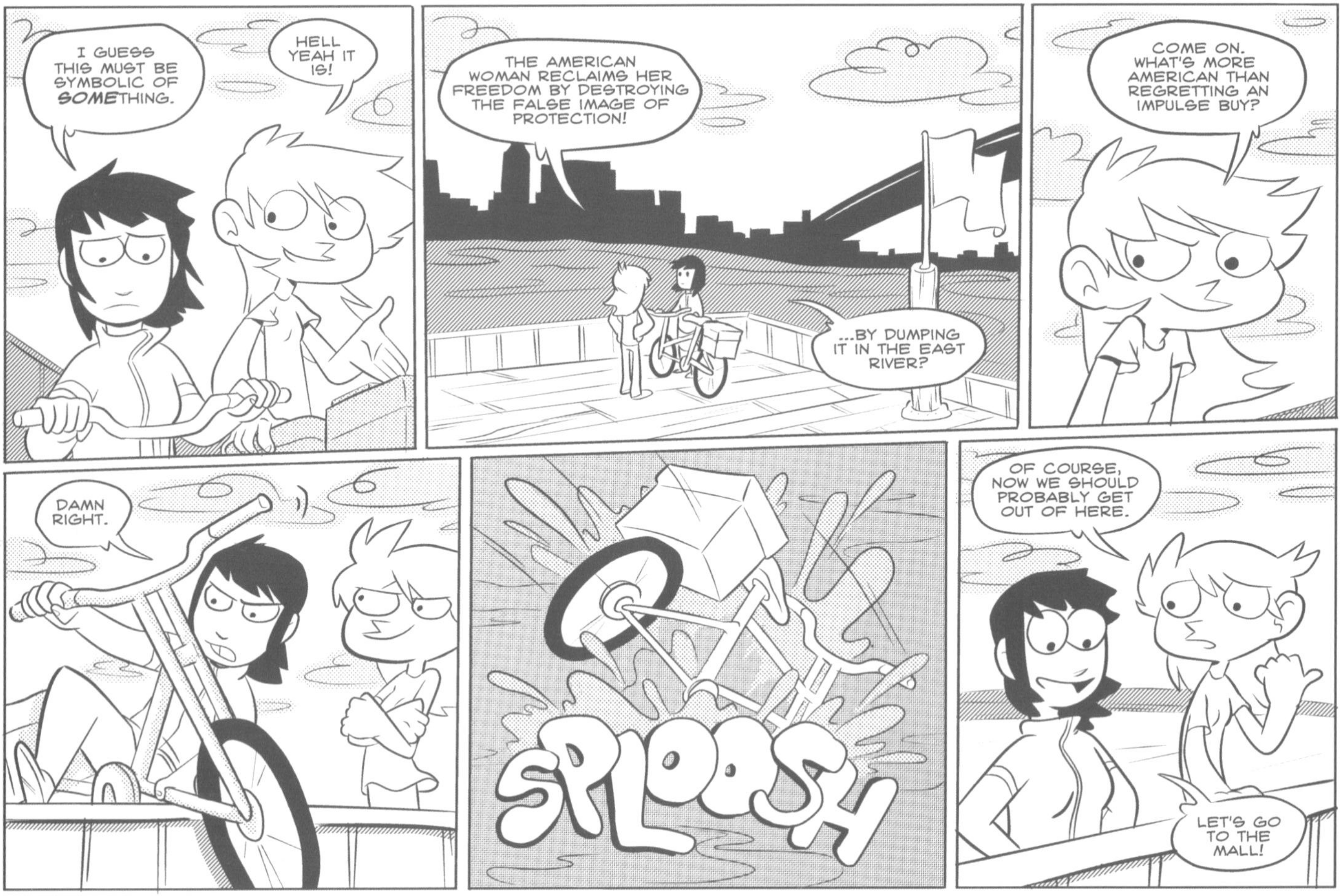
I GUESS THIS MUST BE SYMBOLIC OF SOMETHING.
HELL YEAH IT IS!
THE AMERICAN WOMAN RECLAIMS HER FREEDOM BY DESTROYING THE FALSE IMAGE OF PROTECTION!
...BY DUMPING IT IN THE EAST RIVER?
COME ON. WHAT'S MORE AMERICAN THAN REGRETTING AN IMPULSE BUY?
DAMN RIGHT.
SPLOOSH
OF COURSE, NOW WE SHOULD PROBABLY GET OUT OF HERE.
LET'S GO TO THE MALL!

bake 'n' bake

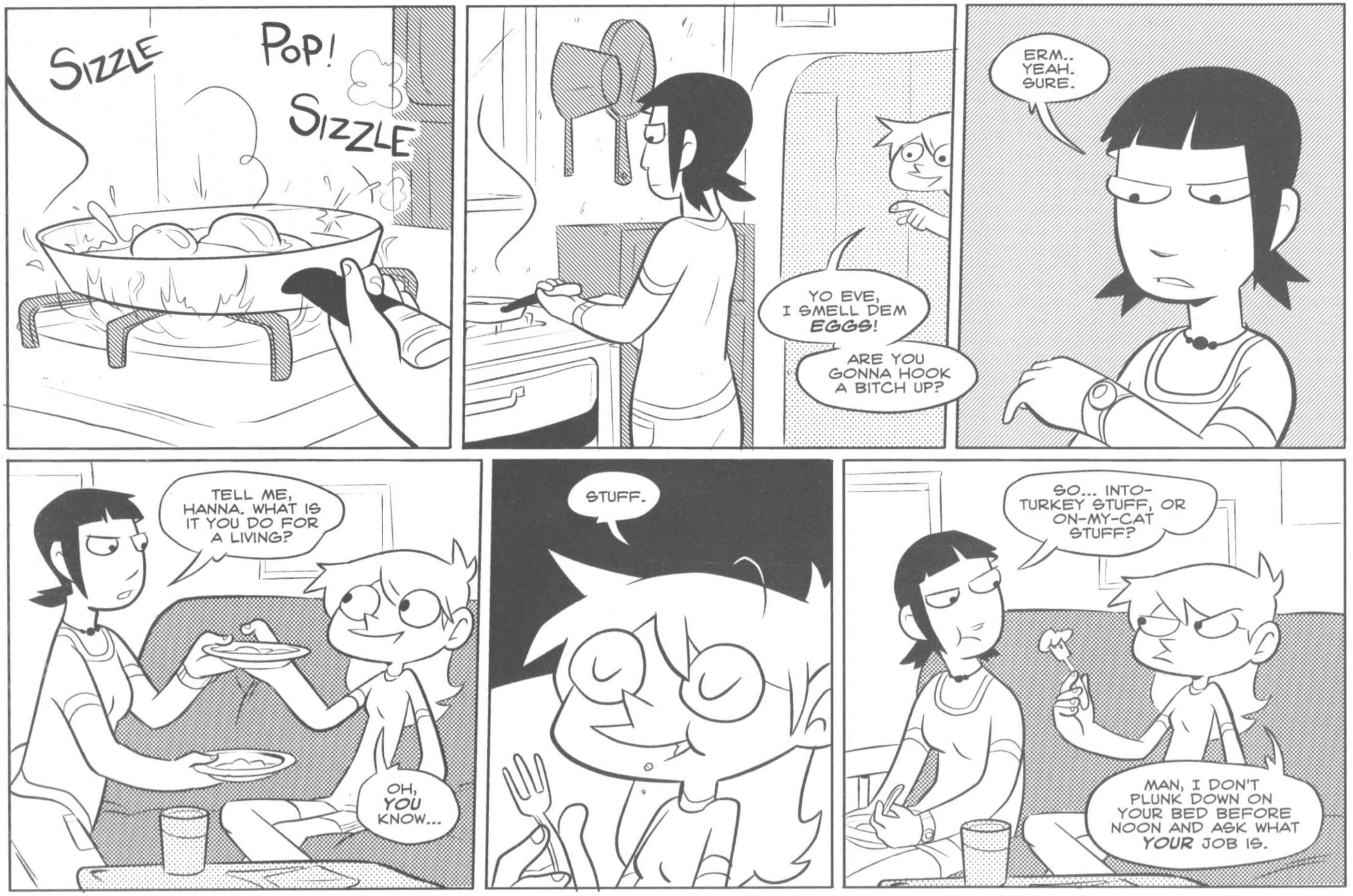
SIZZLE
POP!
SIZZLE
YO EVE, I SMELL DEM EGGS!
ARE YOU GONNA HOOK A BITCH UP?
ERM.. YEAH. SURE.
TELL ME, HANNA. WHAT IS IT YOU DO FOR A LIVING?
OH, YOU KNOW...
STUFF.
SO... INTO-TURKEY STUFF, OR ON-MY-CAT STUFF?
MAN, I DON'T PLUNK DOWN ON YOUR BED BEFORE NOON AND ASK WHAT YOUR JOB IS.

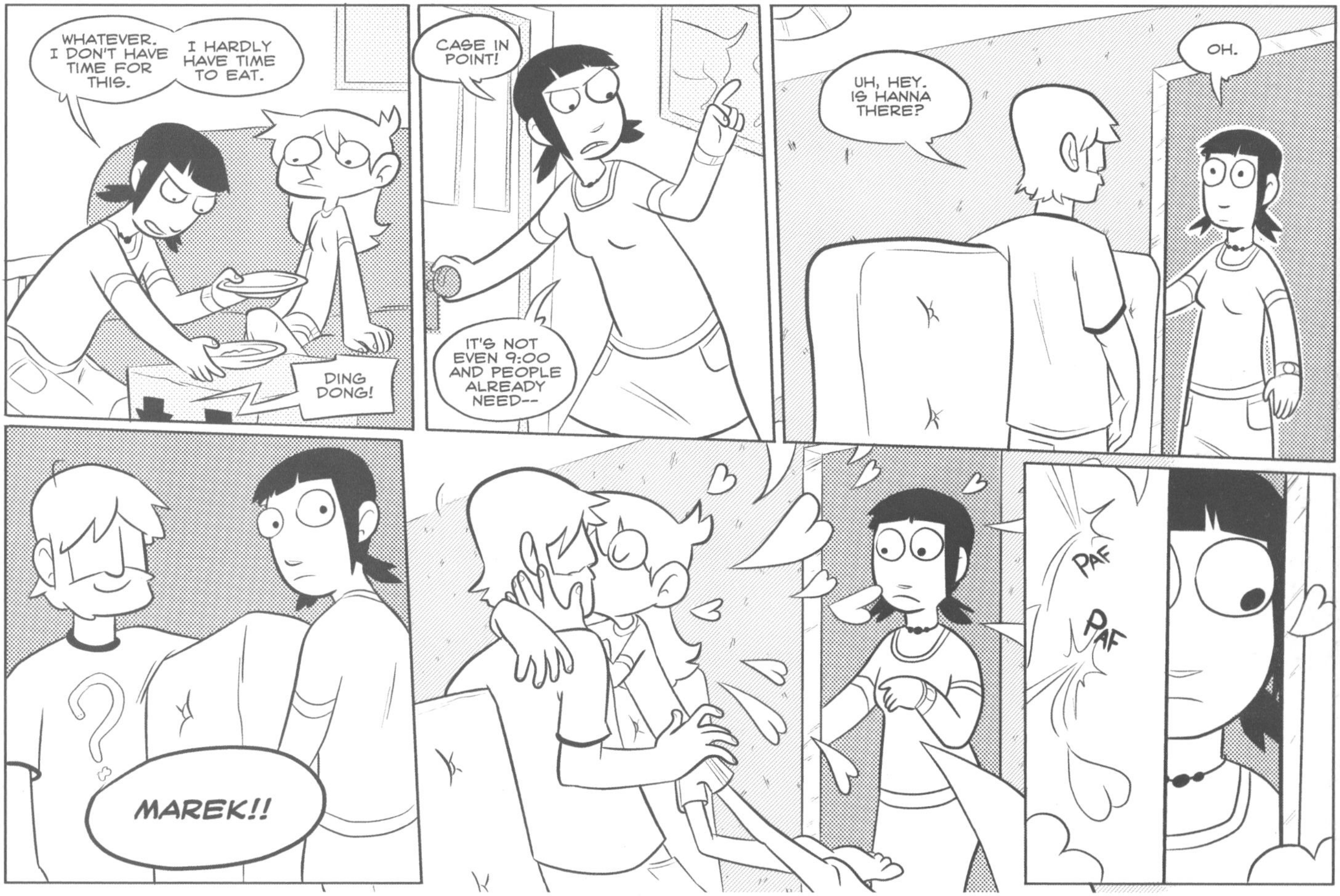
WHATEVER. I DON'T HAVE TIME FOR THIS.
I HARDLY HAVE TIME TO EAT.
DING DONG!
CASE IN POINT!
IT'S NOT EVEN 9:00 AND PEOPLE ALREADY NEED--
UH, HEY. IS HANNA THERE?
OH.
MAREK!!
PAF
PAF

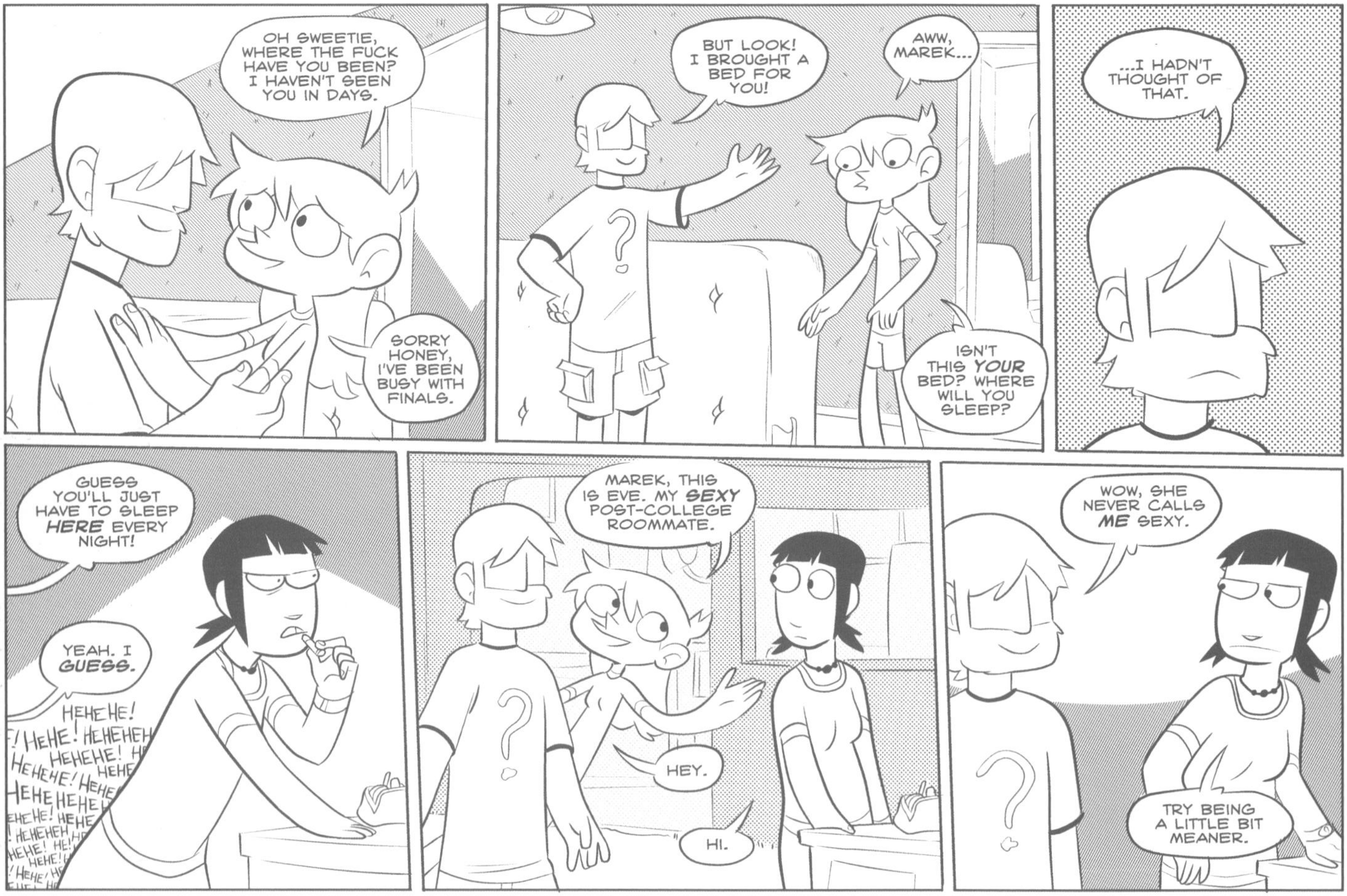
OH SWEETIE, WHERE THE FUCK HAVE YOU BEEN? I HAVEN'T SEEN YOU IN DAYS.
SORRY HONEY, I'VE BEEN BUSY WITH FINALS.
BUT LOOK! I BROUGHT A BED FOR YOU!
AWW, MAREK...
ISN'T THIS YOUR BED? WHERE WILL YOU SLEEP?
...I HADN'T THOUGHT OF THAT.
GUESS YOU'LL JUST HAVE TO SLEEP HERE EVERY NIGHT!
YEAH. I GUESS.
HEHEHE!
MAREK, THIS IS EVE. MY SEXY POST-COLLEGE ROOMMATE.
HEY.
HI.
WOW, SHE NEVER CALLS ME SEXY.
TRY BEING A LITTLE BIT MEANER.

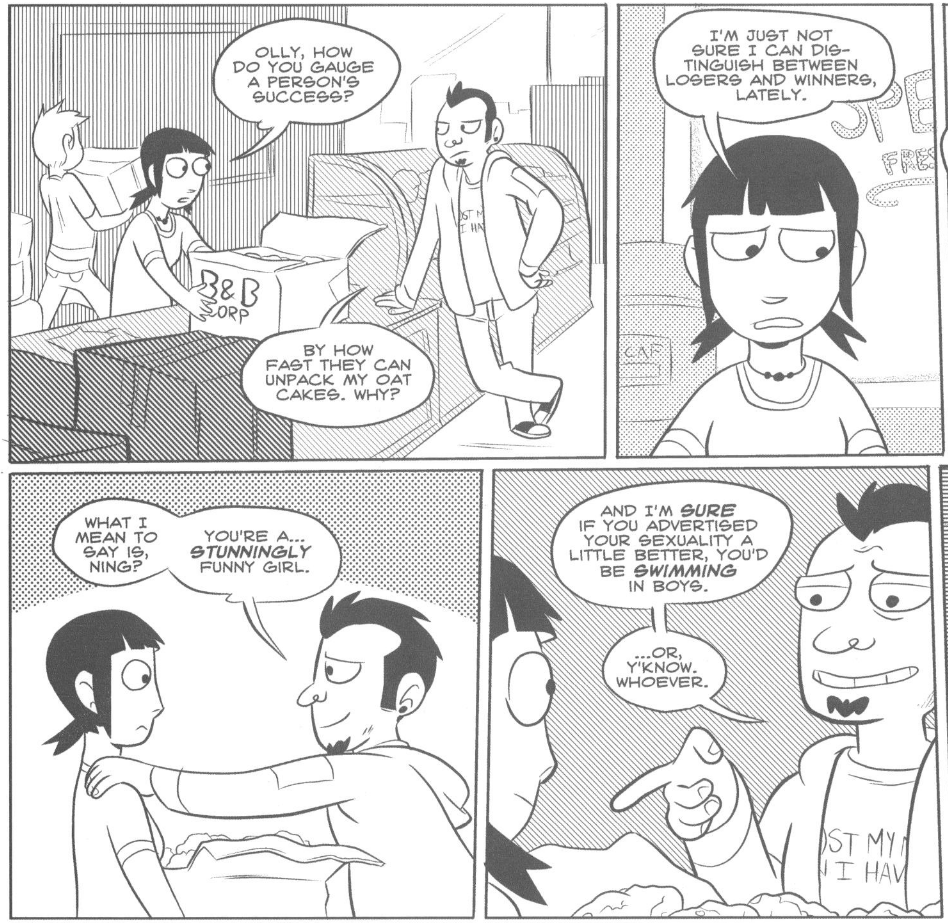
OLLY, HOW DO YOU GAUGE A PERSON'S SUCCESS?
BY HOW FAST THEY CAN UNPACK MY OAT CAKES. WHY?
I'M JUST NOT SURE I CAN DISTINGUISH BETWEEN LOSERS AND WINNERS, LATELY.
NING, I FOUNDED OLLY'S ORGANIX ON A SIMPLE NOTION.
THAT YOU CAN TAKE A PRODUCT NO ONE WANTS, CONVINCE THEM THEY WANT IT, AND SELL IT AT A PREMIUM.
WHAT I MEAN TO SAY IS, NING?
YOU'RE A... STUNNINGLY FUNNY GIRL.
AND I'M SURE IF YOU ADVERTISED YOUR SEXUALITY A LITTLE BETTER, YOU'D BE SWIMMING IN BOYS.
...OR, Y'KNOW. WHOEVER.
THAT'S NOT AT ALL WHAT I WAS TALKING ABOUT.
THEN MY FIRST ANSWER STILL STANDS. GET BACK TO WORK.

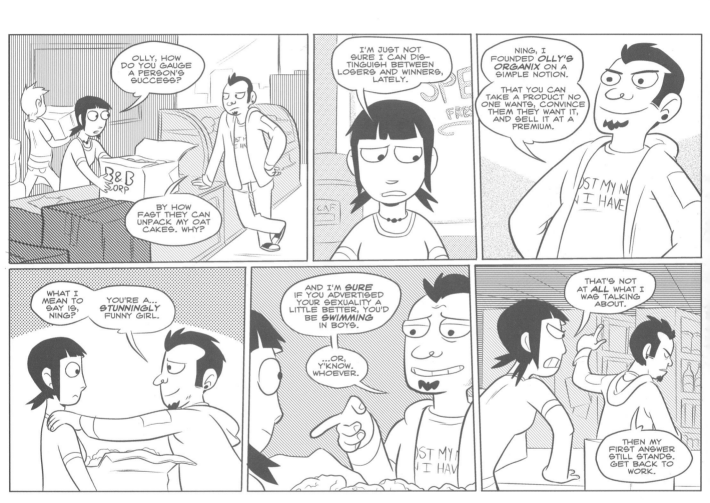

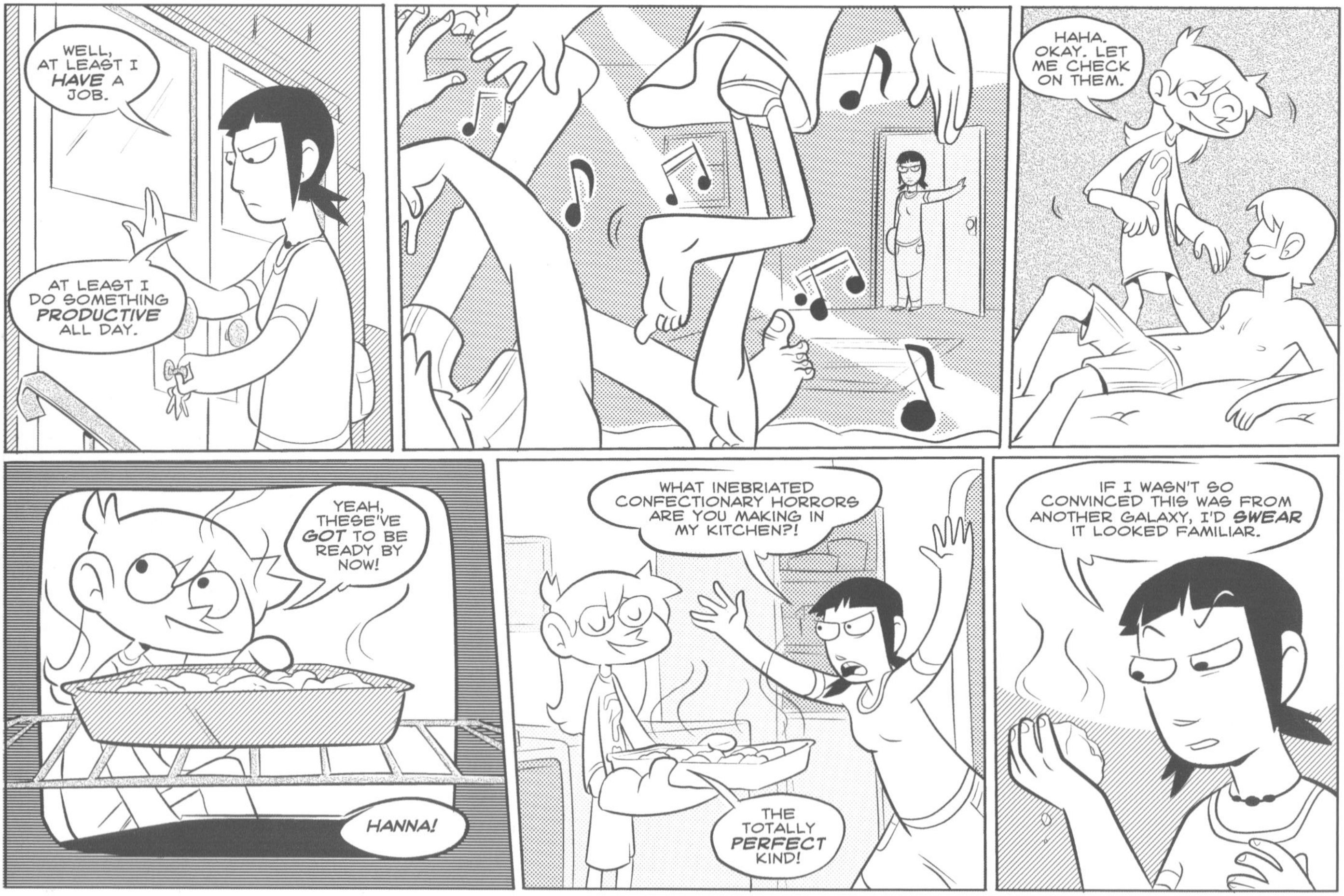
WELL, AT LEAST I HAVE A JOB.
AT LEAST I DO SOMETHING PRODUCTIVE ALL DAY.
HAHA. OKAY. LET ME CHECK ON THEM.
YEAH, THESE'VE GOT TO BE READY BY NOW!
HANNA!
WHAT INEBRIATED CONFECTIONARY HORRORS ARE YOU MAKING IN MY KITCHEN?!
THE TOTALLY PERFECT KIND!
IF I WASN'T SO CONVINCED THIS WAS FROM ANOTHER GALAXY, I'D SWEAR IT LOOKED FAMILIAR.

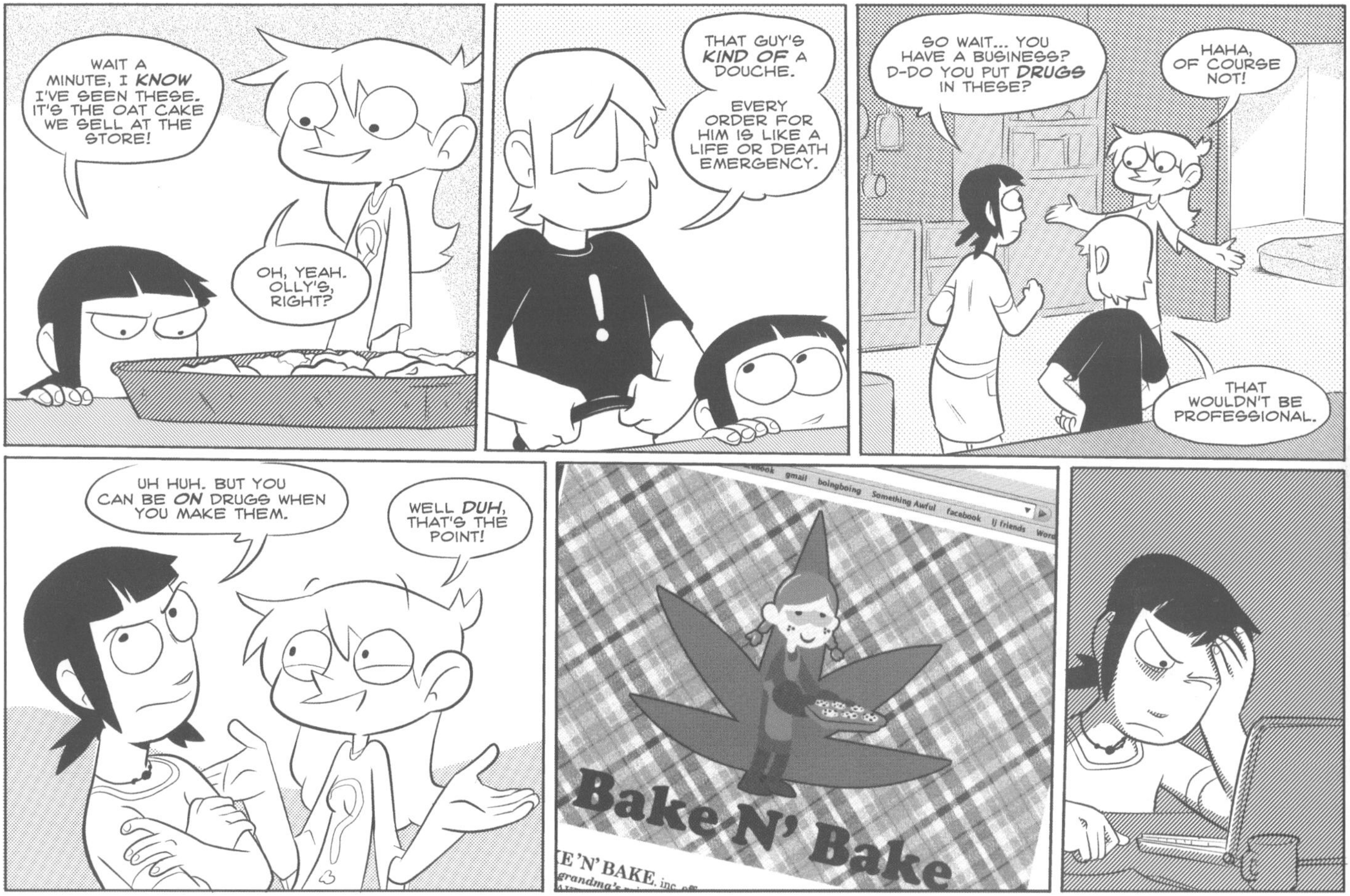
WAIT A MINUTE, I KNOW I'VE SEEN THESE. IT'S THE OAT CAKE WE SELL AT THE STORE!
OH, YEAH. OLLY'S, RIGHT?
THAT GUY'S KIND OF A DOUCHE.
EVERY ORDER FOR HIM IS LIKE A LIFE OR DEATH EMERGENCY.
SO WAIT... YOU HAVE A BUSINESS? D-DO YOU PUT DRUGS IN THESE?
HAHA, OF COURSE NOT!
THAT WOULDN'T BE PROFESSIONAL.
UH HUH. BUT YOU CAN BE ON DRUGS WHEN YOU MAKE THEM.
WELL DUH, THAT'S THE POINT!
gmail
boingboing
Something Awful
facebook
lj friends
Bake N' Bake
E 'N' BAKE, inc.

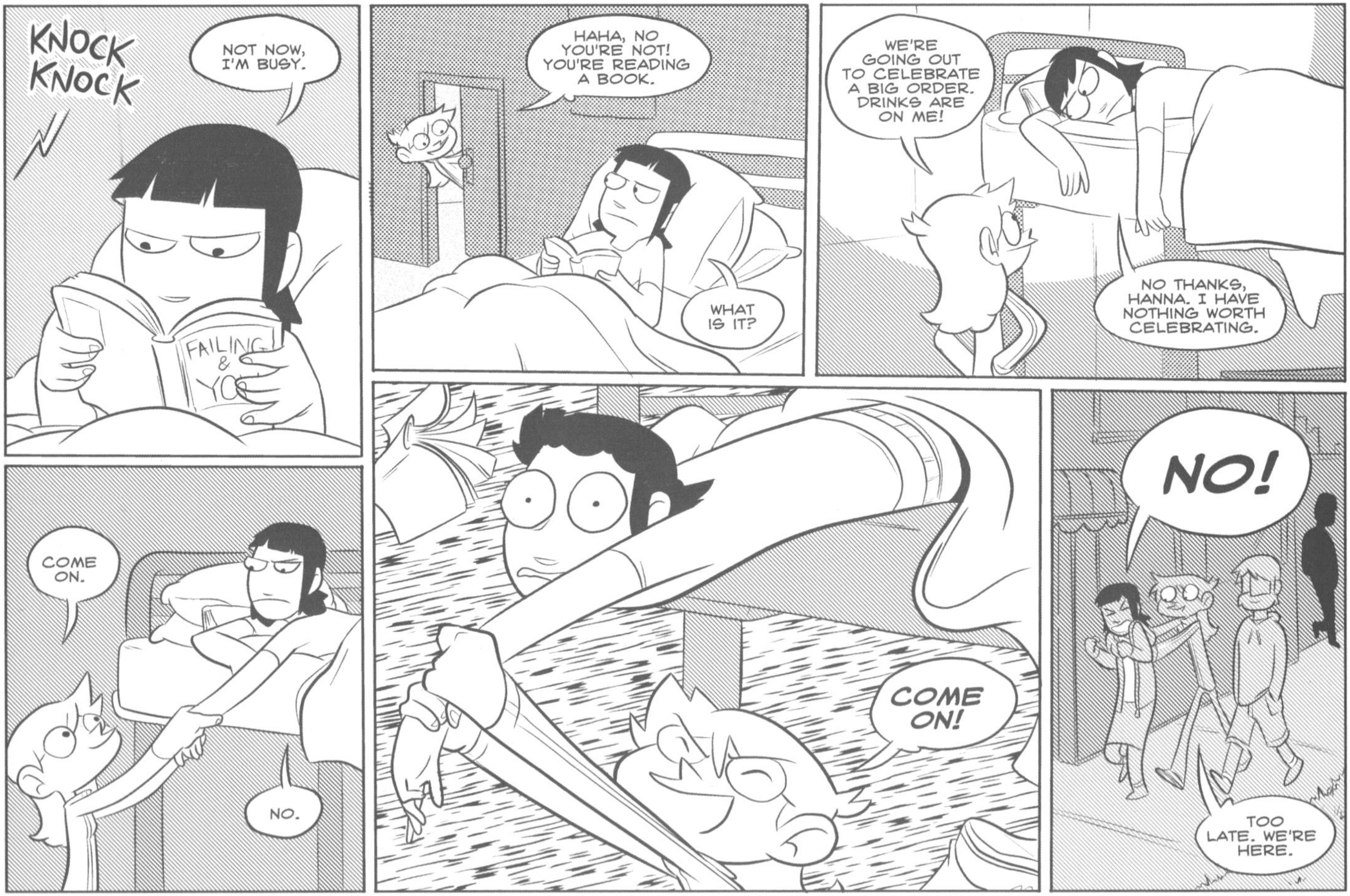
KNOCK KNOCK
NOT NOW, I'M BUSY.
FAILING & YO
HAHA, NO YOU'RE NOT! YOU'RE READING A BOOK.
WHAT IS IT?
WE'RE GOING OUT TO CELEBRATE A BIG ORDER. DRINKS ARE ON ME!
NO THANKS, HANNA. I HAVE NOTHING WORTH CELEBRATING.
COME ON.
NO.
COME ON!
NO!
TOO LATE. WE'RE HERE.

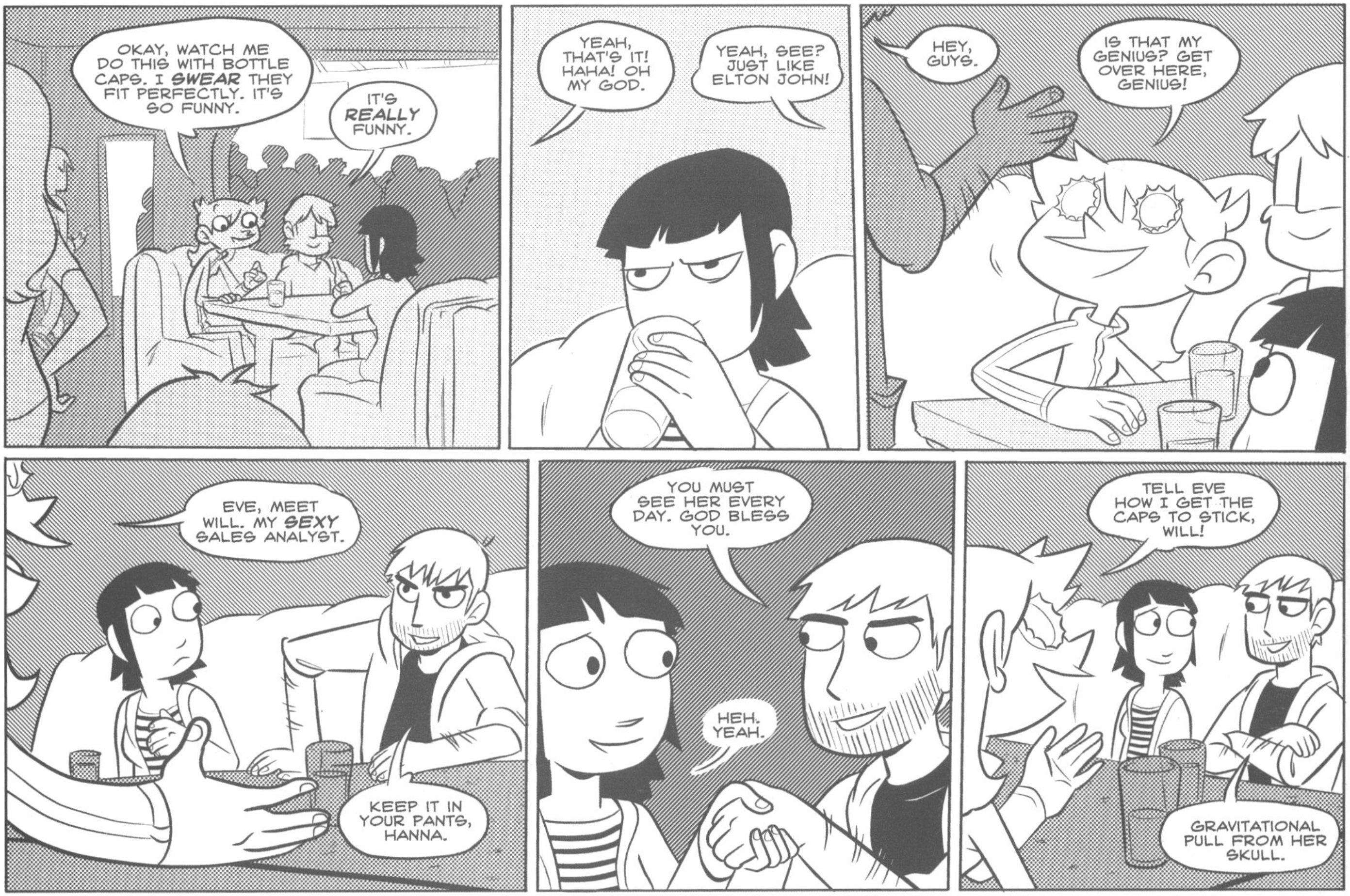
OKAY, WATCH ME DO THIS WITH BOTTLE CAPS. I SWEAR THEY FIT PERFECTLY. IT'S SO FUNNY.
IT'S REALLY FUNNY.
YEAH, THAT'S IT! HAHA! OH MY GOD.
YEAH, SEE? JUST LIKE ELTON JOHN!
HEY, GUYS.
IS THAT MY GENIUS? GET OVER HERE, GENIUS!
EVE, MEET WILL. MY SEXY SALES ANALYST.
KEEP IT IN YOUR PANTS, HANNA.
YOU MUST SEE HER EVERY DAY. GOD BLESS YOU.
HEH. YEAH.
TELL EVE HOW I GET THE CAPS TO STICK, WILL!
GRAVITATIONAL PULL FROM HER SKULL.

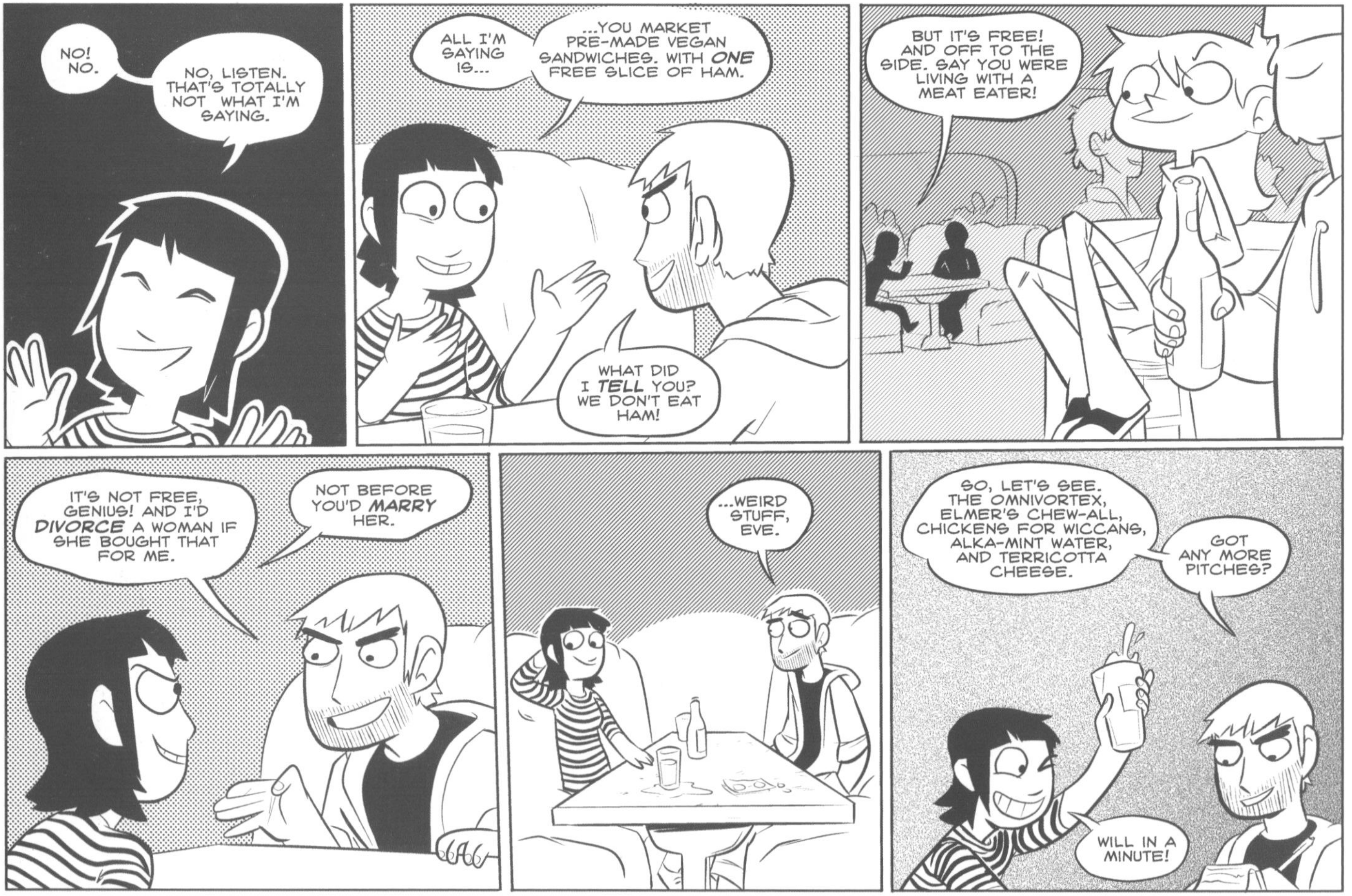
NO! NO.
NO, LISTEN. THAT'S TOTALLY NOT WHAT I'M SAYING.
ALL I'M SAYING IS...
...YOU MARKET PRE-MADE VEGAN SANDWICHES. WITH ONE FREE SLICE OF HAM.
WHAT DID I TELL YOU? WE DON'T EAT HAM!
BUT IT'S FREE! AND OFF TO THE SIDE. SAY YOU WERE LIVING WITH A MEAT EATER!
IT'S NOT FREE, GENIUS! AND I'D DIVORCE A WOMAN IF SHE BOUGHT THAT FOR ME.
NOT BEFORE YOU'D MARRY HER.
...WEIRD STUFF, EVE.
SO, LET'S SEE. THE OMNIVORTEX, ELMER'S CHEW-ALL, CHICKENS FOR WICCANS, ALKA-MINT WATER, AND TERRICOTTA CHEESE.
GOT ANY MORE PITCHES?
WILL IN A MINUTE!

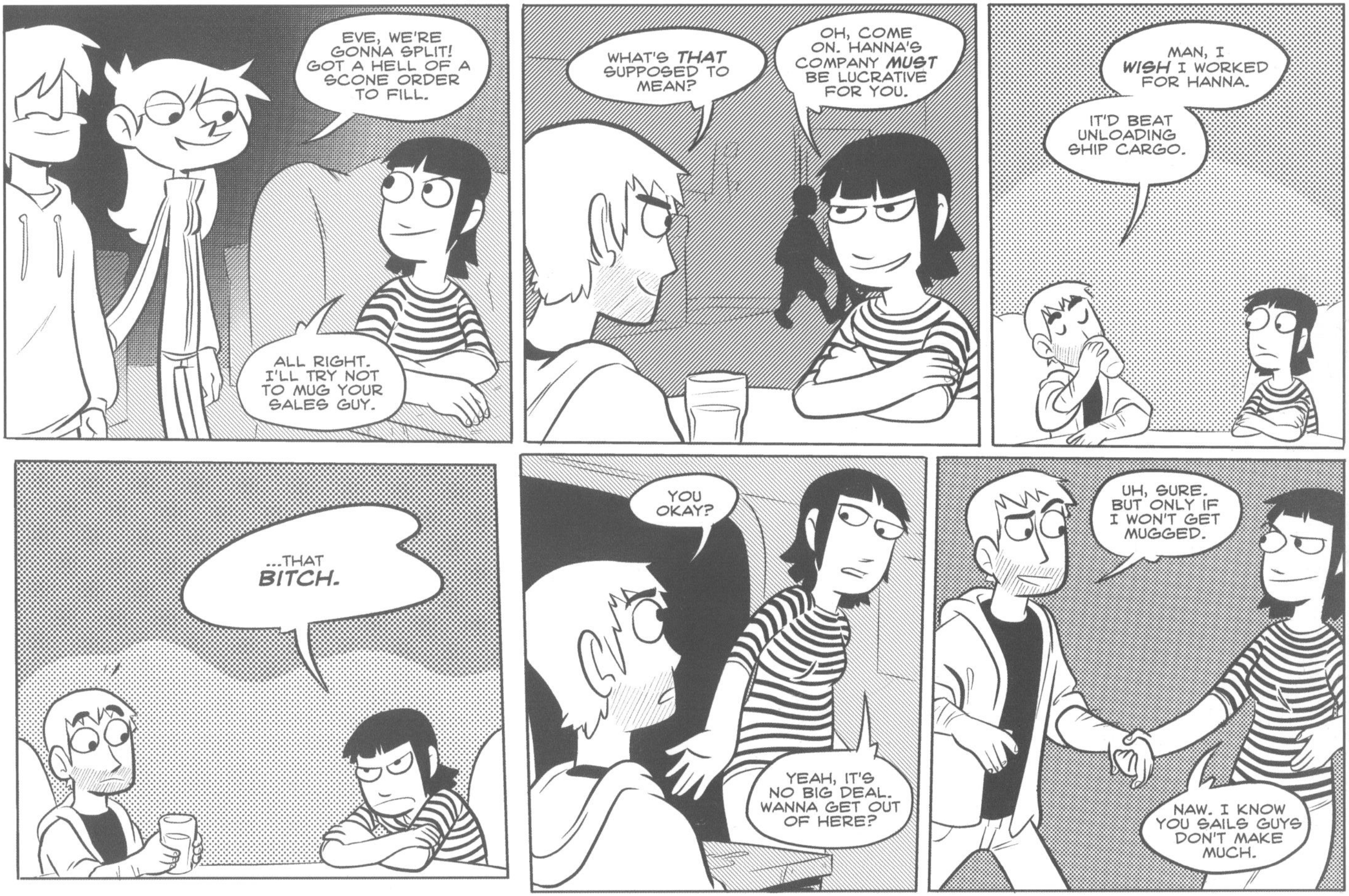
EVE, WE'RE GONNA SPLIT! GOT A HELL OF A SCONE ORDER TO FILL.
ALL RIGHT. I'LL TRY NOT TO MUG YOUR SALES GUY.
WHAT'S THAT SUPPOSED TO MEAN?
OH, COME ON. HANNA'S COMPANY MUST BE LUCRATIVE FOR YOU.
MAN, I WISH I WORKED FOR HANNA.
IT'D BEAT UNLOADING SHIP CARGO.
...THAT BITCH.
YOU OKAY?
YEAH, IT'S NO BIG DEAL. WANNA GET OUT OF HERE?
UH, SURE. BUT ONLY IF I WON'T GET MUGGED.
NAW. I KNOW YOU SAILS GUYS DON'T MAKE MUCH.

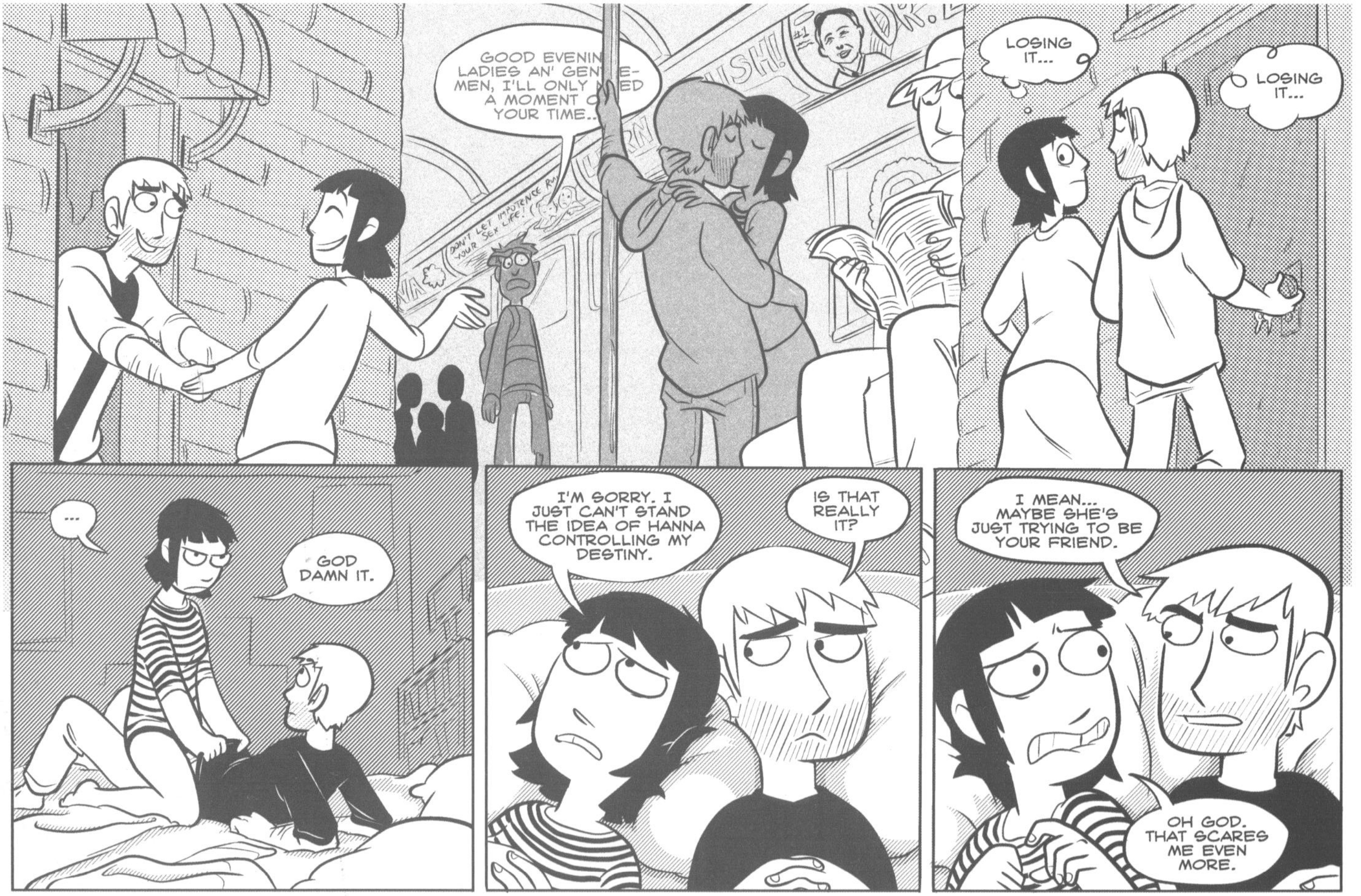
GOOD EVENING LADIES AN' GENTLEMEN, I'LL ONLY NEED A MOMENT OF YOUR TIME...
LOSING IT...
LOSING IT...
...
GOD DAMN IT.
I'M SORRY. I JUST CAN'T STAND THE IDEA OF HANNA CONTROLLING MY DESTINY.
IS THAT REALLY IT?
I MEAN... MAYBE SHE'S JUST TRYING TO BE YOUR FRIEND.
OH GOD. THAT SCARES ME EVEN MORE.

EXCUSE ME, YOUNG MAN!
WOULD YOU HAVE THE TIME?
I SURE DO! IT'S HALF PAST NOON.
GOODNESS! AREN'T YOU IN A HAPPY MOOD TODAY!
YEP. I MET THE SURLIEST GIRL LAST NIGHT.
OH MY!

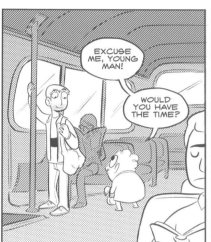

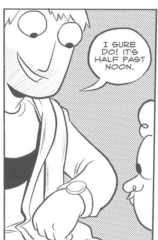

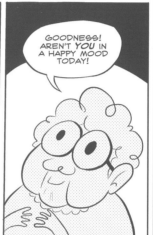

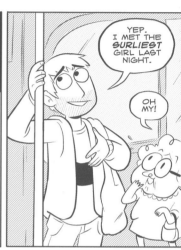

under the bodhi tree

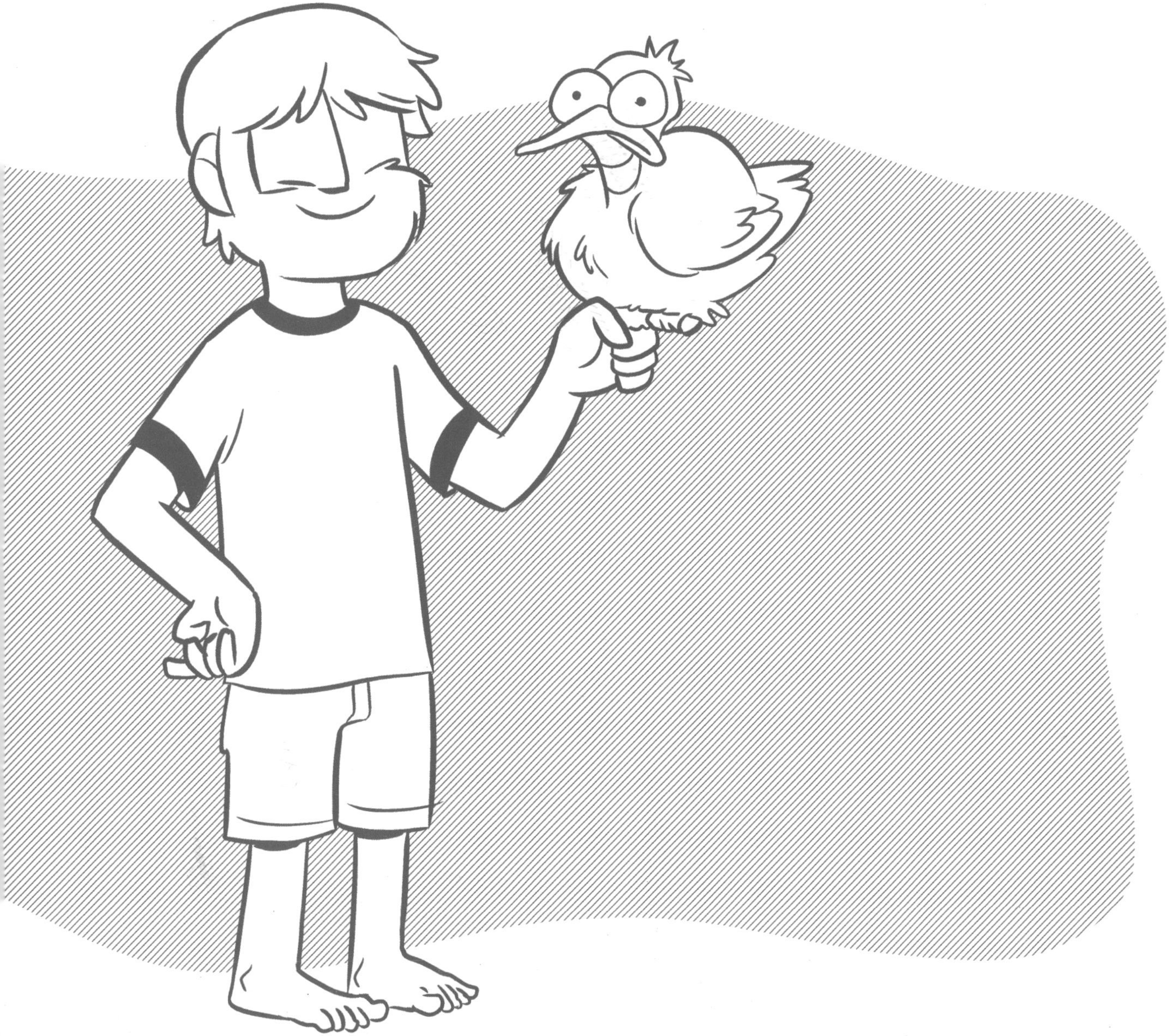

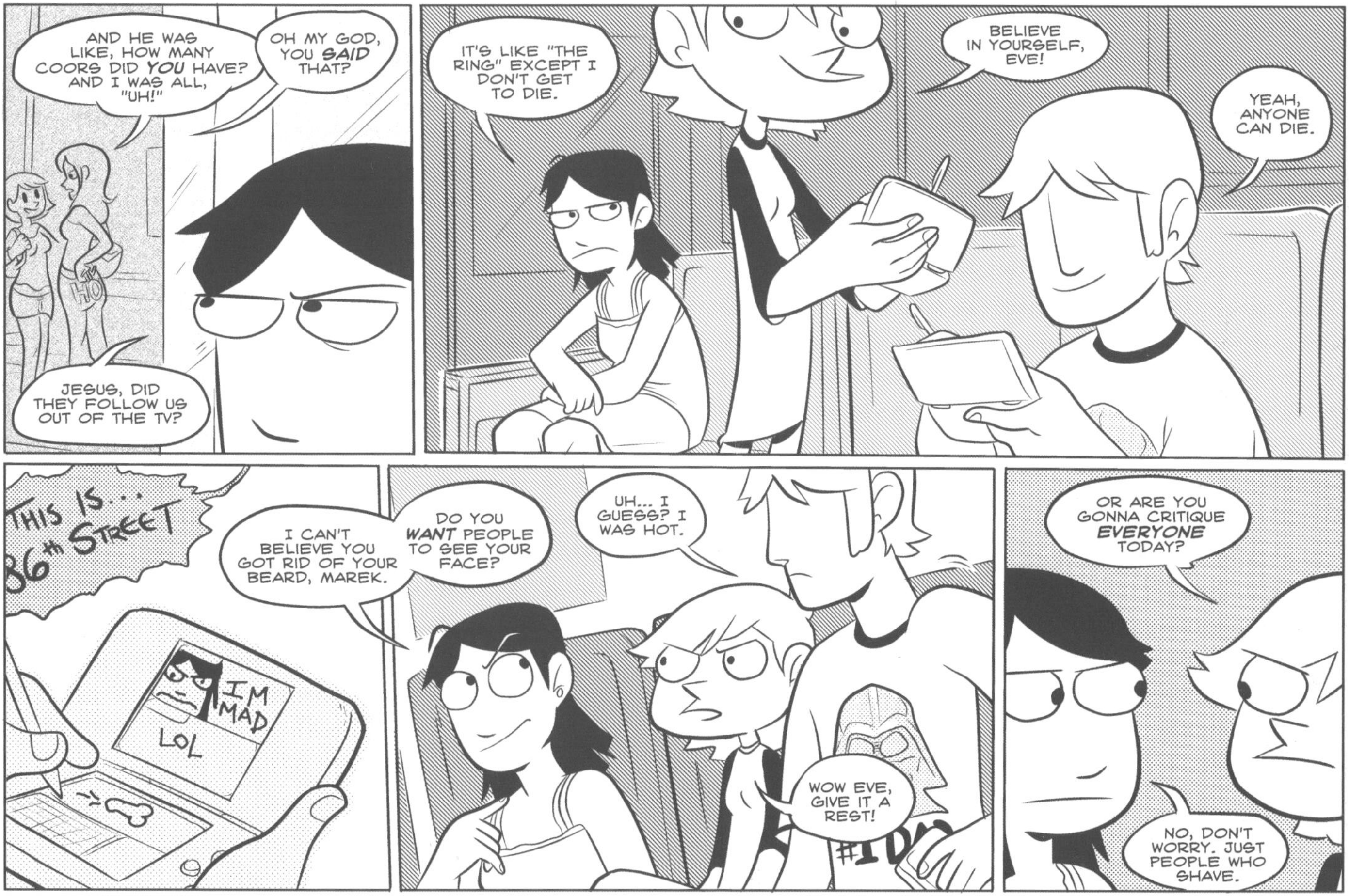
AND HE WAS LIKE, HOW MANY COORS DID *YOU* HAVE? AND I WAS ALL, "UH!"
OH MY GOD, YOU *SAID* THAT?
HO
JESUS, DID THEY FOLLOW US OUT OF THE TV?
IT'S LIKE "THE RING" EXCEPT I DON'T GET TO DIE.
BELIEVE IN YOURSELF, EVE!
YEAH, ANYONE CAN DIE.
THIS IS... 86th STREET
IM MAD
LOL
I CAN'T BELIEVE YOU GOT RID OF YOUR BEARD, MAREK.
DO YOU *WANT* PEOPLE TO SEE YOUR FACE?
UH... I GUESS? I WAS HOT.
WOW EVE, GIVE IT A REST!
OR ARE YOU GONNA CRITIQUE *EVERYONE* TODAY?
NO, DON'T WORRY. JUST PEOPLE WHO SHAVE.

WELCOME TO MY SUPAH MARKET! CASH ONLY.
IS YOUR BREAD GLUTEN FREE? I HAVE A DISEASE, MISS.
JEREMY! WHERE DID YOU HEAR THAT TRASH?!
THE MAN IN THE STORE.
GOD DAMN IT!
I SWEAR I'M GOING TO CLOCK THE NEXT GRANOLA-FACED, TREE-FUCKING HIPPIE I SEE.

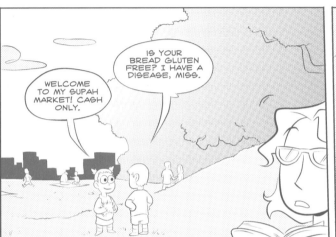

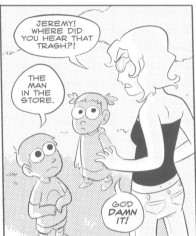

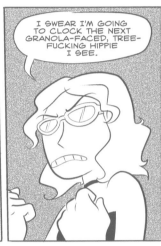

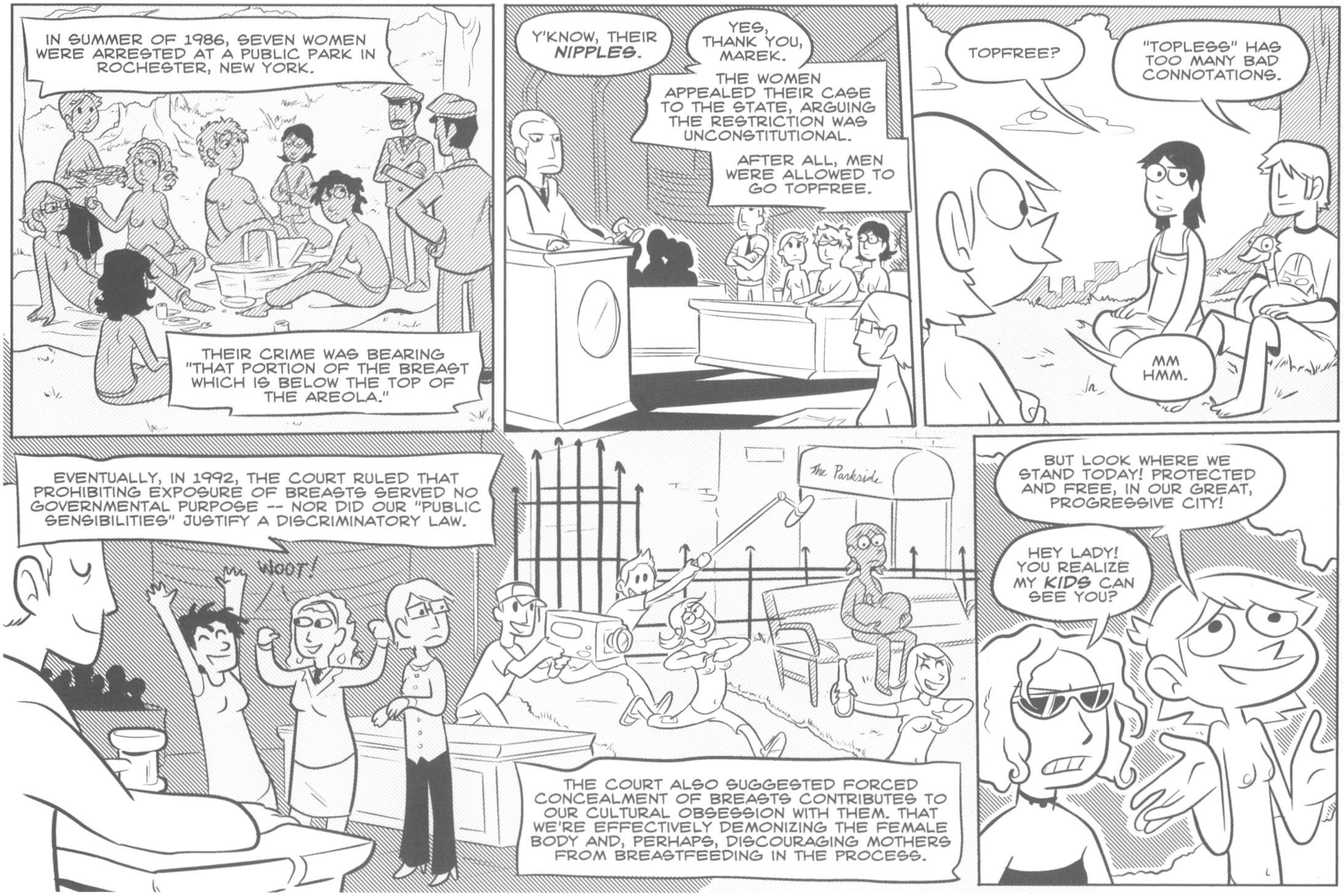
IN SUMMER OF 1986, SEVEN WOMEN WERE ARRESTED AT A PUBLIC PARK IN ROCHESTER, NEW YORK.
THEIR CRIME WAS BEARING "THAT PORTION OF THE BREAST WHICH IS BELOW THE TOP OF THE AREOLA."
Y'KNOW, THEIR *NIPPLES.*
YES, THANK YOU, MAREK.
THE WOMEN APPEALED THEIR CASE TO THE STATE, ARGUING THE RESTRICTION WAS UNCONSTITUTIONAL.
AFTER ALL, MEN WERE ALLOWED TO GO TOPFREE.
TOPFREE?
"TOPLESS" HAS TOO MANY BAD CONNOTATIONS.
MM HMM.
EVENTUALLY, IN 1992, THE COURT RULED THAT PROHIBITING EXPOSURE OF BREASTS SERVED NO GOVERNMENTAL PURPOSE -- NOR DID OUR "PUBLIC SENSIBILITIES" JUSTIFY A DISCRIMINATORY LAW.
WOOT!
The Parkside
THE COURT ALSO SUGGESTED FORCED CONCEALMENT OF BREASTS CONTRIBUTES TO OUR CULTURAL OBSESSION WITH THEM. THAT WE'RE EFFECTIVELY DEMONIZING THE FEMALE BODY AND, PERHAPS, DISCOURAGING MOTHERS FROM BREASTFEEDING IN THE PROCESS.
BUT LOOK WHERE WE STAND TODAY! PROTECTED AND FREE, IN OUR GREAT, PROGRESSIVE CITY!
HEY LADY! YOU REALIZE MY *KIDS* CAN SEE YOU?

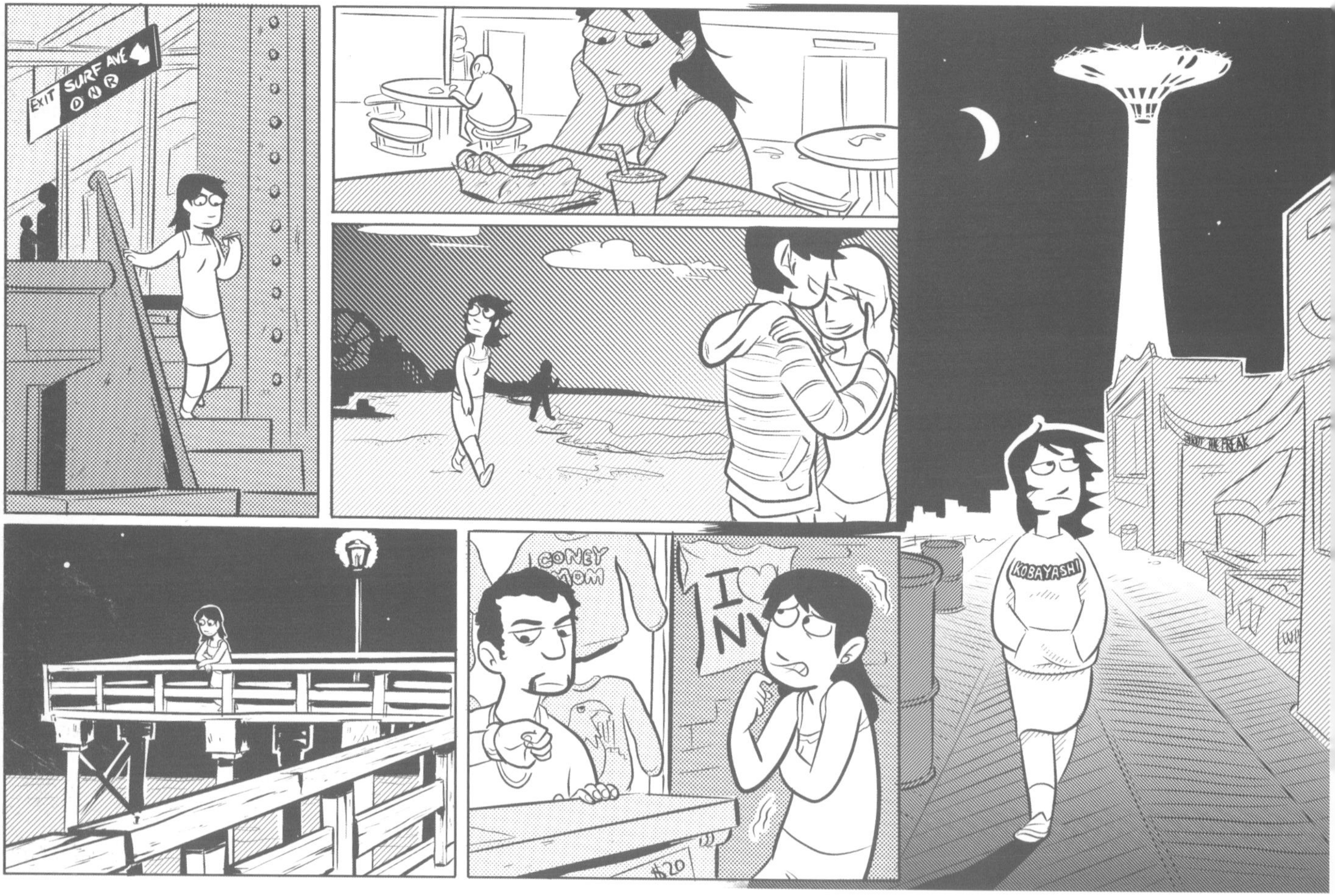
EXIT
SURF AVE
D N R
CONEY MOM
I ♥ NY
KOBAYASHI
$20

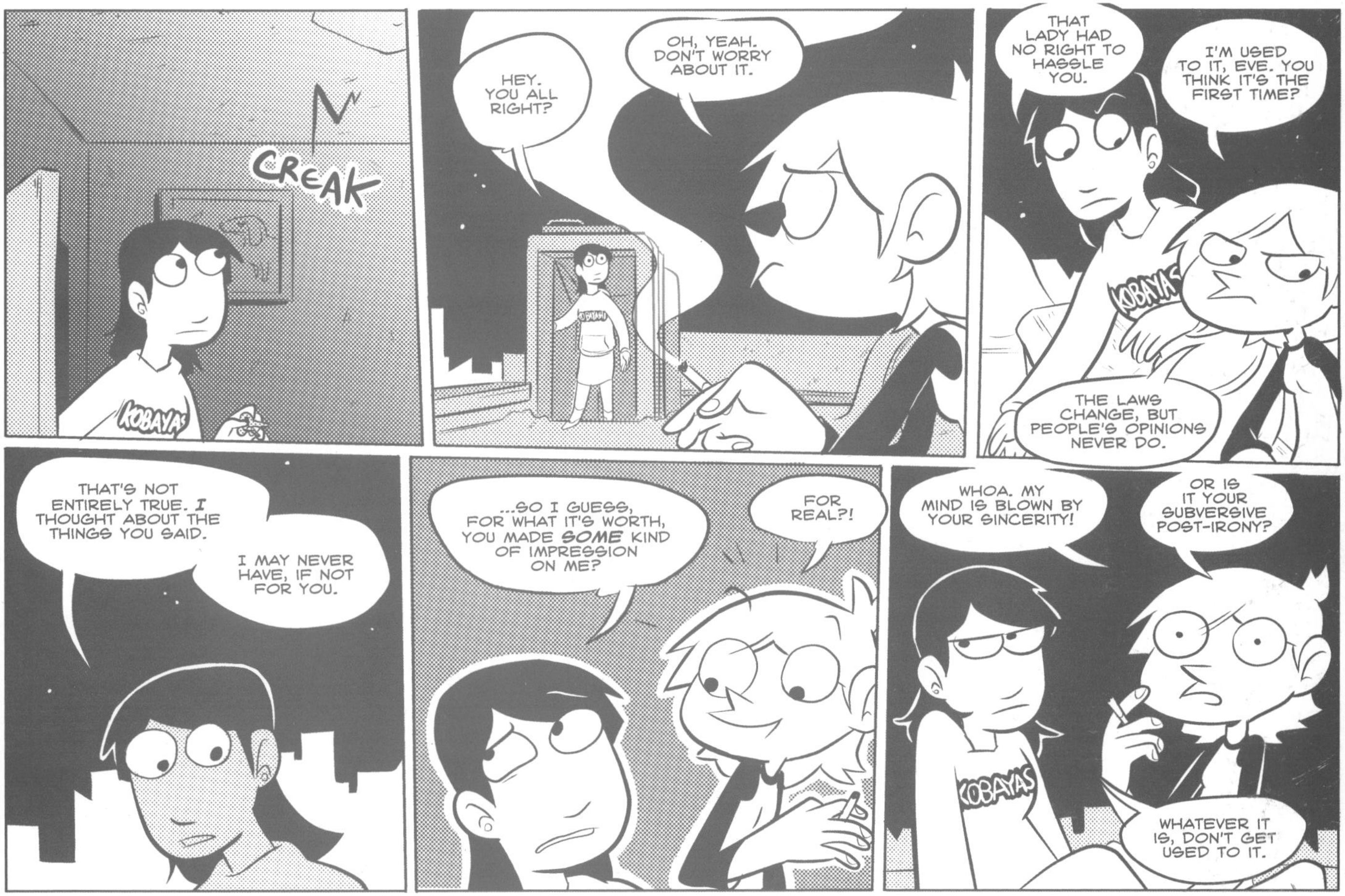
CREAK
HEY. YOU ALL RIGHT?
OH, YEAH. DON'T WORRY ABOUT IT.
THAT LADY HAD NO RIGHT TO HASSLE YOU.
I'M USED TO IT, EVE. YOU THINK IT'S THE FIRST TIME?
THE LAWS CHANGE, BUT PEOPLE'S OPINIONS NEVER DO.
THAT'S NOT ENTIRELY TRUE. I THOUGHT ABOUT THE THINGS YOU SAID.
I MAY NEVER HAVE, IF NOT FOR YOU.
...SO I GUESS, FOR WHAT IT'S WORTH, YOU MADE SOME KIND OF IMPRESSION ON ME?
FOR REAL?!
WHOA. MY MIND IS BLOWN BY YOUR SINCERITY!
OR IS IT YOUR SUBVERSIVE POST-IRONY?
WHATEVER IT IS, DON'T GET USED TO IT.

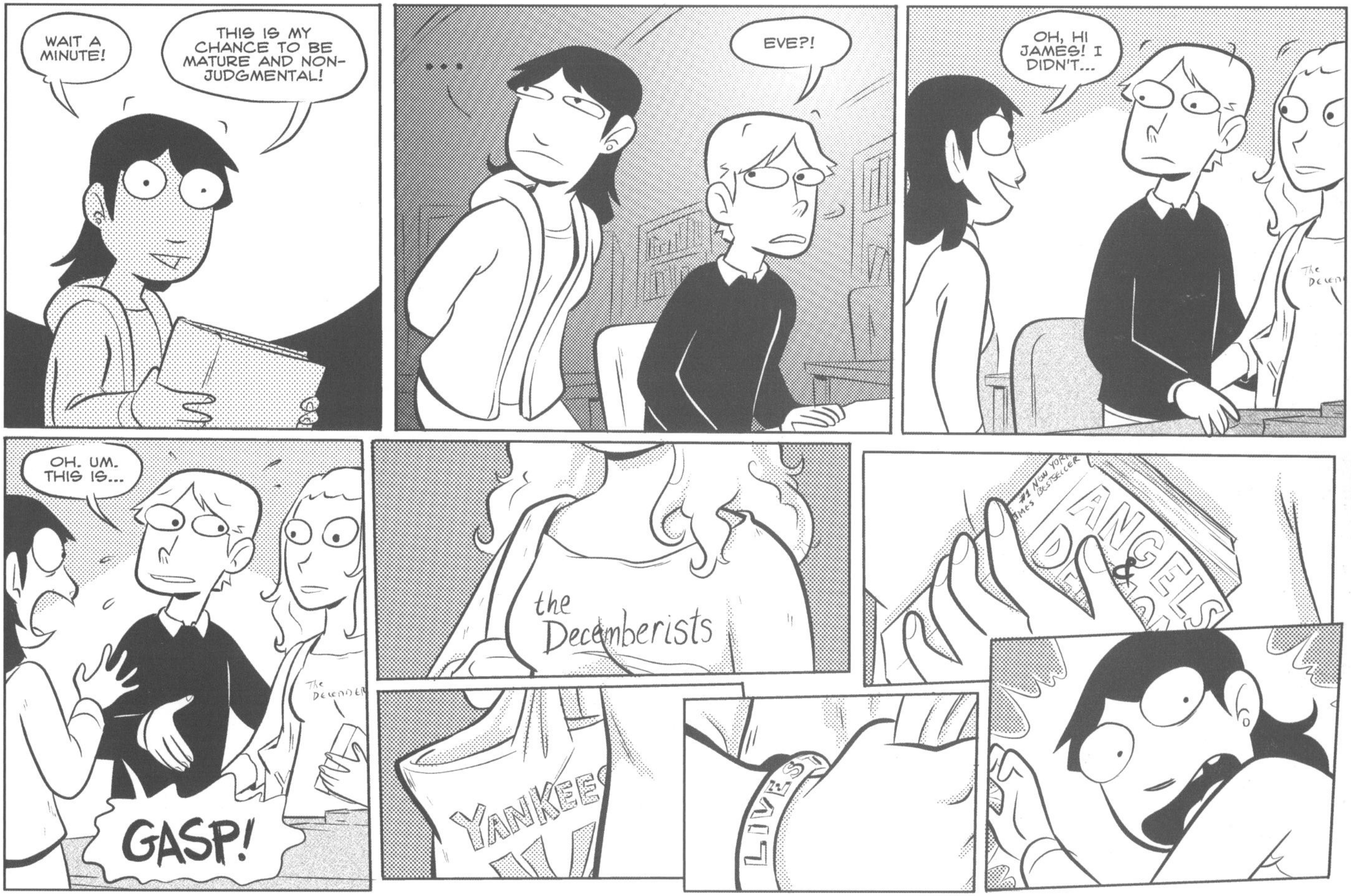
WAIT A MINUTE!
THIS IS MY CHANCE TO BE MATURE AND NON-JUDGMENTAL!
...
EVE?!
OH, HI JAMES! I DIDN'T...
OH. UM. THIS IS...
GASP!
the Decemberists
#1 NEW YORK TIMES BESTSELLER
ANGELS &
YANKEES
LIVEST

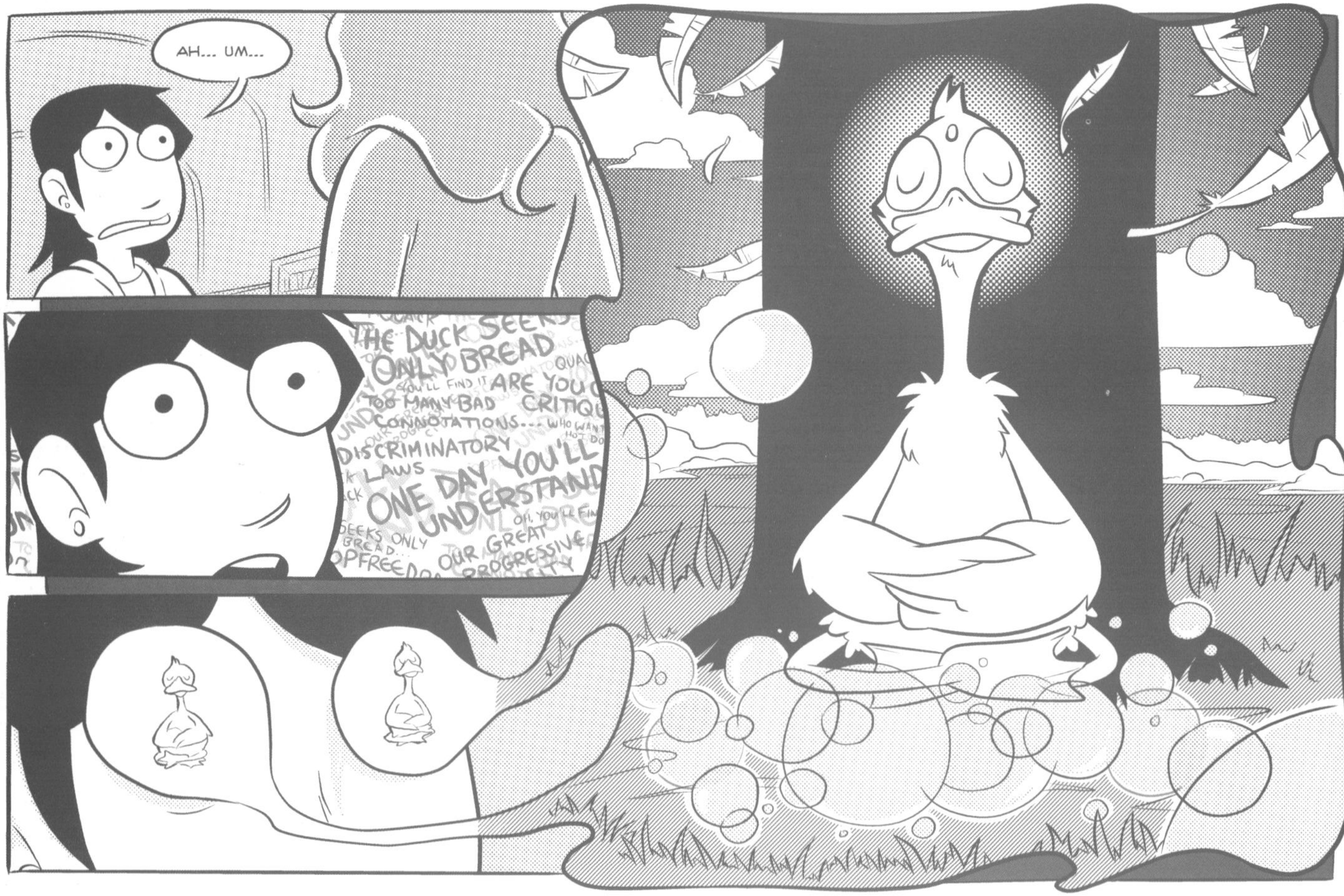
AH... UM...
THE DUCK SEEKS ONLY BREAD
YOU'LL FIND IT
ARE YOU
TOO MANY BAD CONNOTATIONS...
DISCRIMINATORY LAWS
ONE DAY YOU'LL UNDERSTAND
SEEKS ONLY BREAD...
OUR GREAT

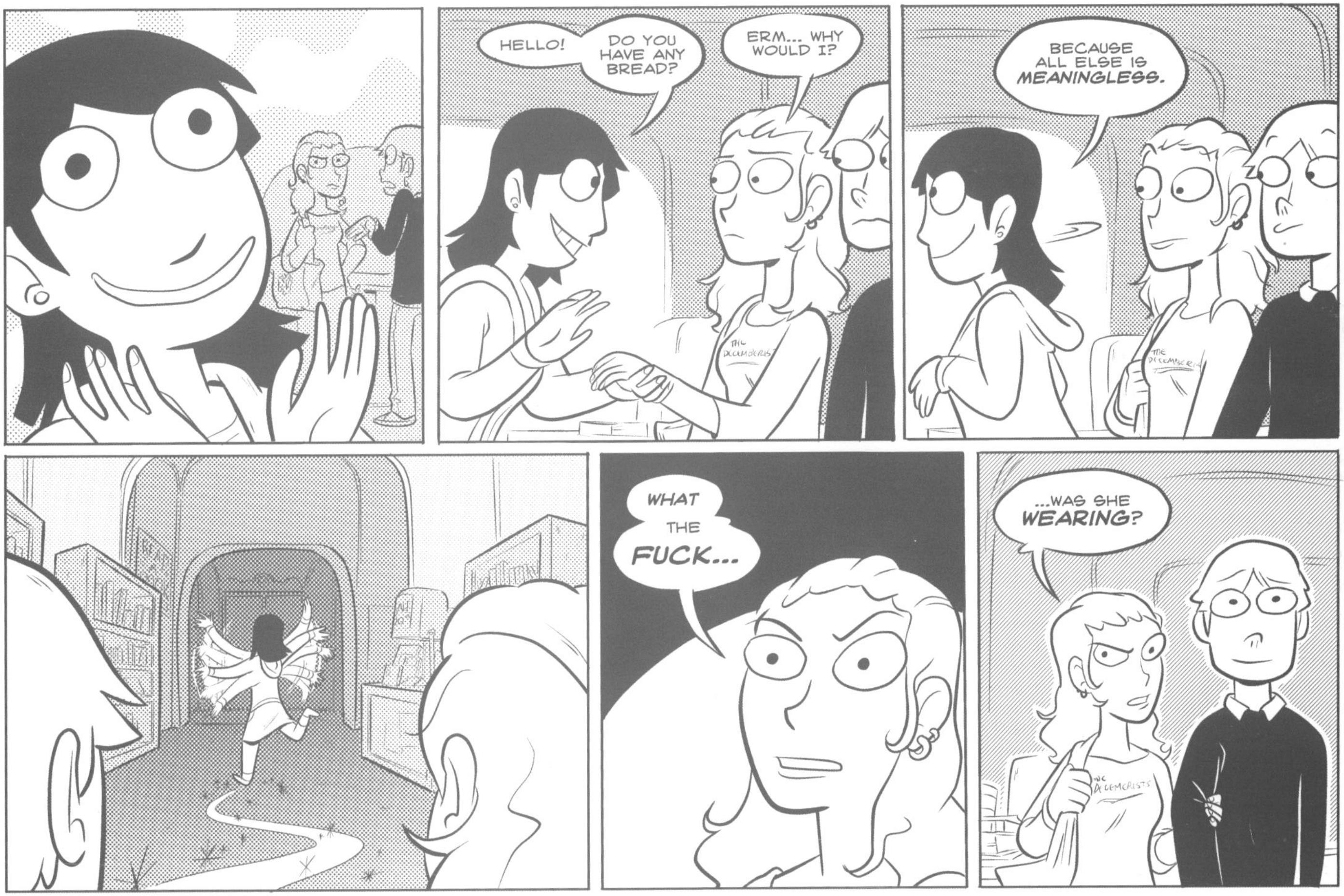
HELLO!
DO YOU HAVE ANY BREAD?
ERM... WHY WOULD I?
BECAUSE ALL ELSE IS *MEANINGLESS.*
WHAT THE *FUCK...*
...WAS SHE *WEARING?*

grocery misconduct

LOOK, OLLY, *I* KNOW THINGS ARE OKAY. YOU DON'T NEED TO CONVINCE *ME*.

THE GUYS, WELL...

...HAVE NO FAITH IN ME.

THEY... WE JUST NEED TO HEAR SOMETHING GOOD. ANYTHING GOOD.

I DON'T KNOW HOW ELSE TO SAY IT, OLLY.

BUT SEE, MARK, I WAS *GETTING* TO THAT!

AWW MAN, WE'RE GONNA HAVE A GREAT YEAR!

BECAUSE... I'M LAUNCHING A BRAND-NEW AD CAMPAIGN!

HOLD STILL, GOD DAMN YOU...

THAT'S THE BEAUTY OF IT! IT'S ONE OF THOSE CANCEROUS MARKETING THINGS.

IT CAN'T FAIL! IN A FEW SHORT MONTHS, *OLLY'S ORGANIX* WILL BE NAILING MORE FINANCIAL GOALS THAN AN OVERAMBITIOUS CAREER SLUT!

YOU ARE? IS THAT IN THE BUDGET?

KRAK

AAAAAAA
AA
AAAA
AA
AA
A
A
AAA
A
A

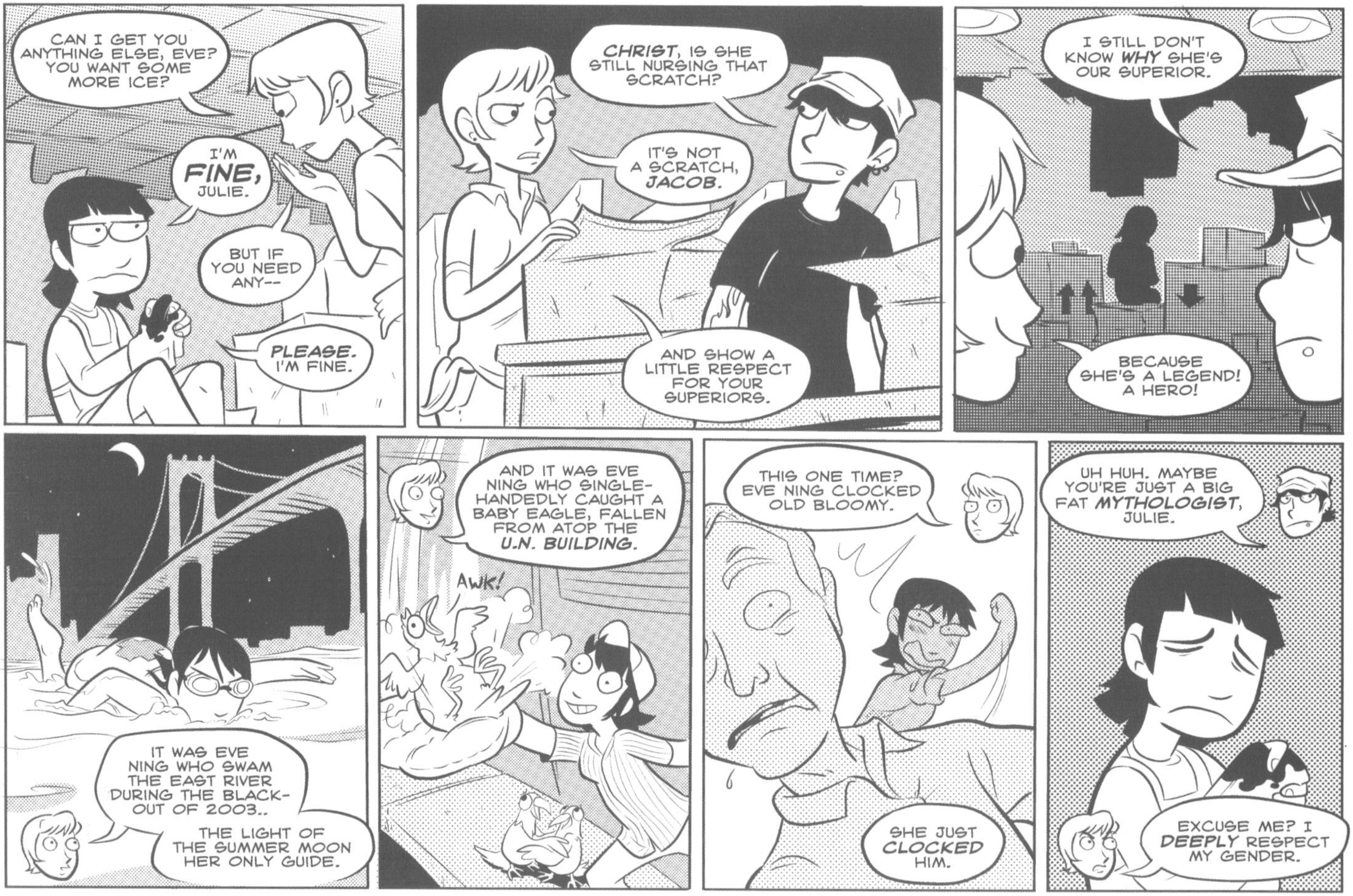
CAN I GET YOU ANYTHING ELSE, EVE? YOU WANT SOME MORE ICE?
I'M FINE, JULIE.
BUT IF YOU NEED ANY--
PLEASE. I'M FINE.
CHRIST, IS SHE STILL NURSING THAT SCRATCH?
IT'S NOT A SCRATCH, JACOB.
AND SHOW A LITTLE RESPECT FOR YOUR SUPERIORS.
I STILL DON'T KNOW WHY SHE'S OUR SUPERIOR.
BECAUSE SHE'S A LEGEND! A HERO!
IT WAS EVE NING WHO SWAM THE EAST RIVER DURING THE BLACK-OUT OF 2003..
THE LIGHT OF THE SUMMER MOON HER ONLY GUIDE.
AND IT WAS EVE NING WHO SINGLE-HANDEDLY CAUGHT A BABY EAGLE, FALLEN FROM ATOP THE U.N. BUILDING.
AWK!
THIS ONE TIME? EVE NING CLOCKED OLD BLOOMY.
SHE JUST CLOCKED HIM.
UH HUH. MAYBE YOU'RE JUST A BIG FAT MYTHOLOGIST, JULIE.
EXCUSE ME? I DEEPLY RESPECT MY GENDER.

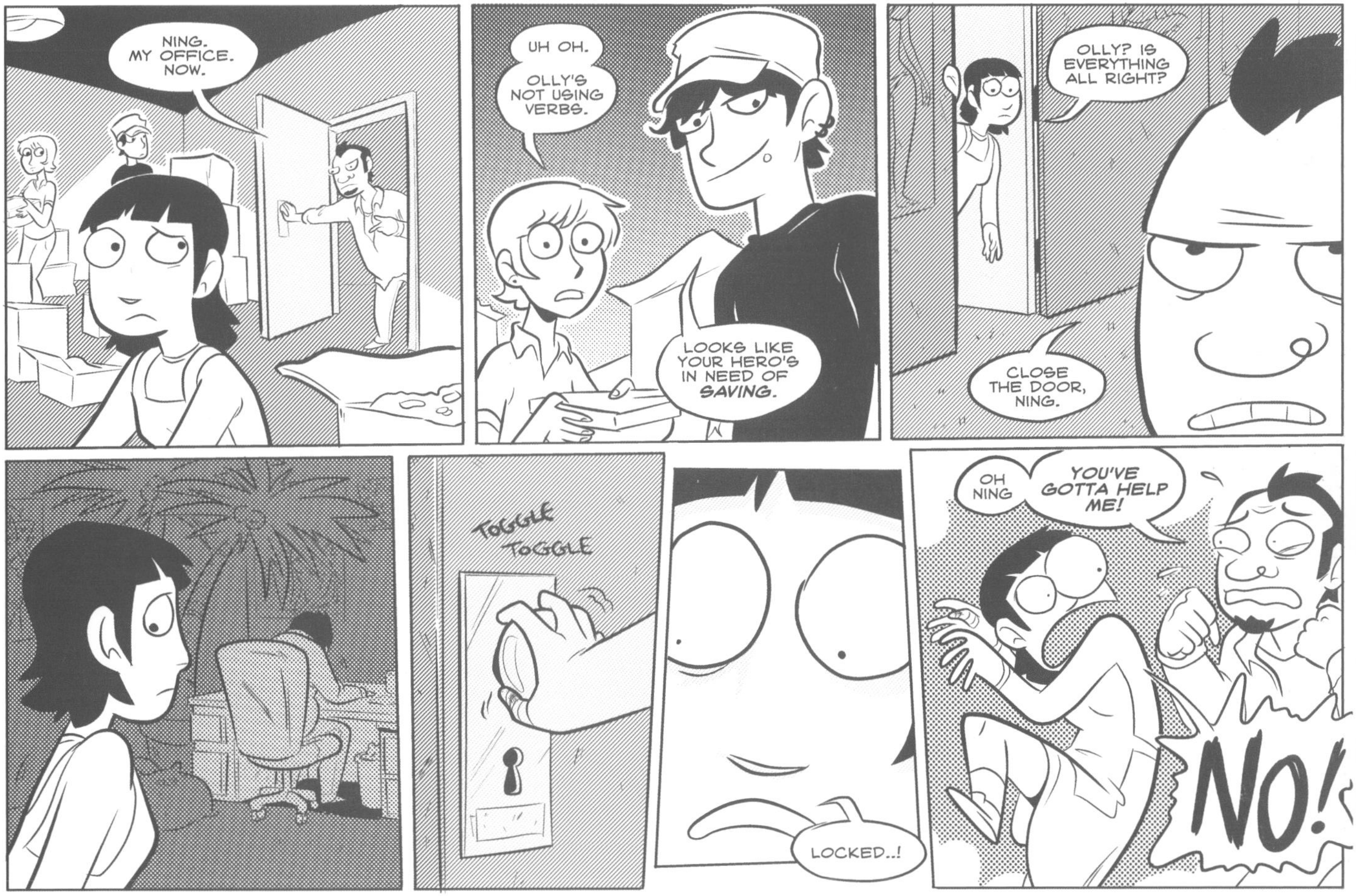
NING. MY OFFICE. NOW.
UH OH.
OLLY'S NOT USING VERBS.
LOOKS LIKE YOUR HERO'S IN NEED OF SAVING.
OLLY? IS EVERYTHING ALL RIGHT?
CLOSE THE DOOR, NING.
TOGGLE TOGGLE
LOCKED..!
OH NING
YOU'VE GOTTA HELP ME!
NO!

AWW, C'MON MANUEL...

I'M *REALLY* ON A DEADLINE HERE.

GLUG!

DING! DING!

oLLyOrG69: hows it coming
Ningrate: give me 20
oLLyOrG69: brb
oLLyOrG69: wats up
oLLyOrG69: hello?
oLLyOrG69: anything new, ning?
oLLyOrG69: brb
oLLyOrG69: wats up

NOT SHINY ENOUGH

ADD MORE SHINE!!

OLLY'S ORGANIX

THE FUKKEN SHIT

9: hows
ive me
9: brb
9: wats
9: hello
9: anyth
9: brb
9: wats

HEY OLLY... HOW'S...*THIS*... LOOK?

oLLyOrG69: ...
dont waste my time, ning

YOU ... GOTTA DELETE ... THAT SWEARING.

COME TO WHAT I *MEANT* BY "BED," ASSHOLE.

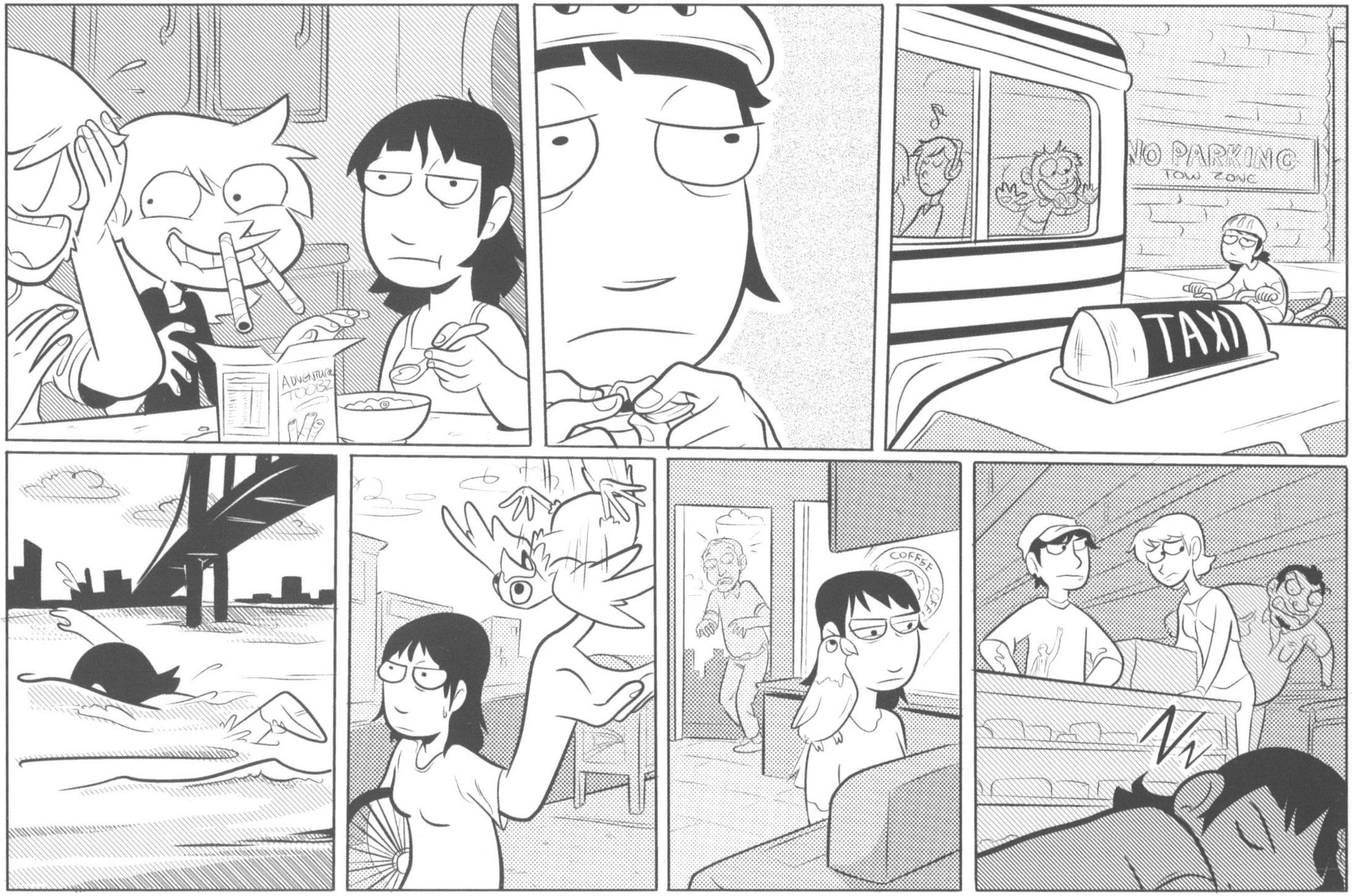
NO PARKING
TOW ZONE
TAXI

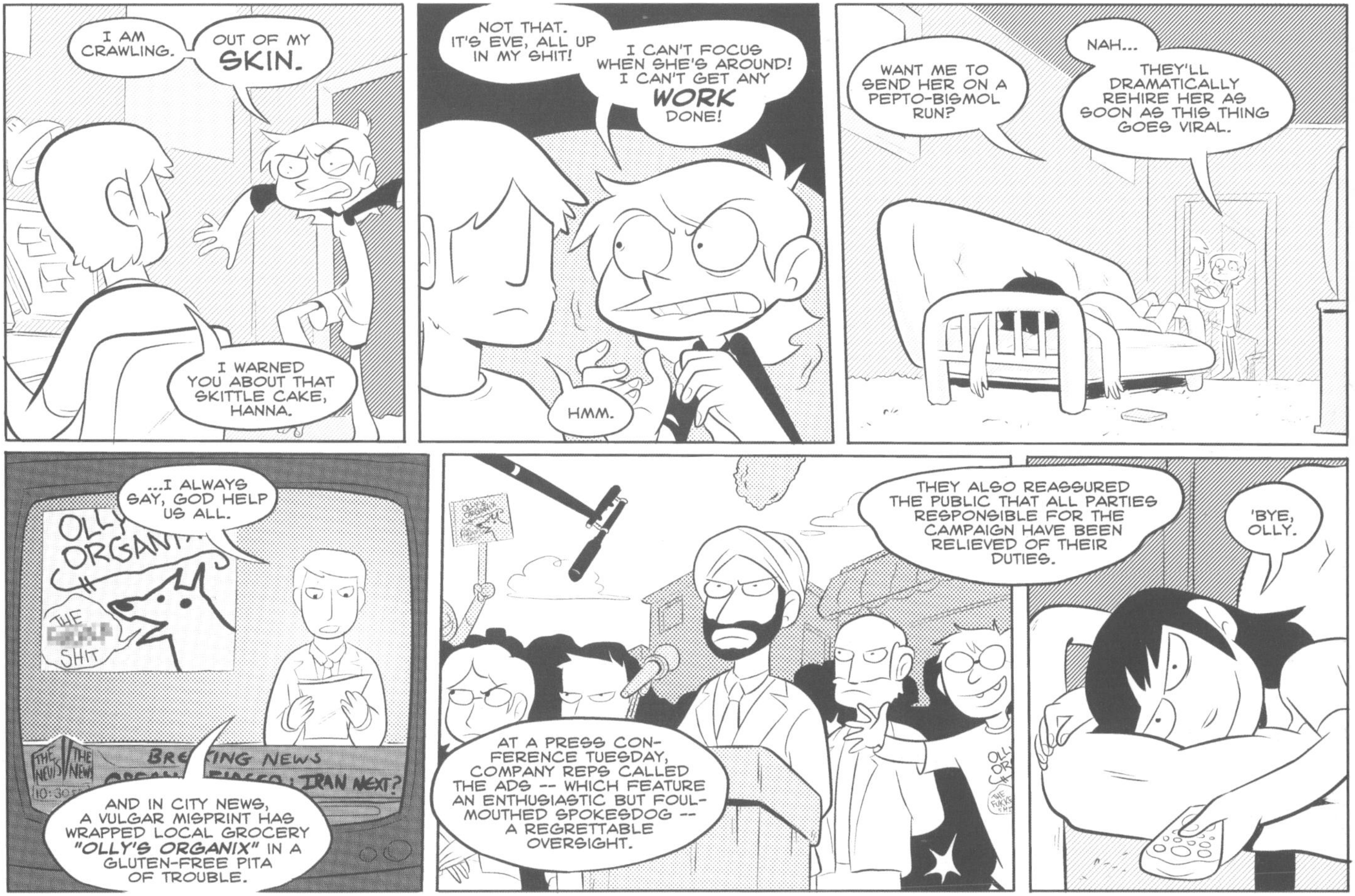
I AM CRAWLING.
OUT OF MY SKIN.
I WARNED YOU ABOUT THAT SKITTLE CAKE, HANNA.
NOT THAT. IT'S EVE, ALL UP IN MY SHIT!
I CAN'T FOCUS WHEN SHE'S AROUND! I CAN'T GET ANY WORK DONE!
HMM.
WANT ME TO SEND HER ON A PEPTO-BISMOL RUN?
NAH...
THEY'LL DRAMATICALLY REHIRE HER AS SOON AS THIS THING GOES VIRAL.
...I ALWAYS SAY, GOD HELP US ALL.
IRAN NEXT?
AND IN CITY NEWS, A VULGAR MISPRINT HAS WRAPPED LOCAL GROCERY "OLLY'S ORGANIX" IN A GLUTEN-FREE PITA OF TROUBLE.
AT A PRESS CONFERENCE TUESDAY, COMPANY REPS CALLED THE ADS -- WHICH FEATURE AN ENTHUSIASTIC BUT FOUL-MOUTHED SPOKESDOG -- A REGRETTABLE OVERSIGHT.
THEY ALSO REASSURED THE PUBLIC THAT ALL PARTIES RESPONSIBLE FOR THE CAMPAIGN HAVE BEEN RELIEVED OF THEIR DUTIES.
'BYE, OLLY.

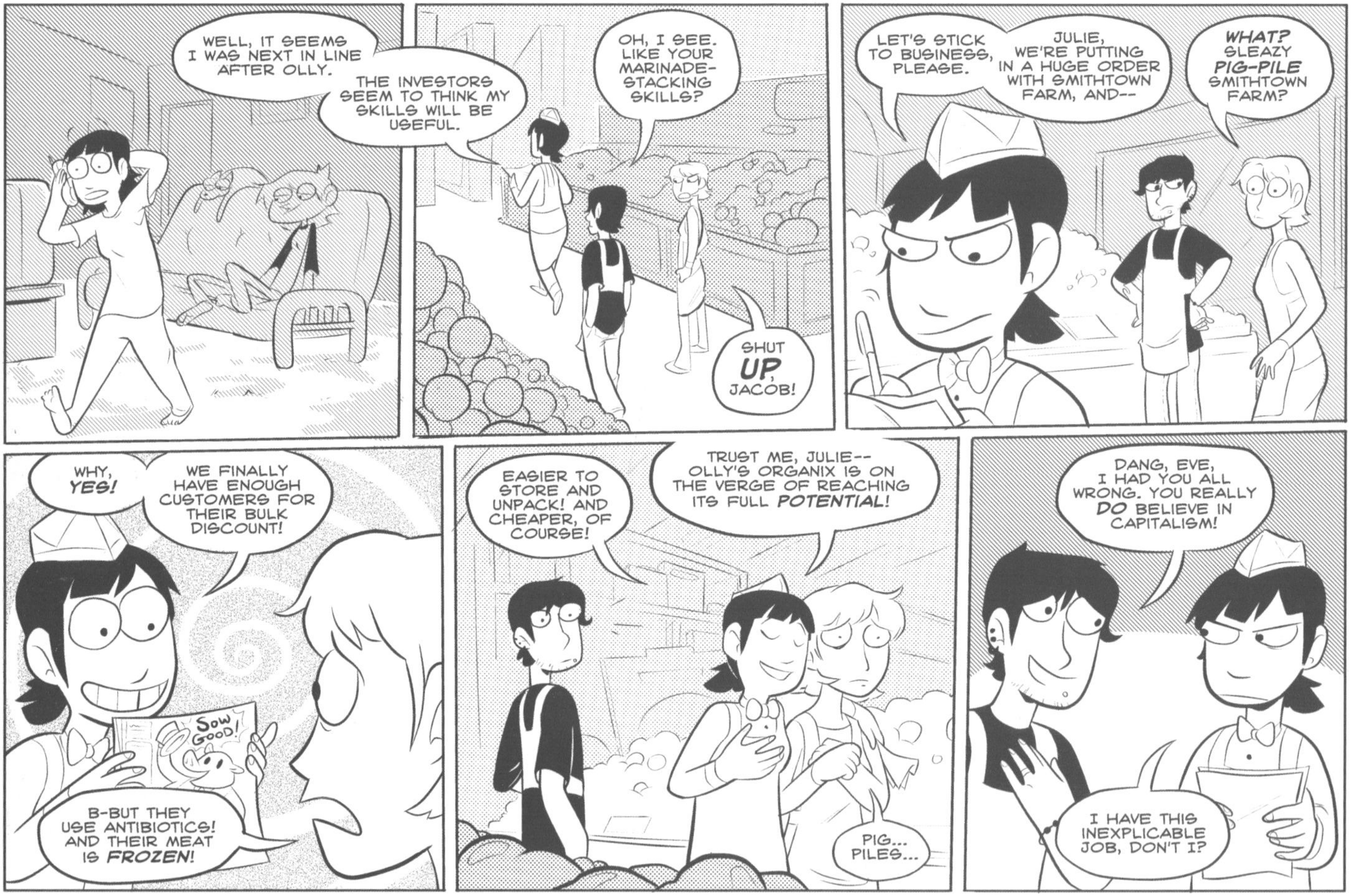
WELL, IT SEEMS I WAS NEXT IN LINE AFTER OLLY.
THE INVESTORS SEEM TO THINK MY SKILLS WILL BE USEFUL.
OH, I SEE. LIKE YOUR MARINADE-STACKING SKILLS?
SHUT UP, JACOB!
LET'S STICK TO BUSINESS, PLEASE.
JULIE, WE'RE PUTTING IN A HUGE ORDER WITH SMITHTOWN FARM, AND--
WHAT? SLEAZY PIG-PILE SMITHTOWN FARM?
WHY, YES!
WE FINALLY HAVE ENOUGH CUSTOMERS FOR THEIR BULK DISCOUNT!
SOW GOOD!
B-BUT THEY USE ANTIBIOTICS! AND THEIR MEAT IS FROZEN!
EASIER TO STORE AND UNPACK! AND CHEAPER, OF COURSE!
TRUST ME, JULIE-- OLLY'S ORGANIX IS ON THE VERGE OF REACHING ITS FULL POTENTIAL!
PIG... PILES...
DANG, EVE, I HAD YOU ALL WRONG. YOU REALLY DO BELIEVE IN CAPITALISM!
I HAVE THIS INEXPLICABLE JOB, DON'T I?

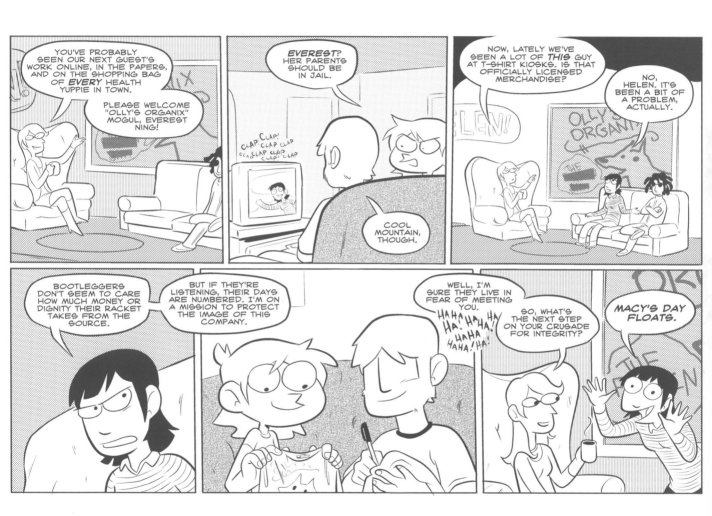

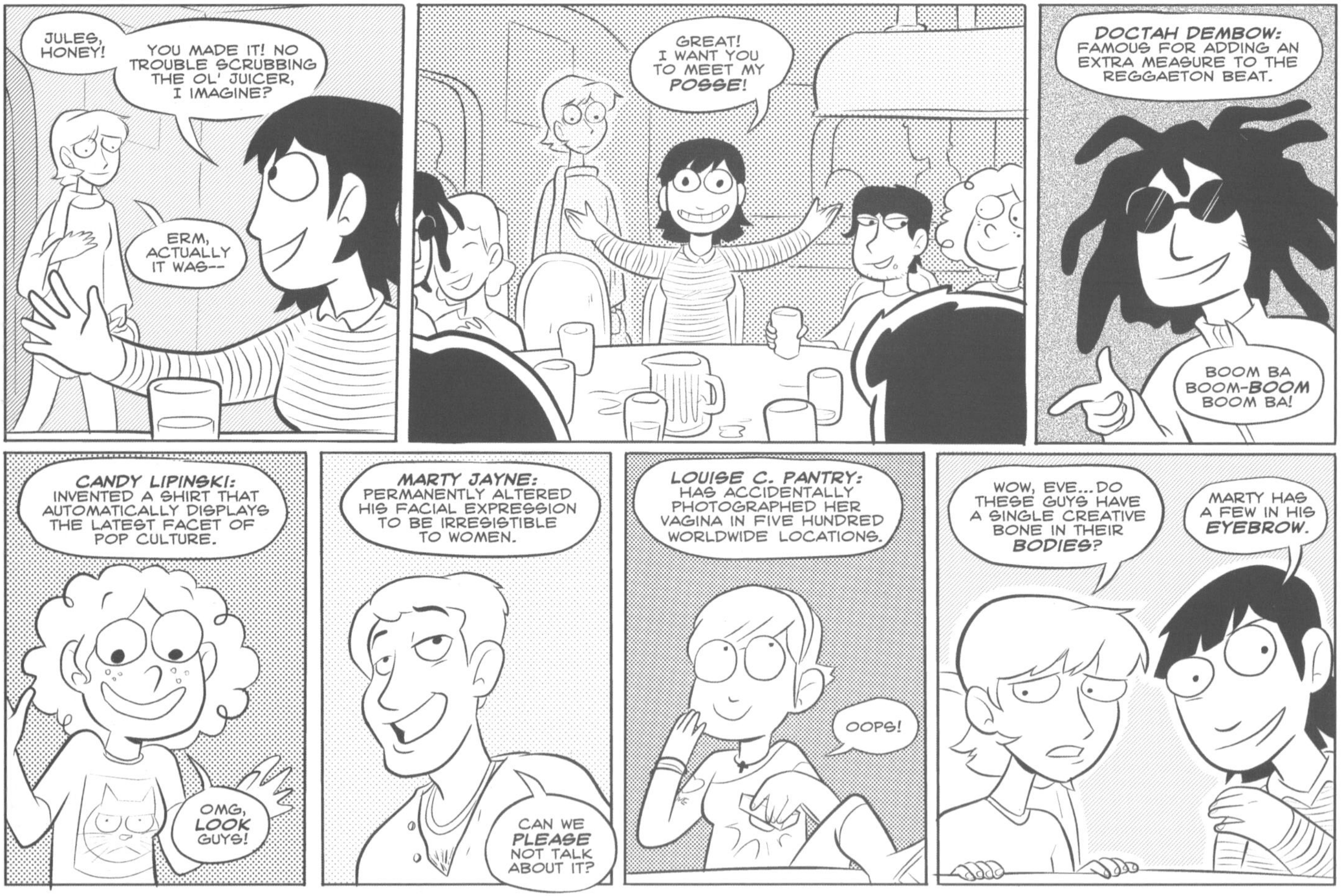
JULES, HONEY!
YOU MADE IT! NO TROUBLE SCRUBBING THE OL' JUICER, I IMAGINE?
ERM, ACTUALLY IT WAS--
GREAT! I WANT YOU TO MEET MY POSSE!
DOCTAH DEMBOW: FAMOUS FOR ADDING AN EXTRA MEASURE TO THE REGGAETON BEAT.
BOOM BA BOOM-BOOM BOOM BA!
CANDY LIPINSKI: INVENTED A SHIRT THAT AUTOMATICALLY DISPLAYS THE LATEST FACET OF POP CULTURE.
OMG, LOOK GUYS!
MARTY JAYNE: PERMANENTLY ALTERED HIS FACIAL EXPRESSION TO BE IRRESISTIBLE TO WOMEN.
CAN WE PLEASE NOT TALK ABOUT IT?
LOUISE C. PANTRY: HAS ACCIDENTALLY PHOTOGRAPHED HER VAGINA IN FIVE HUNDRED WORLDWIDE LOCATIONS.
OOPS!
WOW, EVE...DO THESE GUYS HAVE A SINGLE CREATIVE BONE IN THEIR BODIES?
MARTY HAS A FEW IN HIS EYEBROW.

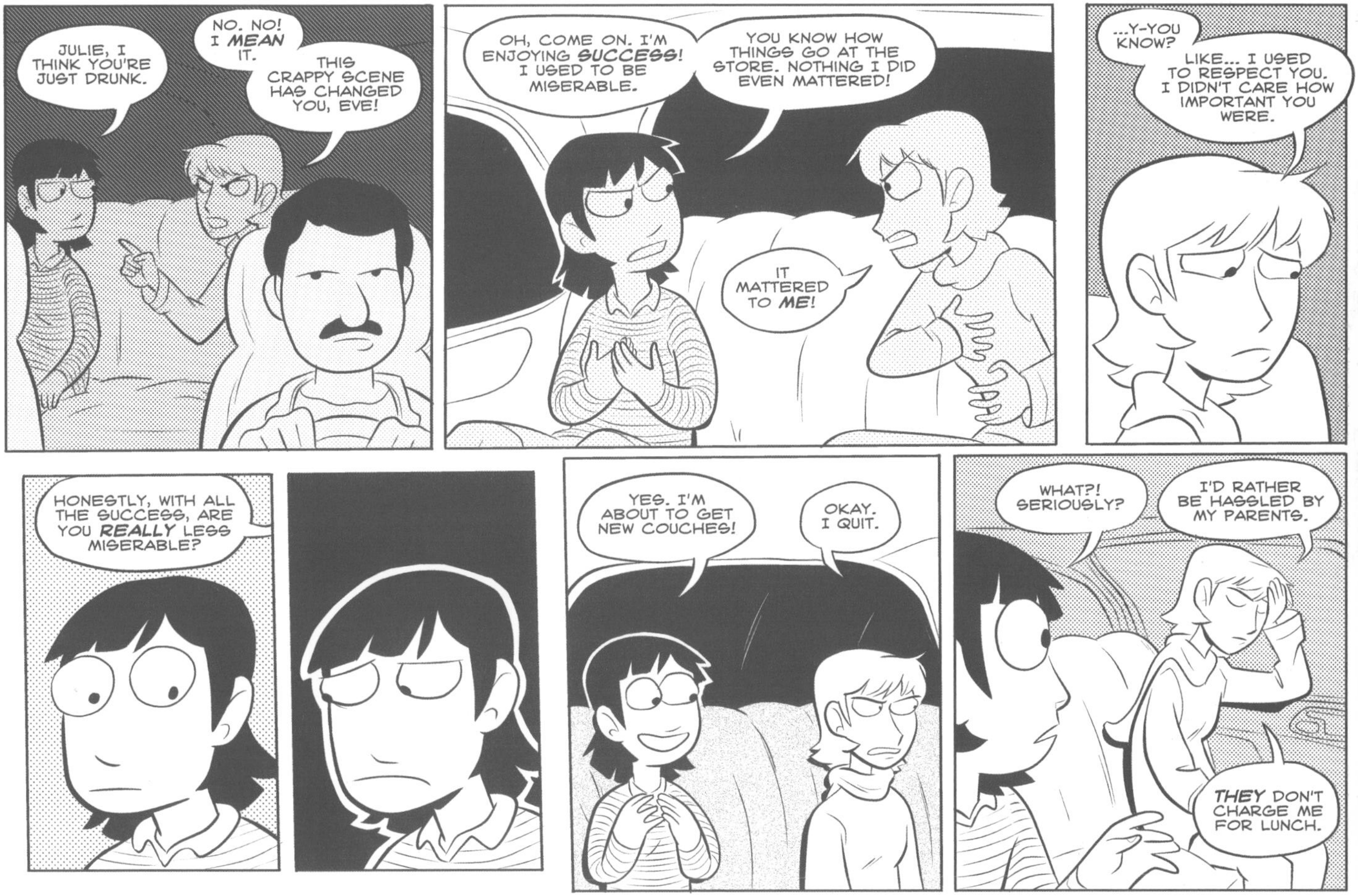
JULIE, I THINK YOU'RE JUST DRUNK.
NO. NO! I MEAN IT.
THIS CRAPPY SCENE HAS CHANGED YOU, EVE!
OH, COME ON. I'M ENJOYING SUCCESS! I USED TO BE MISERABLE.
YOU KNOW HOW THINGS GO AT THE STORE. NOTHING I DID EVEN MATTERED!
IT MATTERED TO ME!
...Y-YOU KNOW?
LIKE... I USED TO RESPECT YOU. I DIDN'T CARE HOW IMPORTANT YOU WERE.
HONESTLY, WITH ALL THE SUCCESS, ARE YOU REALLY LESS MISERABLE?
YES. I'M ABOUT TO GET NEW COUCHES!
OKAY. I QUIT.
WHAT?! SERIOUSLY?
I'D RATHER BE HASSLED BY MY PARENTS.
THEY DON'T CHARGE ME FOR LUNCH.

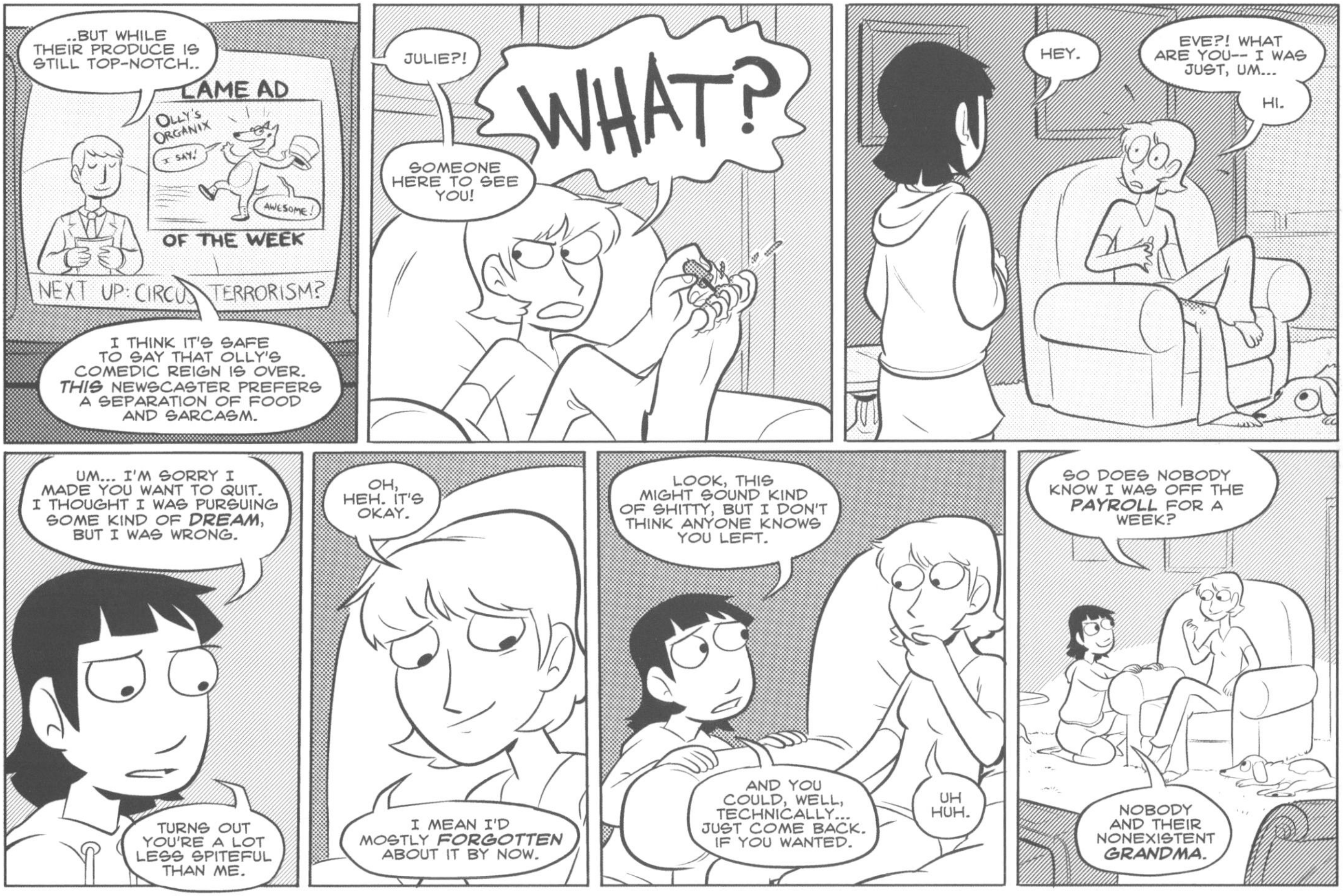

..BUT WHILE THEIR PRODUCE IS STILL TOP-NOTCH..
LAME AD
OLLY'S ORGANIX
I SAY!
AWESOME!
OF THE WEEK
NEXT UP: CIRCUS TERRORISM?
I THINK IT'S SAFE TO SAY THAT OLLY'S COMEDIC REIGN IS OVER. THIS NEWSCASTER PREFERS A SEPARATION OF FOOD AND SARCASM.
JULIE?!
SOMEONE HERE TO SEE YOU!
WHAT?
HEY.
EVE?! WHAT ARE YOU-- I WAS JUST, UM...
HI.
UM... I'M SORRY I MADE YOU WANT TO QUIT. I THOUGHT I WAS PURSUING SOME KIND OF DREAM, BUT I WAS WRONG.
TURNS OUT YOU'RE A LOT LESS SPITEFUL THAN ME.
OH, HEH. IT'S OKAY.
I MEAN I'D MOSTLY FORGOTTEN ABOUT IT BY NOW.
LOOK, THIS MIGHT SOUND KIND OF SHITTY, BUT I DON'T THINK ANYONE KNOWS YOU LEFT.
AND YOU COULD, WELL, TECHNICALLY... JUST COME BACK. IF YOU WANTED.
UH HUH.
SO DOES NOBODY KNOW I WAS OFF THE PAYROLL FOR A WEEK?
NOBODY AND THEIR NONEXISTENT GRANDMA.

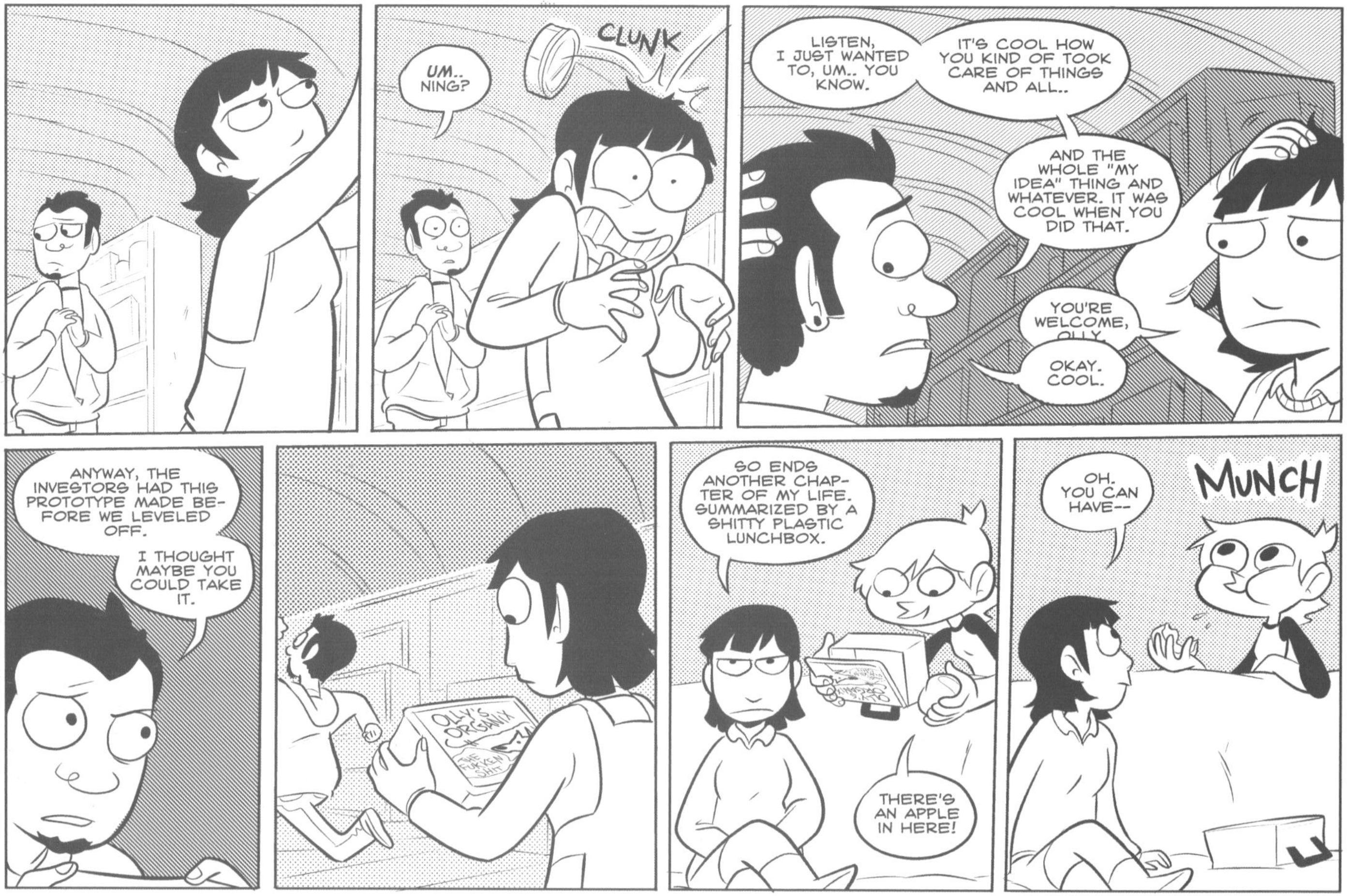
UM.. NING?
CLUNK
LISTEN, I JUST WANTED TO, UM.. YOU KNOW.
IT'S COOL HOW YOU KIND OF TOOK CARE OF THINGS AND ALL..
AND THE WHOLE "MY IDEA" THING AND WHATEVER. IT WAS COOL WHEN YOU DID THAT.
YOU'RE WELCOME,
OKAY. COOL.
ANYWAY, THE INVESTORS HAD THIS PROTOTYPE MADE BE- FORE WE LEVELED OFF.
I THOUGHT MAYBE YOU COULD TAKE IT.
OLLY'S ORGANIX
SO ENDS ANOTHER CHAP- TER OF MY LIFE. SUMMARIZED BY A SHITTY PLASTIC LUNCHBOX.
THERE'S AN APPLE IN HERE!
OH. YOU CAN HAVE--
MUNCH

natural phenomenon

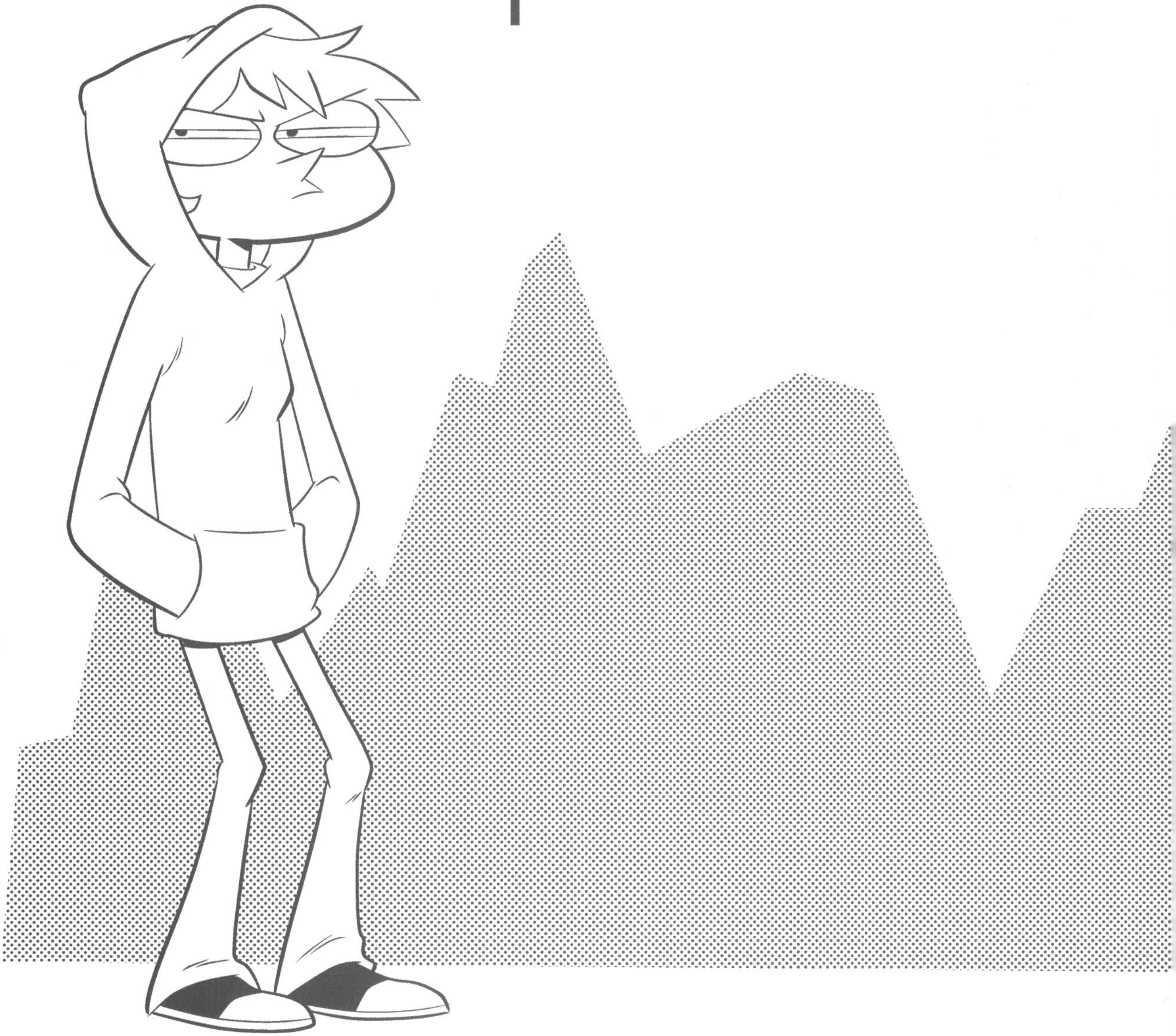

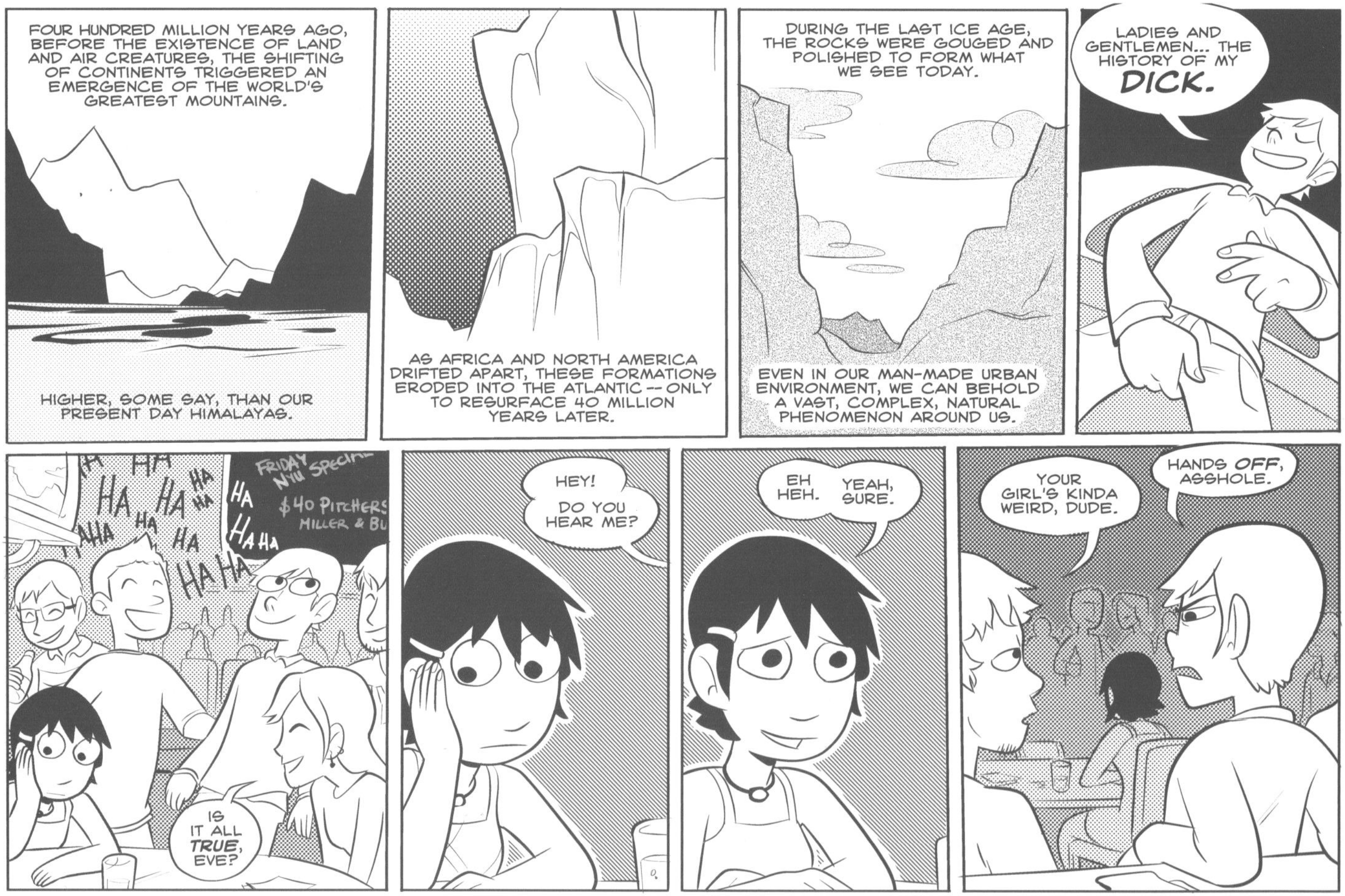
FOUR HUNDRED MILLION YEARS AGO, BEFORE THE EXISTENCE OF LAND AND AIR CREATURES, THE SHIFTING OF CONTINENTS TRIGGERED AN EMERGENCE OF THE WORLD'S GREATEST MOUNTAINS.
HIGHER, SOME SAY, THAN OUR PRESENT DAY HIMALAYAS.
AS AFRICA AND NORTH AMERICA DRIFTED APART, THESE FORMATIONS ERODED INTO THE ATLANTIC -- ONLY TO RESURFACE 40 MILLION YEARS LATER.
DURING THE LAST ICE AGE, THE ROCKS WERE GOUGED AND POLISHED TO FORM WHAT WE SEE TODAY.
EVEN IN OUR MAN-MADE URBAN ENVIRONMENT, WE CAN BEHOLD A VAST, COMPLEX, NATURAL PHENOMENON AROUND US.
LADIES AND GENTLEMEN... THE HISTORY OF MY DICK.
HA HA HA HA HA HA HA HA HA HA HA HA HA HA HAHA
$40 PITCHERS
IS IT ALL TRUE, EVE?
HEY!
DO YOU HEAR ME?
EH HEH.
YEAH, SURE.
YOUR GIRL'S KINDA WEIRD, DUDE.
HANDS OFF, ASSHOLE.

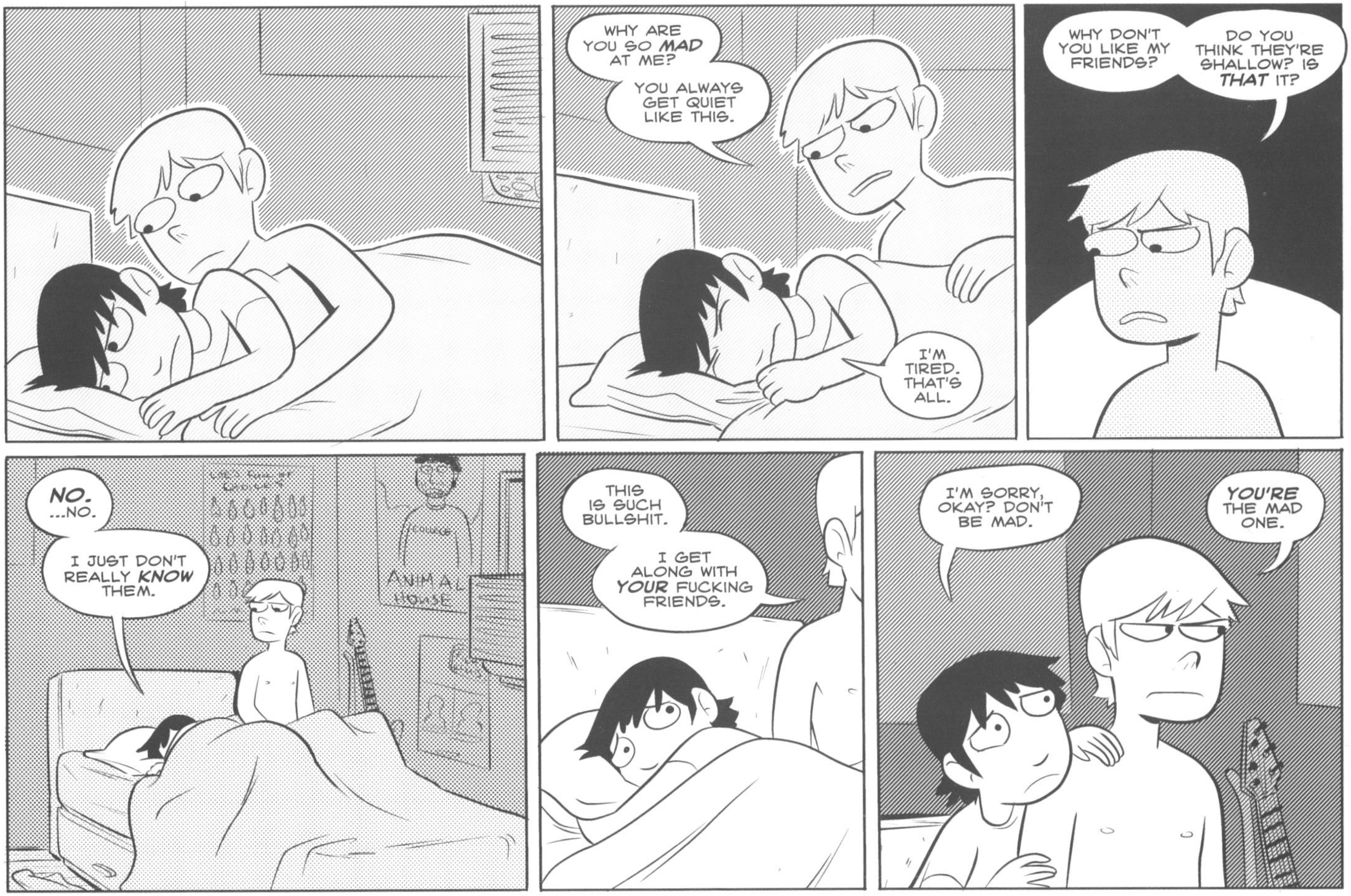
WHY ARE YOU SO **MAD** AT ME?
YOU ALWAYS GET QUIET LIKE THIS.
I'M TIRED. THAT'S ALL.
WHY DON'T YOU LIKE MY FRIENDS?
DO YOU THINK THEY'RE SHALLOW? IS **THAT** IT?
NO. ...NO.
I JUST DON'T REALLY **KNOW** THEM.
ANIMAL HOUSE
THIS IS SUCH BULLSHIT.
I GET ALONG WITH **YOUR** FUCKING FRIENDS.
I'M SORRY, OKAY? DON'T BE MAD.
YOU'RE THE MAD ONE.

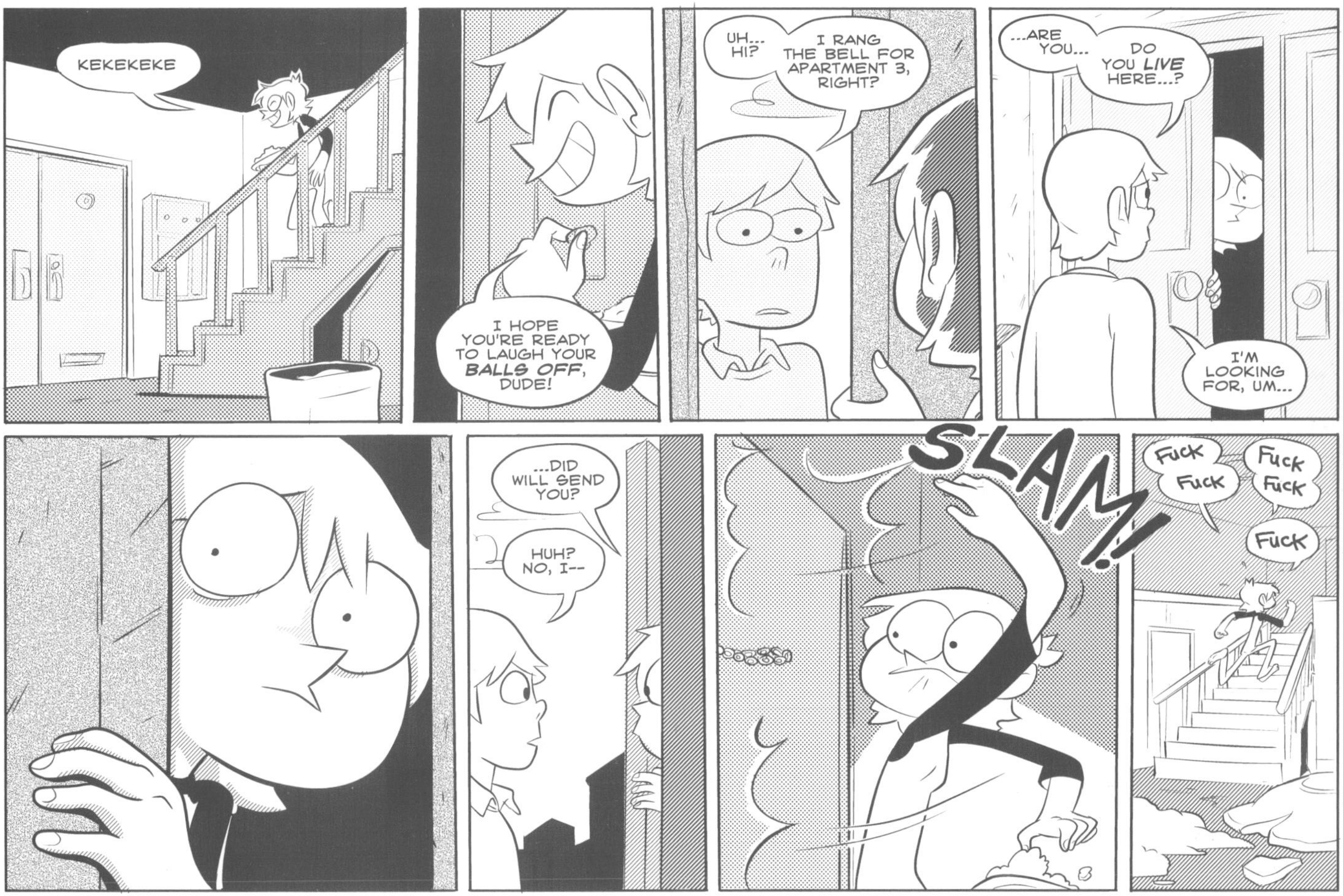
KEKEKEKE
I HOPE YOU'RE READY TO LAUGH YOUR BALLS OFF, DUDE!
UH... HI?
I RANG THE BELL FOR APARTMENT 3, RIGHT?
...ARE YOU...
DO YOU LIVE HERE...?
I'M LOOKING FOR, UM...
...DID WILL SEND YOU?
HUH? NO, I--
SLAM!!
FUCK FUCK
FUCK FUCK
FUCK

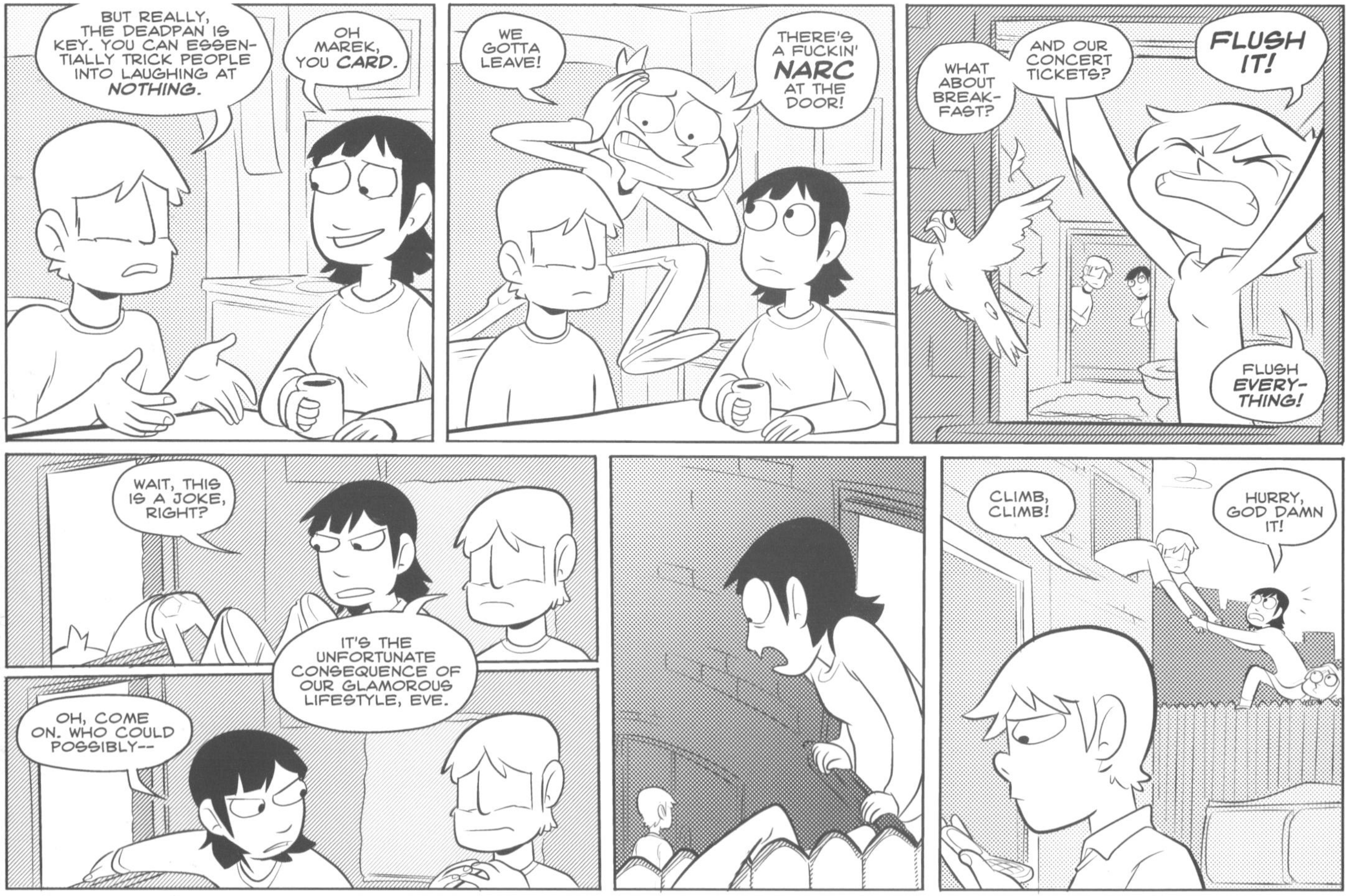
BUT REALLY, THE DEADPAN IS KEY. YOU CAN ESSENTIALLY TRICK PEOPLE INTO LAUGHING AT NOTHING.
OH MAREK, YOU CARD.
WE GOTTA LEAVE!
THERE'S A FUCKIN' NARC AT THE DOOR!
WHAT ABOUT BREAKFAST?
AND OUR CONCERT TICKETS?
FLUSH IT!
FLUSH EVERYTHING!
WAIT, THIS IS A JOKE, RIGHT?
IT'S THE UNFORTUNATE CONSEQUENCE OF OUR GLAMOROUS LIFESTYLE, EVE.
OH, COME ON. WHO COULD POSSIBLY--
CLIMB, CLIMB!
HURRY, GOD DAMN IT!

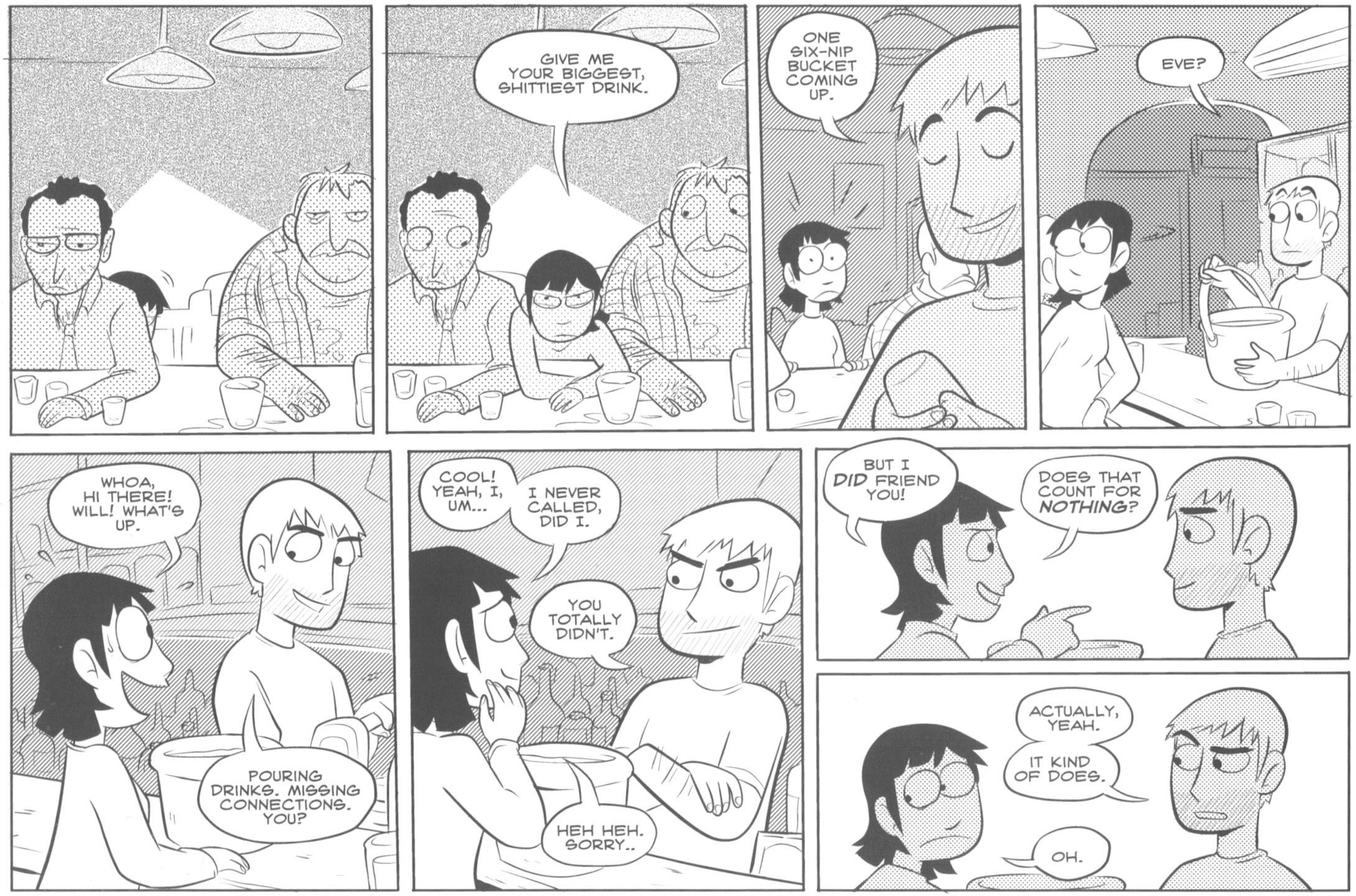
GIVE ME YOUR BIGGEST, SHITTIEST DRINK.
ONE SIX-NIP BUCKET COMING UP.
EVE?
WHOA, HI THERE! WILL! WHAT'S UP.
POURING DRINKS. MISSING CONNECTIONS. YOU?
COOL! YEAH, I, UM...
I NEVER CALLED, DID I.
YOU TOTALLY DIDN'T.
HEH HEH. SORRY..
BUT I DID FRIEND YOU!
DOES THAT COUNT FOR NOTHING?
ACTUALLY, YEAH.
IT KIND OF DOES.
OH.

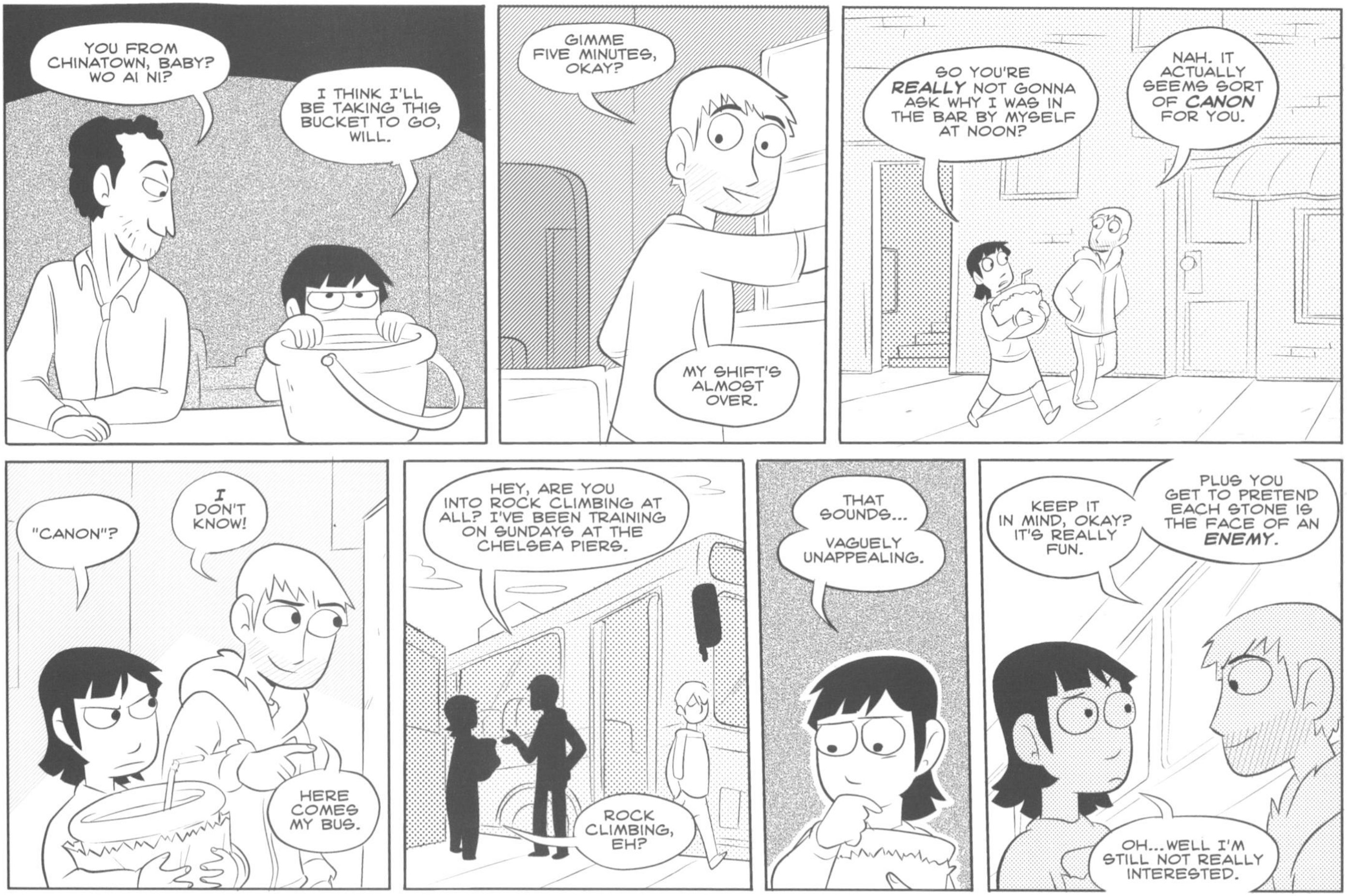
YOU FROM CHINATOWN, BABY? WO AI NI?
I THINK I'LL BE TAKING THIS BUCKET TO GO, WILL.
GIMME FIVE MINUTES, OKAY?
MY SHIFT'S ALMOST OVER.
SO YOU'RE REALLY NOT GONNA ASK WHY I WAS IN THE BAR BY MYSELF AT NOON?
NAH. IT ACTUALLY SEEMS SORT OF CANON FOR YOU.
"CANON"?
I DON'T KNOW!
HERE COMES MY BUS.
HEY, ARE YOU INTO ROCK CLIMBING AT ALL? I'VE BEEN TRAINING ON SUNDAYS AT THE CHELSEA PIERS.
ROCK CLIMBING, EH?
THAT SOUNDS...
VAGUELY UNAPPEALING.
KEEP IT IN MIND, OKAY? IT'S REALLY FUN.
PLUS YOU GET TO PRETEND EACH STONE IS THE FACE OF AN ENEMY.
OH...WELL I'M STILL NOT REALLY INTERESTED.

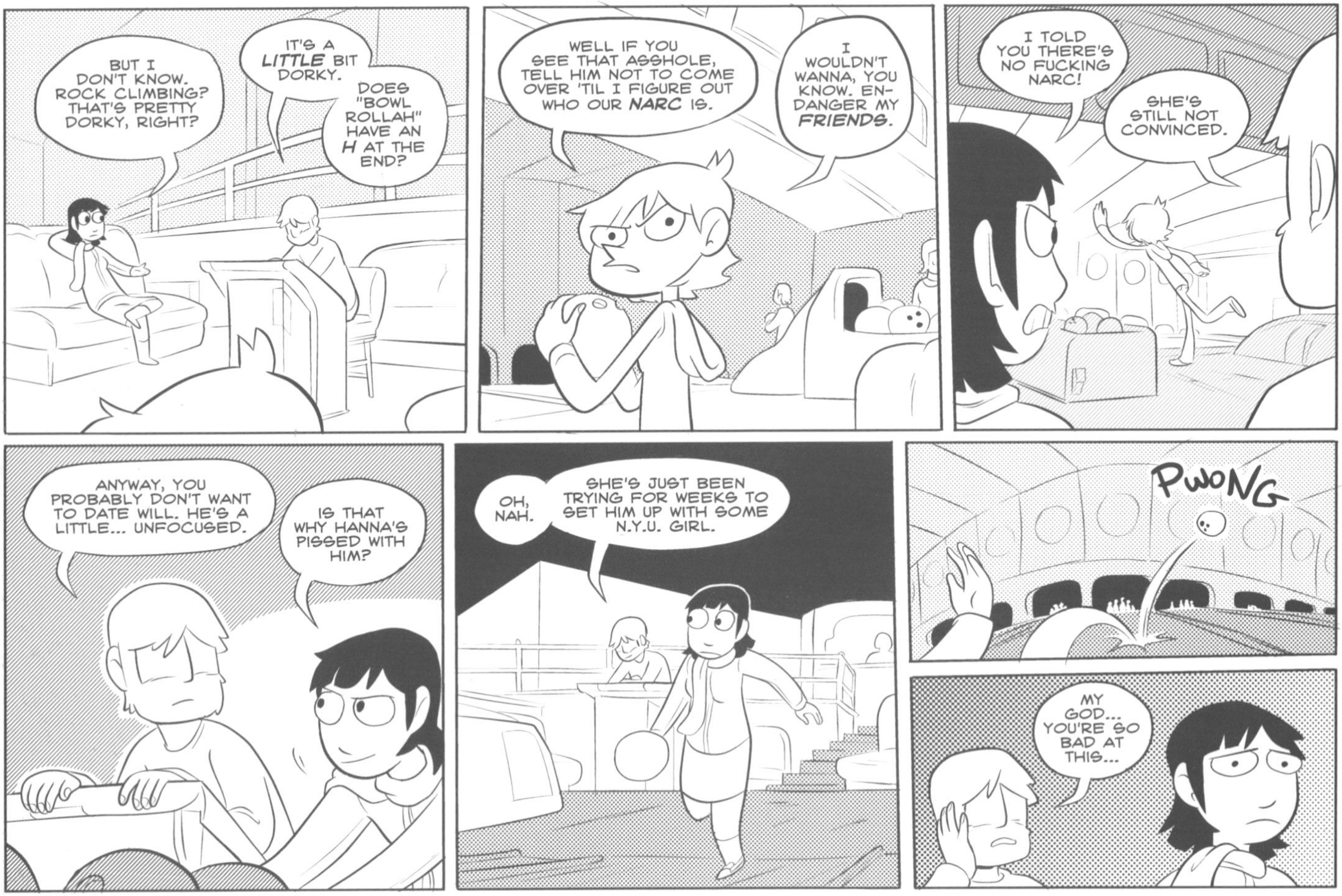
BUT I DON'T KNOW. ROCK CLIMBING? THAT'S PRETTY DORKY, RIGHT?
IT'S A LITTLE BIT DORKY.
DOES "BOWL ROLLAH" HAVE AN H AT THE END?
WELL IF YOU SEE THAT ASSHOLE, TELL HIM NOT TO COME OVER 'TIL I FIGURE OUT WHO OUR NARC IS.
I WOULDN'T WANNA, YOU KNOW. EN-DANGER MY FRIENDS.
I TOLD YOU THERE'S NO FUCKING NARC!
SHE'S STILL NOT CONVINCED.
ANYWAY, YOU PROBABLY DON'T WANT TO DATE WILL. HE'S A LITTLE... UNFOCUSED.
IS THAT WHY HANNA'S PISSED WITH HIM?
OH, NAH.
SHE'S JUST BEEN TRYING FOR WEEKS TO SET HIM UP WITH SOME N.Y.U. GIRL.
PWONG
MY GOD... YOU'RE SO BAD AT THIS...

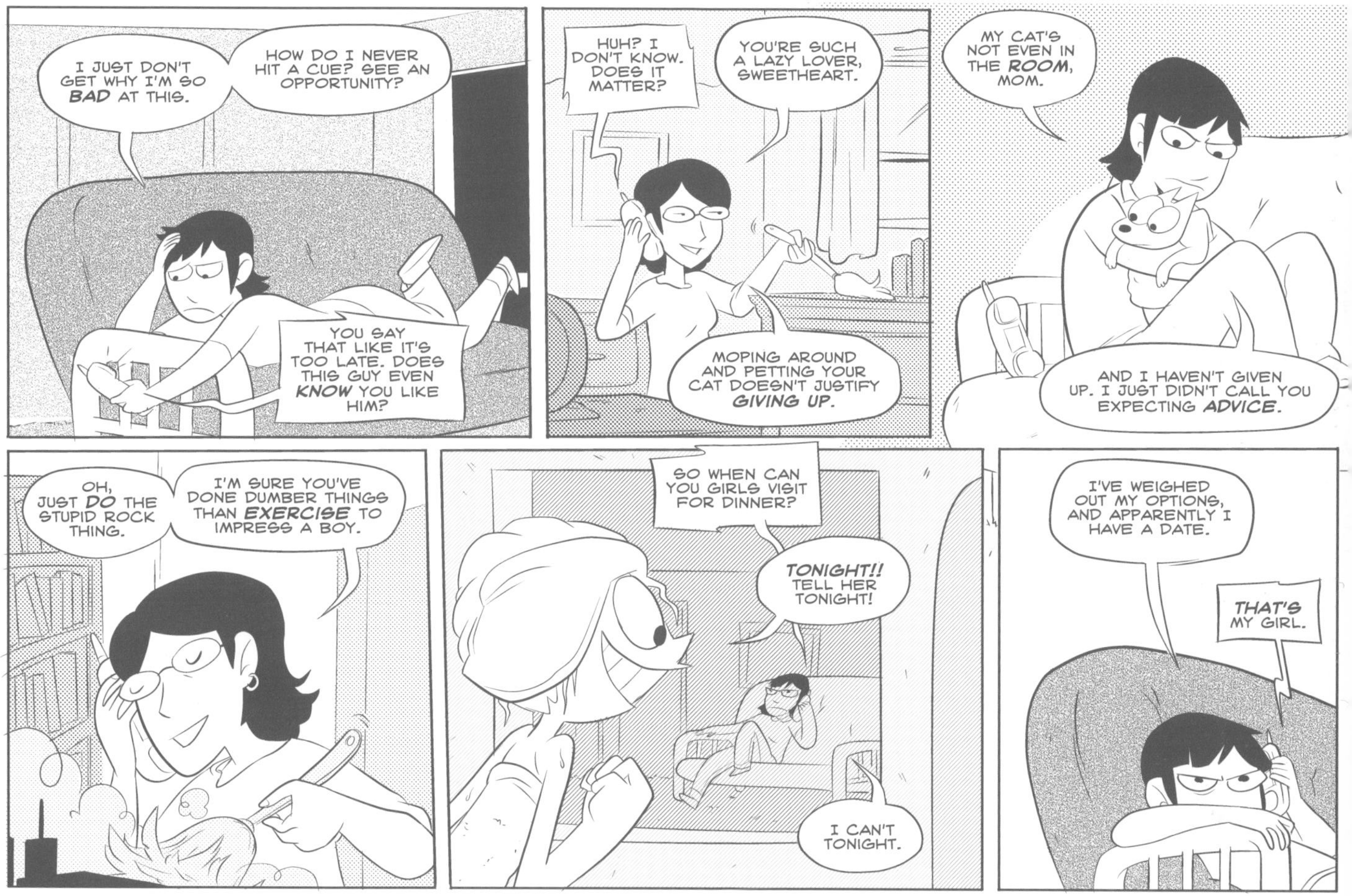
I JUST DON'T GET WHY I'M SO BAD AT THIS.
HOW DO I NEVER HIT A CUE? SEE AN OPPORTUNITY?
YOU SAY THAT LIKE IT'S TOO LATE. DOES THIS GUY EVEN KNOW YOU LIKE HIM?
HUH? I DON'T KNOW. DOES IT MATTER?
YOU'RE SUCH A LAZY LOVER, SWEETHEART.
MOPING AROUND AND PETTING YOUR CAT DOESN'T JUSTIFY GIVING UP.
MY CAT'S NOT EVEN IN THE ROOM, MOM.
AND I HAVEN'T GIVEN UP. I JUST DIDN'T CALL YOU EXPECTING ADVICE.
OH, JUST DO THE STUPID ROCK THING.
I'M SURE YOU'VE DONE DUMBER THINGS THAN EXERCISE TO IMPRESS A BOY.
SO WHEN CAN YOU GIRLS VISIT FOR DINNER?
TONIGHT!! TELL HER TONIGHT!
I CAN'T TONIGHT.
I'VE WEIGHED OUT MY OPTIONS, AND APPARENTLY I HAVE A DATE.
THAT'S MY GIRL.

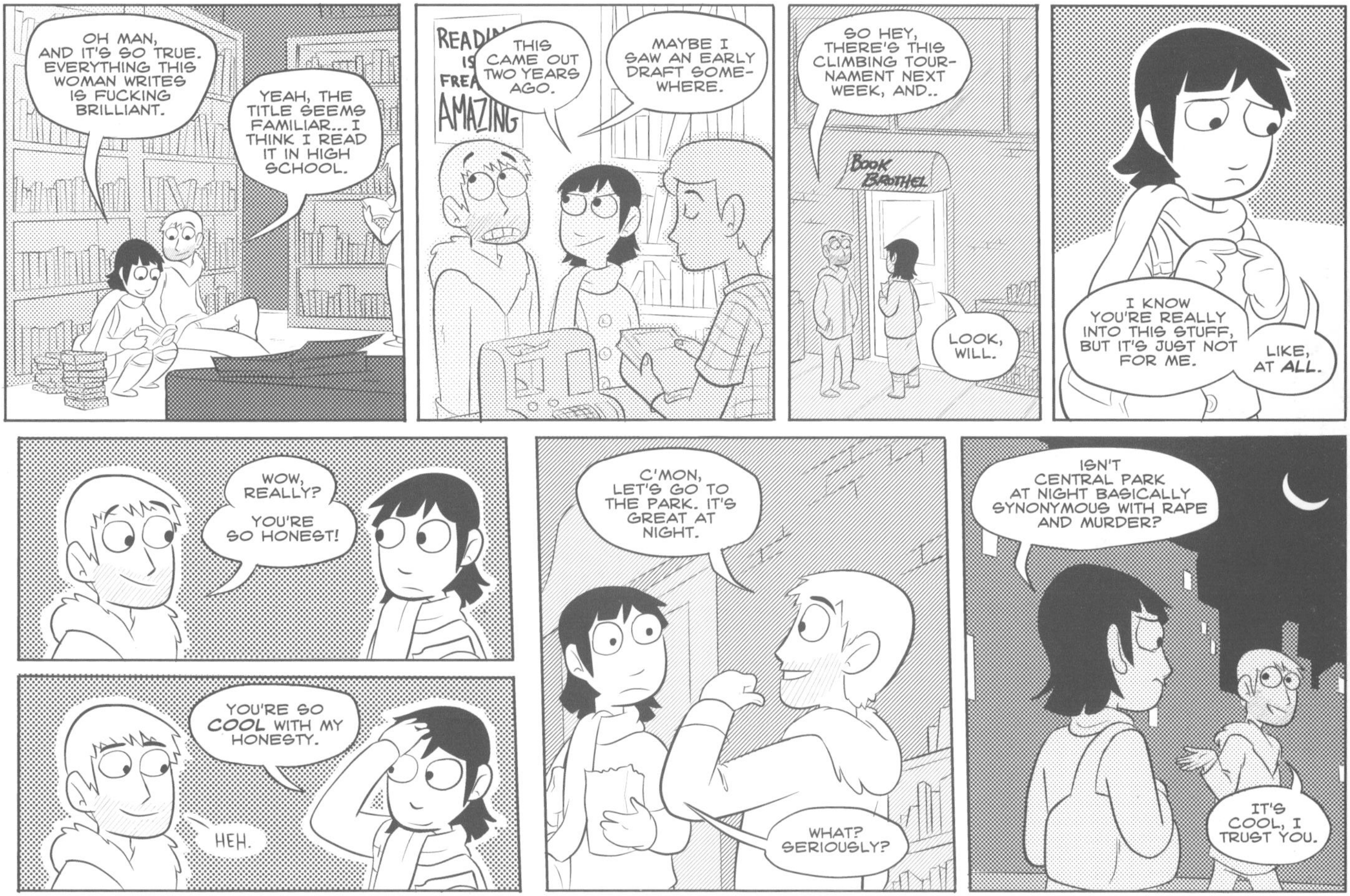
OH MAN, AND IT'S SO TRUE. EVERYTHING THIS WOMAN WRITES IS FUCKING BRILLIANT.
YEAH, THE TITLE SEEMS FAMILIAR... I THINK I READ IT IN HIGH SCHOOL.
READING IS FREA... AMAZING
THIS CAME OUT TWO YEARS AGO.
MAYBE I SAW AN EARLY DRAFT SOME-WHERE.
SO HEY, THERE'S THIS CLIMBING TOUR-NAMENT NEXT WEEK, AND..
BOOK BROTHEL
LOOK, WILL.
I KNOW YOU'RE REALLY INTO THIS STUFF, BUT IT'S JUST NOT FOR ME.
LIKE, AT **ALL**.
WOW, REALLY?
YOU'RE SO HONEST!
YOU'RE SO **COOL** WITH MY HONESTY.
HEH.
C'MON, LET'S GO TO THE PARK. IT'S GREAT AT NIGHT.
WHAT? SERIOUSLY?
ISN'T CENTRAL PARK AT NIGHT BASICALLY SYNONYMOUS WITH RAPE AND MURDER?
IT'S COOL, I TRUST YOU.

..AND THEN, HE SHOWED UP AT MY DOOR. I *RAN*.

RELATIONSHIPS MAKE ME DUMB, WILL. I'VE YET TO FIGURE THEM OUT.

HAS ANYBODY?

FUCKED IF I KNOW.

THAT'S WHY I'M SO INTO ROCKS. THEY'RE SO NEUTRAL. OUR LIVES ARE JUST A SPECK ON THEIR TIMELINE.

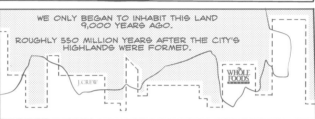

WE ONLY BEGAN TO INHABIT THIS LAND 9,000 YEARS AGO.

ROUGHLY 550 MILLION YEARS AFTER THE CITY'S HIGHLANDS WERE FORMED.

J.CREW

WHOLE FOODS

WE CAN SAY OUR WORLD IS RAPIDLY CHANGING. YET THE FOUNDATION STAYS THE SAME.

IT WAS HERE BEFORE US. IT'LL BE HERE LONG AFTER WE'RE GONE.

THAT'S *ONE* WAY TO END MY STORY.

I PROMISE I'M REALLY INTERESTED.

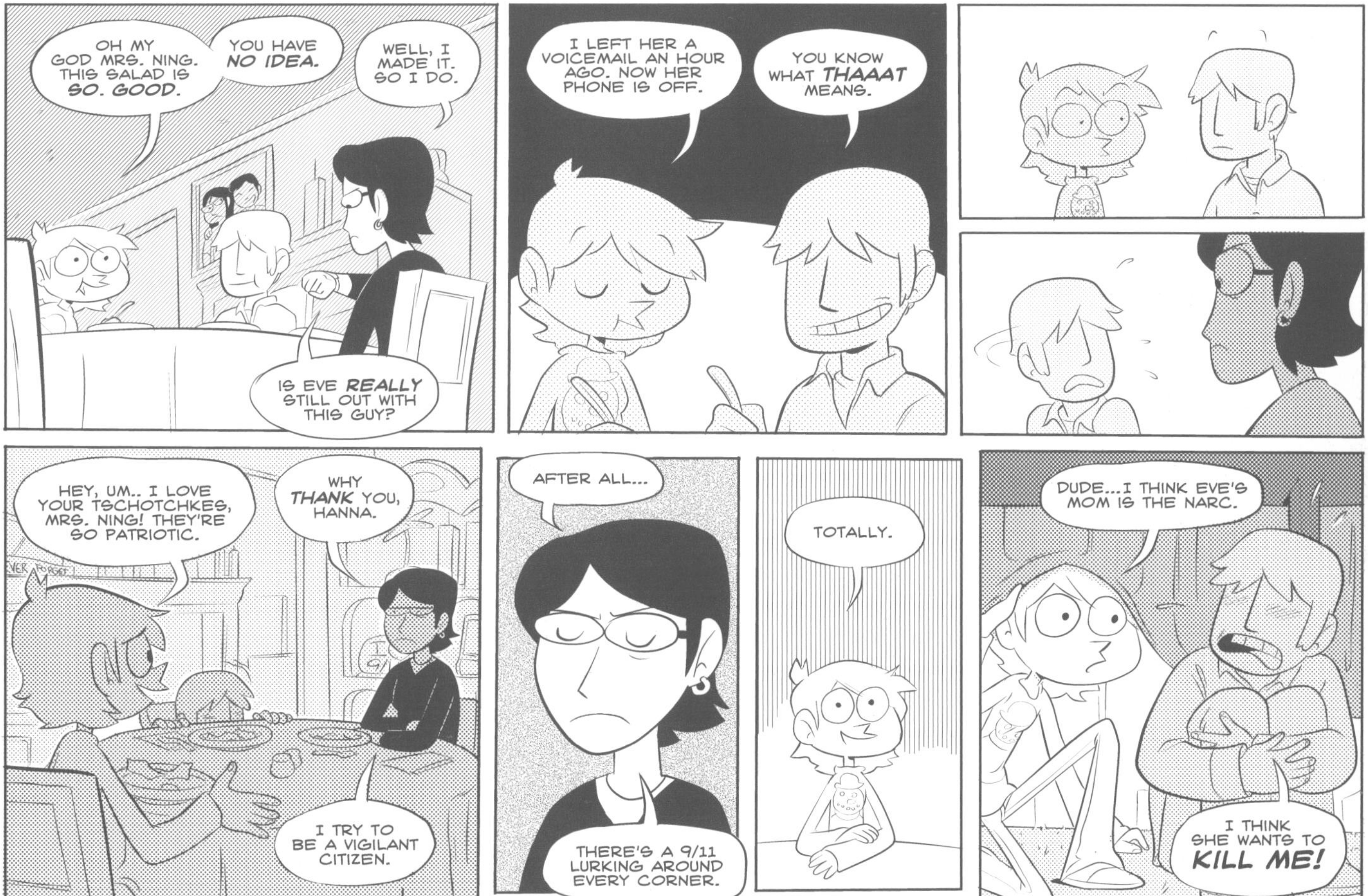
OH MY GOD MRS. NING. THIS SALAD IS SO. GOOD.
YOU HAVE NO IDEA.
WELL, I MADE IT. SO I DO.
IS EVE REALLY STILL OUT WITH THIS GUY?
I LEFT HER A VOICEMAIL AN HOUR AGO. NOW HER PHONE IS OFF.
YOU KNOW WHAT THAAAT MEANS.
HEY, UM.. I LOVE YOUR TSCHOTCHKES, MRS. NING! THEY'RE SO PATRIOTIC.
WHY THANK YOU, HANNA.
I TRY TO BE A VIGILANT CITIZEN.
AFTER ALL...
THERE'S A 9/11 LURKING AROUND EVERY CORNER.
TOTALLY.
DUDE...I THINK EVE'S MOM IS THE NARC.
I THINK SHE WANTS TO KILL ME!

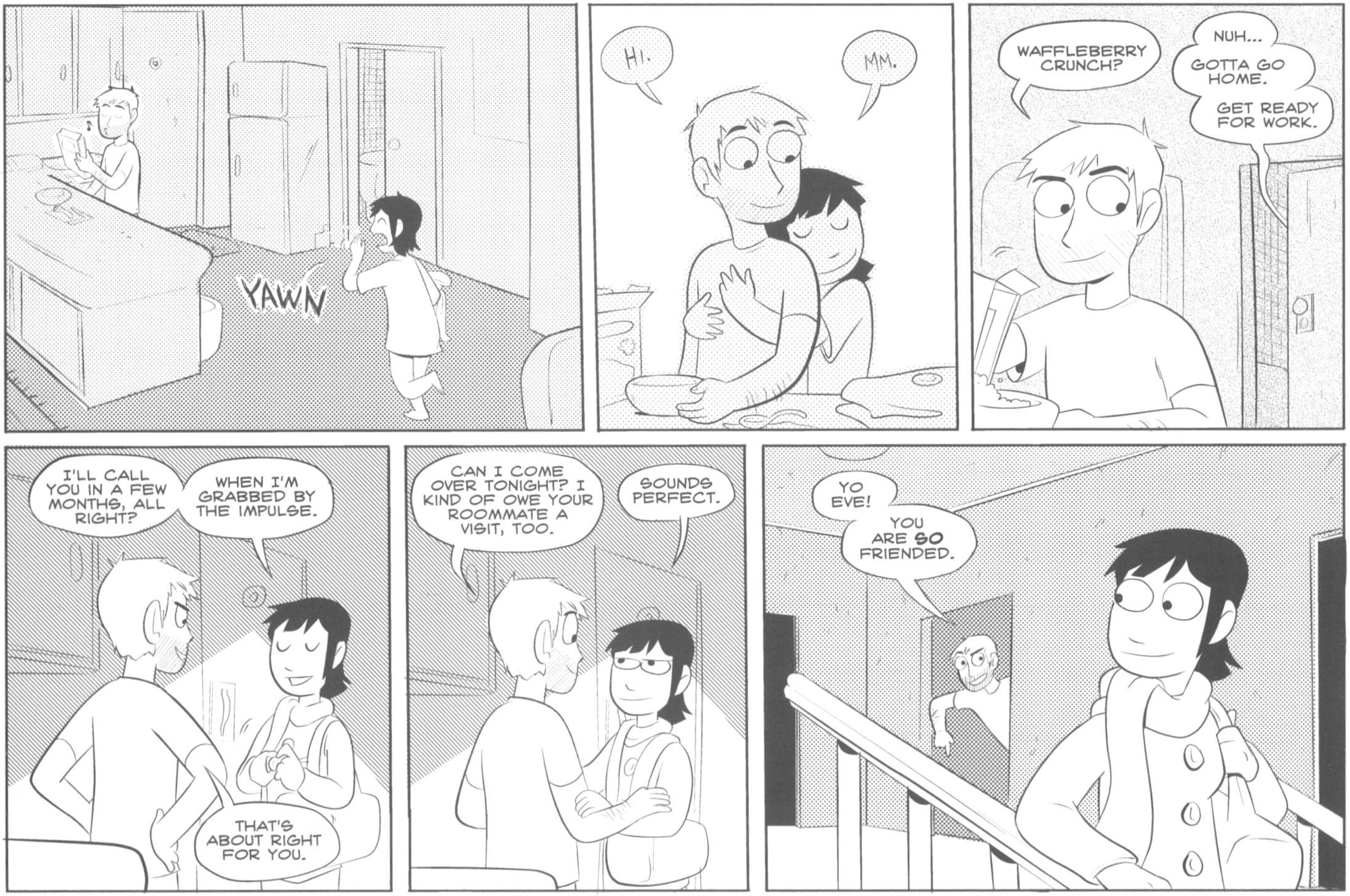
YAWN
HI.
MM.
WAFFLEBERRY CRUNCH?
NUH...
GOTTA GO HOME.
GET READY FOR WORK.
I'LL CALL YOU IN A FEW MONTHS, ALL RIGHT?
WHEN I'M GRABBED BY THE IMPULSE.
THAT'S ABOUT RIGHT FOR YOU.
CAN I COME OVER TONIGHT? I KIND OF OWE YOUR ROOMMATE A VISIT, TOO.
SOUNDS PERFECT.
YO EVE!
YOU ARE **SO** FRIENDED.

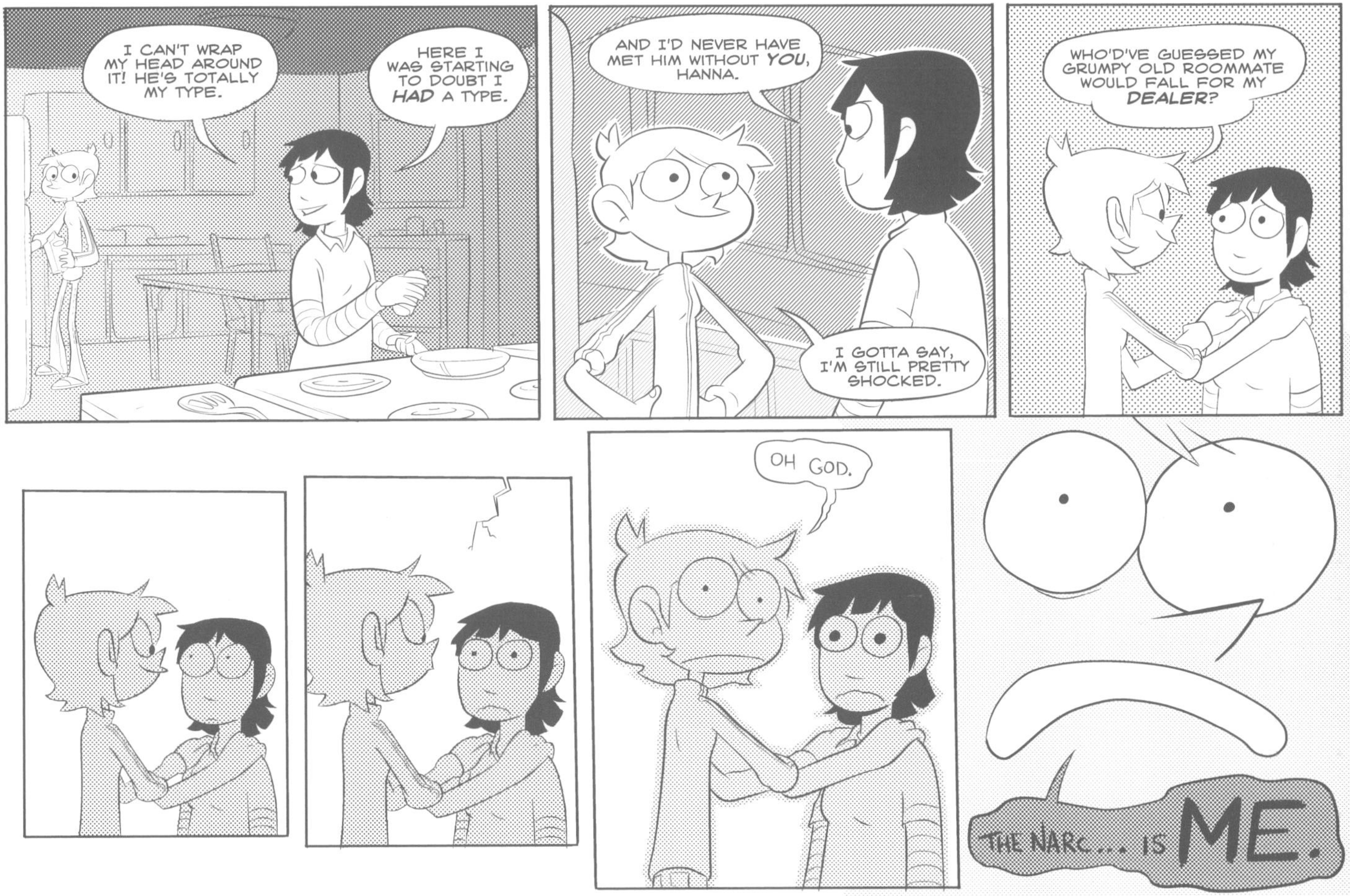
I CAN'T WRAP MY HEAD AROUND IT! HE'S TOTALLY MY TYPE.
HERE I WAS STARTING TO DOUBT I HAD A TYPE.
AND I'D NEVER HAVE MET HIM WITHOUT YOU, HANNA.
I GOTTA SAY, I'M STILL PRETTY SHOCKED.
WHO'D'VE GUESSED MY GRUMPY OLD ROOMMATE WOULD FALL FOR MY DEALER?
OH GOD.
THE NARC... IS ME.

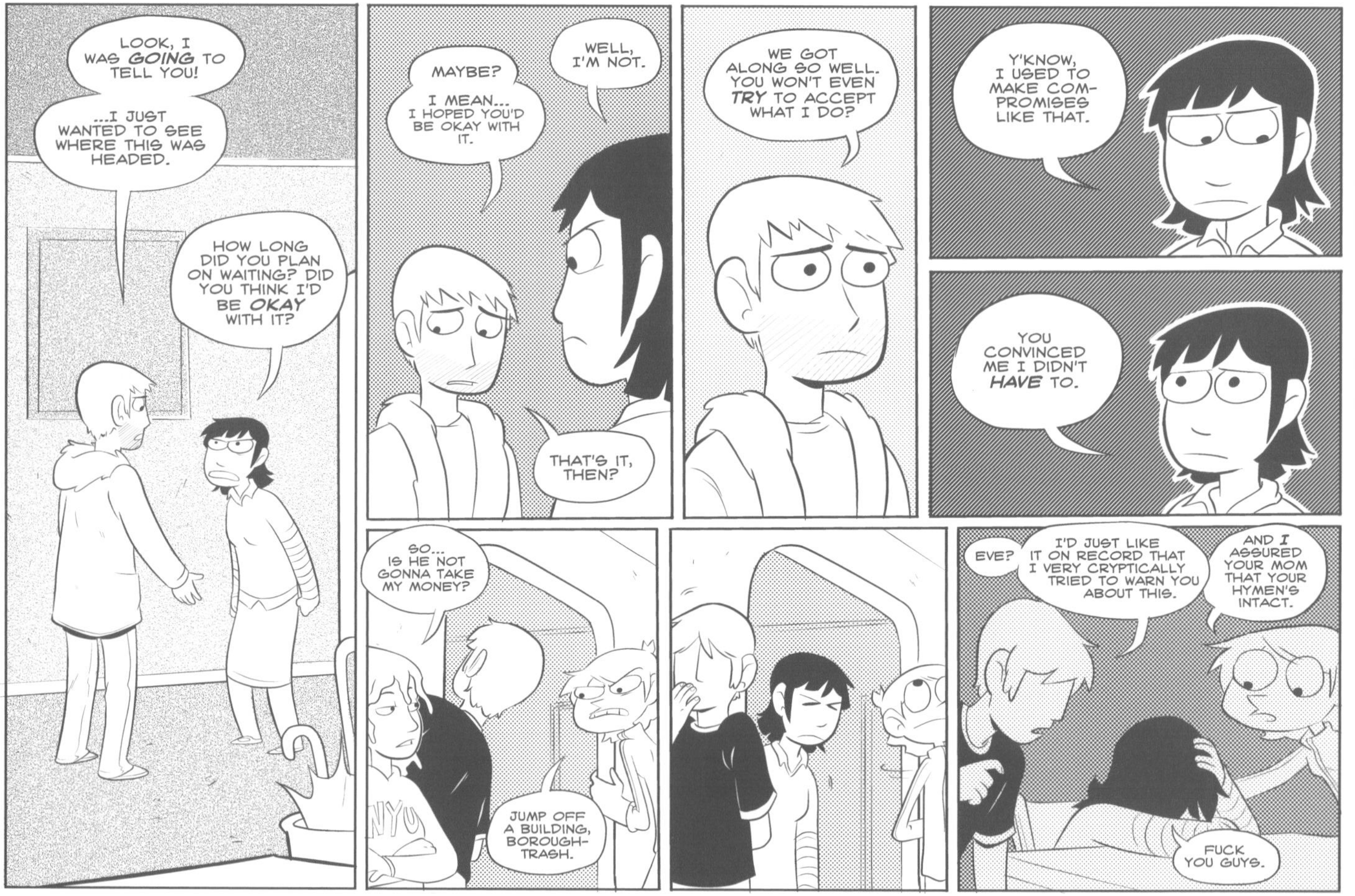
LOOK, I WAS GOING TO TELL YOU!
...I JUST WANTED TO SEE WHERE THIS WAS HEADED.
HOW LONG DID YOU PLAN ON WAITING? DID YOU THINK I'D BE OKAY WITH IT?
WELL, I'M NOT.
MAYBE?
I MEAN... I HOPED YOU'D BE OKAY WITH IT.
THAT'S IT, THEN?
WE GOT ALONG SO WELL. YOU WON'T EVEN TRY TO ACCEPT WHAT I DO?
Y'KNOW, I USED TO MAKE COM-PROMISES LIKE THAT.
YOU CONVINCED ME I DIDN'T HAVE TO.
SO... IS HE NOT GONNA TAKE MY MONEY?
JUMP OFF A BUILDING, BOROUGH-TRASH.
NYU
EVE?
I'D JUST LIKE IT ON RECORD THAT I VERY CRYPTICALLY TRIED TO WARN YOU ABOUT THIS.
AND I ASSURED YOUR MOM THAT YOUR HYMEN'S INTACT.
FUCK YOU GUYS.

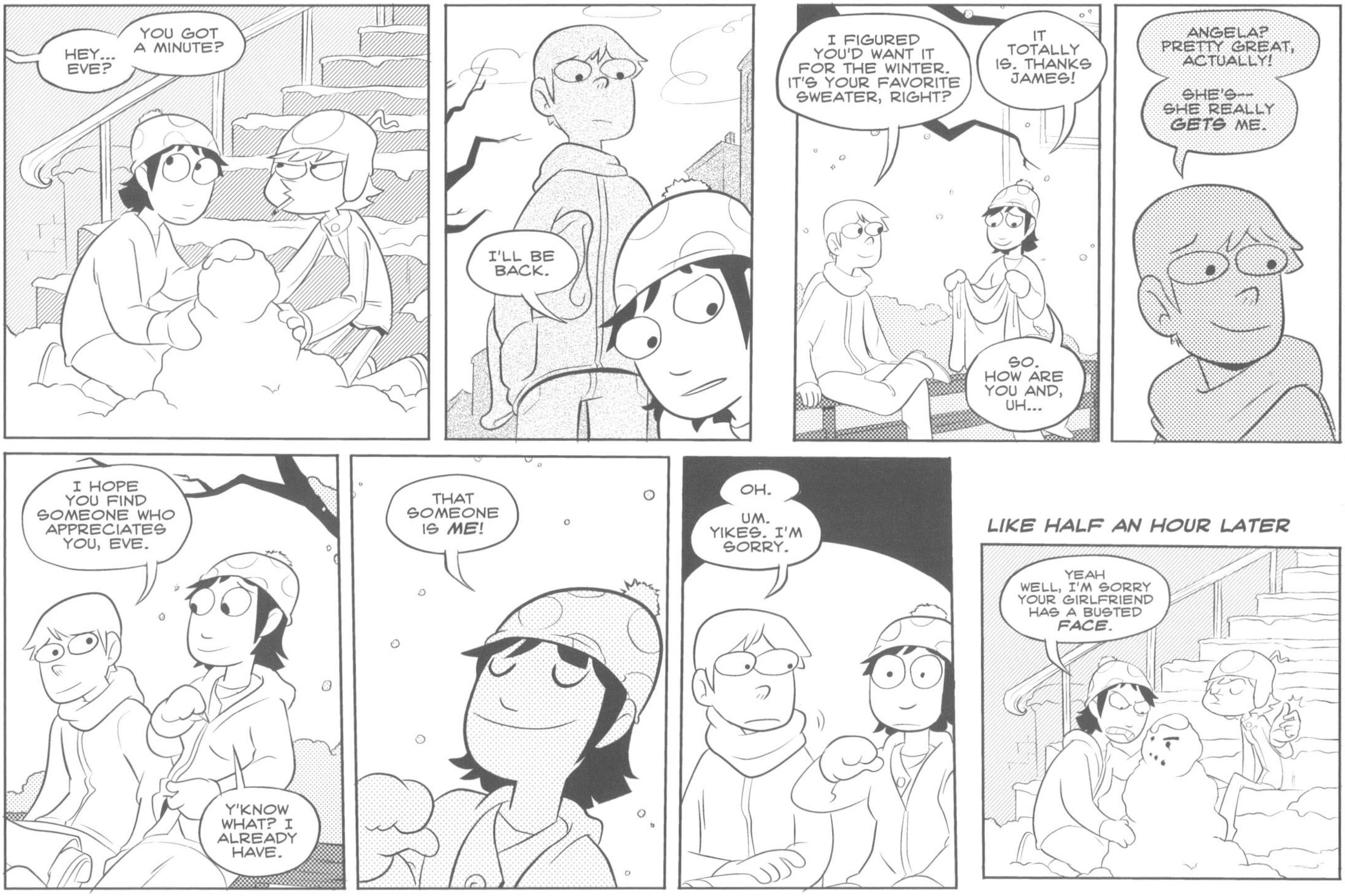
HEY... EVE?
YOU GOT A MINUTE?
I'LL BE BACK.
I FIGURED YOU'D WANT IT FOR THE WINTER. IT'S YOUR FAVORITE SWEATER, RIGHT?
IT TOTALLY IS. THANKS JAMES!
SO. HOW ARE YOU AND, UH...
ANGELA? PRETTY GREAT, ACTUALLY!
SHE'S-- SHE REALLY GETS ME.
I HOPE YOU FIND SOMEONE WHO APPRECIATES YOU, EVE.
Y'KNOW WHAT? I ALREADY HAVE.
THAT SOMEONE IS ME!
OH.
UM. YIKES. I'M SORRY.
LIKE HALF AN HOUR LATER
YEAH WELL, I'M SORRY YOUR GIRLFRIEND HAS A BUSTED FACE.

skate or don't

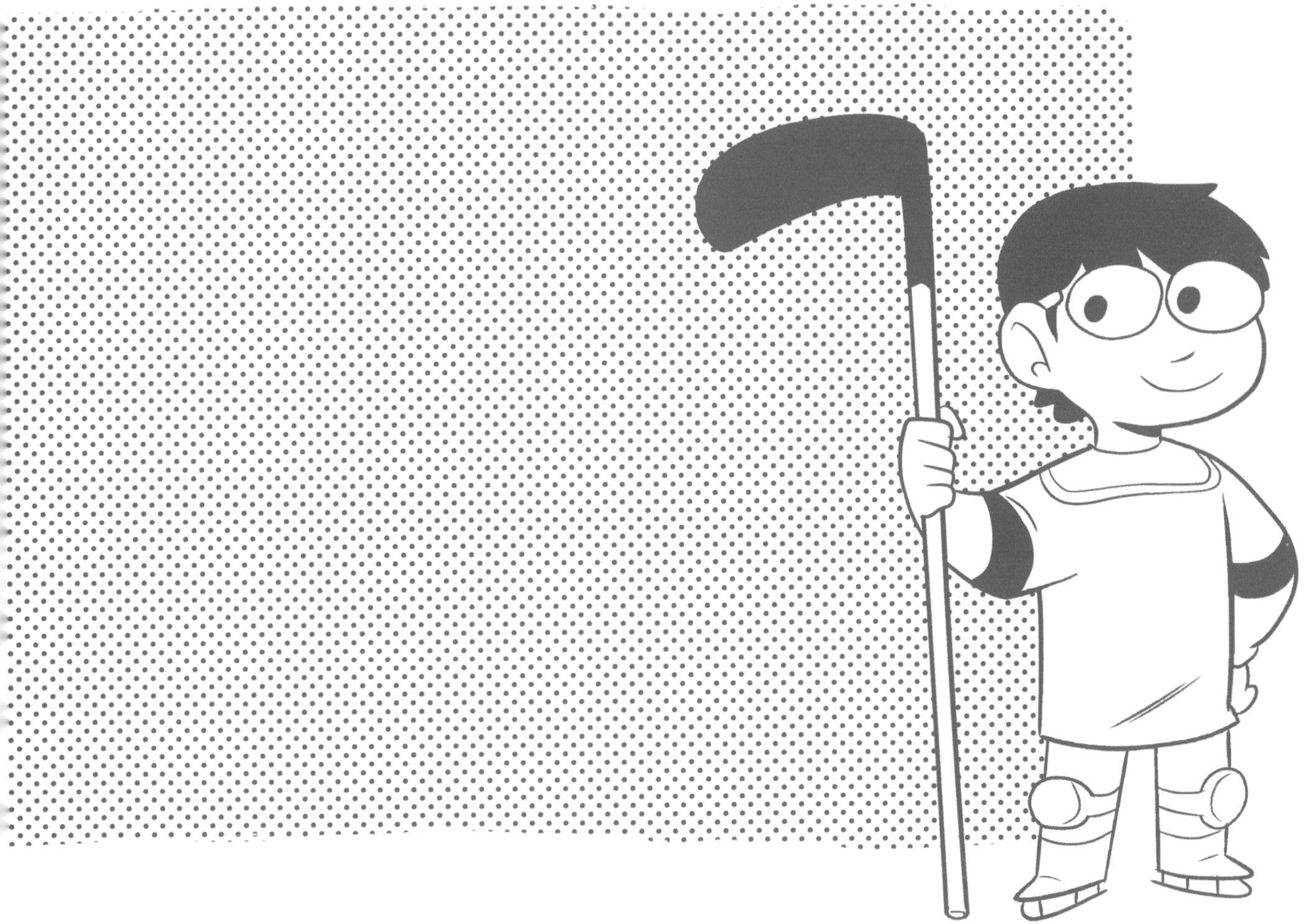

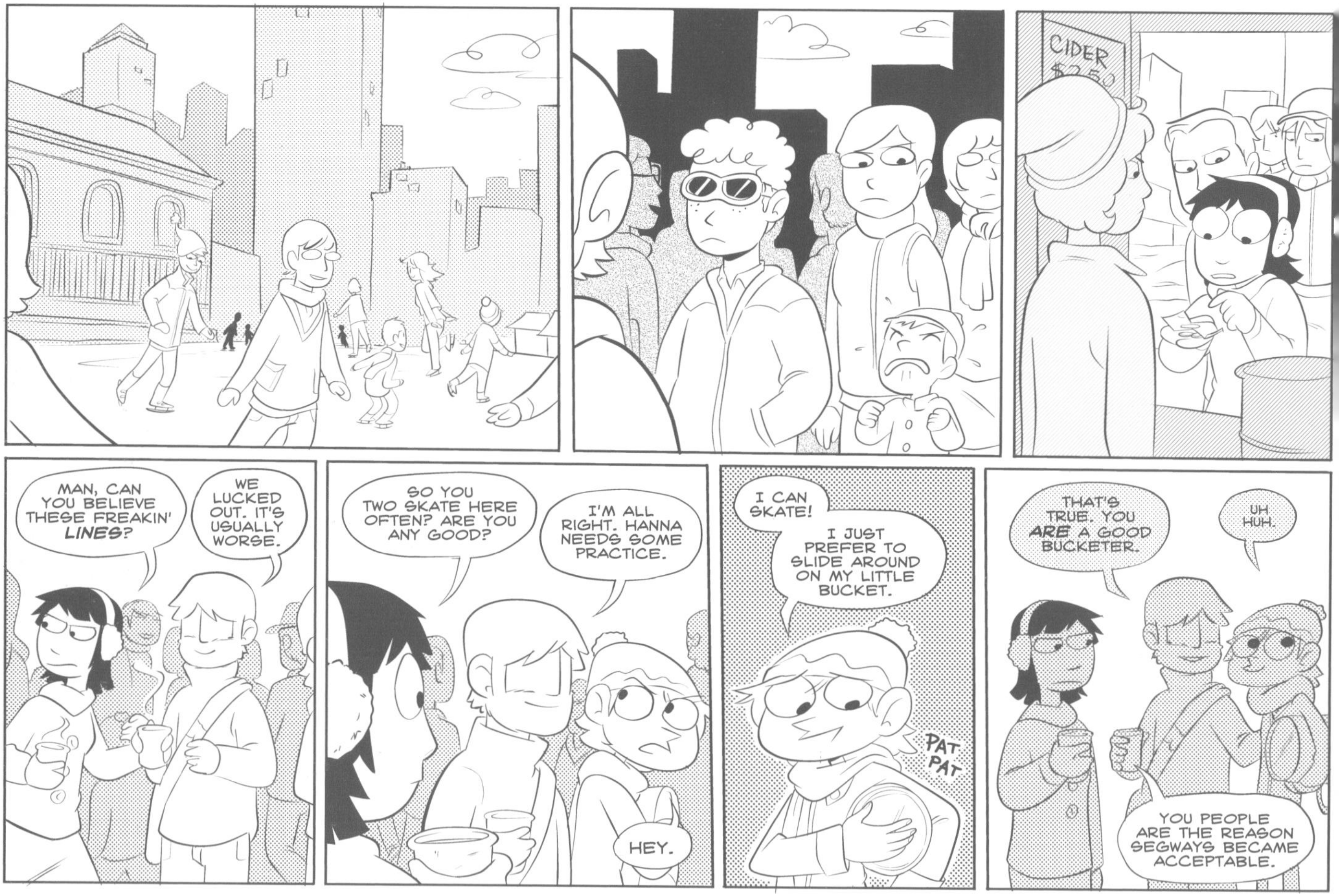
CIDER
MAN, CAN YOU BELIEVE THESE FREAKIN' *LINES*?
WE LUCKED OUT. IT'S USUALLY WORSE.
SO YOU TWO SKATE HERE OFTEN? ARE YOU ANY GOOD?
I'M ALL RIGHT. HANNA NEEDS SOME PRACTICE.
HEY.
I CAN SKATE!
I JUST PREFER TO SLIDE AROUND ON MY LITTLE BUCKET.
PAT PAT
THAT'S TRUE. YOU *ARE* A GOOD BUCKETER.
UH HUH.
YOU PEOPLE ARE THE REASON SEGWAYS BECAME ACCEPTABLE.

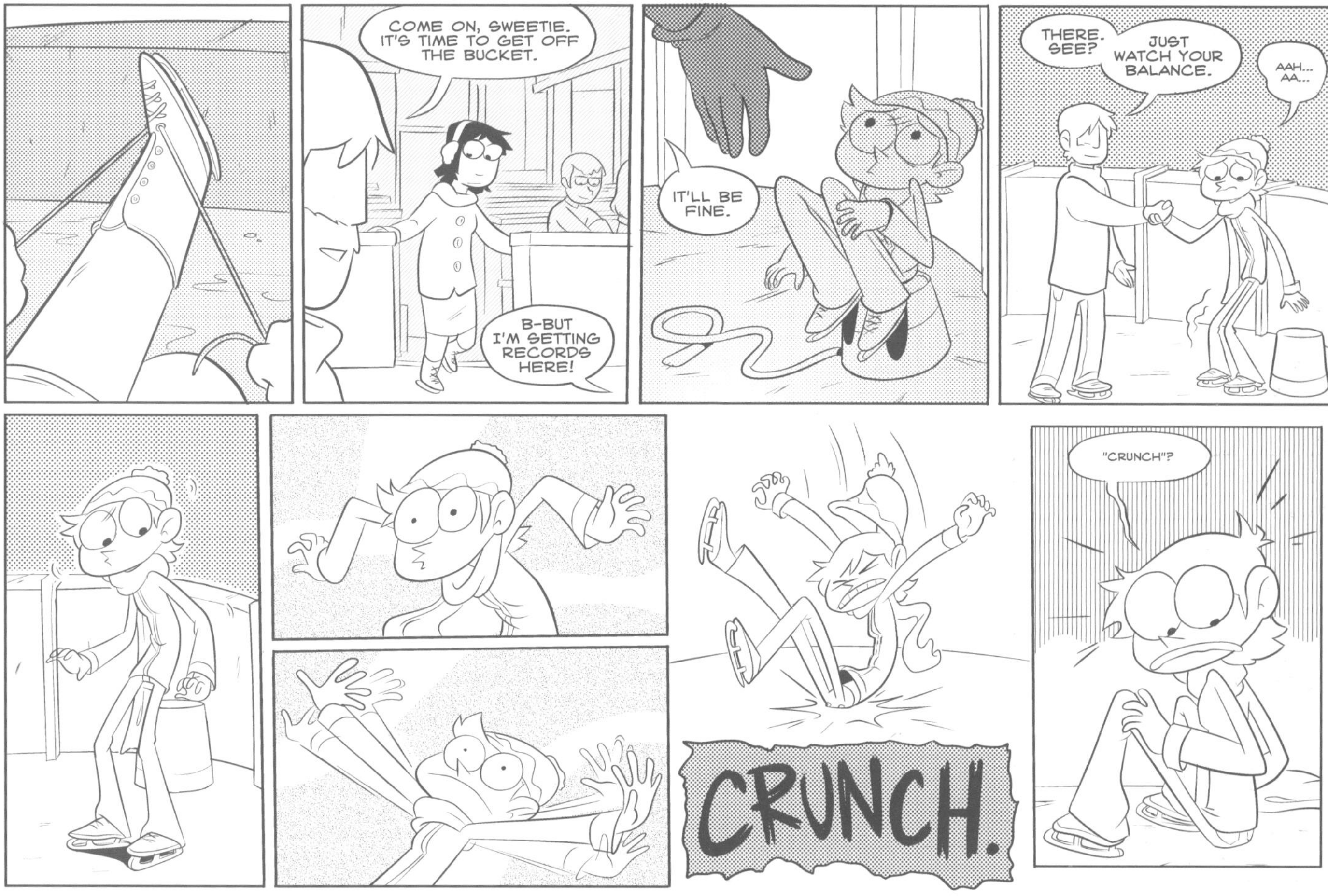
COME ON, SWEETIE. IT'S TIME TO GET OFF THE BUCKET.
B-BUT I'M SETTING RECORDS HERE!
IT'LL BE FINE.
THERE. SEE?
JUST WATCH YOUR BALANCE.
AAH... AA...
CRUNCH.
"CRUNCH"?

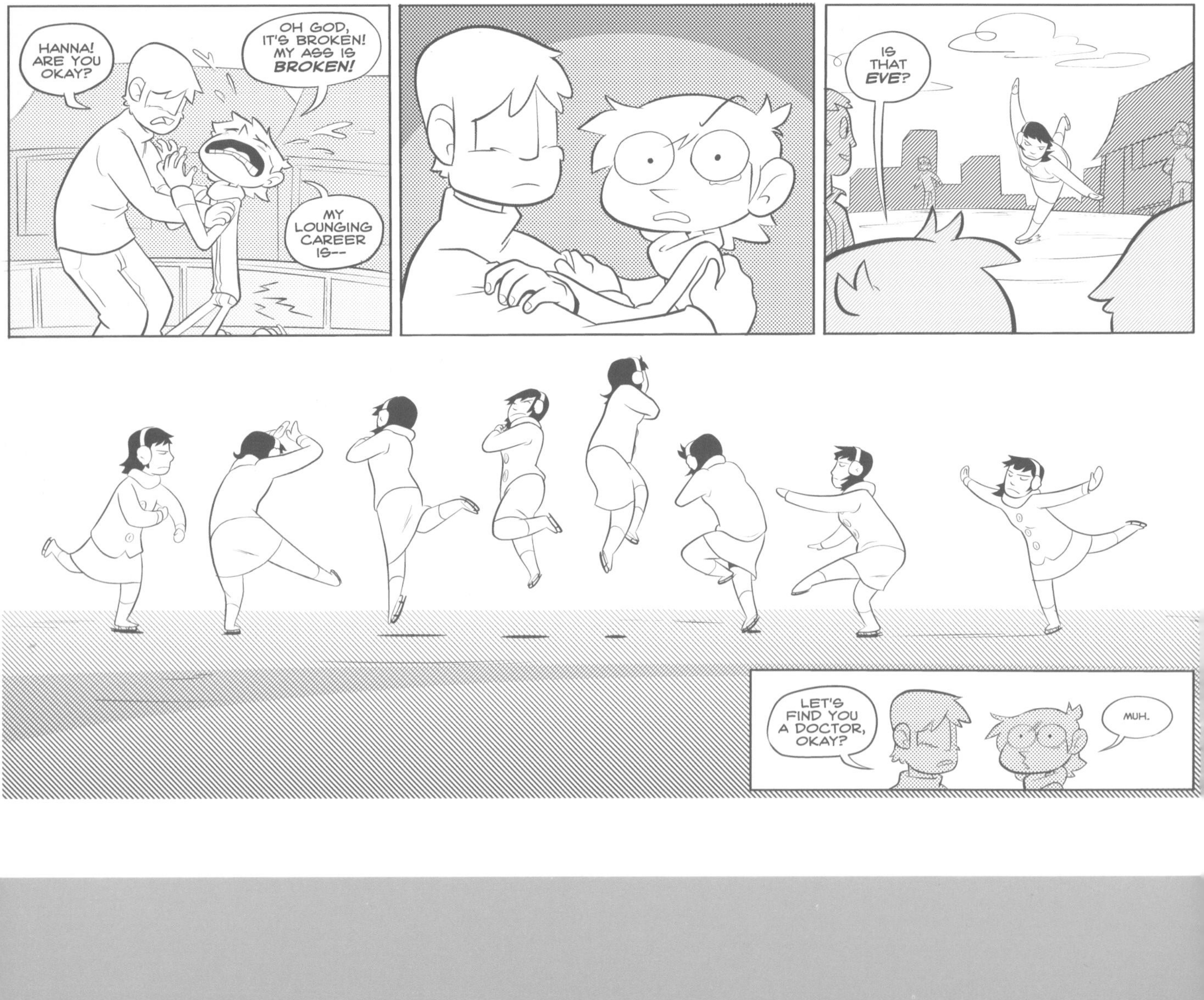
HANNA! ARE YOU OKAY?
OH GOD, IT'S BROKEN! MY ASS IS BROKEN!
MY LOUNGING CAREER IS--
IS THAT EVE?
LET'S FIND YOU A DOCTOR, OKAY?
MUH.

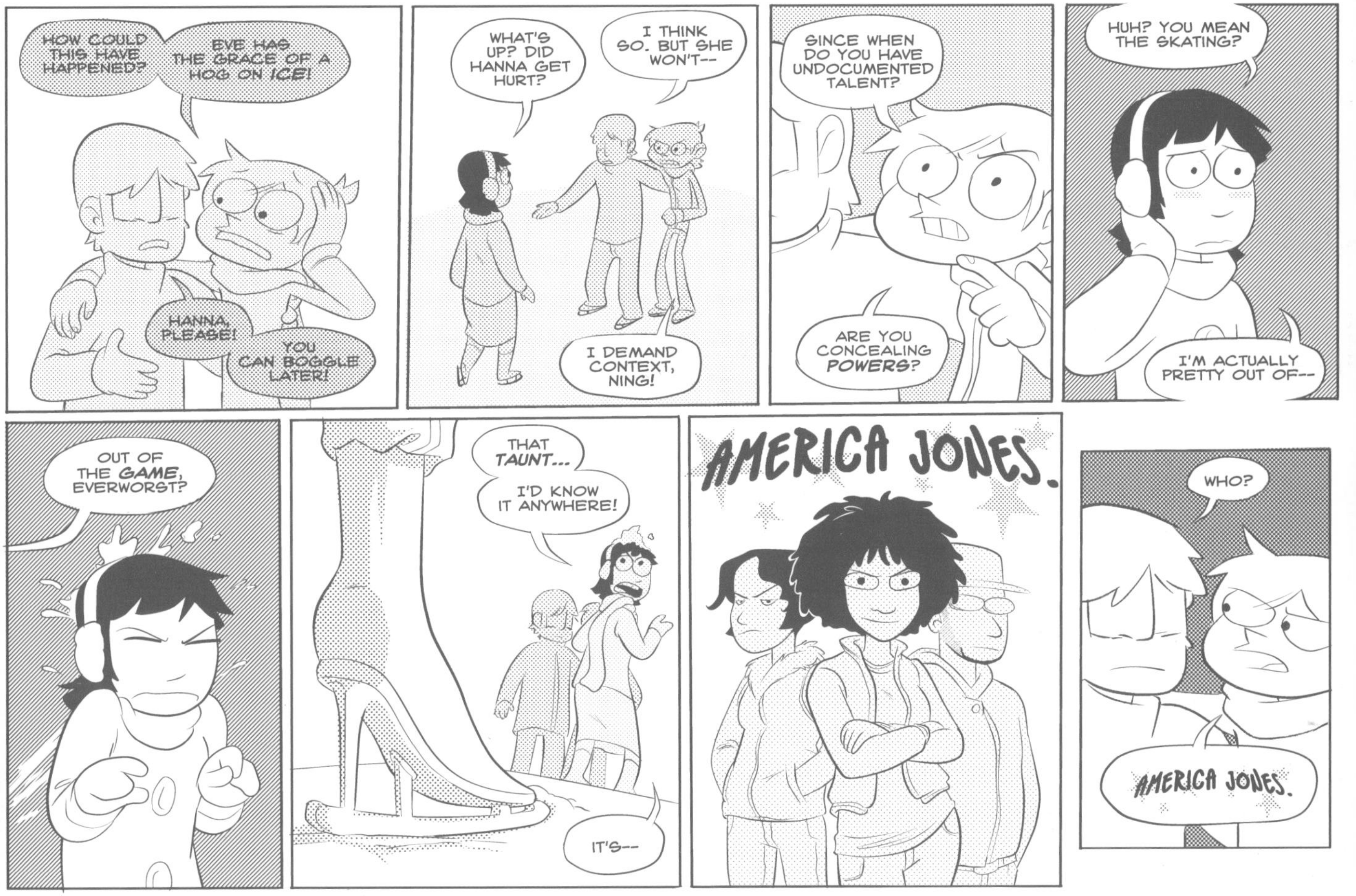
HOW COULD THIS HAVE HAPPENED?
EVE HAS THE GRACE OF A HOG ON *ICE*!
HANNA, PLEASE!
YOU CAN BOGGLE LATER!
WHAT'S UP? DID HANNA GET HURT?
I THINK SO. BUT SHE WON'T--
I DEMAND CONTEXT, NING!
SINCE WHEN DO YOU HAVE UNDOCUMENTED TALENT?
ARE YOU CONCEALING *POWERS*?
HUH? YOU MEAN THE SKATING?
I'M ACTUALLY PRETTY OUT OF--
OUT OF THE *GAME*, EVERWORST?
THAT *TAUNT*...
I'D KNOW IT ANYWHERE!
IT'S--
AMERICA JONES.
WHO?
AMERICA JONES.

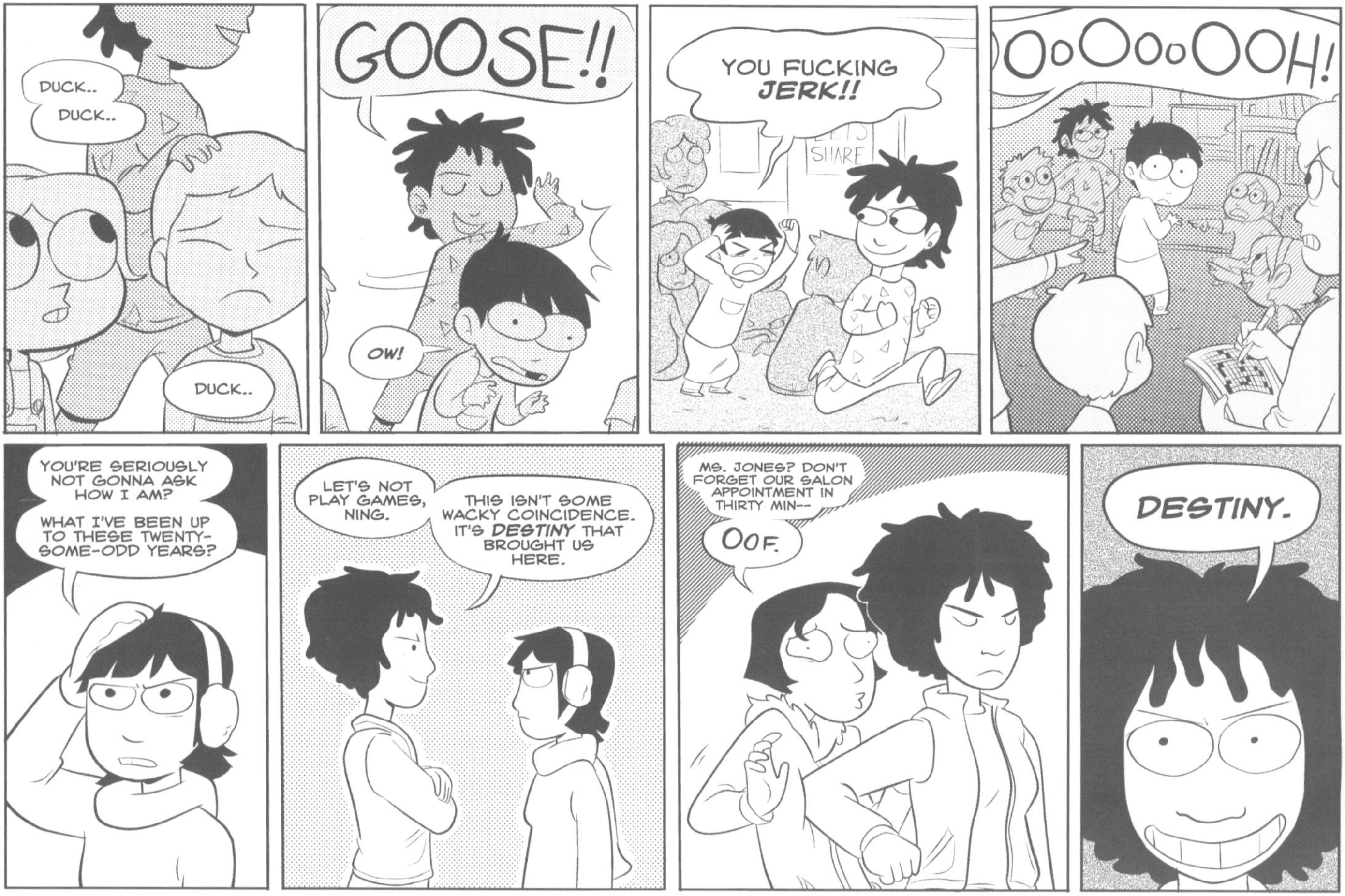
DUCK..
DUCK..
DUCK..
GOOSE!!
OW!
YOU FUCKING JERK!!
LET'S SHARE
OOoOOoOOH!
YOU'RE SERIOUSLY NOT GONNA ASK HOW I AM?
WHAT I'VE BEEN UP TO THESE TWENTY-SOME-ODD YEARS?
LET'S NOT PLAY GAMES, NING.
THIS ISN'T SOME WACKY COINCIDENCE. IT'S DESTINY THAT BROUGHT US HERE.
MS. JONES? DON'T FORGET OUR SALON APPOINTMENT IN THIRTY MIN--
OOF.
DESTINY.

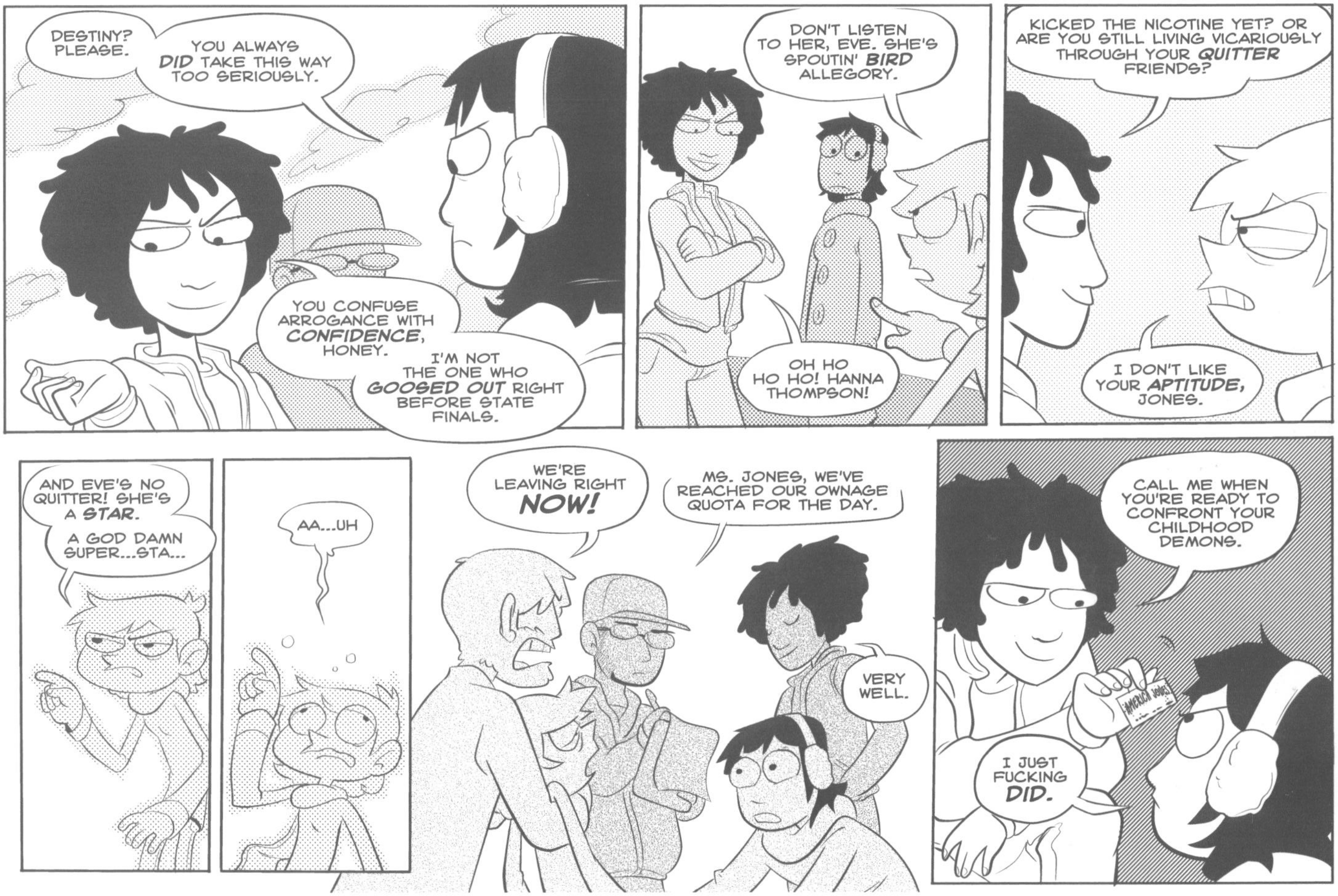
DESTINY? PLEASE.
YOU ALWAYS DID TAKE THIS WAY TOO SERIOUSLY.
YOU CONFUSE ARROGANCE WITH CONFIDENCE, HONEY.
I'M NOT THE ONE WHO GOOSED OUT RIGHT BEFORE STATE FINALS.
DON'T LISTEN TO HER, EVE. SHE'S SPOUTIN' BIRD ALLEGORY.
OH HO HO HO! HANNA THOMPSON!
KICKED THE NICOTINE YET? OR ARE YOU STILL LIVING VICARIOUSLY THROUGH YOUR QUITTER FRIENDS?
I DON'T LIKE YOUR APTITUDE, JONES.
AND EVE'S NO QUITTER! SHE'S A STAR.
A GOD DAMN SUPER...STA...
AA...UH
WE'RE LEAVING RIGHT NOW!
MS. JONES, WE'VE REACHED OUR OWNAGE QUOTA FOR THE DAY.
VERY WELL.
CALL ME WHEN YOU'RE READY TO CONFRONT YOUR CHILDHOOD DEMONS.
I JUST FUCKING DID.

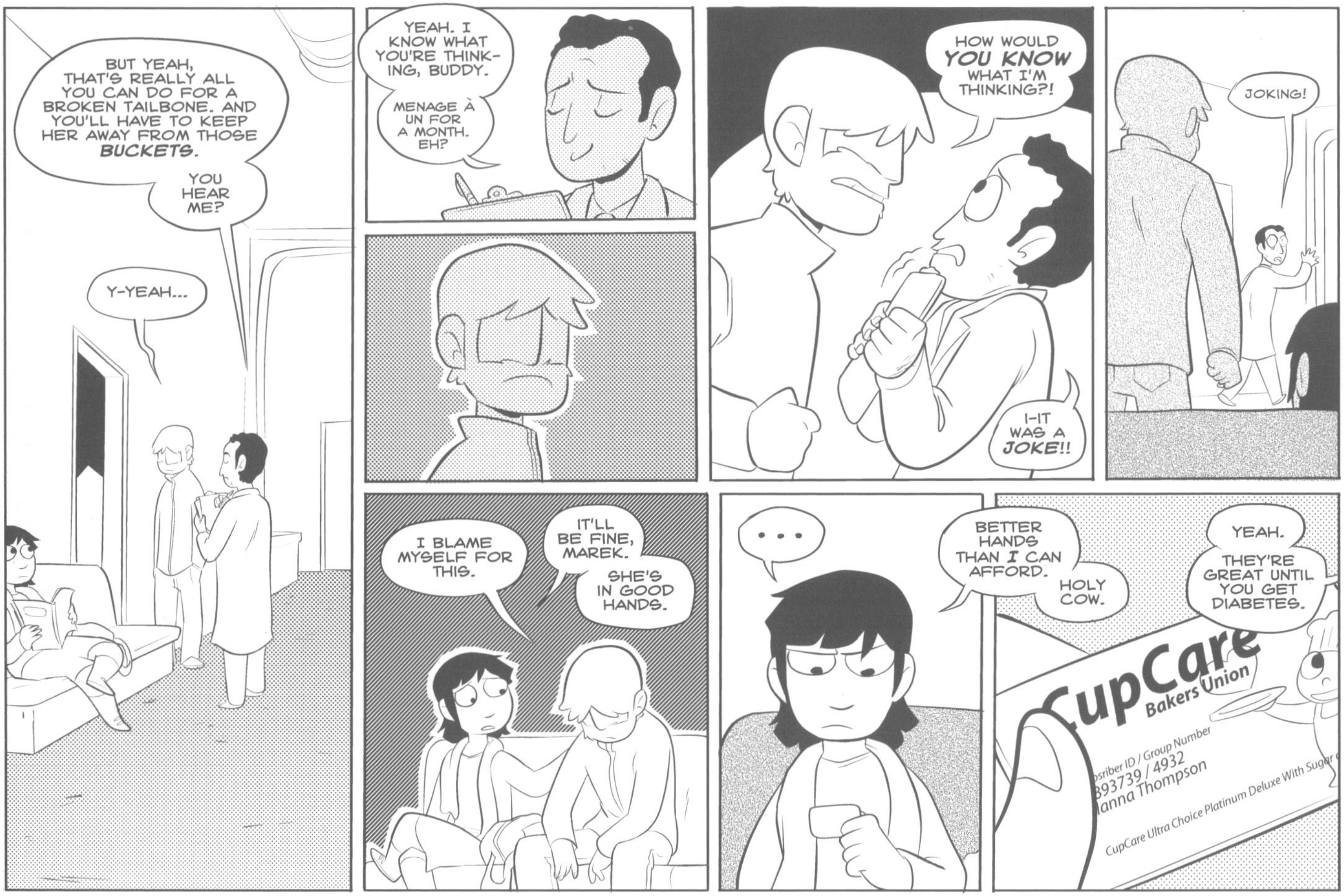
BUT YEAH, THAT'S REALLY ALL YOU CAN DO FOR A BROKEN TAILBONE. AND YOU'LL HAVE TO KEEP HER AWAY FROM THOSE BUCKETS.
YOU HEAR ME?
Y-YEAH...
YEAH. I KNOW WHAT YOU'RE THINKING, BUDDY.
MENAGE À UN FOR A MONTH. EH?
HOW WOULD YOU KNOW WHAT I'M THINKING?!
I-IT WAS A JOKE!!
JOKING!
I BLAME MYSELF FOR THIS.
IT'LL BE FINE, MAREK.
SHE'S IN GOOD HANDS.
...
BETTER HANDS THAN I CAN AFFORD.
HOLY COW.
YEAH.
THEY'RE GREAT UNTIL YOU GET DIABETES.
CupCare
Bakers Union
Group Number
393739 / 4932
Thompson
CupCare Ultra Choice Platinum Deluxe With Sugar

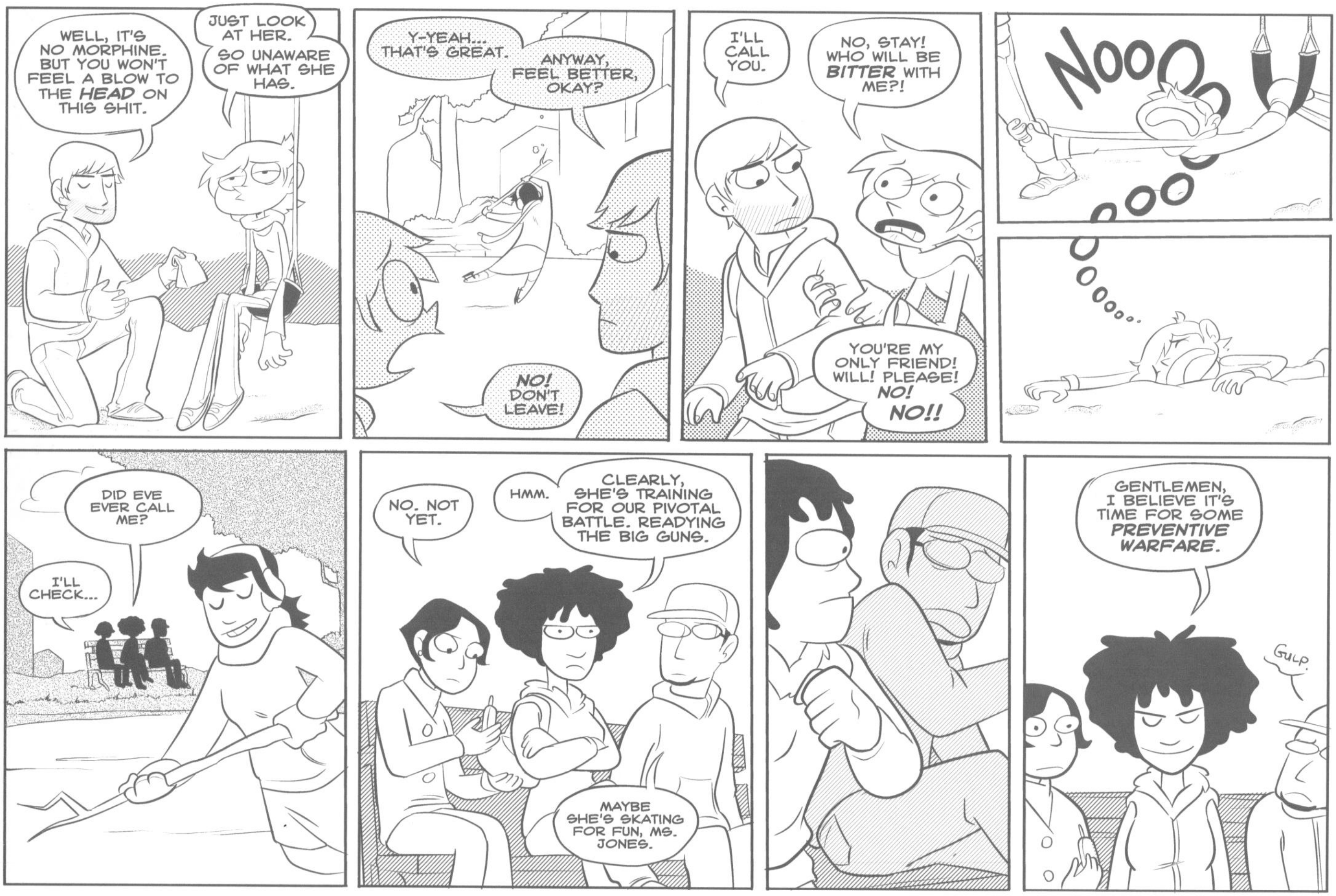
WELL, IT'S NO MORPHINE. BUT YOU WON'T FEEL A BLOW TO THE HEAD ON THIS SHIT.
JUST LOOK AT HER.
SO UNAWARE OF WHAT SHE HAS.
Y-YEAH... THAT'S GREAT.
ANYWAY, FEEL BETTER, OKAY?
NO! DON'T LEAVE!
I'LL CALL YOU.
NO, STAY! WHO WILL BE BITTER WITH ME?!
YOU'RE MY ONLY FRIEND! WILL! PLEASE! NO! NO!!
NOOOOOOOOOOOOOOOO...
DID EVE EVER CALL ME?
I'LL CHECK...
NO. NOT YET.
HMM.
CLEARLY, SHE'S TRAINING FOR OUR PIVOTAL BATTLE. READYING THE BIG GUNS.
MAYBE SHE'S SKATING FOR FUN, MS. JONES.
GENTLEMEN, I BELIEVE IT'S TIME FOR SOME PREVENTIVE WARFARE.
GULP.

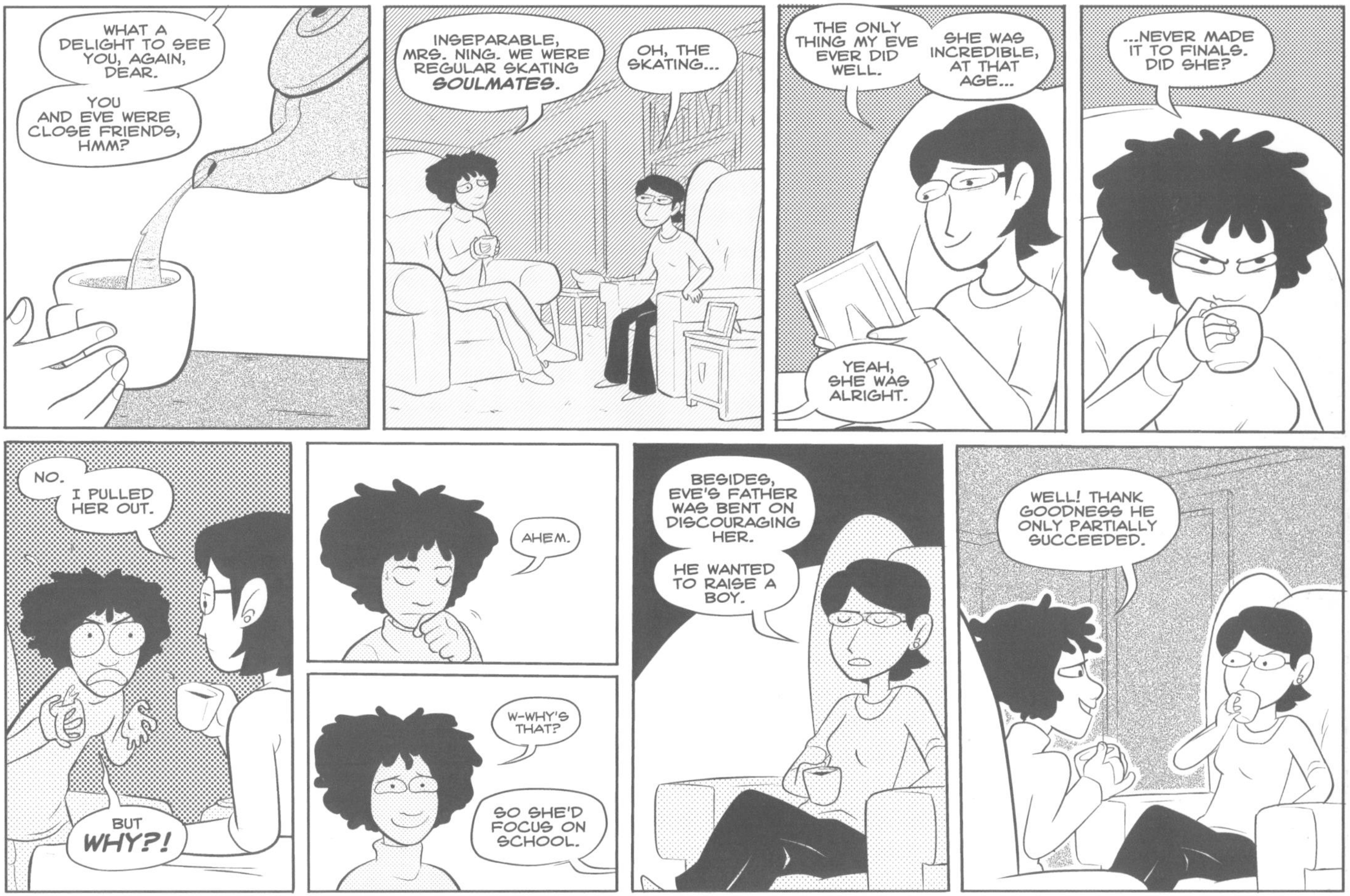
WHAT A DELIGHT TO SEE YOU, AGAIN, DEAR.
YOU AND EVE WERE CLOSE FRIENDS, HMM?
INSEPARABLE, MRS. NING. WE WERE REGULAR SKATING SOULMATES.
OH, THE SKATING...
THE ONLY THING MY EVE EVER DID WELL.
SHE WAS INCREDIBLE, AT THAT AGE...
YEAH, SHE WAS ALRIGHT.
...NEVER MADE IT TO FINALS. DID SHE?
NO. I PULLED HER OUT.
BUT WHY?!
AHEM.
W-WHY'S THAT?
SO SHE'D FOCUS ON SCHOOL.
BESIDES, EVE'S FATHER WAS BENT ON DISCOURAGING HER.
HE WANTED TO RAISE A BOY.
WELL! THANK GOODNESS HE ONLY PARTIALLY SUCCEEDED.

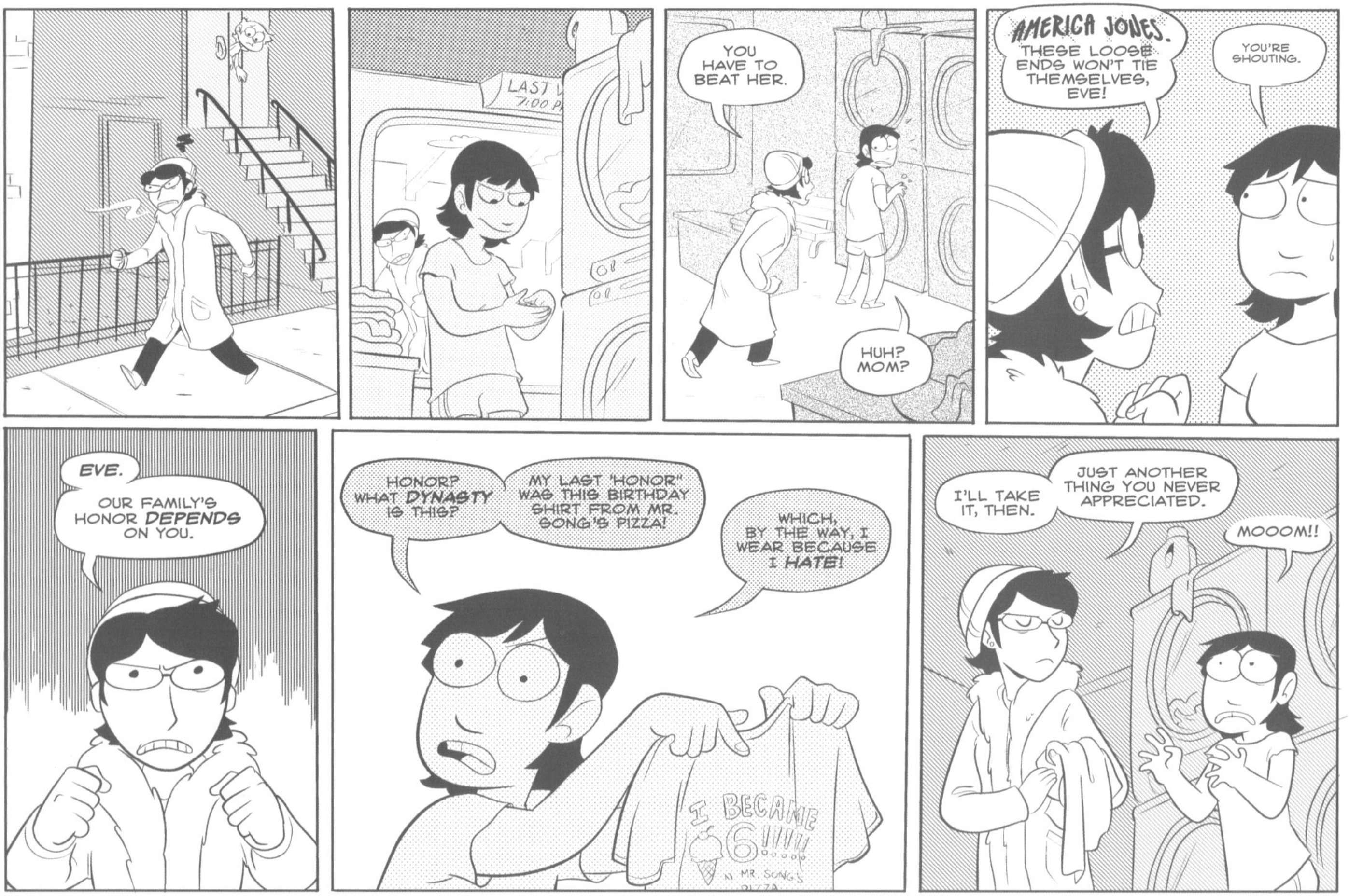
LAST
7:00 P
YOU HAVE TO BEAT HER.
HUH? MOM?
AMERICA JONES.
THESE LOOSE ENDS WON'T TIE THEMSELVES, EVE!
YOU'RE SHOUTING.
EVE.
OUR FAMILY'S HONOR **DEPENDS** ON YOU.
HONOR? WHAT **DYNASTY** IS THIS?
MY LAST "HONOR" WAS THIS BIRTHDAY SHIRT FROM MR. SONG'S PIZZA!
WHICH, BY THE WAY, I WEAR BECAUSE I **HATE**!
I BECAME 6!!!!!
AT MR. SONG'S
JUST ANOTHER THING YOU NEVER APPRECIATED.
I'LL TAKE IT, THEN.
MOOOM!!

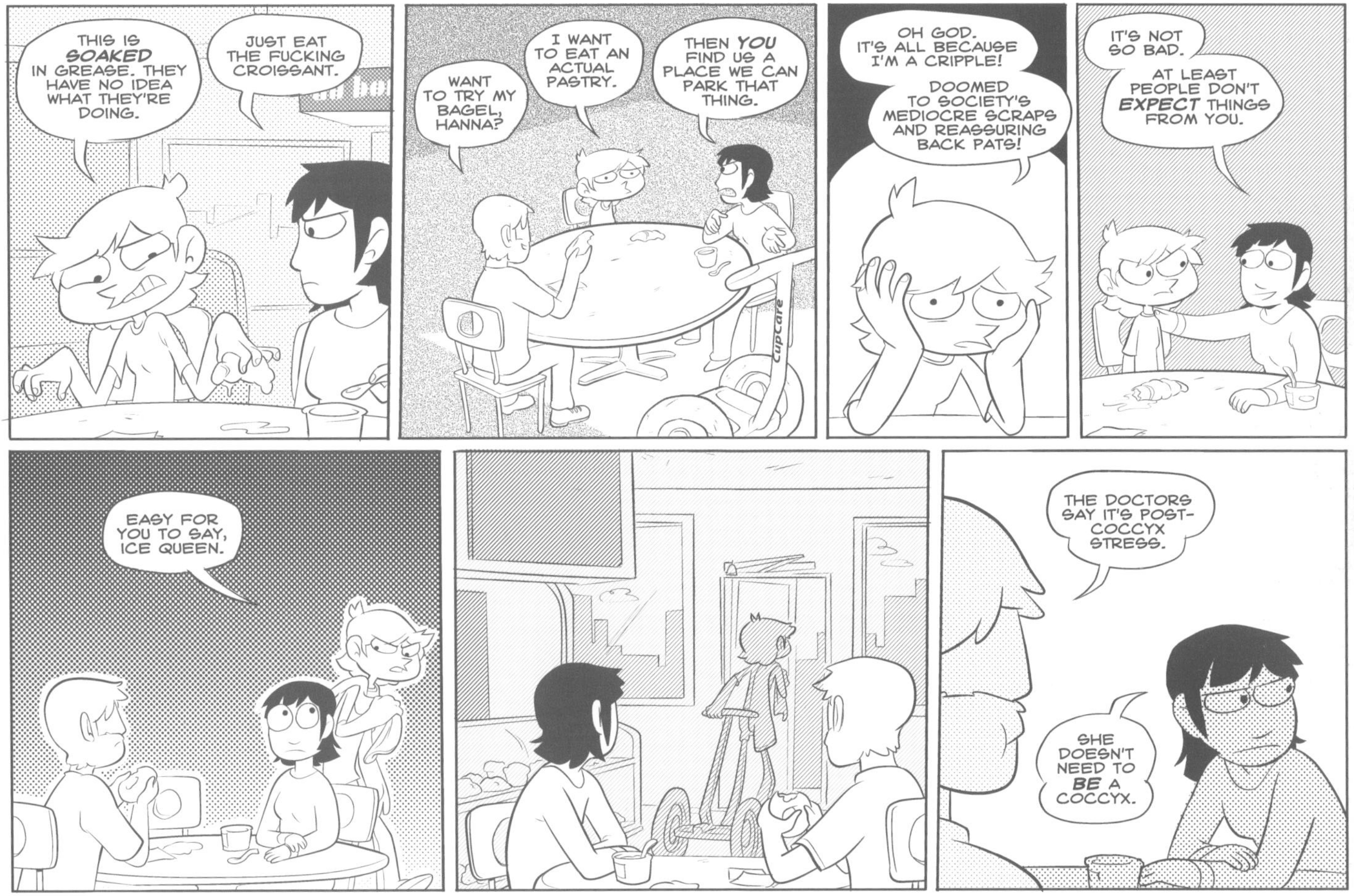
THIS IS SOAKED IN GREASE. THEY HAVE NO IDEA WHAT THEY'RE DOING.
JUST EAT THE FUCKING CROISSANT.
WANT TO TRY MY BAGEL, HANNA?
I WANT TO EAT AN ACTUAL PASTRY.
THEN YOU FIND US A PLACE WE CAN PARK THAT THING.
OH GOD. IT'S ALL BECAUSE I'M A CRIPPLE!
DOOMED TO SOCIETY'S MEDIOCRE SCRAPS AND REASSURING BACK PATS!
IT'S NOT SO BAD.
AT LEAST PEOPLE DON'T EXPECT THINGS FROM YOU.
EASY FOR YOU TO SAY, ICE QUEEN.
THE DOCTORS SAY IT'S POST-COCCYX STRESS.
SHE DOESN'T NEED TO BE A COCCYX.

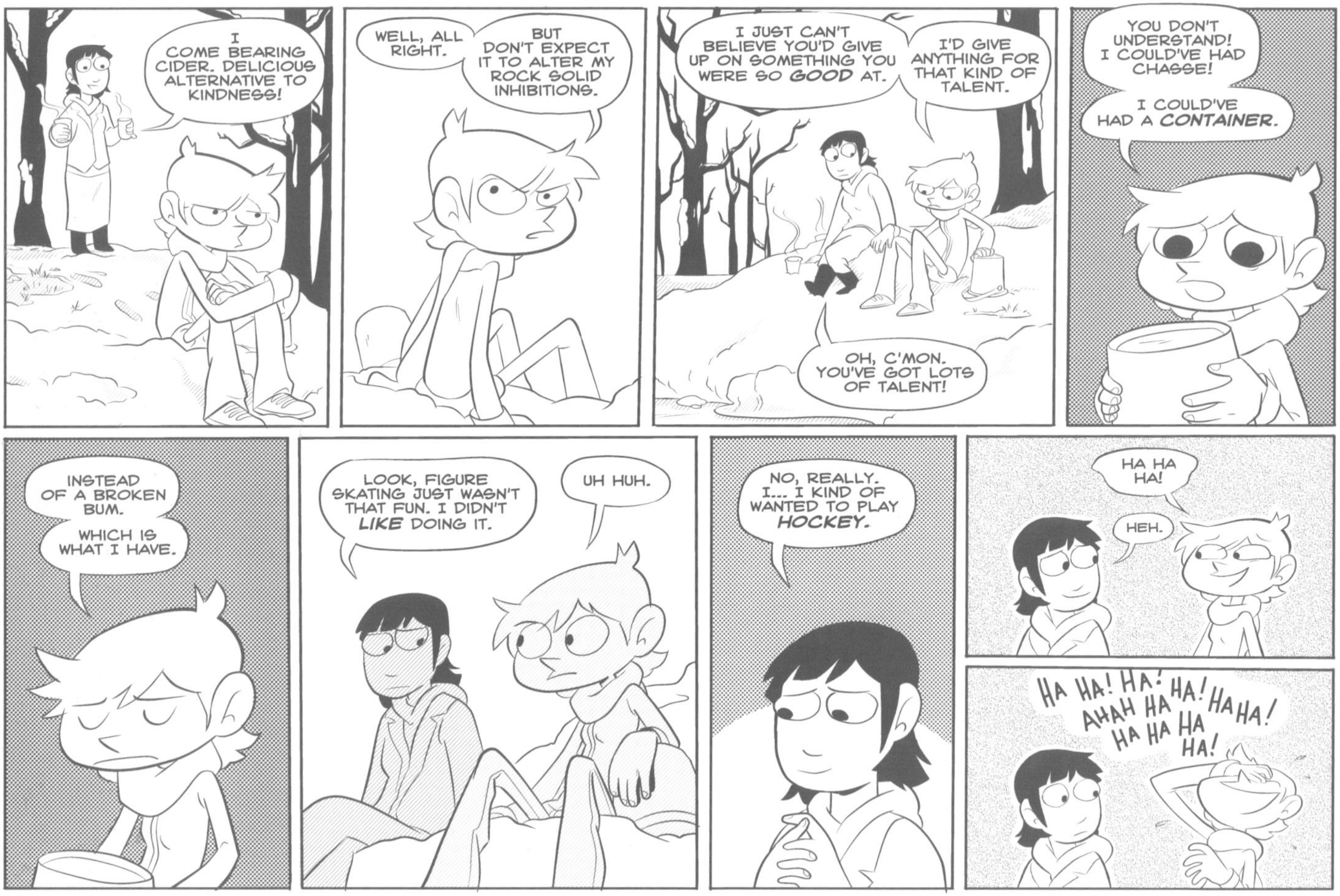
I COME BEARING CIDER. DELICIOUS ALTERNATIVE TO KINDNESS!
WELL, ALL RIGHT.
BUT DON'T EXPECT IT TO ALTER MY ROCK SOLID INHIBITIONS.
I JUST CAN'T BELIEVE YOU'D GIVE UP ON SOMETHING YOU WERE SO GOOD AT.
I'D GIVE ANYTHING FOR THAT KIND OF TALENT.
OH, C'MON. YOU'VE GOT LOTS OF TALENT!
YOU DON'T UNDERSTAND! I COULD'VE HAD CHASSE!
I COULD'VE HAD A CONTAINER.
INSTEAD OF A BROKEN BUM.
WHICH IS WHAT I HAVE.
LOOK, FIGURE SKATING JUST WASN'T THAT FUN. I DIDN'T LIKE DOING IT.
UH HUH.
NO, REALLY. I... I KIND OF WANTED TO PLAY HOCKEY.
HA HA HA!
HEH.
HA HA! HA! HA! HA HA! AHAH HA HA HA HA HA!

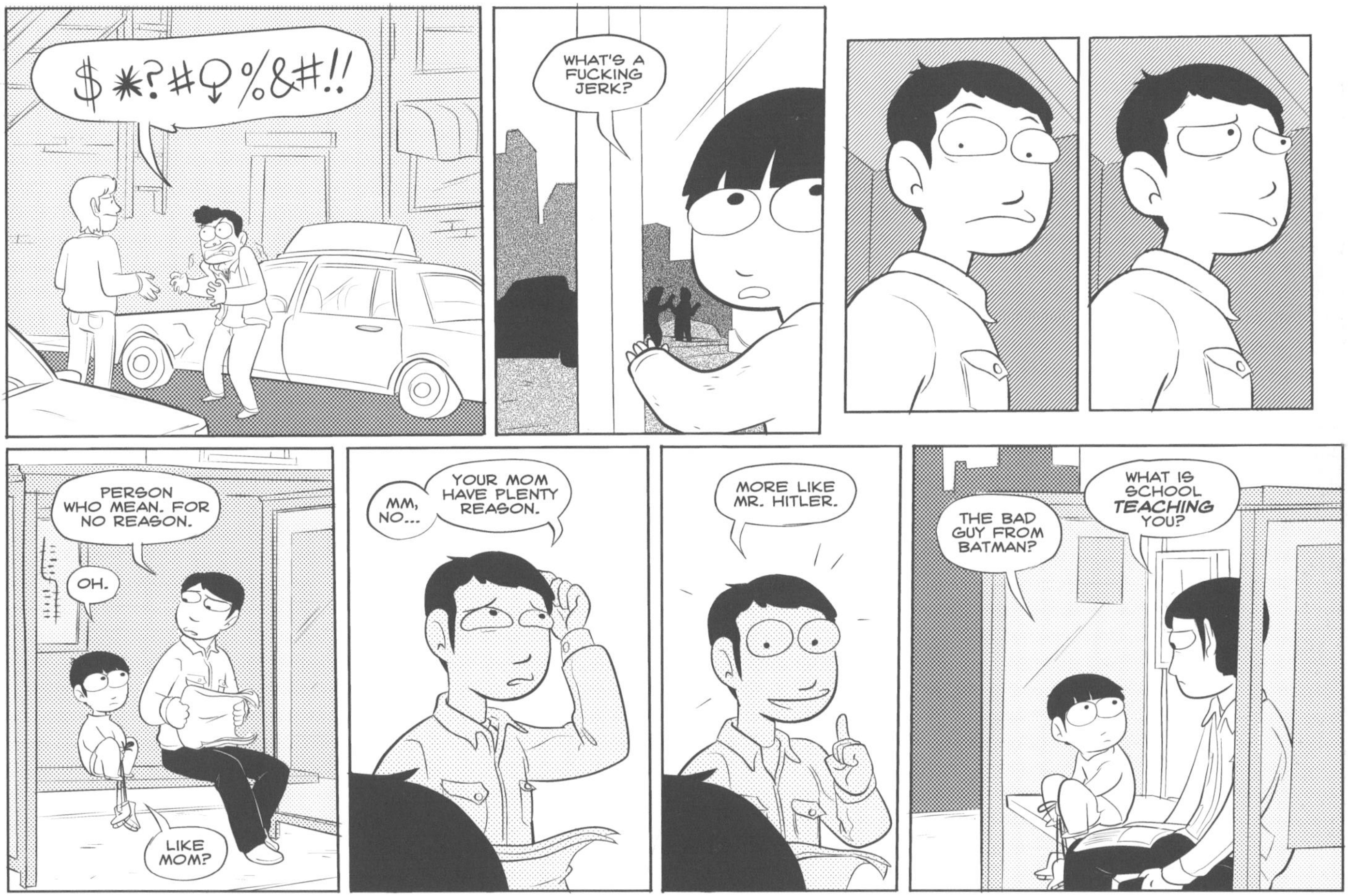
$*?#♀%&#!!
WHAT'S A FUCKING JERK?
PERSON WHO MEAN. FOR NO REASON.
OH.
LIKE MOM?
MM, NO...
YOUR MOM HAVE PLENTY REASON.
MORE LIKE MR. HITLER.
THE BAD GUY FROM BATMAN?
WHAT IS SCHOOL *TEACHING* YOU?

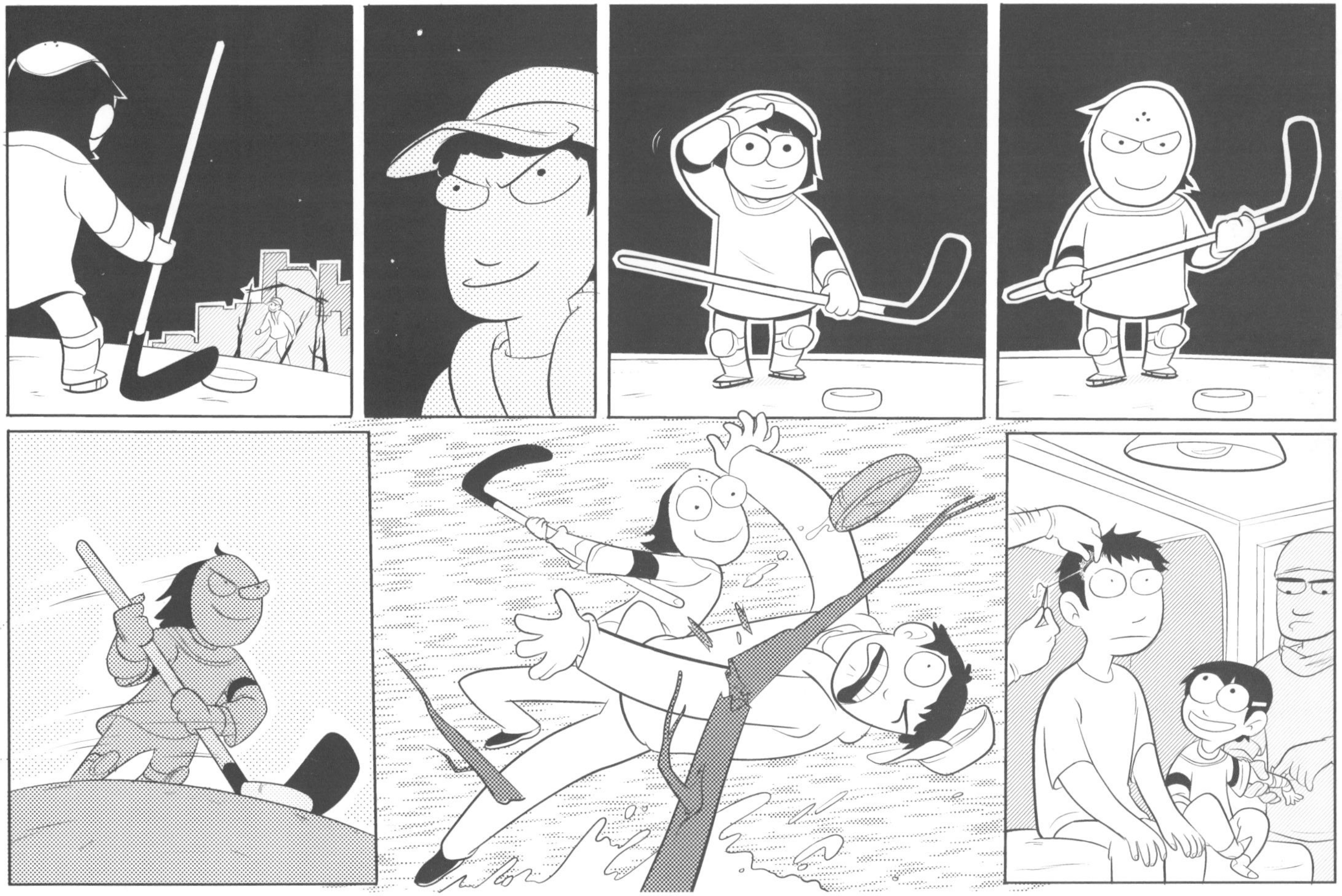

DID YOU WEAR A NUT GUARD?

NO.

DID YOU KNOCK OUT ALL YOUR TEETH?

NO.

WERE YOU IN LOVE WITH WAYNE GRETZKY?

...SHUT UP.

IS THIS *REALLY* SO HARD TO BELIEVE? DIDN'T YOU HAVE KID HEROES?

WELL, SURE. I WANTED TO BE THE NEXT MICHELANGELO.

BUT, YOU KNOW, THE *TURTLE*.

NO WONDER WE FORGET OUR DREAMS.

REALITY MAKES THEM SEEM *STUPID* BY COMPARISON.

AT LEAST WE STILL HAVE OUR VIOLENT URGES, RIGHT?

YEAH, RIGHT. I COULDN'T RUN OVER A BUG IF IT WAS SITTING UNDER MY WHEE--

PAF!

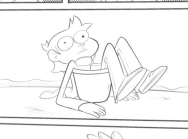

WOGGLE

WOGGLE

WOGGLE

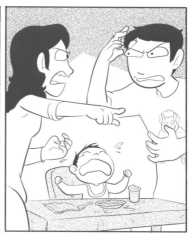

THIS IS

STUPID!!

YOU NEED TO KNOW WHY, AMERICA? YOU NEED TO KNOW WHY I *FUCKING QUIT?!*

I-IT WAS REALLY MORE OF A FLEETING CURIOSITY.

THAN ANYTHING.

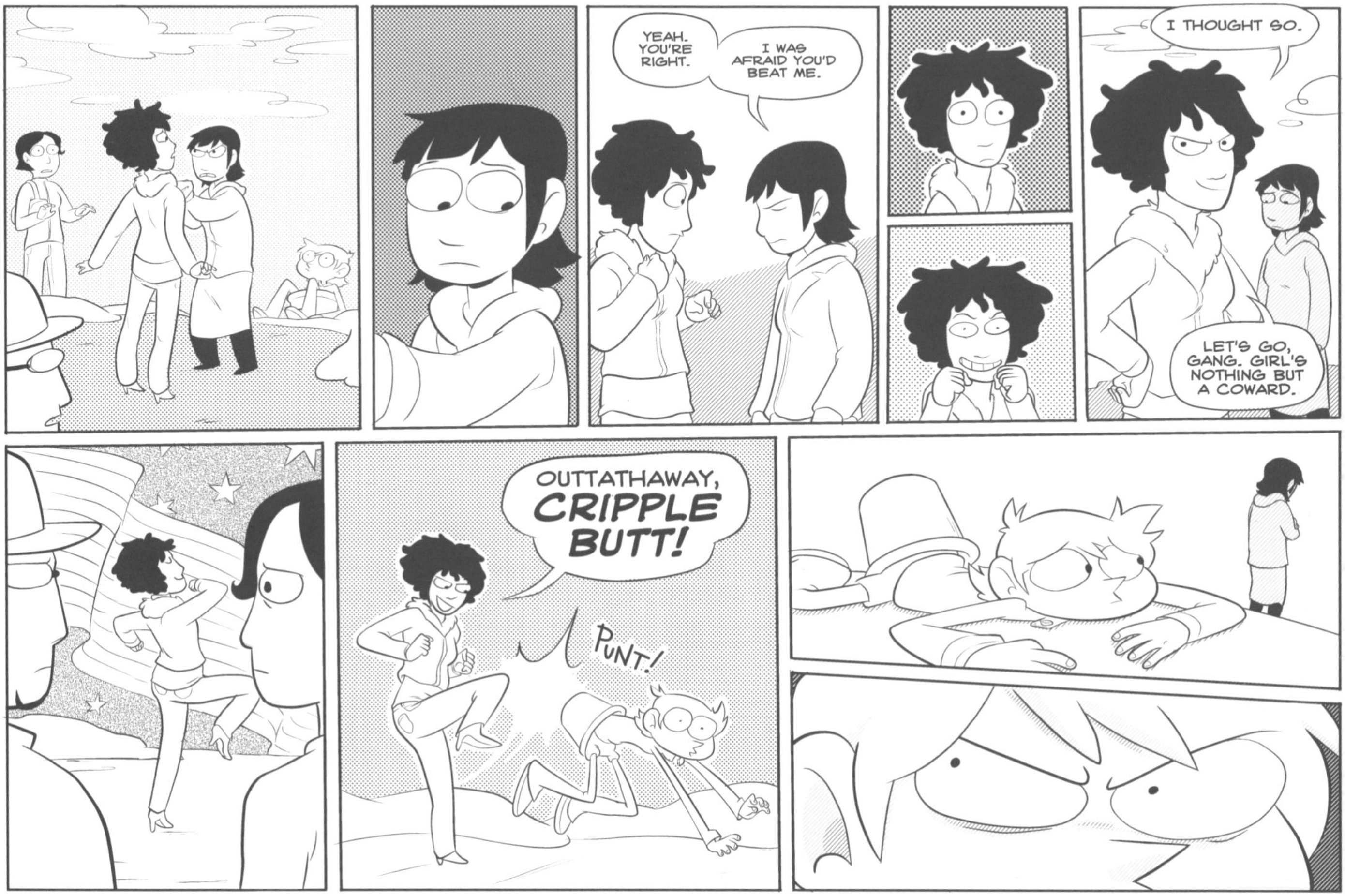
YEAH. YOU'RE RIGHT.
I WAS AFRAID YOU'D BEAT ME.
I THOUGHT SO.
LET'S GO, GANG. GIRL'S NOTHING BUT A COWARD.
OUTTATHAWAY, CRIPPLE BUTT!
PUNT!

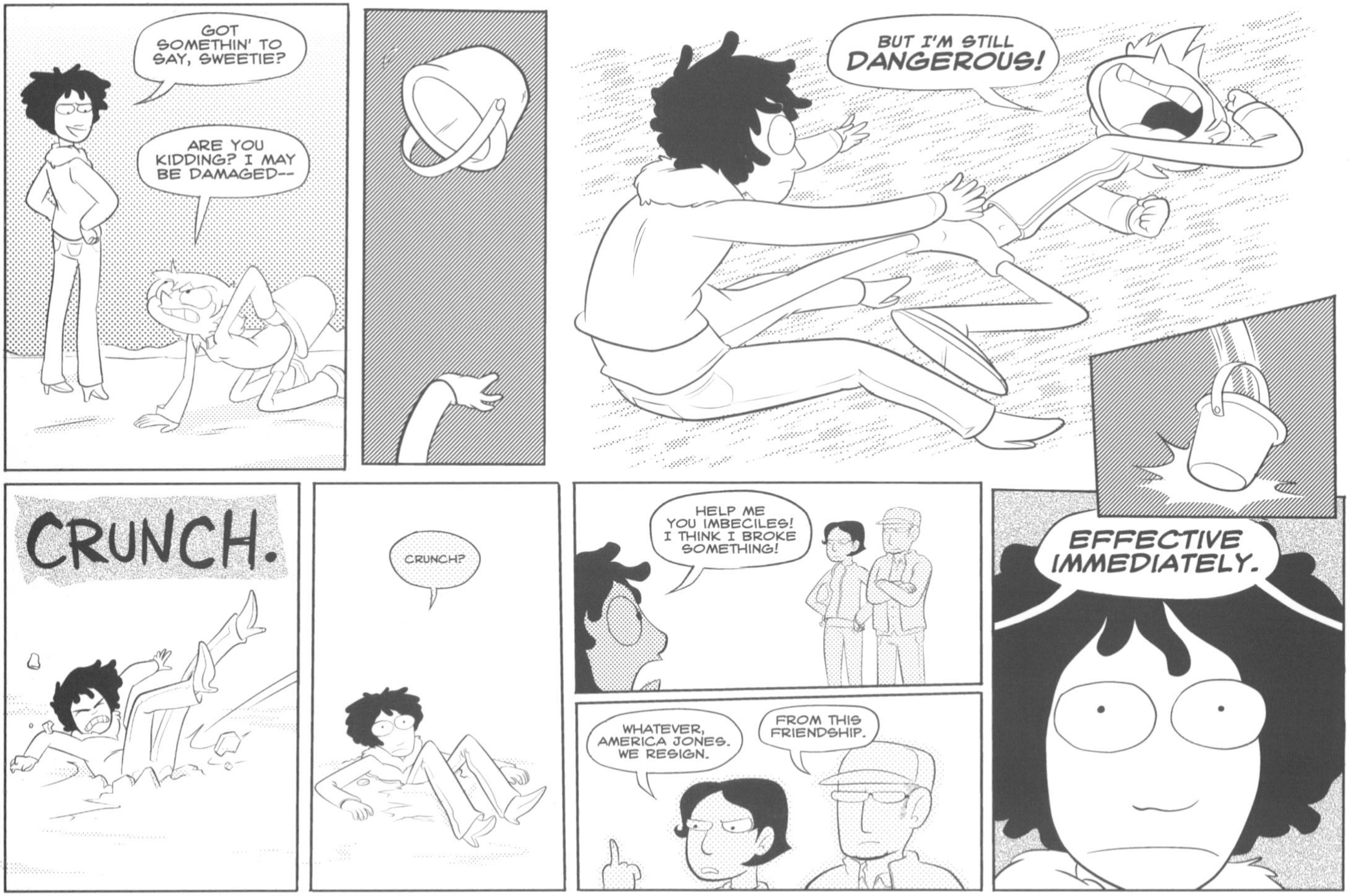
GOT SOMETHIN' TO SAY, SWEETIE?
ARE YOU KIDDING? I MAY BE DAMAGED--
BUT I'M STILL DANGEROUS!
CRUNCH.
CRUNCH?
HELP ME YOU IMBECILES! I THINK I BROKE SOMETHING!
WHATEVER, AMERICA JONES. WE RESIGN.
FROM THIS FRIENDSHIP.
EFFECTIVE IMMEDIATELY.

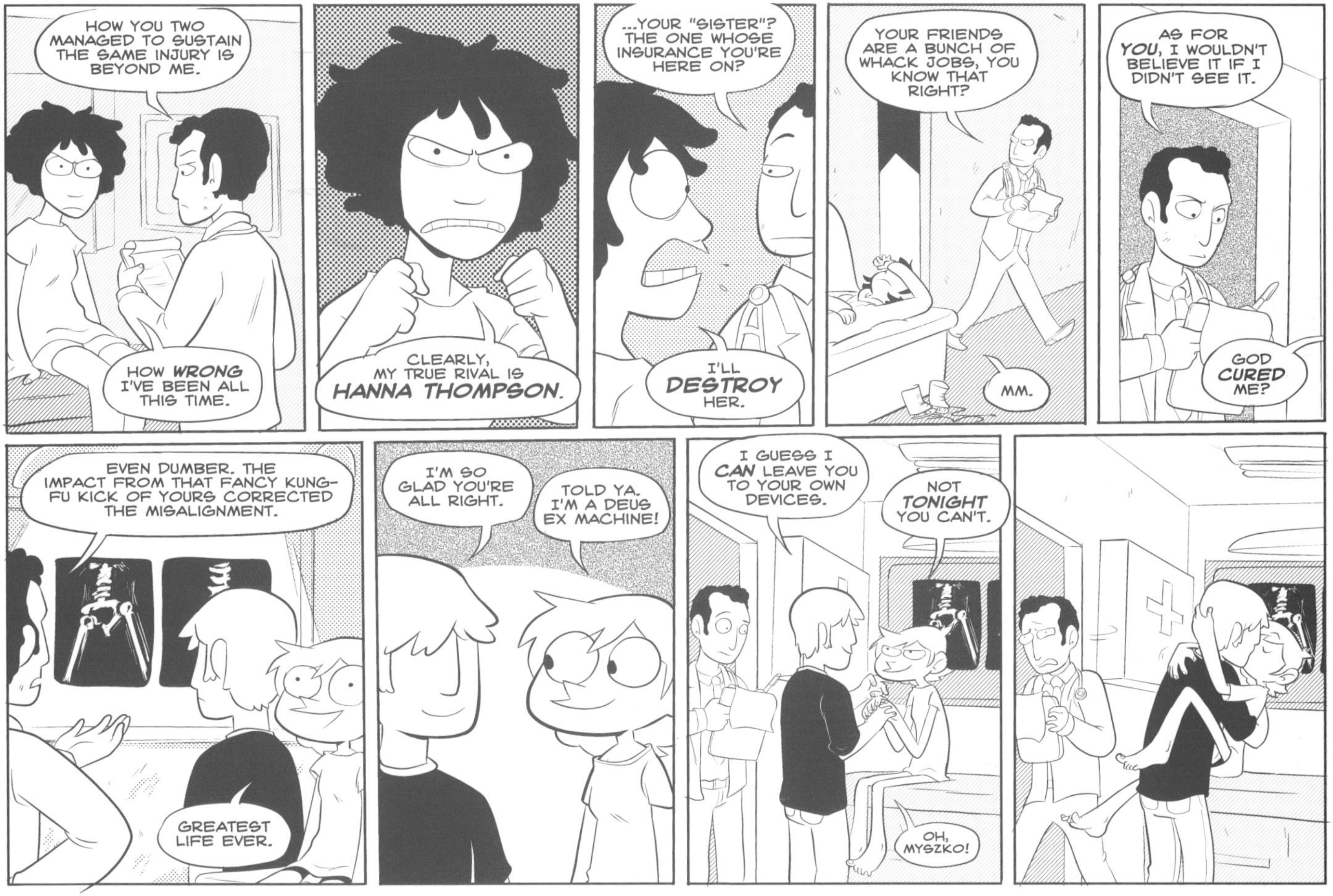
HOW YOU TWO MANAGED TO SUSTAIN THE SAME INJURY IS BEYOND ME.
HOW WRONG I'VE BEEN ALL THIS TIME.
CLEARLY, MY TRUE RIVAL IS HANNA THOMPSON.
...YOUR "SISTER"? THE ONE WHOSE INSURANCE YOU'RE HERE ON?
I'LL DESTROY HER.
YOUR FRIENDS ARE A BUNCH OF WHACK JOBS, YOU KNOW THAT RIGHT?
MM.
AS FOR YOU, I WOULDN'T BELIEVE IT IF I DIDN'T SEE IT.
GOD CURED ME?
EVEN DUMBER. THE IMPACT FROM THAT FANCY KUNG-FU KICK OF YOURS CORRECTED THE MISALIGNMENT.
GREATEST LIFE EVER.
I'M SO GLAD YOU'RE ALL RIGHT.
TOLD YA. I'M A DEUS EX MACHINE!
I GUESS I CAN LEAVE YOU TO YOUR OWN DEVICES.
NOT TONIGHT YOU CAN'T.
OH, MYSZKO!

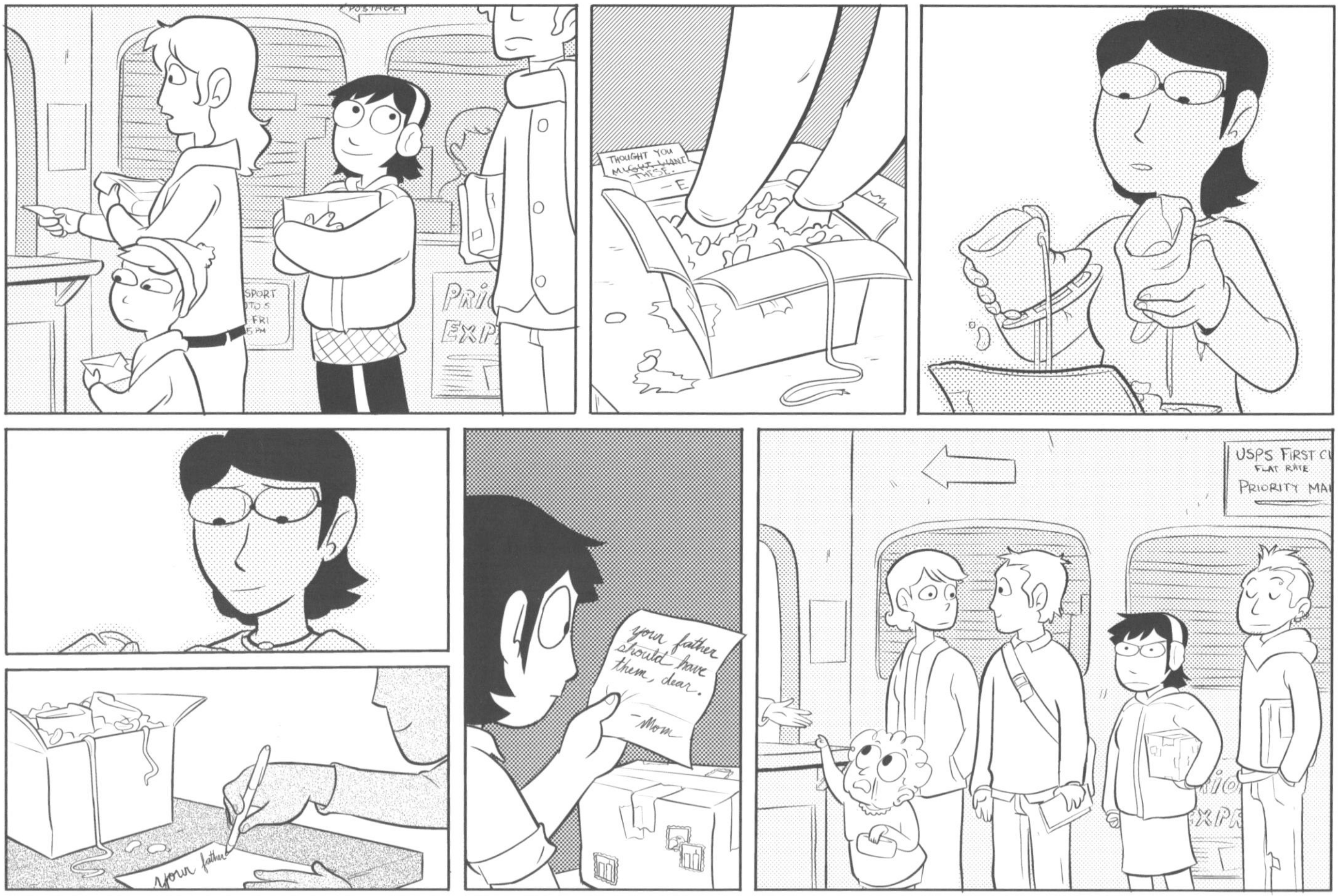
POSTAGE
THOUGHT YOU MIGHT WANT THESE.
—E
your father should have them, dear.
—Mom
USPS FIRST C
FLAT RATE
PRIORITY MAI

our brooklynian life

WHY DO YOU LIKE THIS PLACE ON WEEKENDS? IT'S GOT MORE TOOLS THAN A HARDWARE STORE.

TOOLS ARE USEFUL. *AND* THEY FIX THINGS ONCE IN A WHILE.

Y'KNOW, WILL STILL ASKS ABOUT YOU.

WHAT? HE DOES? TELL HIM I'M DEAD.

I COULDN'T DO THAT.

HE'S MY FRIEND.

HE'S YOUR *DRUG* DEALER.

HEAD UP!

THE TWO AREN'T MUTUALLY EXCLUSIVE, YOU KNOW.

YEAH, WELL, NEITHER ARE DRINKING AND PREGNANCY.

SO WHAT'S THIS JACKET YOU'RE SO EXCITED ABOUT?

ONLY THE HOTTEST OF THE SEASON.

YOU COULDN'T KNIT A FINER FABRIC OUT OF JOHN GALLIANO'S *PUBES*.

RIGHT, I SHOULD'VE KNOWN. ANOTHER COUTURE OF DUTY.

THIS IS WHY I'M *HAUTE*.

UMPH

UMPH

UMPH

UMPH

127

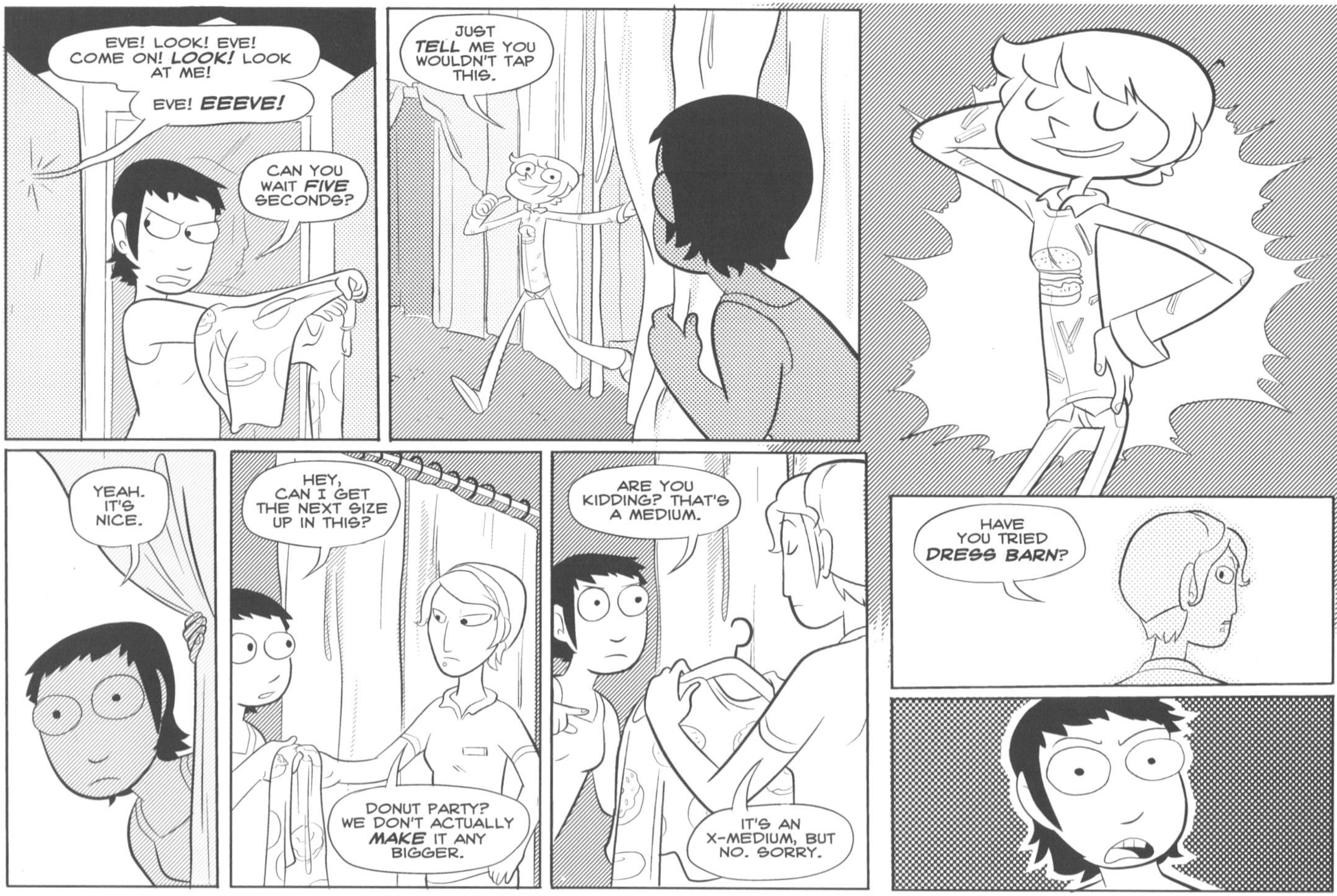
EVE! LOOK! EVE! COME ON! LOOK! LOOK AT ME!
EVE! EEEVE!
CAN YOU WAIT FIVE SECONDS?
JUST TELL ME YOU WOULDN'T TAP THIS.
YEAH. IT'S NICE.
HEY, CAN I GET THE NEXT SIZE UP IN THIS?
DONUT PARTY? WE DON'T ACTUALLY MAKE IT ANY BIGGER.
ARE YOU KIDDING? THAT'S A MEDIUM.
IT'S AN X-MEDIUM, BUT NO. SORRY.
HAVE YOU TRIED DRESS BARN?

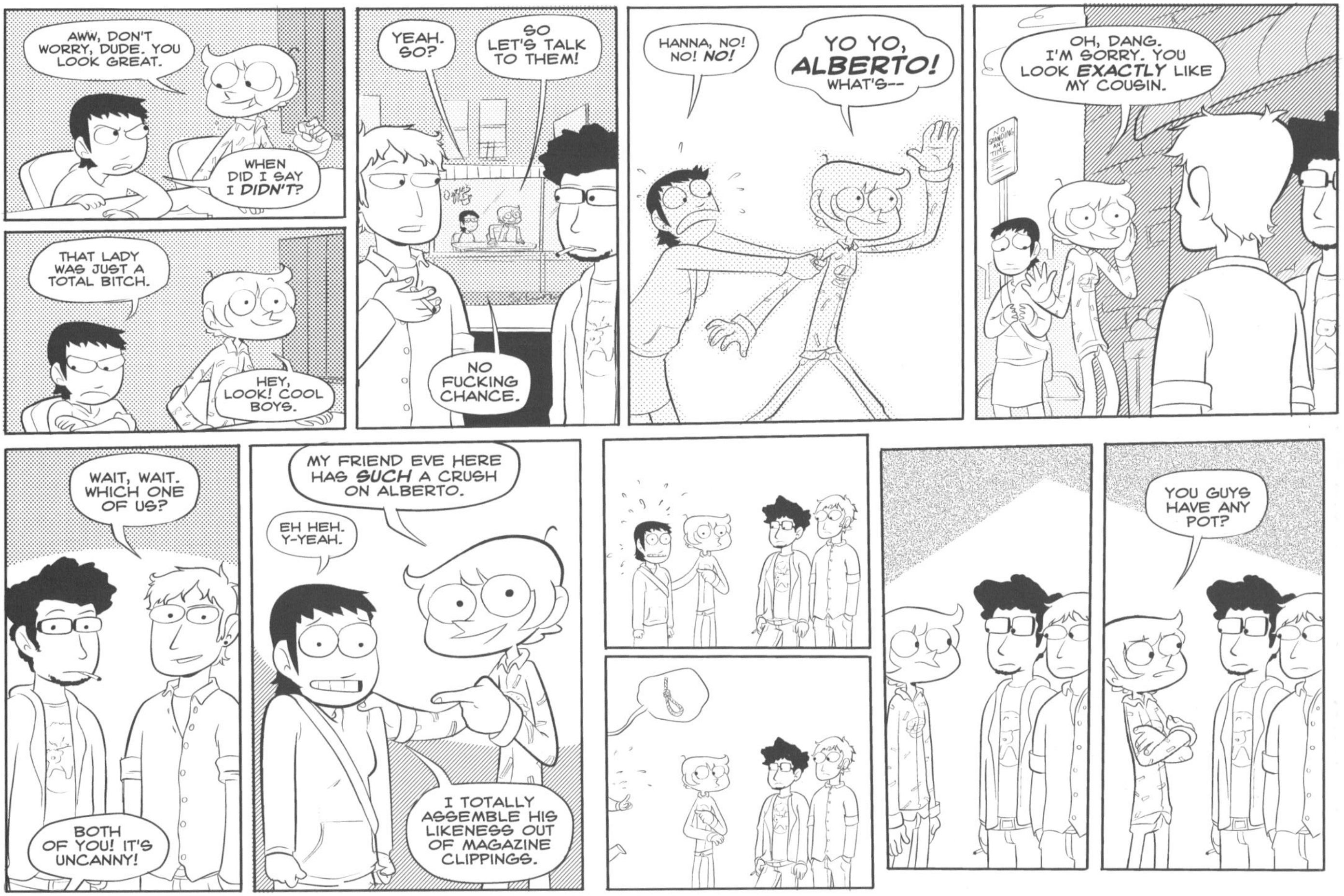
AWW, DON'T WORRY, DUDE. YOU LOOK GREAT.
WHEN DID I SAY I *DIDN'T*?
THAT LADY WAS JUST A TOTAL BITCH.
HEY, LOOK! COOL BOYS.
YEAH. SO?
SO LET'S TALK TO THEM!
NO FUCKING CHANCE.
HANNA, NO! NO! *NO!*
YO YO, *ALBERTO!* WHAT'S--
OH, DANG. I'M SORRY. YOU LOOK *EXACTLY* LIKE MY COUSIN.
NO STANDING ANY TIME
WAIT, WAIT. WHICH ONE OF US?
BOTH OF YOU! IT'S UNCANNY!
MY FRIEND EVE HERE HAS *SUCH* A CRUSH ON ALBERTO.
EH HEH. Y-YEAH.
I TOTALLY ASSEMBLE HIS LIKENESS OUT OF MAGAZINE CLIPPINGS.
YOU GUYS HAVE ANY POT?

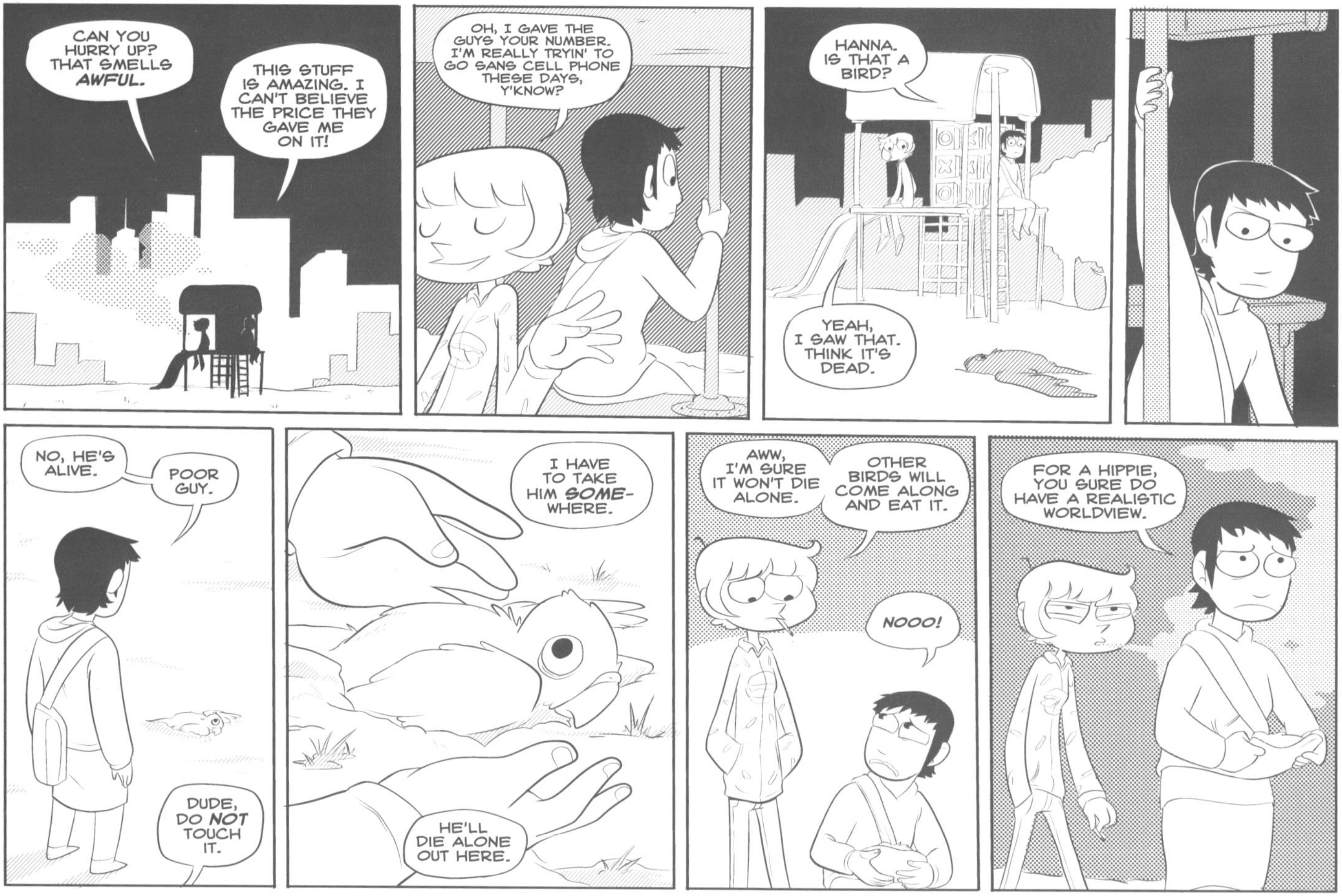
CAN YOU HURRY UP? THAT SMELLS **AWFUL.**
THIS STUFF IS AMAZING. I CAN'T BELIEVE THE PRICE THEY GAVE ME ON IT!
OH, I GAVE THE GUYS YOUR NUMBER. I'M REALLY TRYIN' TO GO SANS CELL PHONE THESE DAYS, Y'KNOW?
HANNA. IS THAT A BIRD?
YEAH, I SAW THAT. THINK IT'S DEAD.
NO, HE'S ALIVE.
POOR GUY.
DUDE, DO **NOT** TOUCH IT.
I HAVE TO TAKE HIM **SOME**-WHERE.
HE'LL DIE ALONE OUT HERE.
AWW, I'M SURE IT WON'T DIE ALONE.
OTHER BIRDS WILL COME ALONG AND EAT IT.
NOOO!
FOR A HIPPIE, YOU SURE DO HAVE A REALISTIC WORLDVIEW.

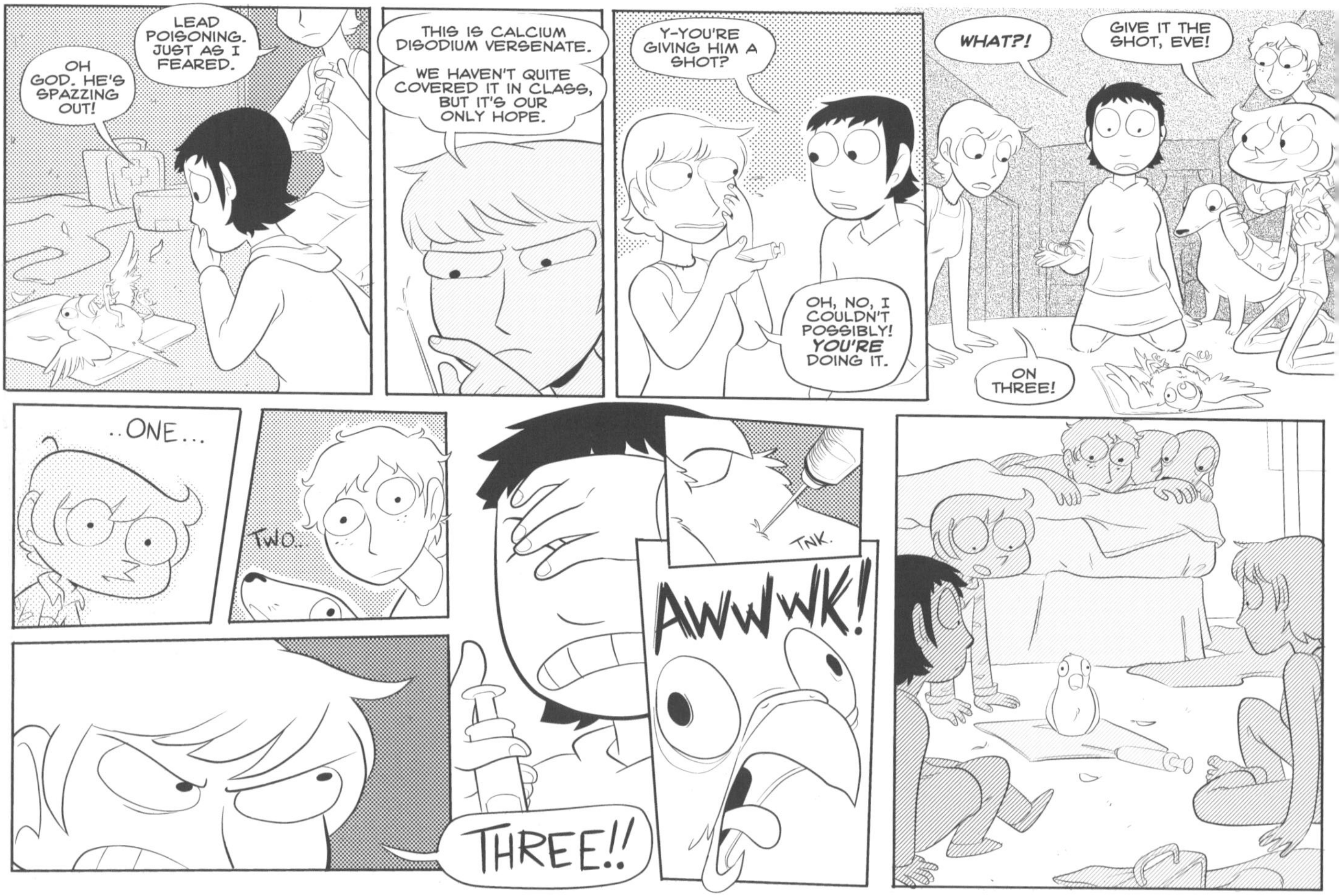
OH GOD. HE'S SPAZZING OUT!
LEAD POISONING. JUST AS I FEARED.
THIS IS CALCIUM DISODIUM VERSENATE.
WE HAVEN'T QUITE COVERED IT IN CLASS, BUT IT'S OUR ONLY HOPE.
Y-YOU'RE GIVING HIM A SHOT?
OH, NO, I COULDN'T POSSIBLY! *YOU'RE* DOING IT.
WHAT?!
GIVE IT THE SHOT, EVE!
ON THREE!
..ONE...
TWO..
TNK.
AWWWK!
THREE!!

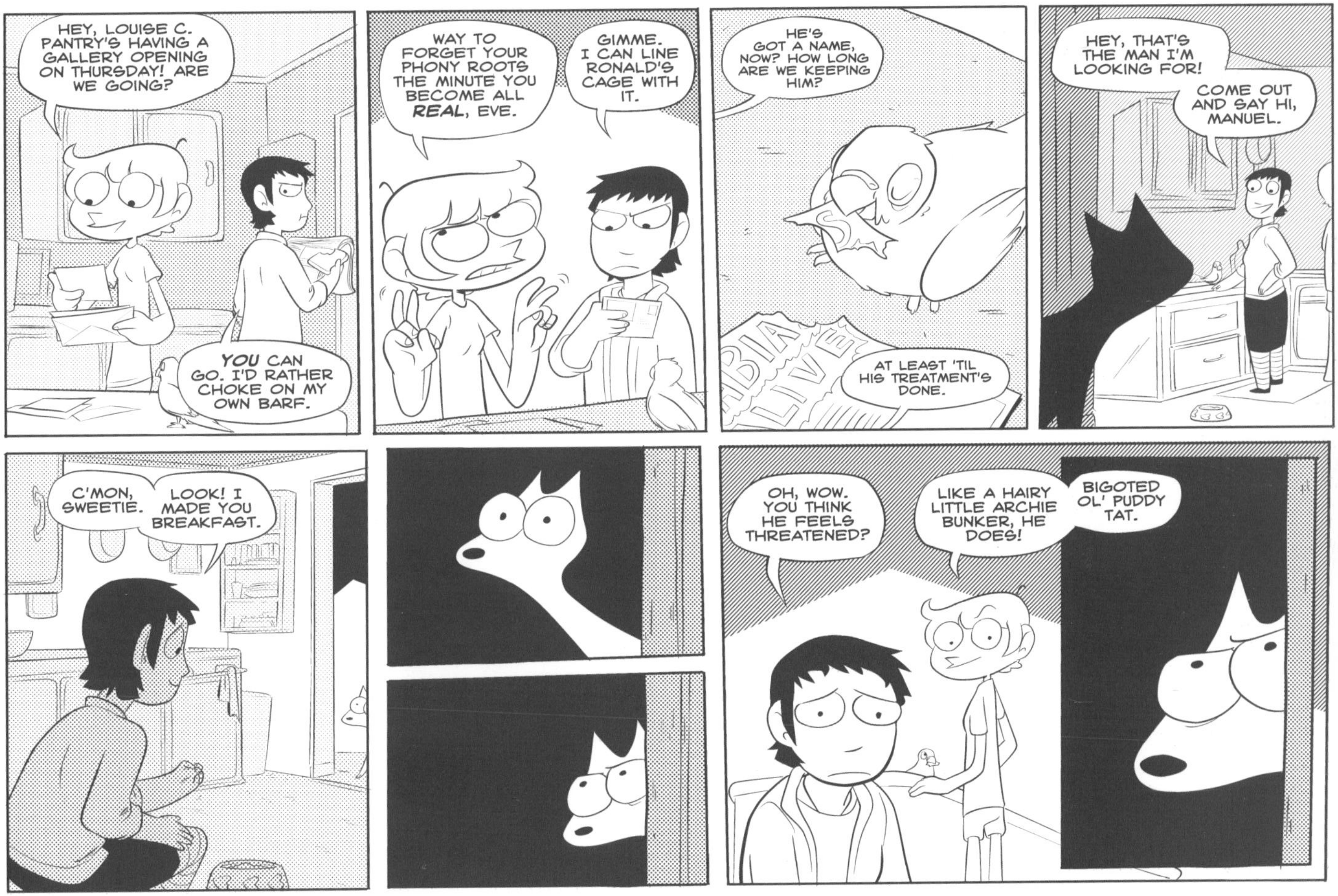
HEY, LOUISE C. PANTRY'S HAVING A GALLERY OPENING ON THURSDAY! ARE WE GOING?
YOU CAN GO. I'D RATHER CHOKE ON MY OWN BARF.
WAY TO FORGET YOUR PHONY ROOTS THE MINUTE YOU BECOME ALL REAL, EVE.
GIMME. I CAN LINE RONALD'S CAGE WITH IT.
HE'S GOT A NAME, NOW? HOW LONG ARE WE KEEPING HIM?
AT LEAST 'TIL HIS TREATMENT'S DONE.
HEY, THAT'S THE MAN I'M LOOKING FOR!
COME OUT AND SAY HI, MANUEL.
C'MON, SWEETIE.
LOOK! I MADE YOU BREAKFAST.
OH, WOW. YOU THINK HE FEELS THREATENED?
LIKE A HAIRY LITTLE ARCHIE BUNKER, HE DOES!
BIGOTED OL' PUDDY TAT.

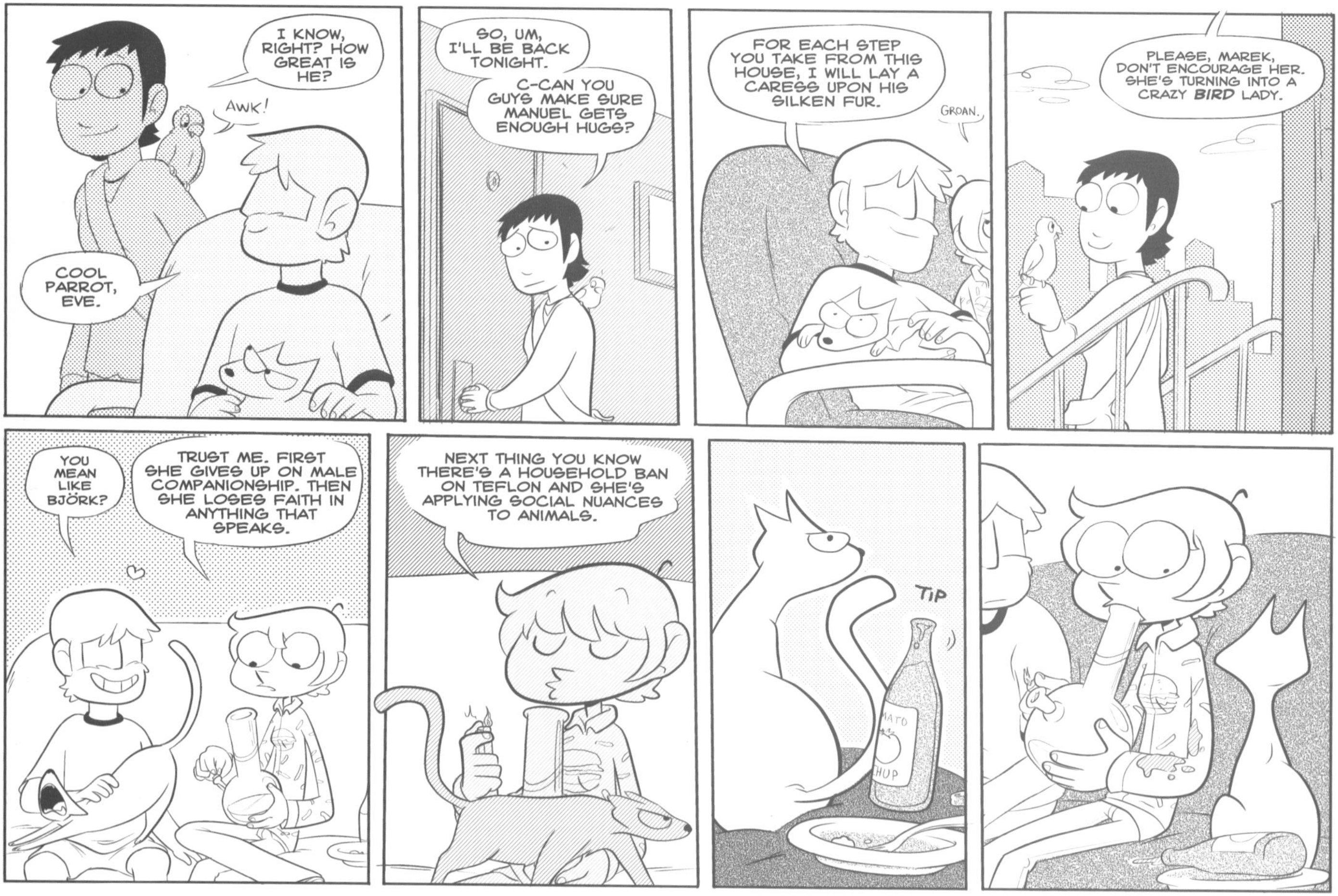
I KNOW, RIGHT? HOW GREAT IS HE?
AWK!
COOL PARROT, EVE.
SO, UM, I'LL BE BACK TONIGHT.
C-CAN YOU GUYS MAKE SURE MANUEL GETS ENOUGH HUGS?
FOR EACH STEP YOU TAKE FROM THIS HOUSE, I WILL LAY A CARESS UPON HIS SILKEN FUR.
GROAN.
PLEASE, MAREK, DON'T ENCOURAGE HER. SHE'S TURNING INTO A CRAZY BIRD LADY.
YOU MEAN LIKE BJÖRK?
TRUST ME. FIRST SHE GIVES UP ON MALE COMPANIONSHIP. THEN SHE LOSES FAITH IN ANYTHING THAT SPEAKS.
NEXT THING YOU KNOW THERE'S A HOUSEHOLD BAN ON TEFLON AND SHE'S APPLYING SOCIAL NUANCES TO ANIMALS.
TIP

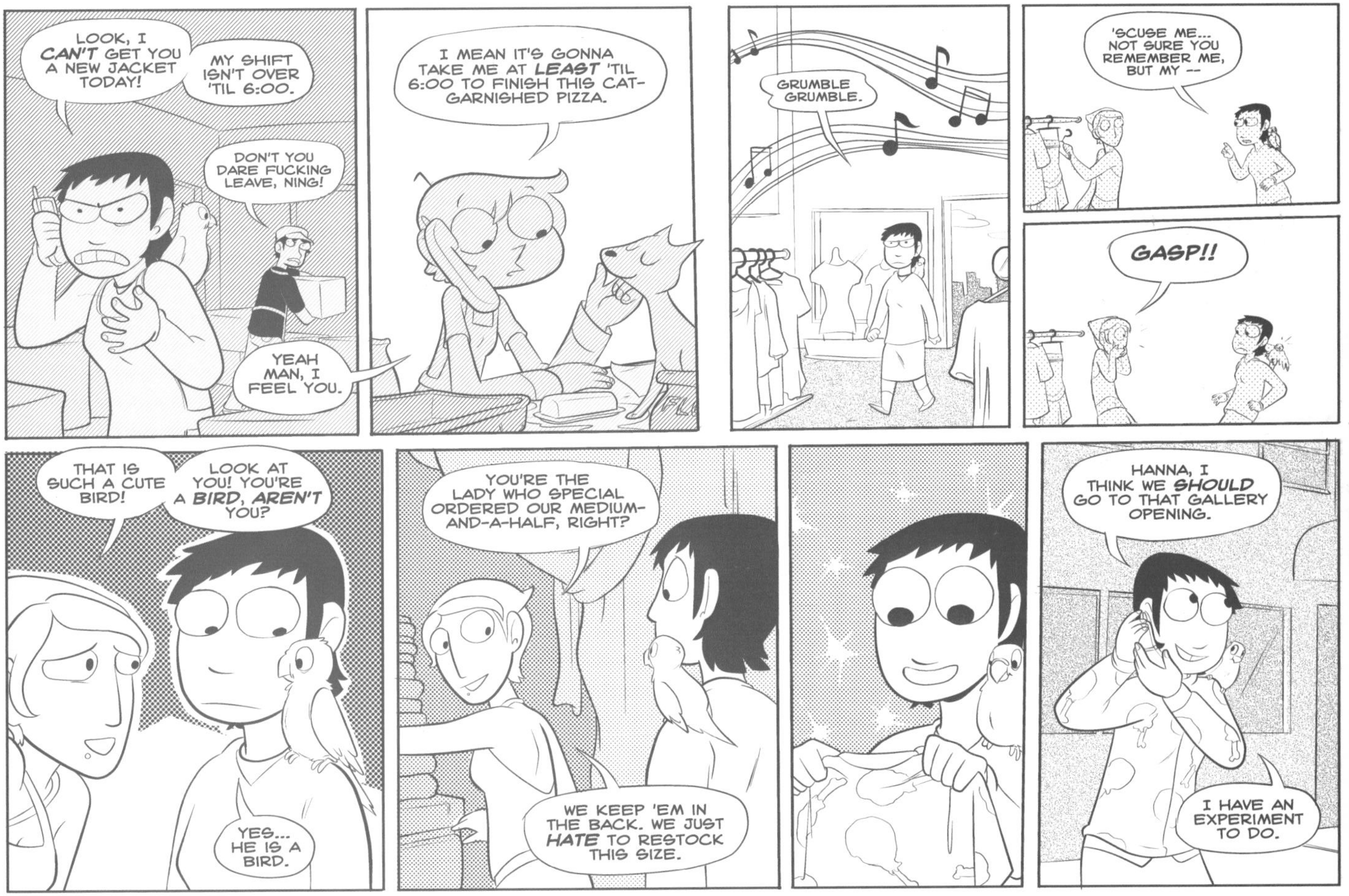
LOOK, I CAN'T GET YOU A NEW JACKET TODAY!
MY SHIFT ISN'T OVER 'TIL 6:00.
DON'T YOU DARE FUCKING LEAVE, NING!
YEAH MAN, I FEEL YOU.
I MEAN IT'S GONNA TAKE ME AT LEAST 'TIL 6:00 TO FINISH THIS CAT-GARNISHED PIZZA.
GRUMBLE GRUMBLE.
'SCUSE ME... NOT SURE YOU REMEMBER ME, BUT MY --
GASP!!
THAT IS SUCH A CUTE BIRD!
LOOK AT YOU! YOU'RE A BIRD, AREN'T YOU?
YES... HE IS A BIRD.
YOU'RE THE LADY WHO SPECIAL ORDERED OUR MEDIUM-AND-A-HALF, RIGHT?
WE KEEP 'EM IN THE BACK. WE JUST HATE TO RESTOCK THIS SIZE.
HANNA, I THINK WE SHOULD GO TO THAT GALLERY OPENING.
I HAVE AN EXPERIMENT TO DO.

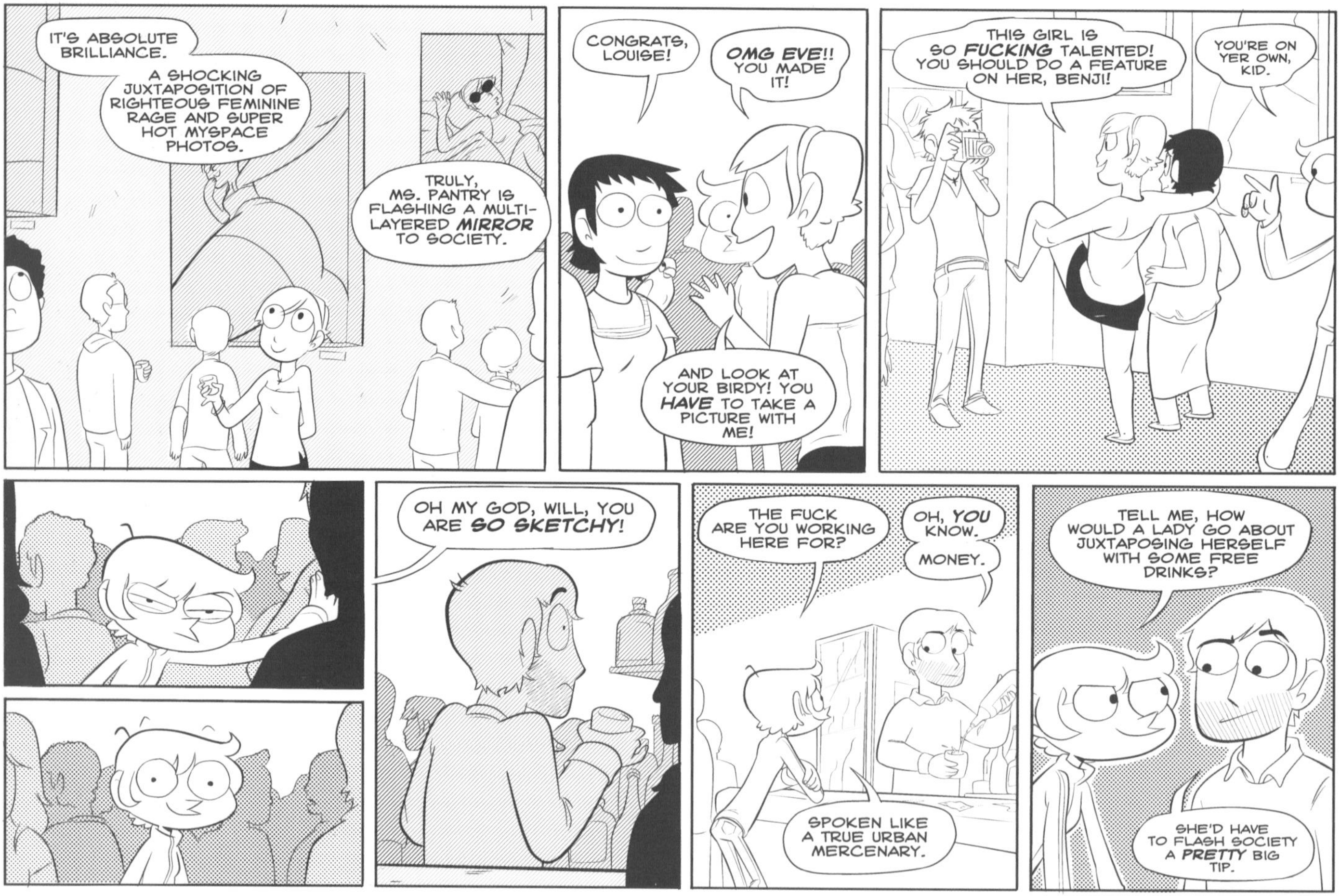
IT'S ABSOLUTE BRILLIANCE.
A SHOCKING JUXTAPOSITION OF RIGHTEOUS FEMININE RAGE AND SUPER HOT MYSPACE PHOTOS.
TRULY, MS. PANTRY IS FLASHING A MULTI-LAYERED *MIRROR* TO SOCIETY.
CONGRATS, LOUISE!
OMG EVE!! YOU MADE IT!
AND LOOK AT YOUR BIRDY! YOU *HAVE* TO TAKE A PICTURE WITH ME!
THIS GIRL IS SO *FUCKING* TALENTED! YOU SHOULD DO A FEATURE ON HER, BENJI!
YOU'RE ON YER OWN, KID.
OH MY GOD, WILL, YOU ARE *SO SKETCHY*!
THE FUCK ARE YOU WORKING HERE FOR?
OH, *YOU* KNOW.
MONEY.
SPOKEN LIKE A TRUE URBAN MERCENARY.
TELL ME, HOW WOULD A LADY GO ABOUT JUXTAPOSING HERSELF WITH SOME FREE DRINKS?
SHE'D HAVE TO FLASH SOCIETY A *PRETTY* BIG TIP.

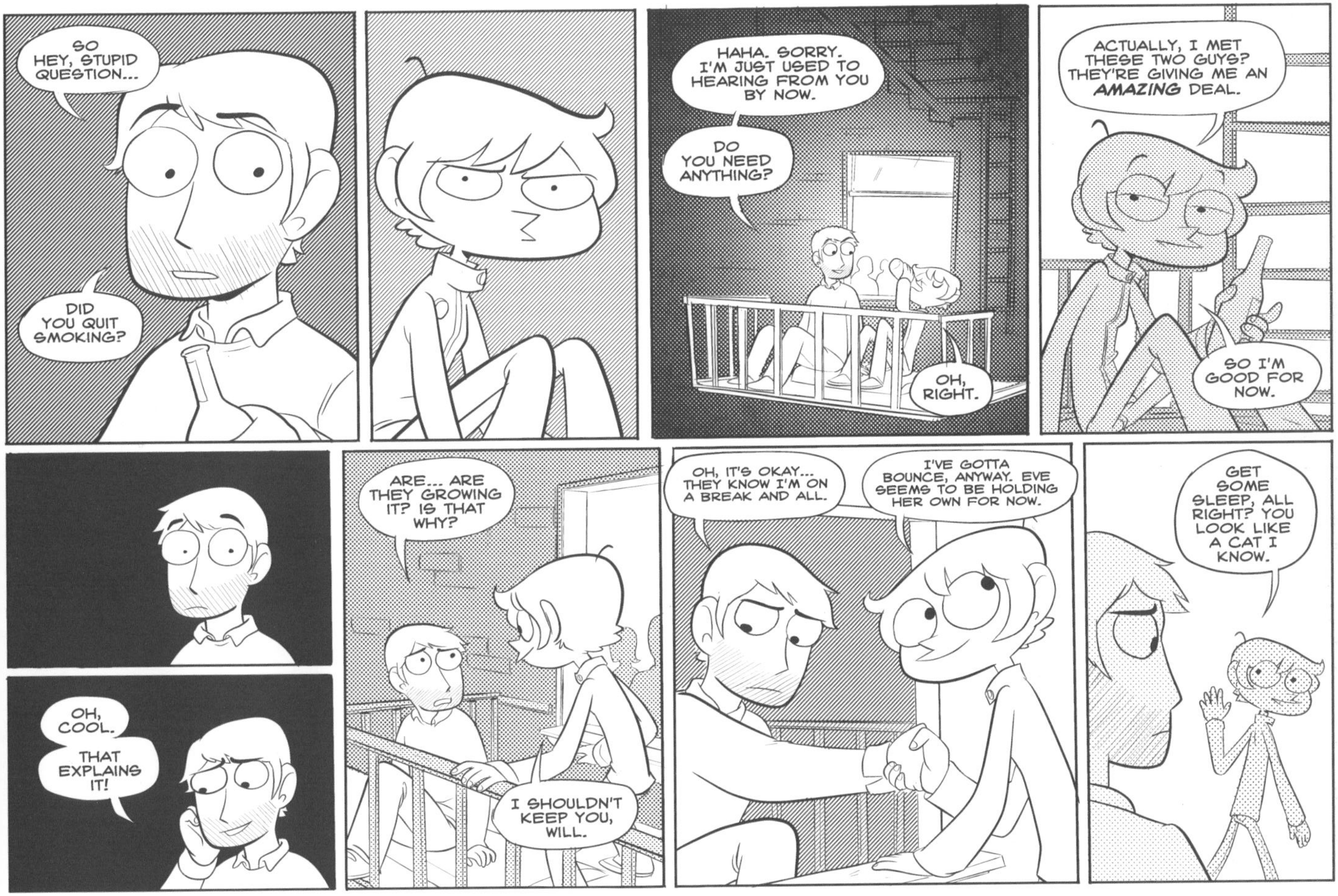
SO HEY, STUPID QUESTION...
DID YOU QUIT SMOKING?
HAHA. SORRY. I'M JUST USED TO HEARING FROM YOU BY NOW.
DO YOU NEED ANYTHING?
OH, RIGHT.
ACTUALLY, I MET THESE TWO GUYS? THEY'RE GIVING ME AN AMAZING DEAL.
SO I'M GOOD FOR NOW.
OH, COOL.
THAT EXPLAINS IT!
ARE... ARE THEY GROWING IT? IS THAT WHY?
I SHOULDN'T KEEP YOU, WILL.
OH, IT'S OKAY... THEY KNOW I'M ON A BREAK AND ALL.
I'VE GOTTA BOUNCE, ANYWAY. EVE SEEMS TO BE HOLDING HER OWN FOR NOW.
GET SOME SLEEP, ALL RIGHT? YOU LOOK LIKE A CAT I KNOW.

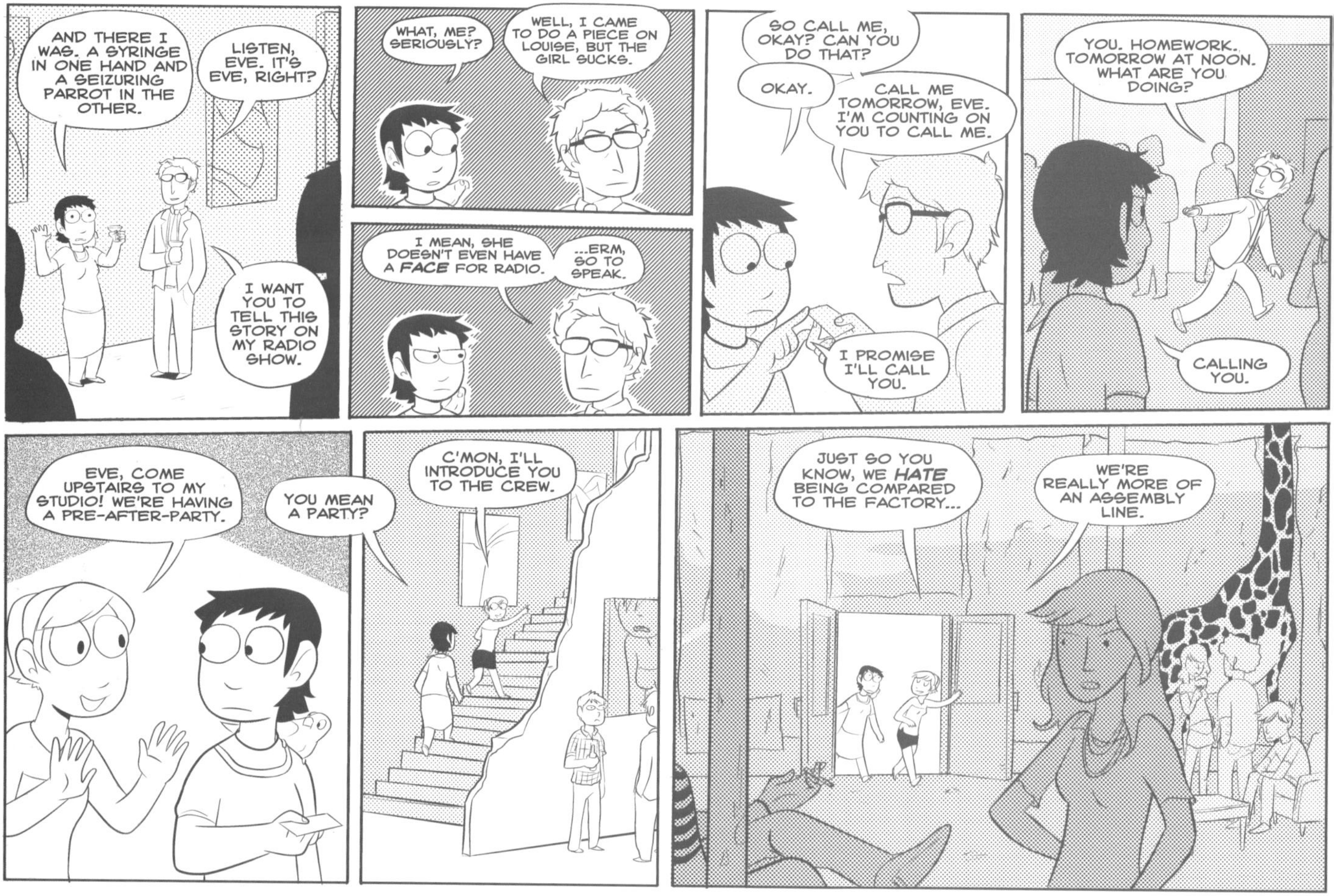
AND THERE I WAS. A SYRINGE IN ONE HAND AND A SEIZURING PARROT IN THE OTHER.
LISTEN, EVE. IT'S EVE, RIGHT?
I WANT YOU TO TELL THIS STORY ON MY RADIO SHOW.
WHAT, ME? SERIOUSLY?
WELL, I CAME TO DO A PIECE ON LOUISE, BUT THE GIRL SUCKS.
I MEAN, SHE DOESN'T EVEN HAVE A FACE FOR RADIO.
...ERM, SO TO SPEAK.
SO CALL ME, OKAY? CAN YOU DO THAT?
OKAY.
CALL ME TOMORROW, EVE. I'M COUNTING ON YOU TO CALL ME.
I PROMISE I'LL CALL YOU.
YOU. HOMEWORK. TOMORROW AT NOON. WHAT ARE YOU DOING?
CALLING YOU.
EVE, COME UPSTAIRS TO MY STUDIO! WE'RE HAVING A PRE-AFTER-PARTY.
YOU MEAN A PARTY?
C'MON, I'LL INTRODUCE YOU TO THE CREW.
JUST SO YOU KNOW, WE HATE BEING COMPARED TO THE FACTORY...
WE'RE REALLY MORE OF AN ASSEMBLY LINE.

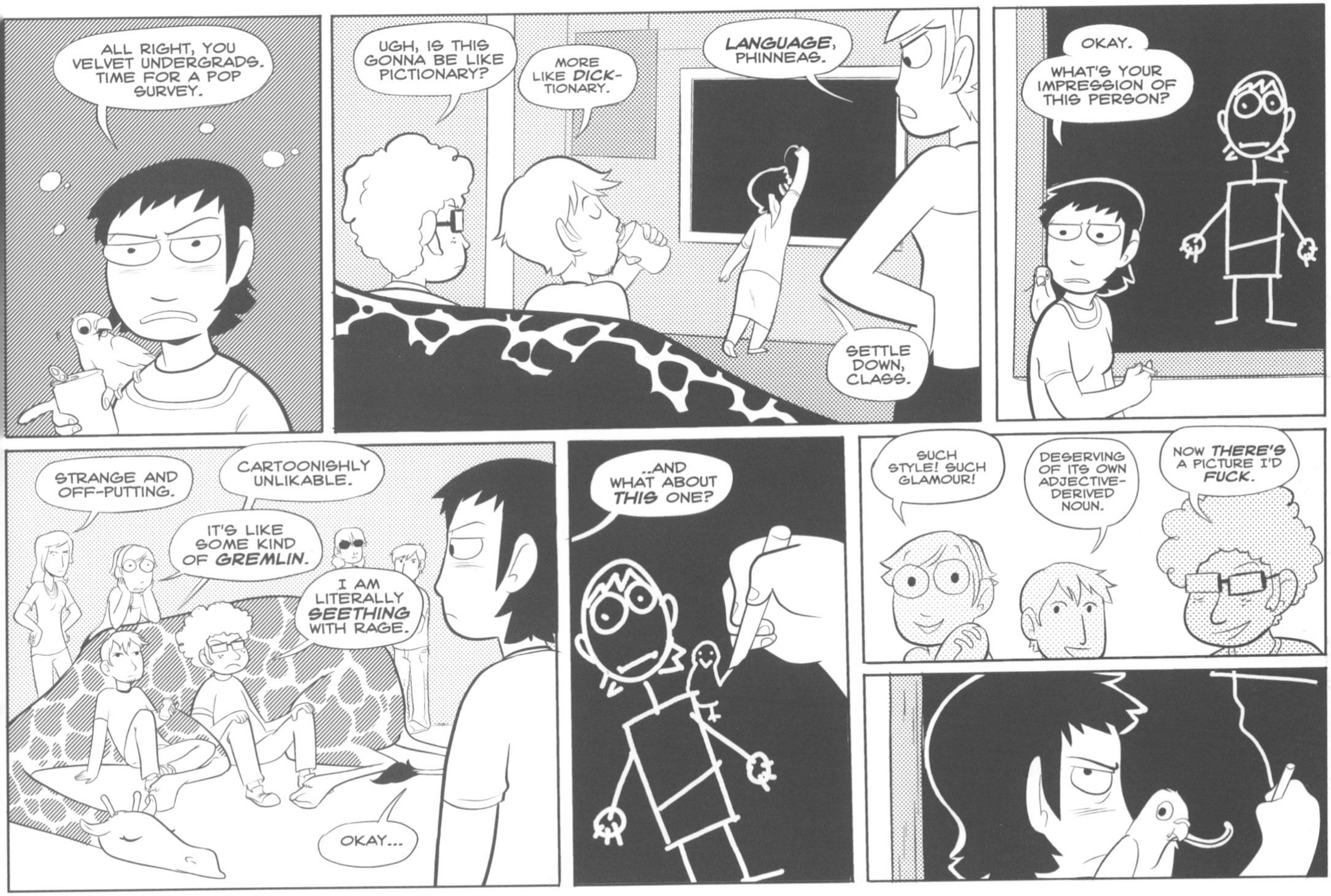
ALL RIGHT, YOU VELVET UNDERGRADS. TIME FOR A POP SURVEY.
UGH, IS THIS GONNA BE LIKE PICTIONARY?
MORE LIKE DICK-TIONARY.
LANGUAGE, PHINNEAS.
SETTLE DOWN, CLASS.
OKAY.
WHAT'S YOUR IMPRESSION OF THIS PERSON?
STRANGE AND OFF-PUTTING.
CARTOONISHLY UNLIKABLE.
IT'S LIKE SOME KIND OF GREMLIN.
I AM LITERALLY SEETHING WITH RAGE.
OKAY...
..AND WHAT ABOUT THIS ONE?
SUCH STYLE! SUCH GLAMOUR!
DESERVING OF ITS OWN ADJECTIVE-DERIVED NOUN.
NOW THERE'S A PICTURE I'D FUCK.

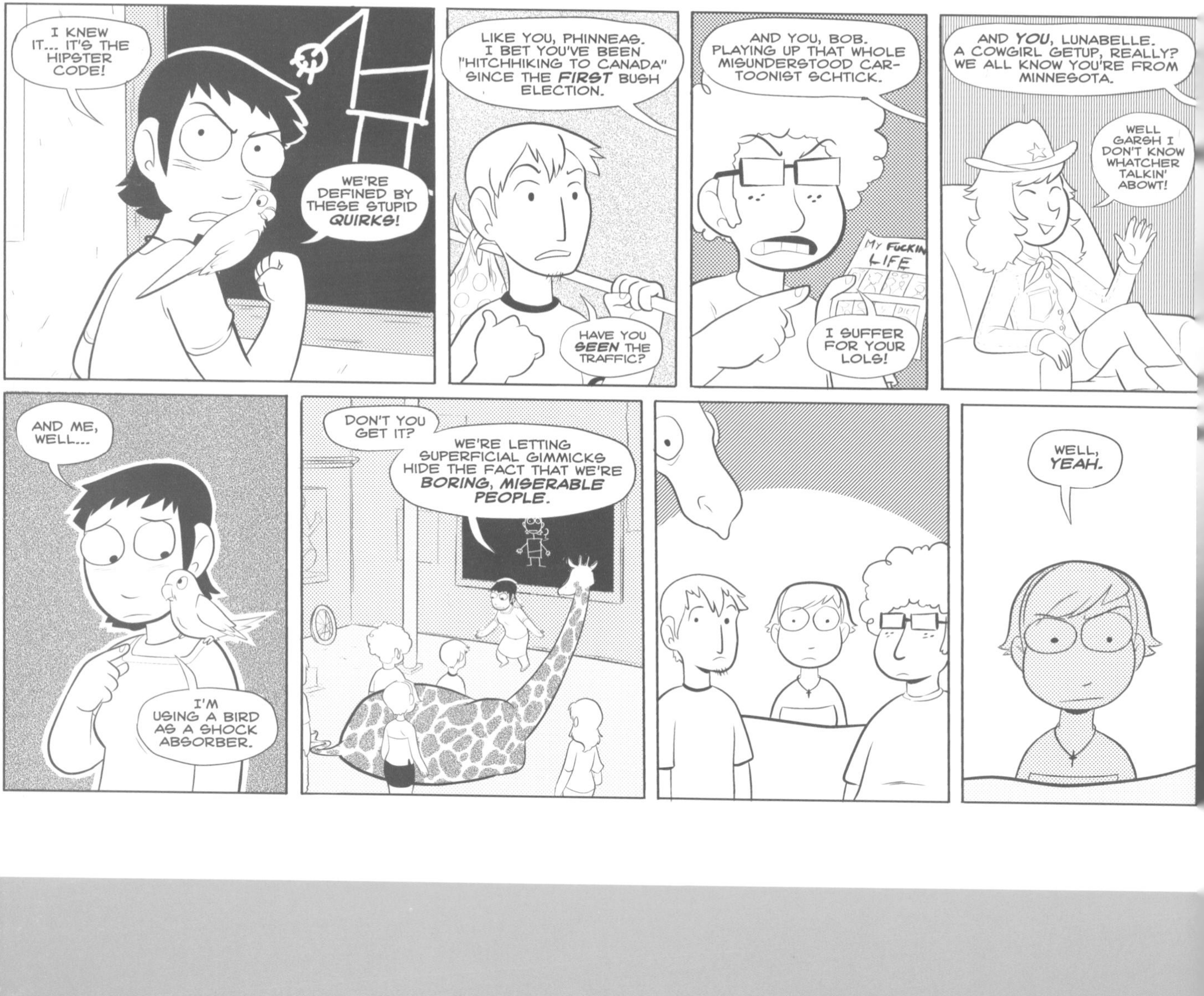
I KNEW IT... IT'S THE HIPSTER CODE!
WE'RE DEFINED BY THESE STUPID QUIRKS!
LIKE YOU, PHINNEAS. I BET YOU'VE BEEN "HITCHHIKING TO CANADA" SINCE THE FIRST BUSH ELECTION.
HAVE YOU SEEN THE TRAFFIC?
AND YOU, BOB. PLAYING UP THAT WHOLE MISUNDERSTOOD CAR-TOONIST SCHTICK.
MY FUCKIN LIFE
I SUFFER FOR YOUR LOLS!
AND YOU, LUNABELLE. A COWGIRL GETUP, REALLY? WE ALL KNOW YOU'RE FROM MINNESOTA.
WELL GARSH I DON'T KNOW WHATCHER TALKIN' ABOWT!
AND ME, WELL...
I'M USING A BIRD AS A SHOCK ABSORBER.
DON'T YOU GET IT?
WE'RE LETTING SUPERFICIAL GIMMICKS HIDE THE FACT THAT WE'RE BORING, MISERABLE PEOPLE.
WELL, YEAH.

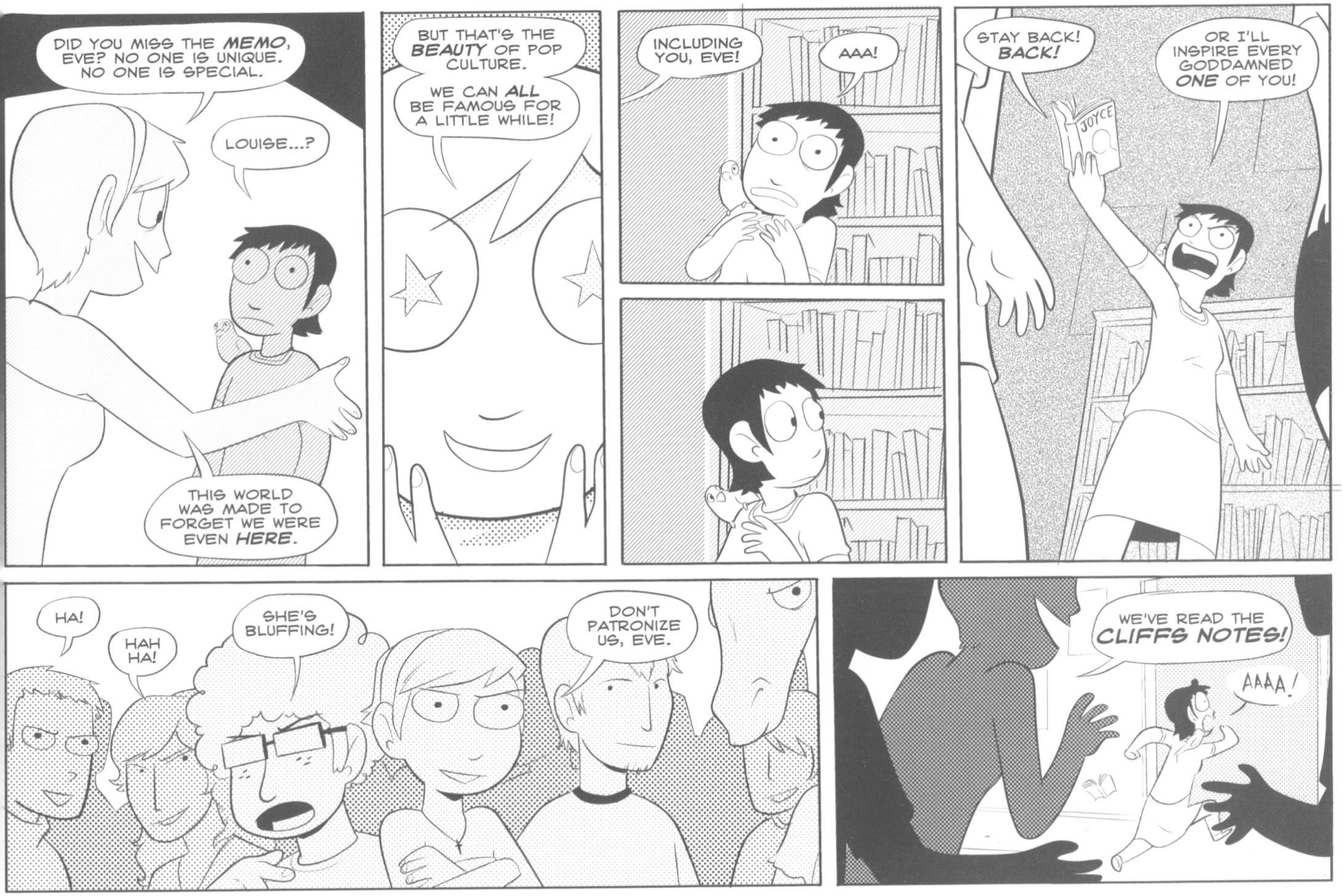
DID YOU MISS THE MEMO, EVE? NO ONE IS UNIQUE. NO ONE IS SPECIAL.
LOUISE...?
THIS WORLD WAS MADE TO FORGET WE WERE EVEN HERE.
BUT THAT'S THE BEAUTY OF POP CULTURE.
WE CAN ALL BE FAMOUS FOR A LITTLE WHILE!
INCLUDING YOU, EVE!
AAA!
STAY BACK! BACK!
OR I'LL INSPIRE EVERY GODDAMNED ONE OF YOU!
JOYCE
HA!
HAH HA!
SHE'S BLUFFING!
DON'T PATRONIZE US, EVE.
WE'VE READ THE CLIFFS NOTES!
AAAA!

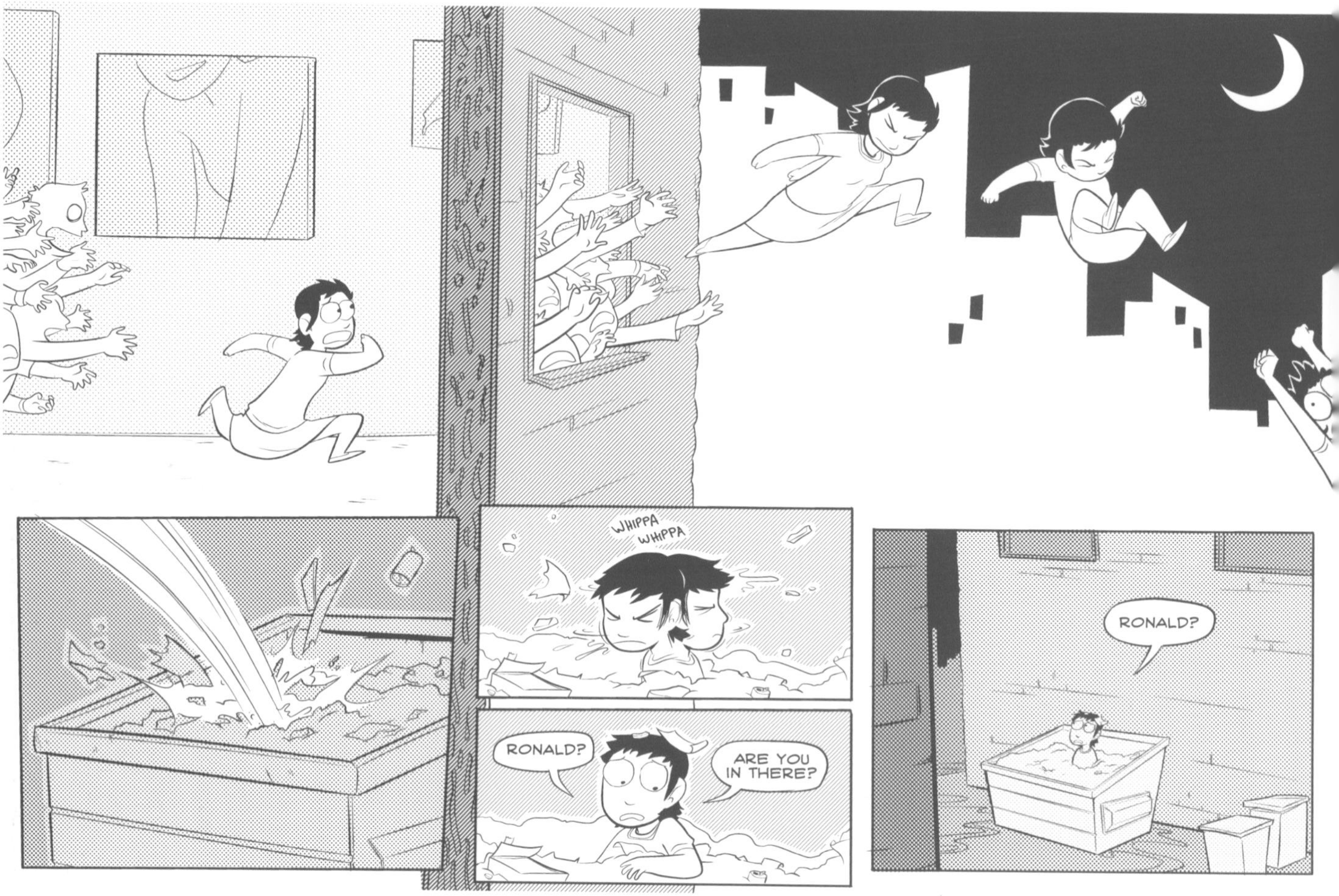
WHIPPA
WHIPPA
RONALD?
ARE YOU IN THERE?
RONALD?

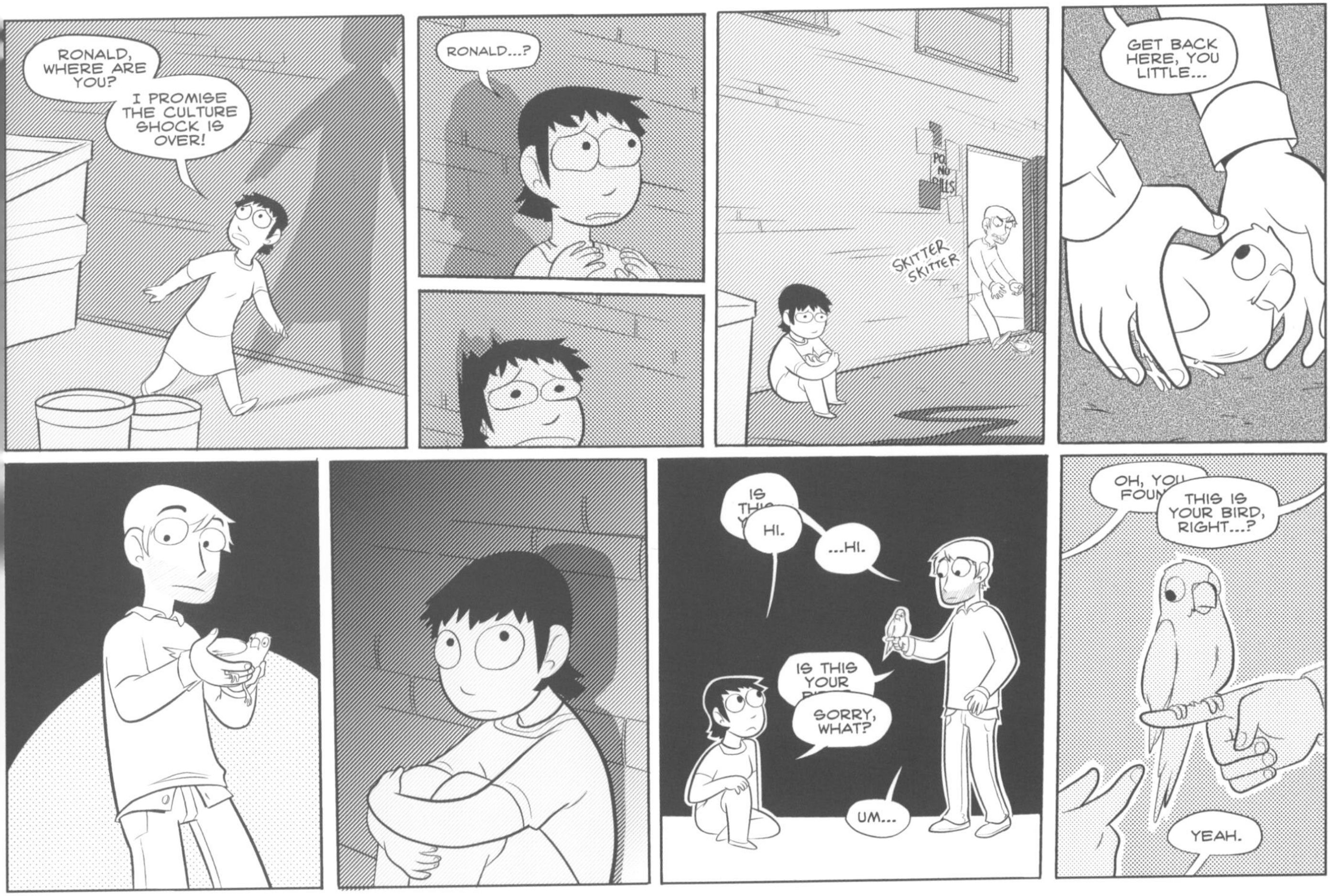
RONALD, WHERE ARE YOU?
I PROMISE THE CULTURE SHOCK IS OVER!
RONALD...?
SKITTER SKITTER
GET BACK HERE, YOU LITTLE...
IS
HI.
...HI.
IS THIS YOUR
SORRY, WHAT?
UM...
OH,
THIS IS YOUR BIRD, RIGHT...?
YEAH.

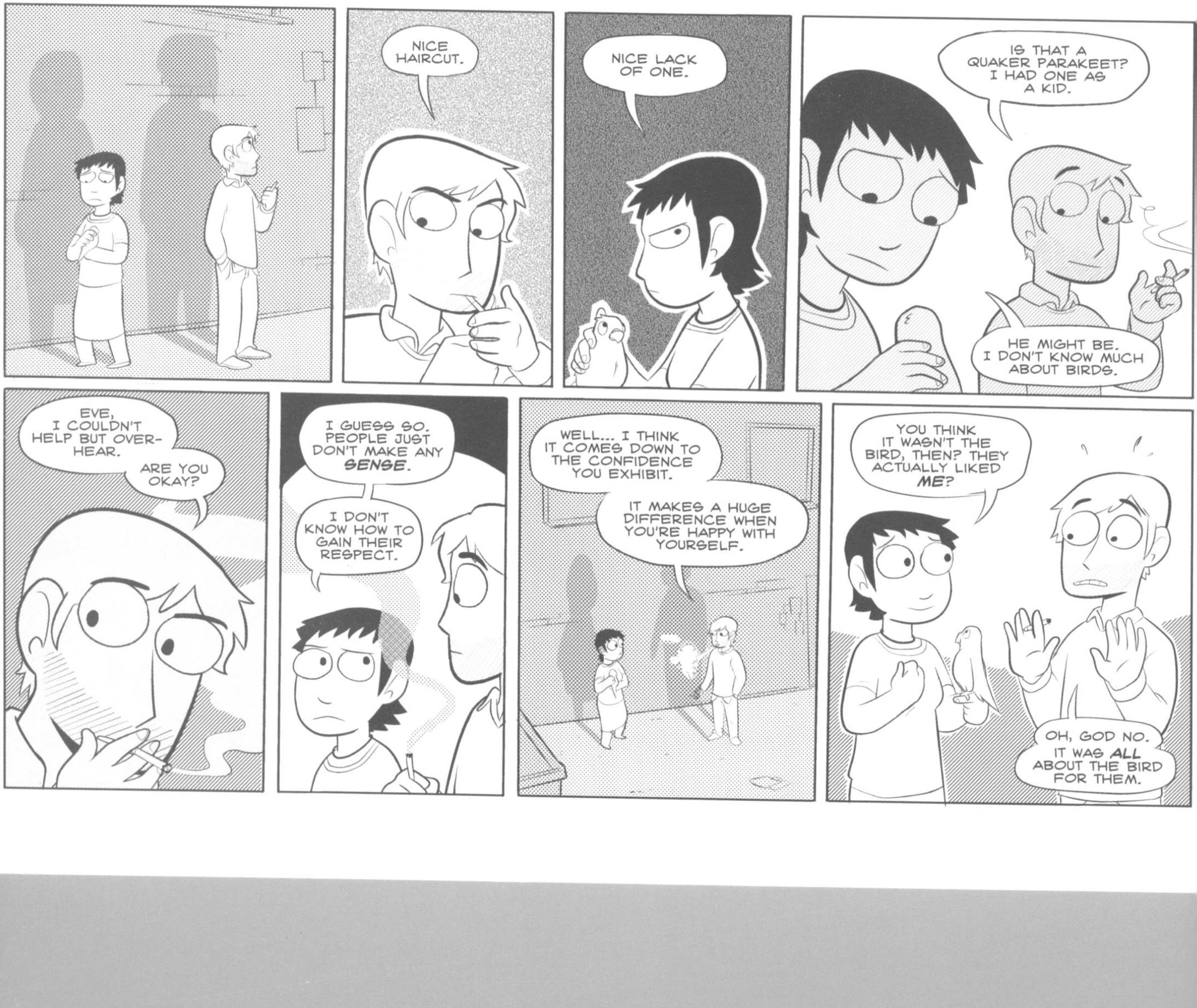
NICE HAIRCUT.
NICE LACK OF ONE.
IS THAT A QUAKER PARAKEET? I HAD ONE AS A KID.
HE MIGHT BE. I DON'T KNOW MUCH ABOUT BIRDS.
EVE, I COULDN'T HELP BUT OVER-HEAR.
ARE YOU OKAY?
I GUESS SO. PEOPLE JUST DON'T MAKE ANY SENSE.
I DON'T KNOW HOW TO GAIN THEIR RESPECT.
WELL... I THINK IT COMES DOWN TO THE CONFIDENCE YOU EXHIBIT.
IT MAKES A HUGE DIFFERENCE WHEN YOU'RE HAPPY WITH YOURSELF.
YOU THINK IT WASN'T THE BIRD, THEN? THEY ACTUALLY LIKED ME?
OH, GOD NO. IT WAS ALL ABOUT THE BIRD FOR THEM.

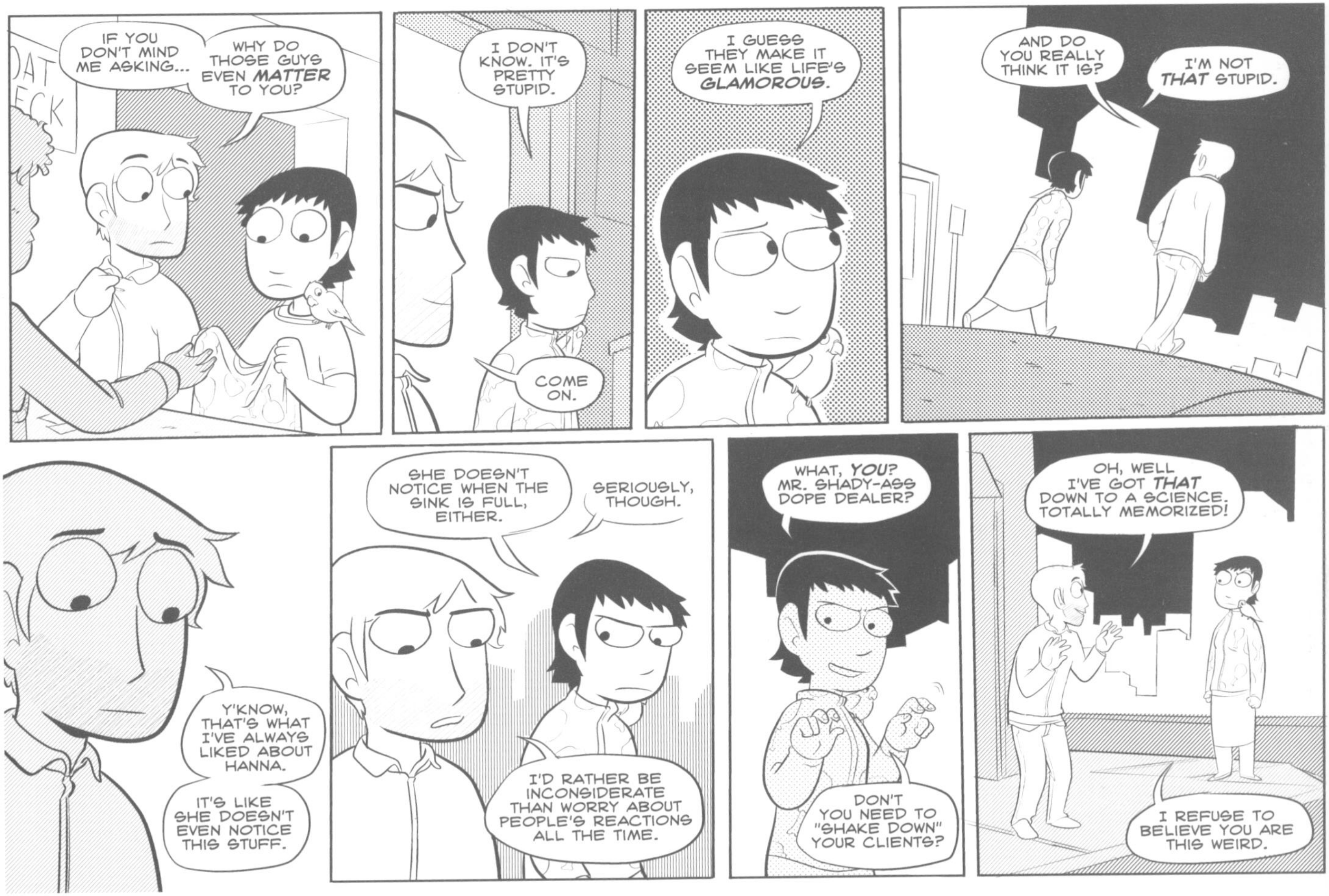
IF YOU DON'T MIND ME ASKING...
WHY DO THOSE GUYS EVEN MATTER TO YOU?
I DON'T KNOW. IT'S PRETTY STUPID.
COME ON.
I GUESS THEY MAKE IT SEEM LIKE LIFE'S GLAMOROUS.
AND DO YOU REALLY THINK IT IS?
I'M NOT THAT STUPID.
Y'KNOW, THAT'S WHAT I'VE ALWAYS LIKED ABOUT HANNA.
IT'S LIKE SHE DOESN'T EVEN NOTICE THIS STUFF.
SHE DOESN'T NOTICE WHEN THE SINK IS FULL, EITHER.
SERIOUSLY, THOUGH.
I'D RATHER BE INCONSIDERATE THAN WORRY ABOUT PEOPLE'S REACTIONS ALL THE TIME.
WHAT, YOU? MR. SHADY-ASS DOPE DEALER?
DON'T YOU NEED TO "SHAKE DOWN" YOUR CLIENTS?
OH, WELL I'VE GOT THAT DOWN TO A SCIENCE. TOTALLY MEMORIZED!
I REFUSE TO BELIEVE YOU ARE THIS WEIRD.

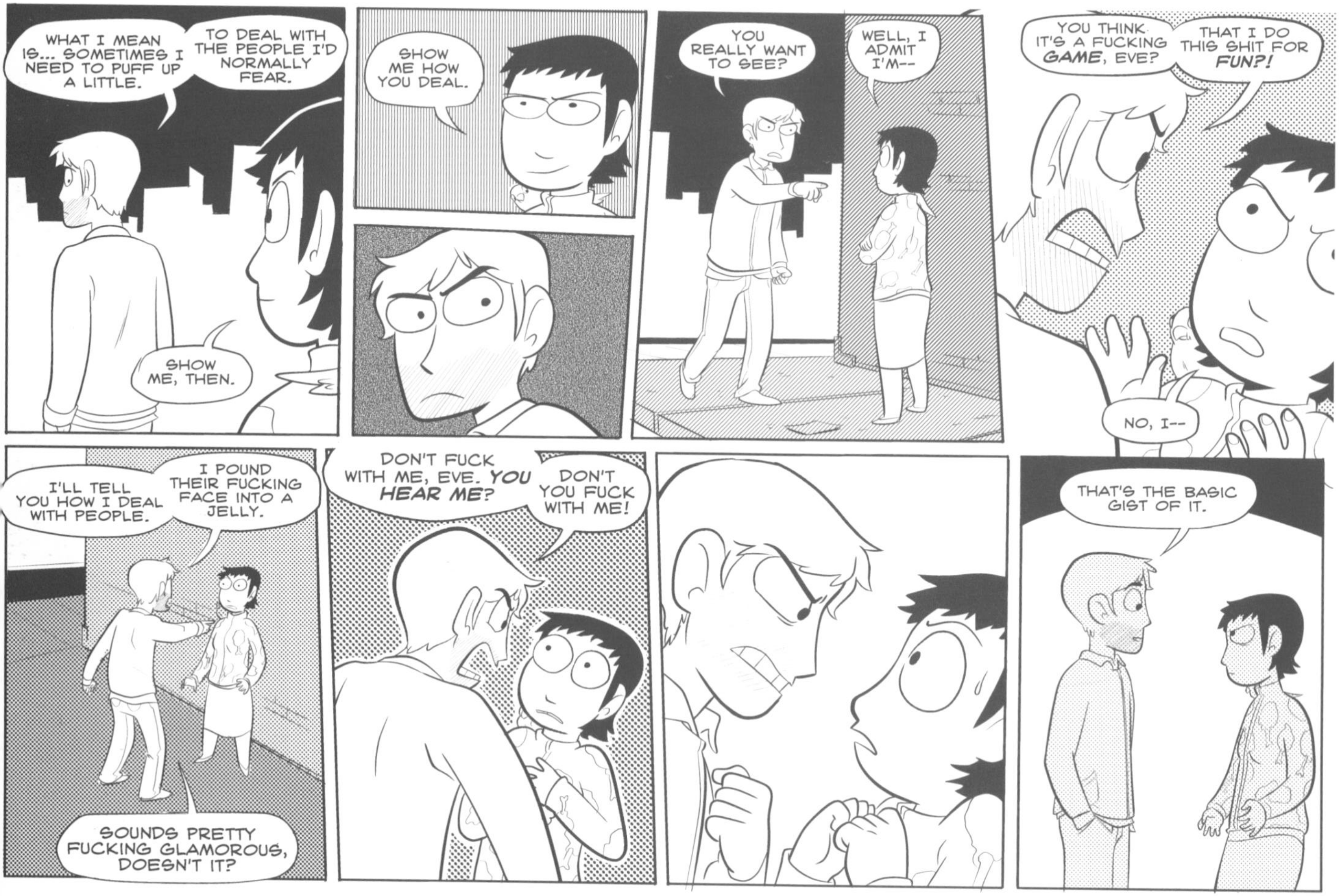
WHAT I MEAN IS... SOMETIMES I NEED TO PUFF UP A LITTLE.
TO DEAL WITH THE PEOPLE I'D NORMALLY FEAR.
SHOW ME, THEN.
SHOW ME HOW YOU DEAL.
YOU REALLY WANT TO SEE?
WELL, I ADMIT I'M--
YOU THINK IT'S A FUCKING GAME, EVE?
THAT I DO THIS SHIT FOR FUN?!
NO, I--
I'LL TELL YOU HOW I DEAL WITH PEOPLE.
I POUND THEIR FUCKING FACE INTO A JELLY.
SOUNDS PRETTY FUCKING GLAMOROUS, DOESN'T IT?
DON'T FUCK WITH ME, EVE. YOU HEAR ME?
DON'T YOU FUCK WITH ME!
THAT'S THE BASIC GIST OF IT.

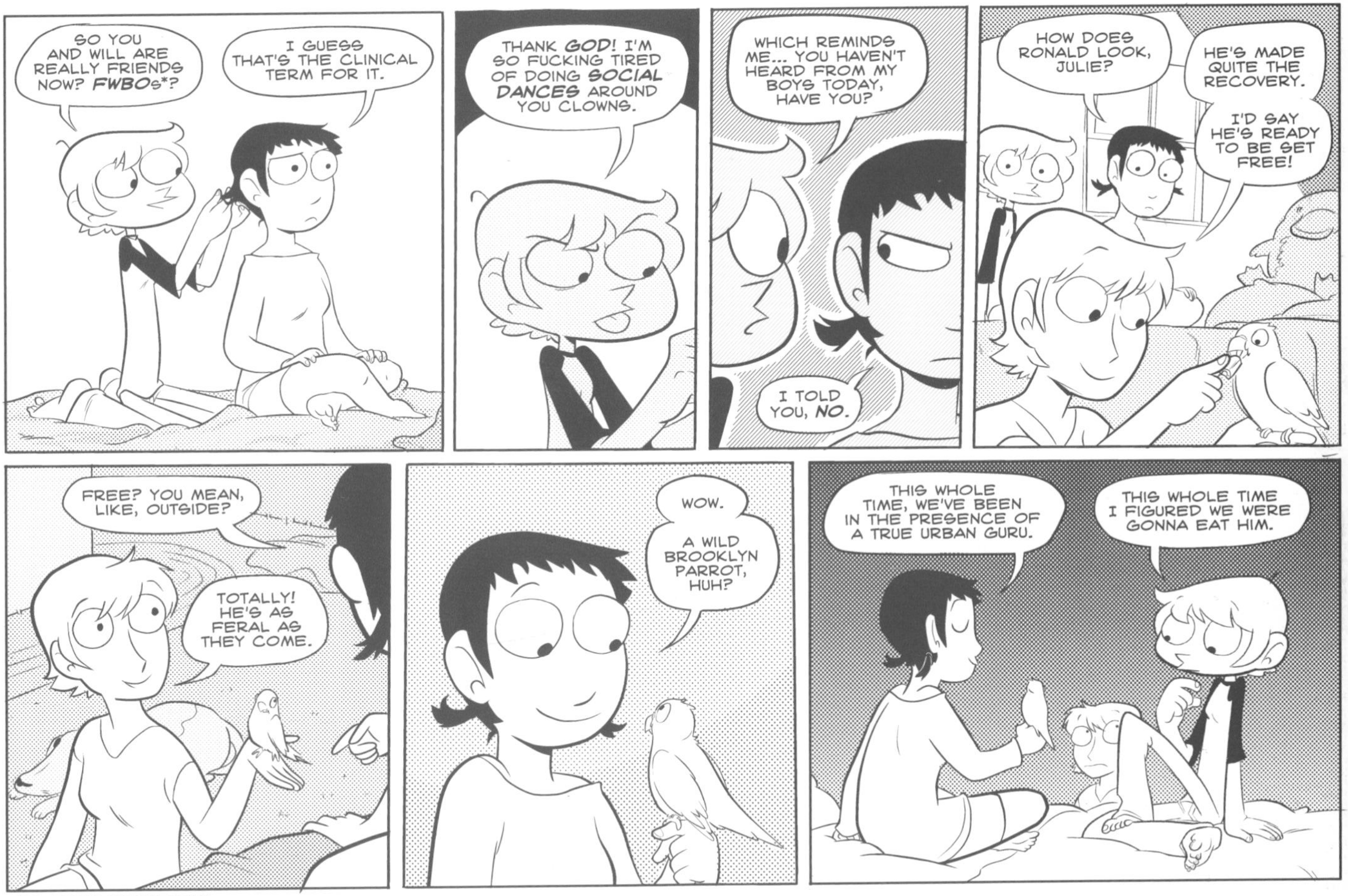
SO YOU AND WILL ARE REALLY FRIENDS NOW? FWBOs*?
I GUESS THAT'S THE CLINICAL TERM FOR IT.
THANK GOD! I'M SO FUCKING TIRED OF DOING SOCIAL DANCES AROUND YOU CLOWNS.
WHICH REMINDS ME... YOU HAVEN'T HEARD FROM MY BOYS TODAY, HAVE YOU?
I TOLD YOU, NO.
HOW DOES RONALD LOOK, JULIE?
HE'S MADE QUITE THE RECOVERY.
I'D SAY HE'S READY TO BE SET FREE!
FREE? YOU MEAN, LIKE, OUTSIDE?
TOTALLY! HE'S AS FERAL AS THEY COME.
WOW.
A WILD BROOKLYN PARROT, HUH?
THIS WHOLE TIME, WE'VE BEEN IN THE PRESENCE OF A TRUE URBAN GURU.
THIS WHOLE TIME I FIGURED WE WERE GONNA EAT HIM.

*ED – FRIENDS WHO BONED ONCE

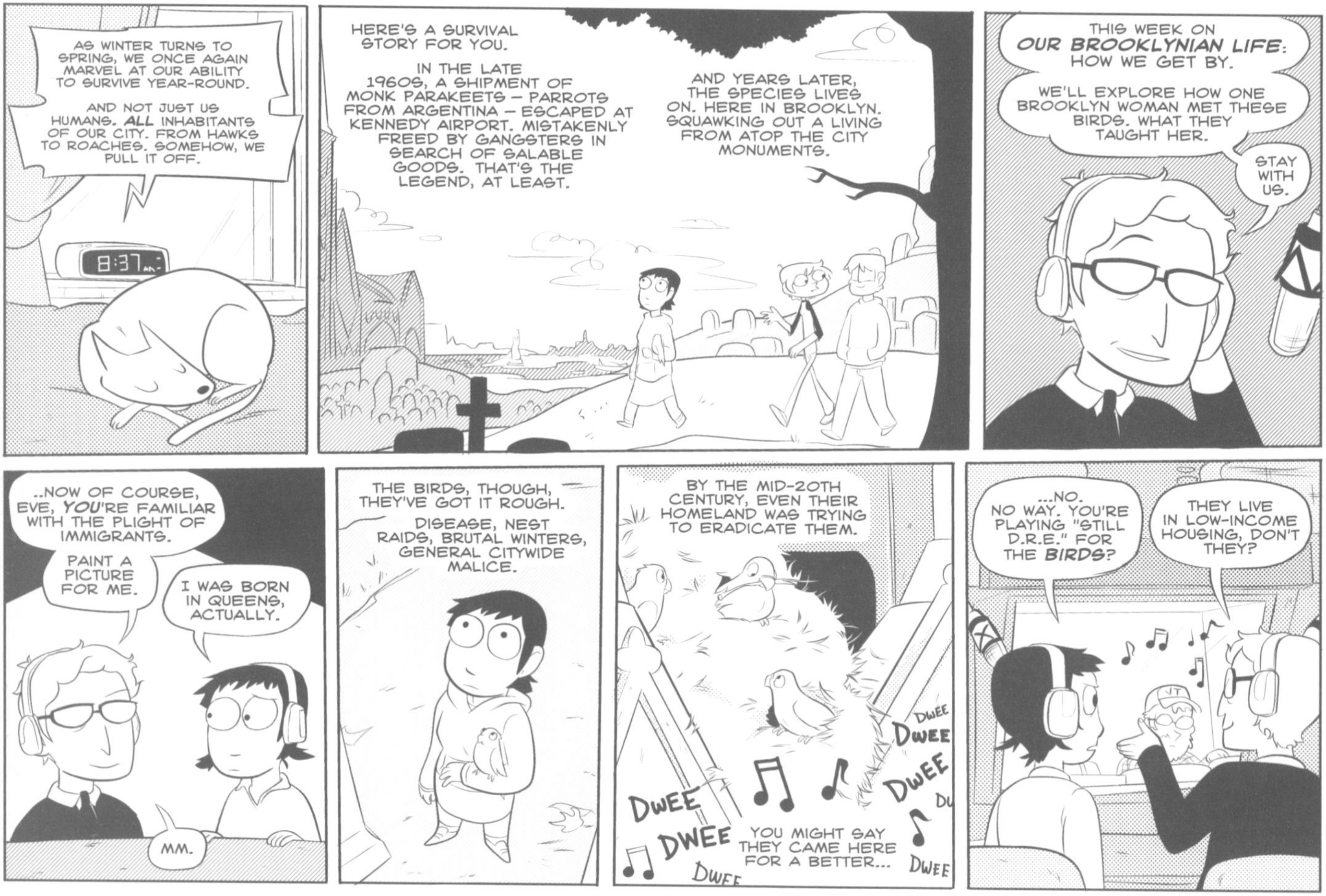
AS WINTER TURNS TO SPRING, WE ONCE AGAIN MARVEL AT OUR ABILITY TO SURVIVE YEAR-ROUND.
AND NOT JUST US HUMANS. ALL INHABITANTS OF OUR CITY. FROM HAWKS TO ROACHES. SOMEHOW, WE PULL IT OFF.
8:37
HERE'S A SURVIVAL STORY FOR YOU.
IN THE LATE 1960S, A SHIPMENT OF MONK PARAKEETS – PARROTS FROM ARGENTINA – ESCAPED AT KENNEDY AIRPORT. MISTAKENLY FREED BY GANGSTERS IN SEARCH OF SALABLE GOODS. THAT'S THE LEGEND, AT LEAST.
AND YEARS LATER, THE SPECIES LIVES ON. HERE IN BROOKLYN. SQUAWKING OUT A LIVING FROM ATOP THE CITY MONUMENTS.
THIS WEEK ON OUR BROOKLYNIAN LIFE: HOW WE GET BY.
WE'LL EXPLORE HOW ONE BROOKLYN WOMAN MET THESE BIRDS. WHAT THEY TAUGHT HER.
STAY WITH US.
..NOW OF COURSE, EVE, YOU'RE FAMILIAR WITH THE PLIGHT OF IMMIGRANTS.
PAINT A PICTURE FOR ME.
I WAS BORN IN QUEENS, ACTUALLY.
MM.
THE BIRDS, THOUGH, THEY'VE GOT IT ROUGH.
DISEASE, NEST RAIDS, BRUTAL WINTERS, GENERAL CITYWIDE MALICE.
BY THE MID-20TH CENTURY, EVEN THEIR HOMELAND WAS TRYING TO ERADICATE THEM.
DWEE
DWEE
DWEE
DWEE
DWEE
YOU MIGHT SAY THEY CAME HERE FOR A BETTER...
DWEE
...NO. NO WAY. YOU'RE PLAYING "STILL D.R.E." FOR THE BIRDS?
THEY LIVE IN LOW-INCOME HOUSING, DON'T THEY?

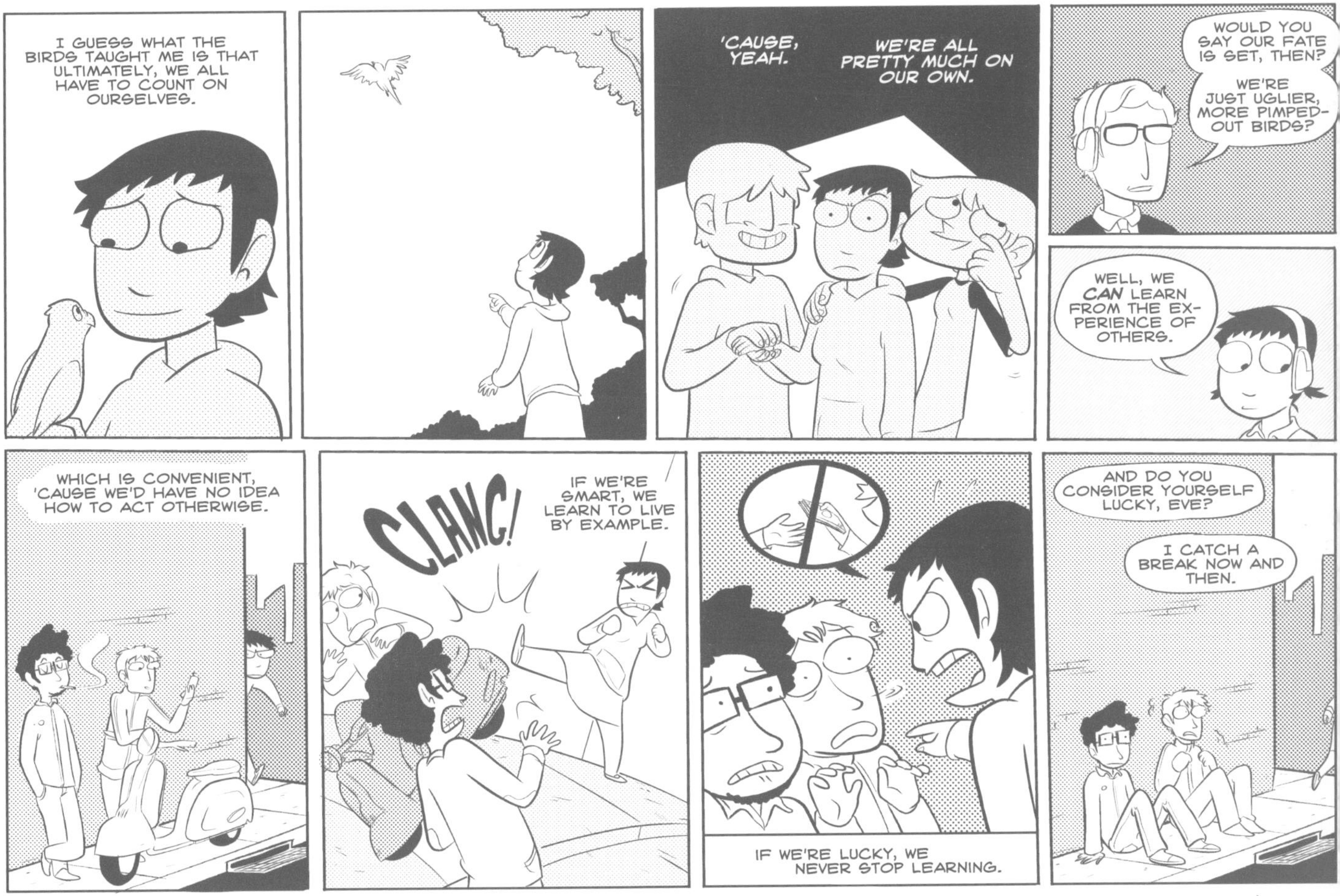
I GUESS WHAT THE BIRDS TAUGHT ME IS THAT ULTIMATELY, WE ALL HAVE TO COUNT ON OURSELVES.
'CAUSE, YEAH.
WE'RE ALL PRETTY MUCH ON OUR OWN.
WOULD YOU SAY OUR FATE IS SET, THEN?
WE'RE JUST UGLIER, MORE PIMPED-OUT BIRDS?
WELL, WE CAN LEARN FROM THE EXPERIENCE OF OTHERS.
WHICH IS CONVENIENT, 'CAUSE WE'D HAVE NO IDEA HOW TO ACT OTHERWISE.
CLANG!
IF WE'RE SMART, WE LEARN TO LIVE BY EXAMPLE.
IF WE'RE LUCKY, WE NEVER STOP LEARNING.
AND DO YOU CONSIDER YOURSELF LUCKY, EVE?
I CATCH A BREAK NOW AND THEN.

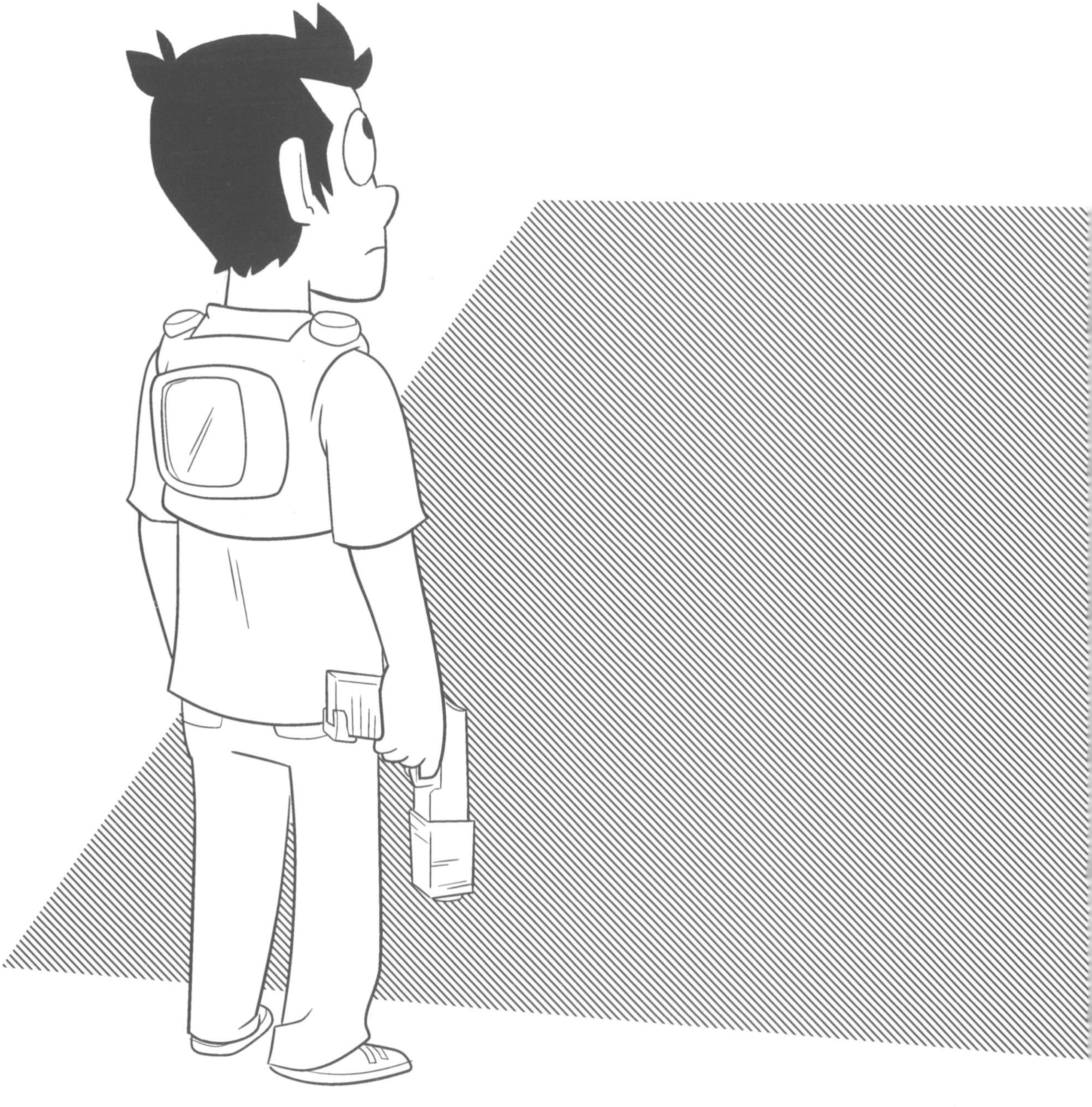

tag

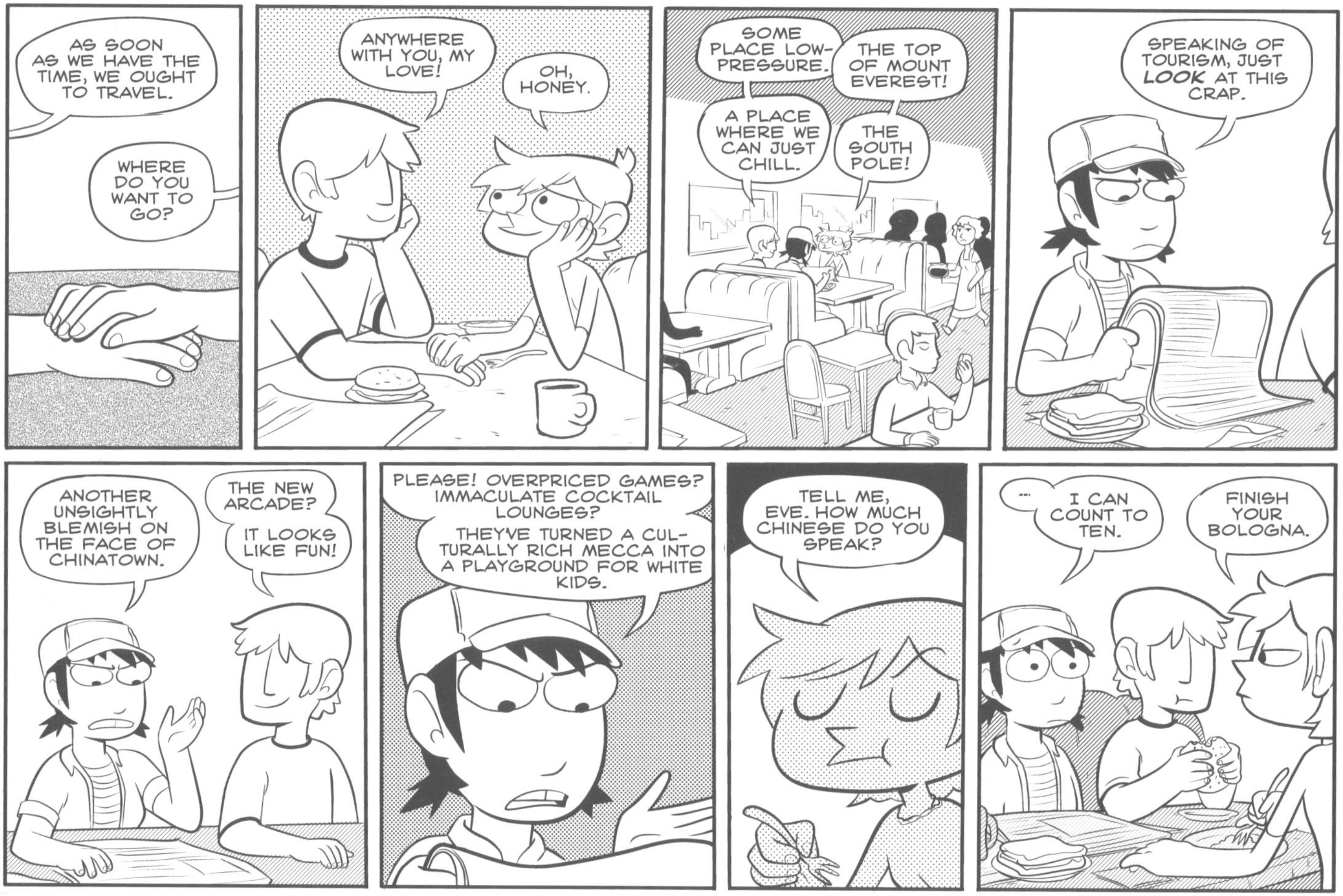
AS SOON AS WE HAVE THE TIME, WE OUGHT TO TRAVEL.
WHERE DO YOU WANT TO GO?
ANYWHERE WITH YOU, MY LOVE!
OH, HONEY.
SOME PLACE LOW-PRESSURE.
THE TOP OF MOUNT EVEREST!
A PLACE WHERE WE CAN JUST CHILL.
THE SOUTH POLE!
SPEAKING OF TOURISM, JUST LOOK AT THIS CRAP.
ANOTHER UNSIGHTLY BLEMISH ON THE FACE OF CHINATOWN.
THE NEW ARCADE?
IT LOOKS LIKE FUN!
PLEASE! OVERPRICED GAMES? IMMACULATE COCKTAIL LOUNGES?
THEY'VE TURNED A CULTURALLY RICH MECCA INTO A PLAYGROUND FOR WHITE KIDS.
TELL ME, EVE. HOW MUCH CHINESE DO YOU SPEAK?
...
I CAN COUNT TO TEN.
FINISH YOUR BOLOGNA.

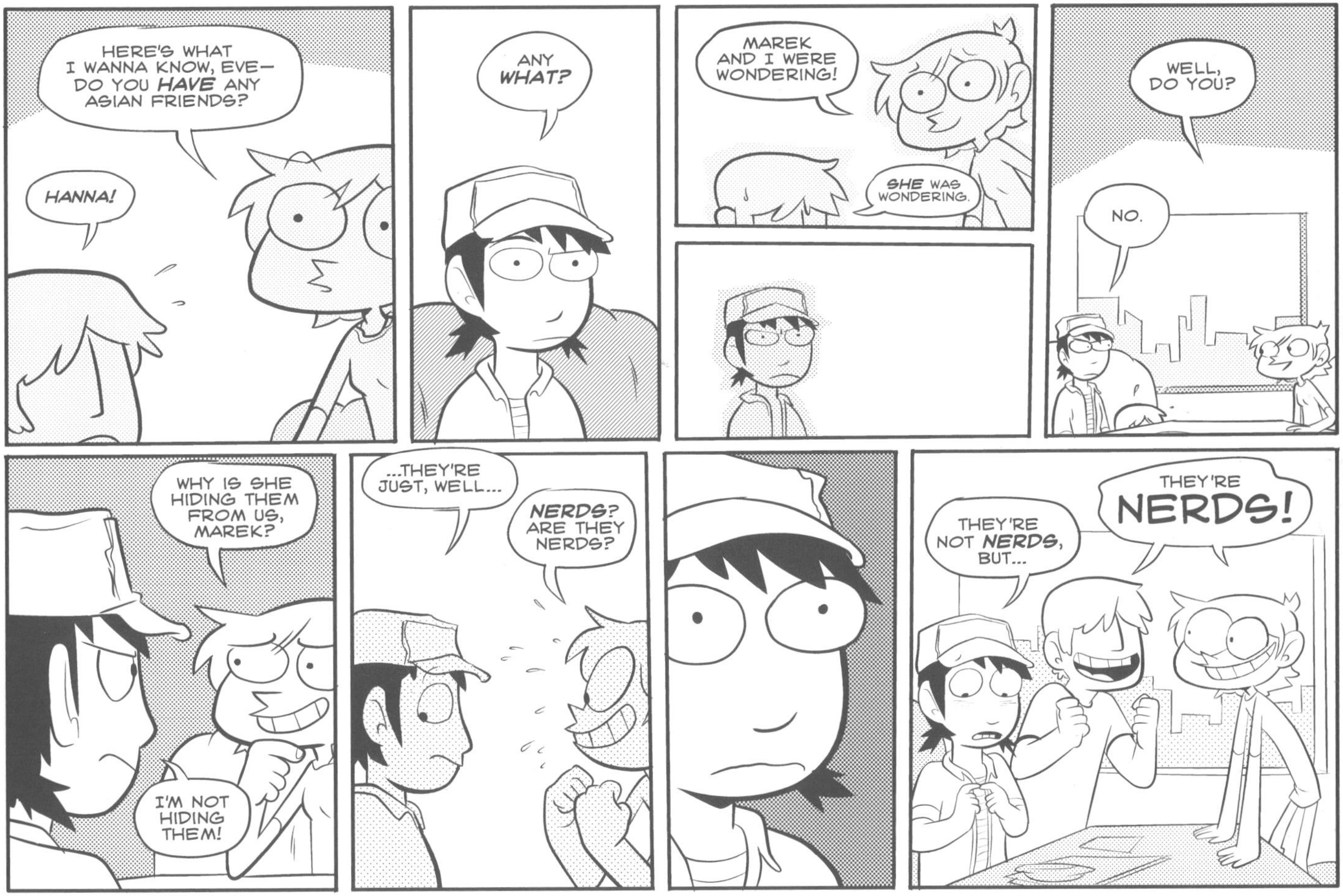
HERE'S WHAT I WANNA KNOW, EVE— DO YOU HAVE ANY ASIAN FRIENDS?
HANNA!
ANY WHAT?
MAREK AND I WERE WONDERING!
SHE WAS WONDERING.
WELL, DO YOU?
NO.
WHY IS SHE HIDING THEM FROM US, MAREK?
I'M NOT HIDING THEM!
...THEY'RE JUST, WELL...
NERDS? ARE THEY NERDS?
THEY'RE NOT NERDS, BUT...
THEY'RE NERDS!

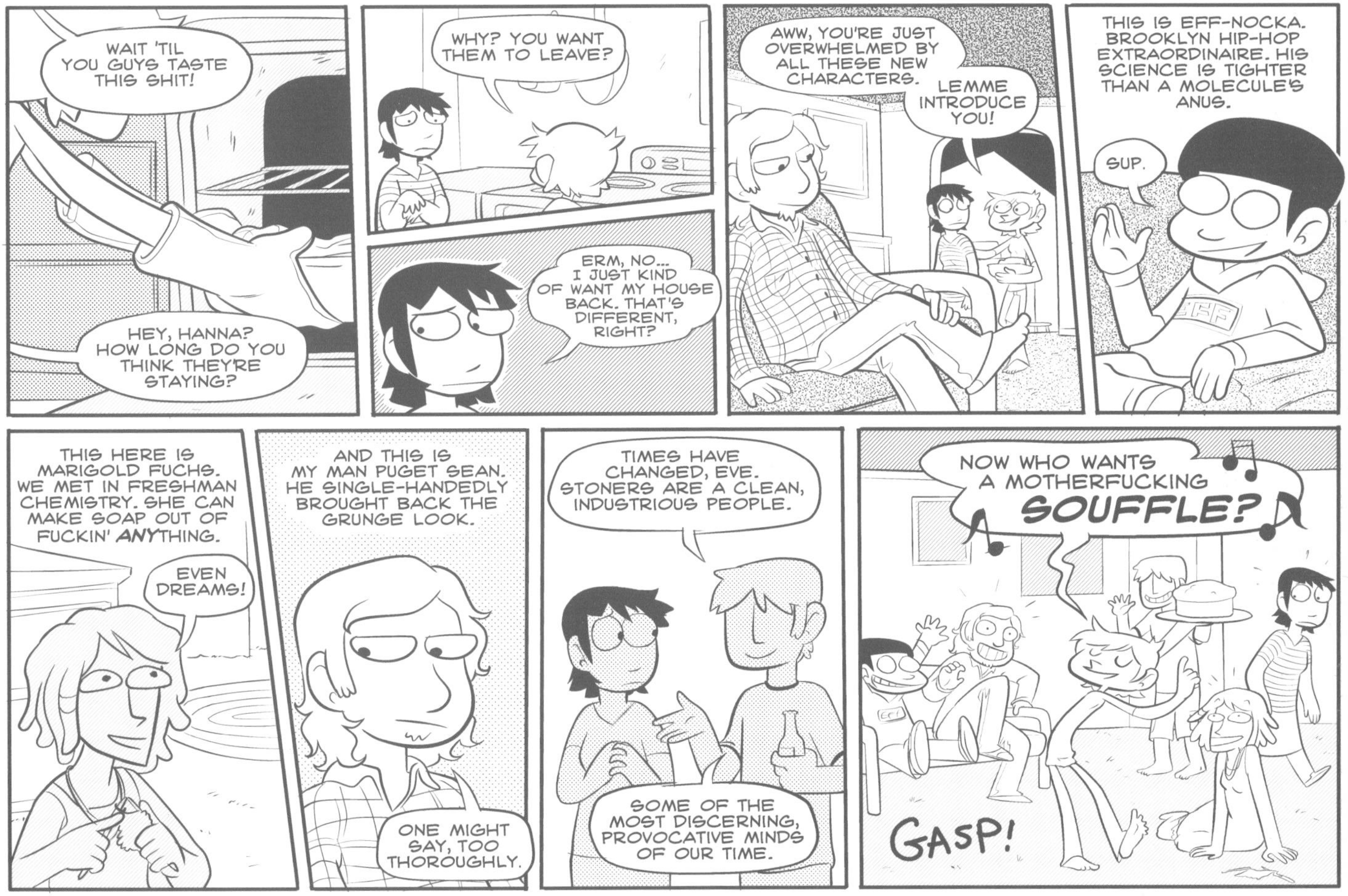
WAIT 'TIL YOU GUYS TASTE THIS SHIT!
HEY, HANNA? HOW LONG DO YOU THINK THEY'RE STAYING?
WHY? YOU WANT THEM TO LEAVE?
ERM, NO... I JUST KIND OF WANT MY HOUSE BACK. THAT'S DIFFERENT, RIGHT?
AWW, YOU'RE JUST OVERWHELMED BY ALL THESE NEW CHARACTERS.
LEMME INTRODUCE YOU!
THIS IS EFF-NOCKA. BROOKLYN HIP-HOP EXTRAORDINAIRE. HIS SCIENCE IS TIGHTER THAN A MOLECULE'S ANUS.
SUP.
THIS HERE IS MARIGOLD FUCHS. WE MET IN FRESHMAN CHEMISTRY. SHE CAN MAKE SOAP OUT OF FUCKIN' ANYTHING.
EVEN DREAMS!
AND THIS IS MY MAN PUGET SEAN. HE SINGLE-HANDEDLY BROUGHT BACK THE GRUNGE LOOK.
ONE MIGHT SAY, TOO THOROUGHLY.
TIMES HAVE CHANGED, EVE. STONERS ARE A CLEAN, INDUSTRIOUS PEOPLE.
SOME OF THE MOST DISCERNING, PROVOCATIVE MINDS OF OUR TIME.
NOW WHO WANTS A MOTHERFUCKING SOUFFLE?
GASP!

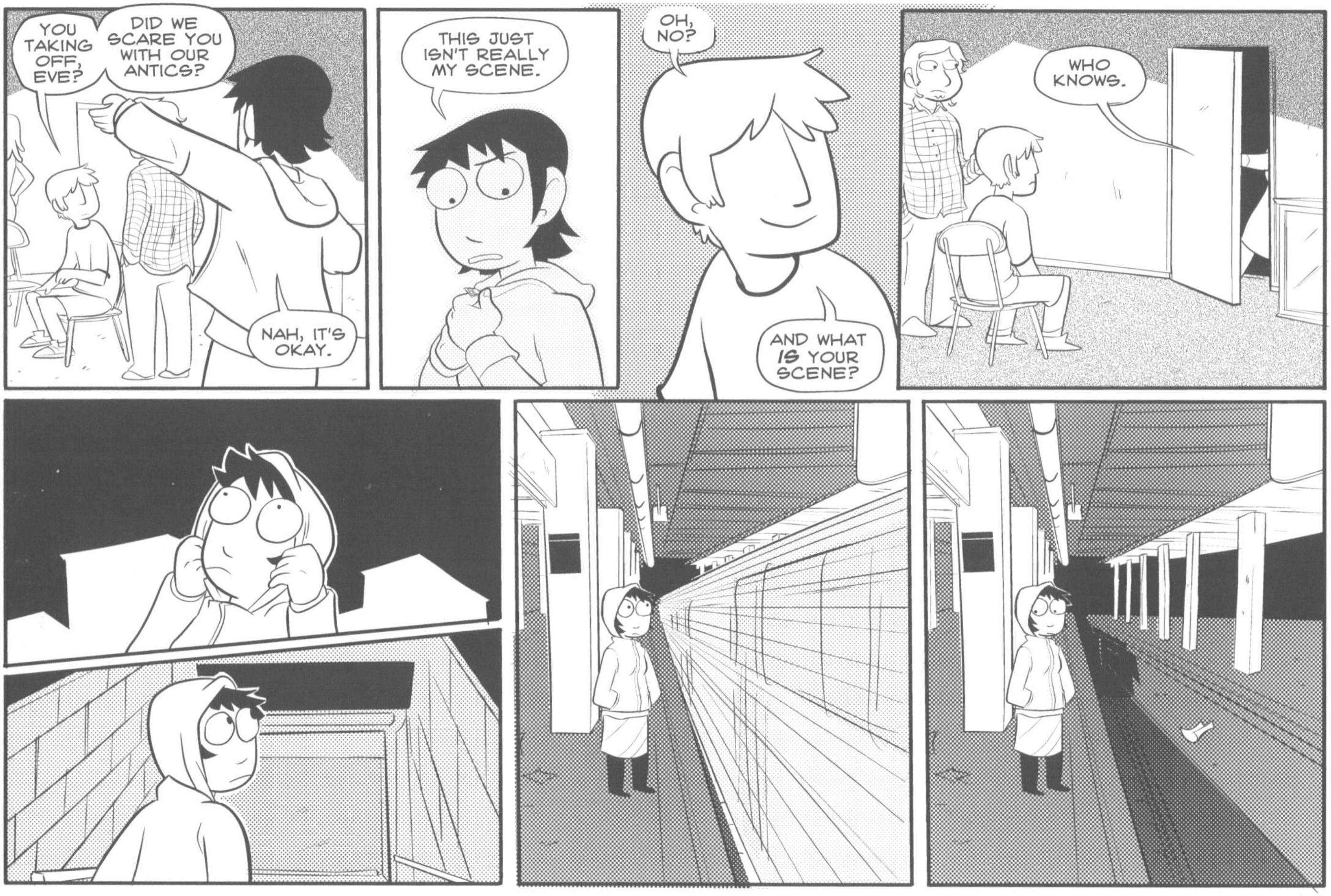
YOU TAKING OFF, EVE?
DID WE SCARE YOU WITH OUR ANTICS?
NAH, IT'S OKAY.
THIS JUST ISN'T REALLY MY SCENE.
OH, NO?
AND WHAT IS YOUR SCENE?
WHO KNOWS.

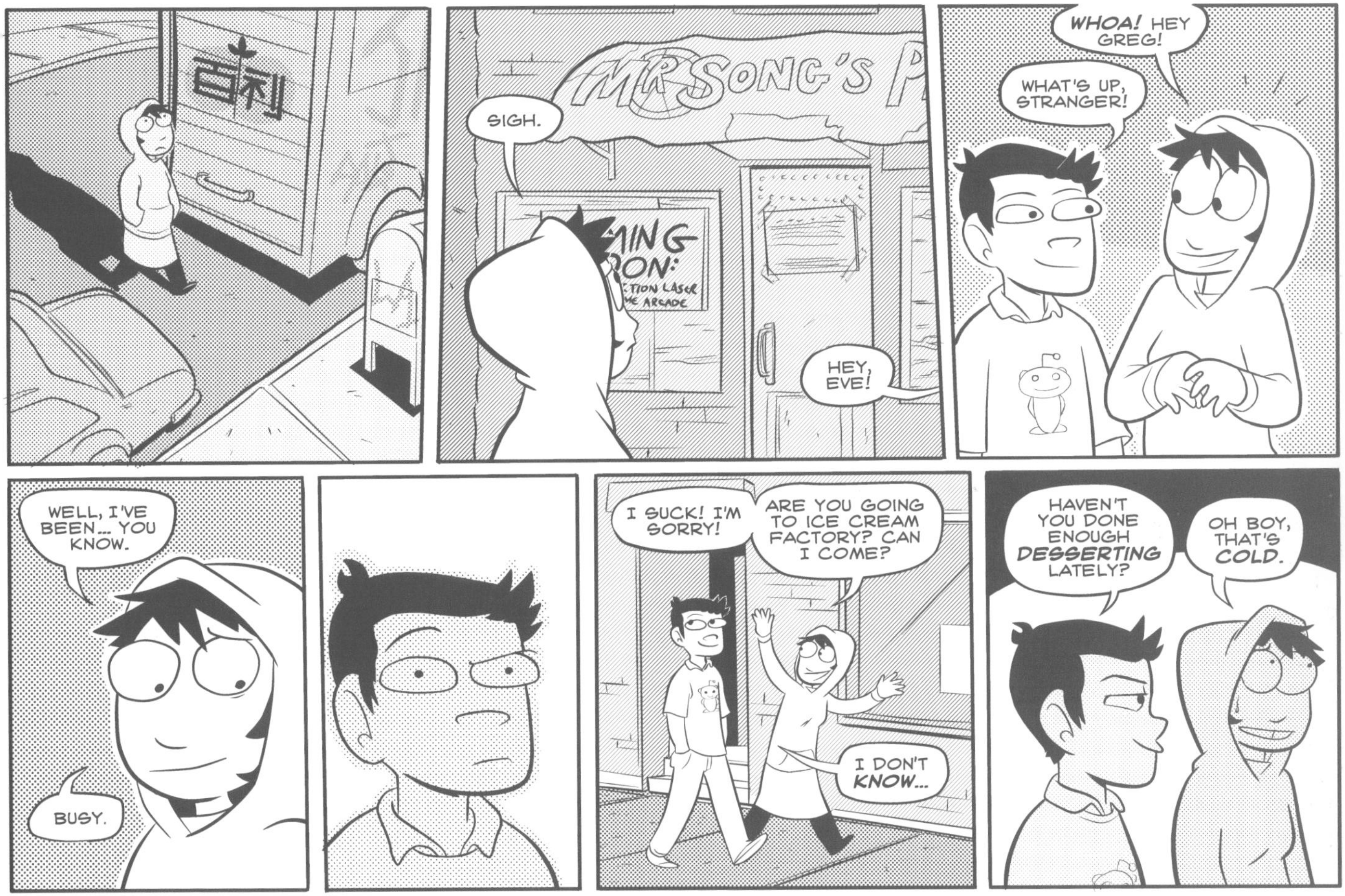
MR SONG'S
SIGH.
HEY, EVE!
WHOA! HEY GREG!
WHAT'S UP, STRANGER!
WELL, I'VE BEEN... YOU KNOW.
BUSY.
I SUCK! I'M SORRY!
ARE YOU GOING TO ICE CREAM FACTORY? CAN I COME?
I DON'T KNOW...
HAVEN'T YOU DONE ENOUGH DESSERTING LATELY?
OH BOY, THAT'S COLD.

HEY GUYS!

LOOK WHO I FOUND!

WELL, WELL.

WHAT'VE YOU BEEN DOING? YOU NEVER CALL ME!

JUST WORKING AT THE SHOP, Y'KNOW?

IT GETS HECTIC.

YOU MISSED AN EPIC GAME LAST FRIDAY, EVE.

TOTALLY! AND DID YOU SEE *LOST*? YOU'RE WATCHING LOST, RIGHT?

ERM, NO...

YOU'RE OUTTA THE LOOP, NING!

I'M HERE TONIGHT, AREN'T I?

Y'KNOW WHO'S COMING TONIGHT, RIGHT?

DOES SHE KNOW, GREG?

WHO'S COMING?

OH. UM.

...PARK.

HE'S BACK FROM SCHOOL.

IS THAT SUPPOSED TO BE A BIG DEAL OR SOMETHING?

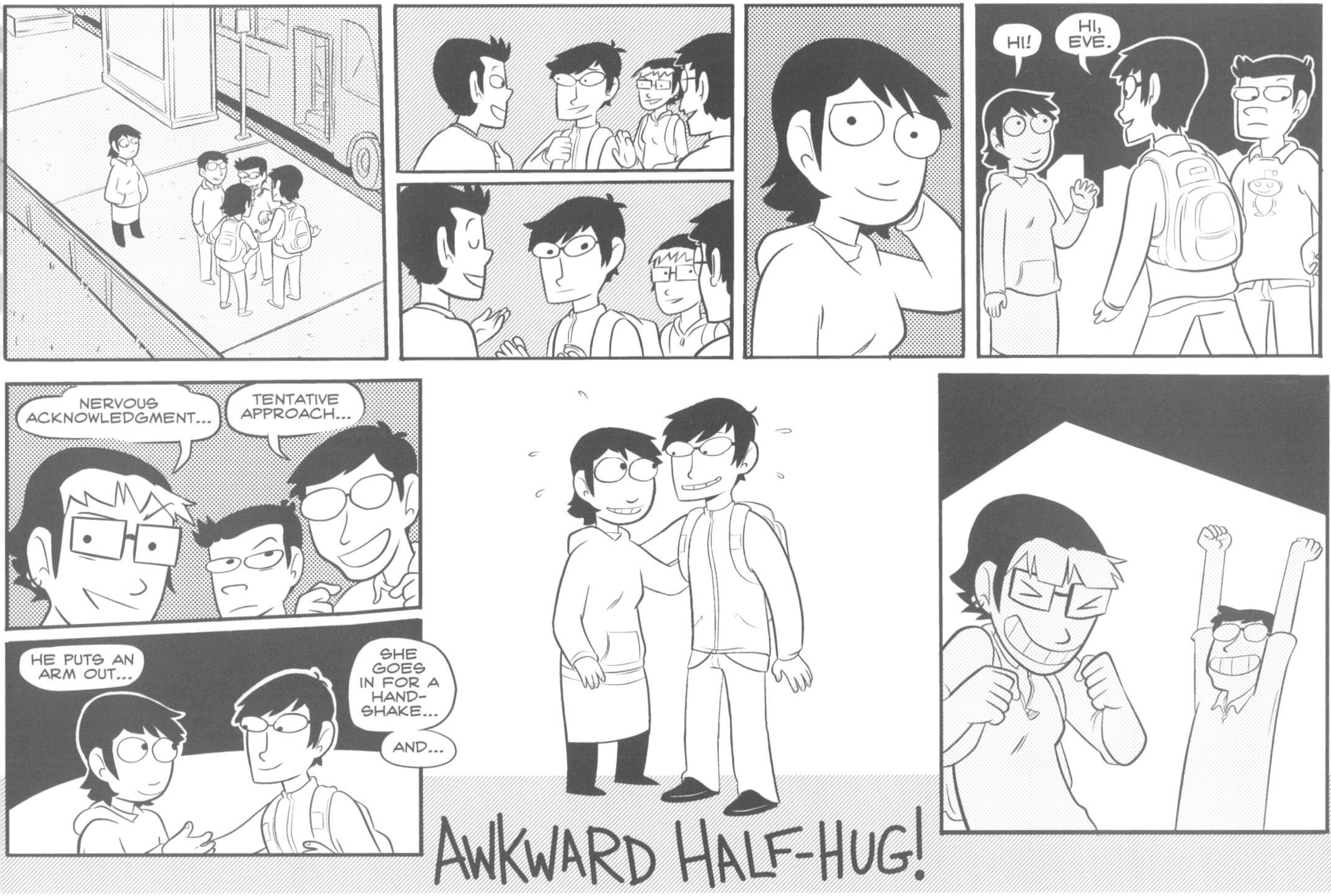
HI!
HI, EVE.
NERVOUS ACKNOWLEDGMENT...
TENTATIVE APPROACH...
HE PUTS AN ARM OUT...
SHE GOES IN FOR A HAND-SHAKE...
AND...
AWKWARD HALF-HUG!

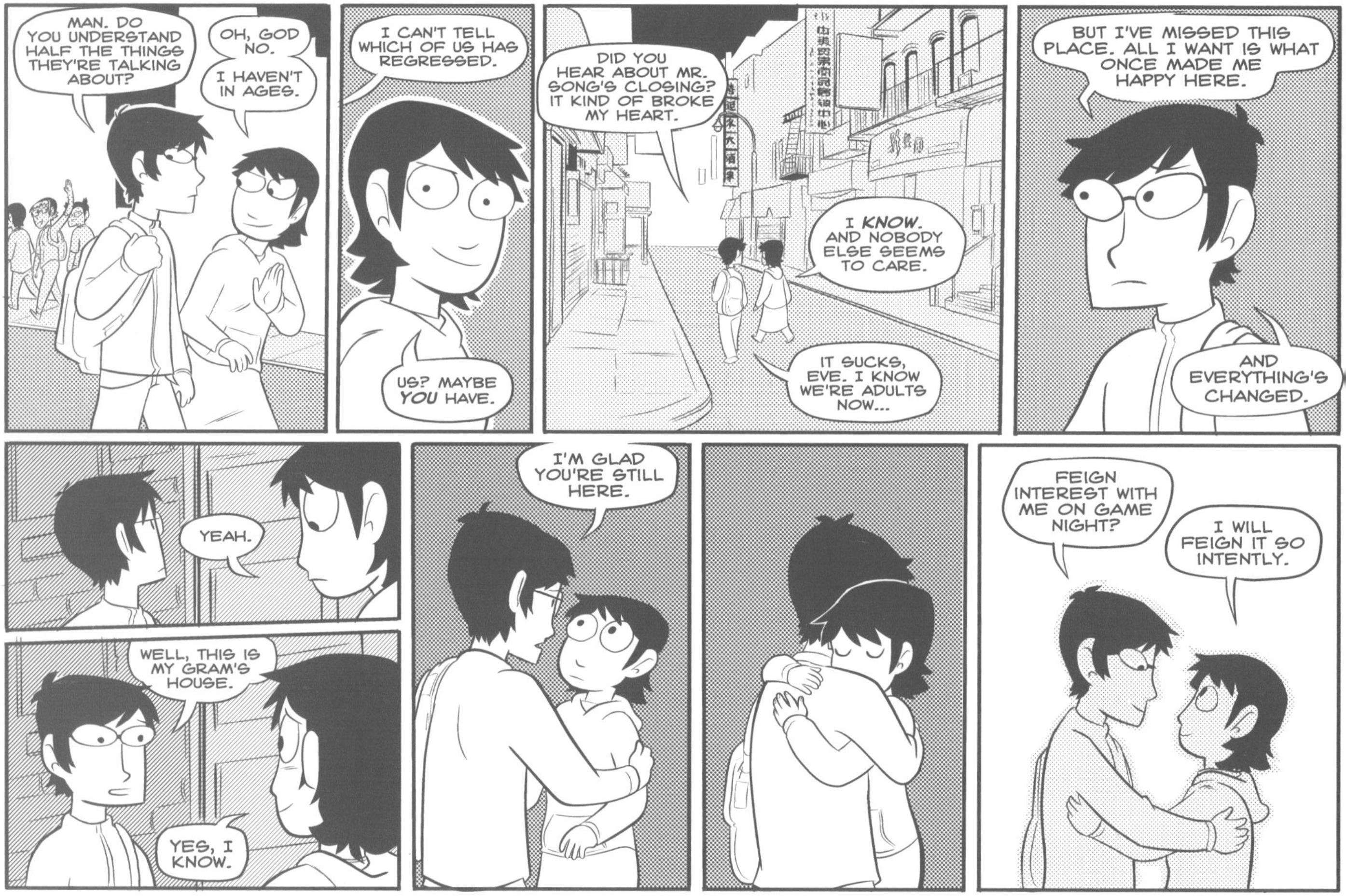
MAN. DO YOU UNDERSTAND HALF THE THINGS THEY'RE TALKING ABOUT?
OH, GOD NO.
I HAVEN'T IN AGES.
I CAN'T TELL WHICH OF US HAS REGRESSED.
US? MAYBE YOU HAVE.
DID YOU HEAR ABOUT MR. SONG'S CLOSING? IT KIND OF BROKE MY HEART.
I KNOW. AND NOBODY ELSE SEEMS TO CARE.
IT SUCKS, EVE. I KNOW WE'RE ADULTS NOW...
BUT I'VE MISSED THIS PLACE. ALL I WANT IS WHAT ONCE MADE ME HAPPY HERE.
AND EVERYTHING'S CHANGED.
YEAH.
WELL, THIS IS MY GRAM'S HOUSE.
YES, I KNOW.
I'M GLAD YOU'RE STILL HERE.
FEIGN INTEREST WITH ME ON GAME NIGHT?
I WILL FEIGN IT SO INTENTLY.

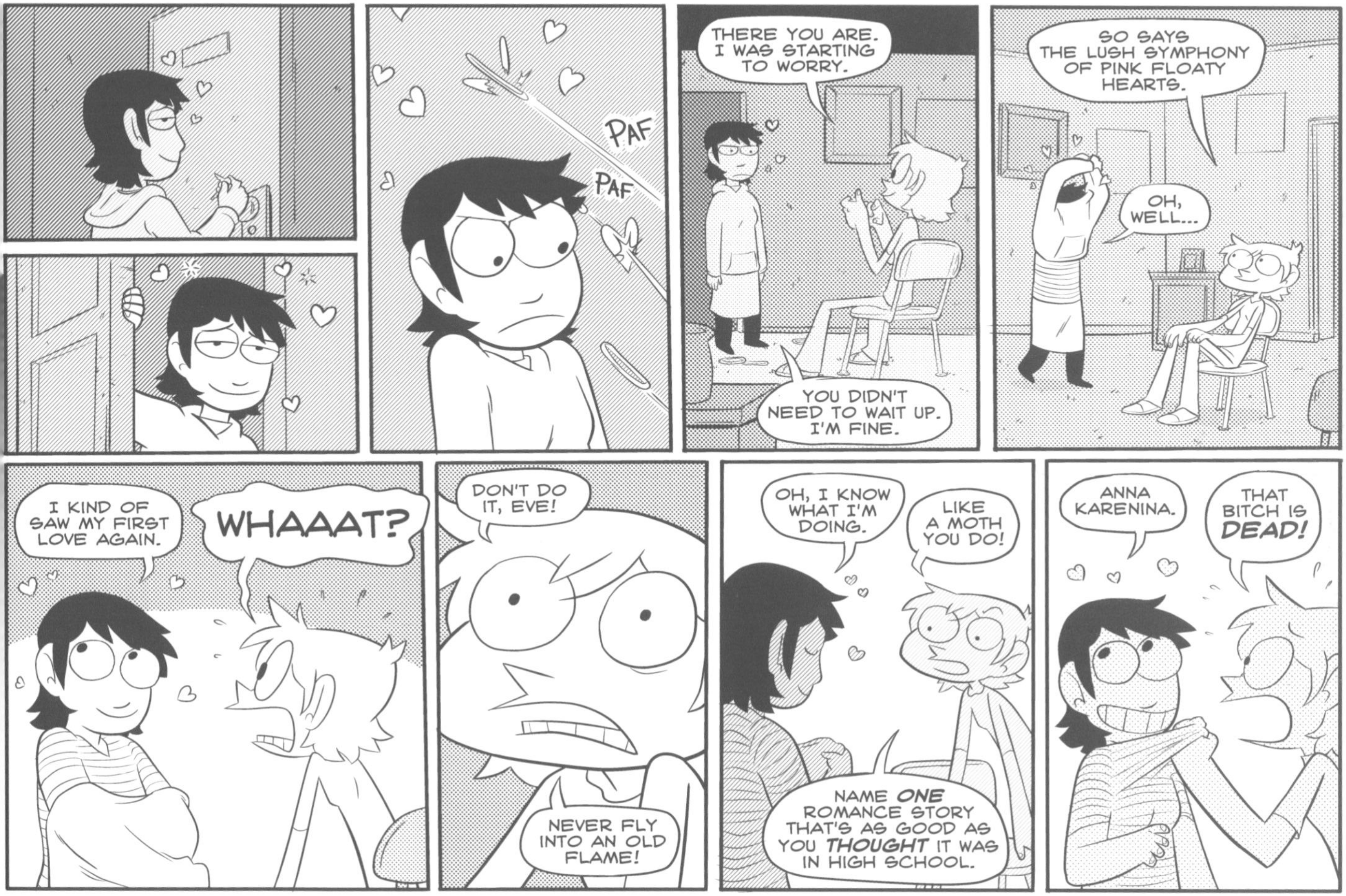
PAF
PAF
THERE YOU ARE. I WAS STARTING TO WORRY.
YOU DIDN'T NEED TO WAIT UP. I'M FINE.
SO SAYS THE LUSH SYMPHONY OF PINK FLOATY HEARTS.
OH, WELL...
I KIND OF SAW MY FIRST LOVE AGAIN.
WHAAAT?
DON'T DO IT, EVE!
NEVER FLY INTO AN OLD FLAME!
OH, I KNOW WHAT I'M DOING.
LIKE A MOTH YOU DO!
NAME ONE ROMANCE STORY THAT'S AS GOOD AS YOU THOUGHT IT WAS IN HIGH SCHOOL.
ANNA KARENINA.
THAT BITCH IS DEAD!

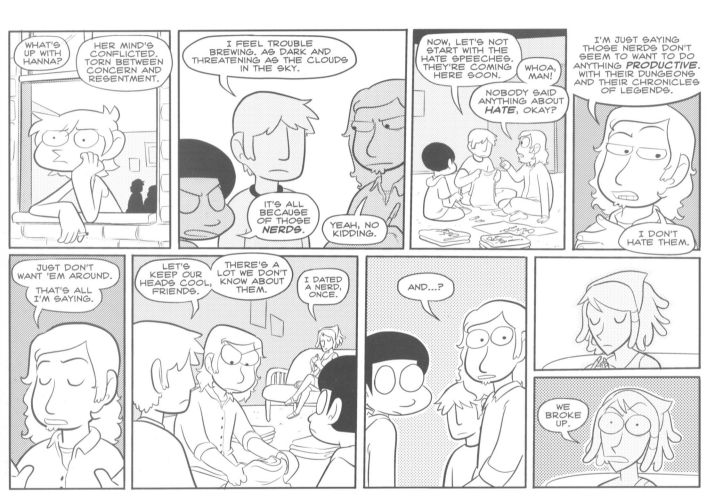

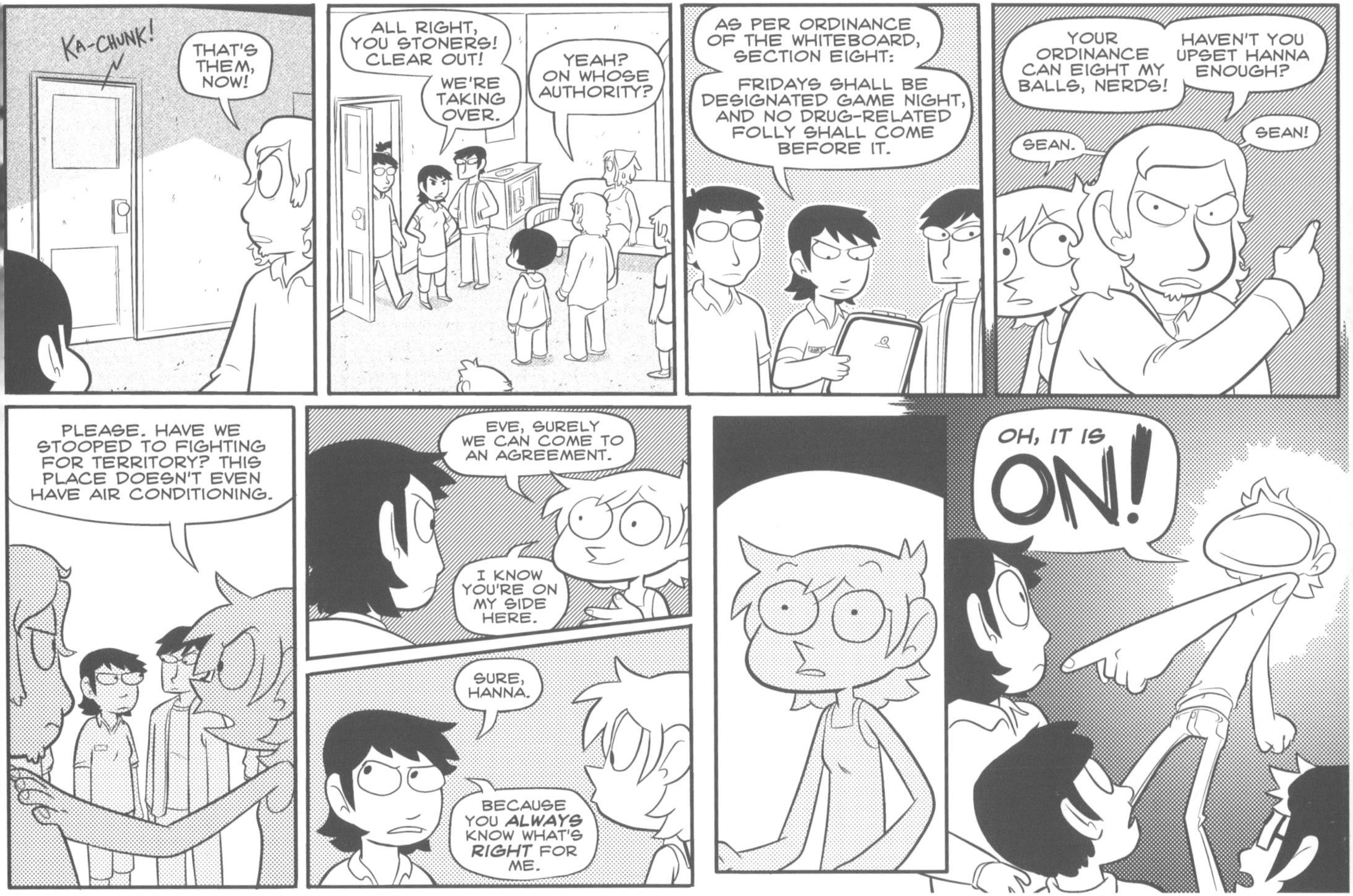
KA-CHUNK!
THAT'S THEM, NOW!
ALL RIGHT, YOU STONERS! CLEAR OUT!
WE'RE TAKING OVER.
YEAH? ON WHOSE AUTHORITY?
AS PER ORDINANCE OF THE WHITEBOARD, SECTION EIGHT:
FRIDAYS SHALL BE DESIGNATED GAME NIGHT, AND NO DRUG-RELATED FOLLY SHALL COME BEFORE IT.
YOUR ORDINANCE CAN EIGHT MY BALLS, NERDS!
HAVEN'T YOU UPSET HANNA ENOUGH?
SEAN.
SEAN!
PLEASE. HAVE WE STOOPED TO FIGHTING FOR TERRITORY? THIS PLACE DOESN'T EVEN HAVE AIR CONDITIONING.
EVE, SURELY WE CAN COME TO AN AGREEMENT.
I KNOW YOU'RE ON MY SIDE HERE.
SURE, HANNA.
BECAUSE YOU ALWAYS KNOW WHAT'S RIGHT FOR ME.
OH, IT IS ON!

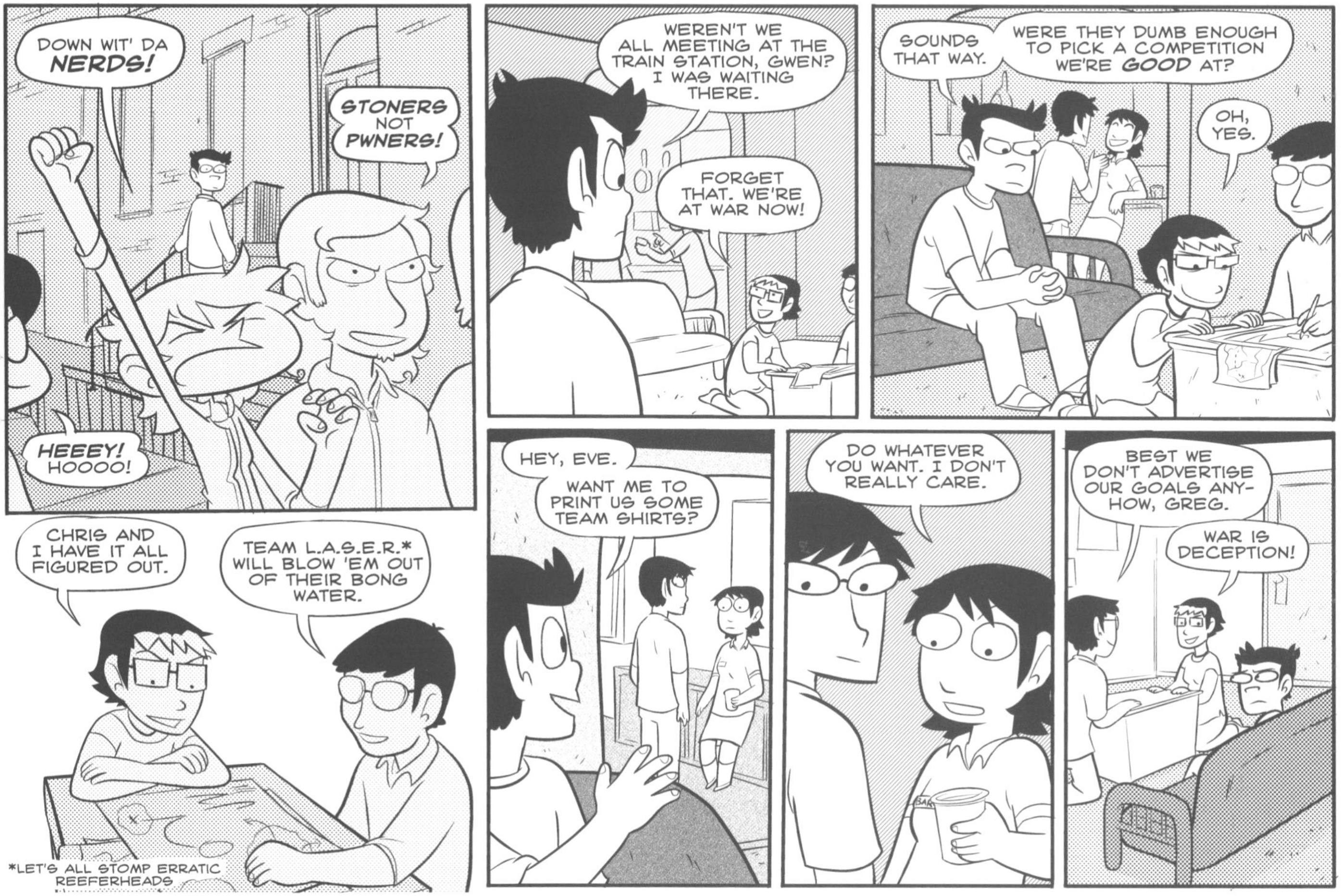
DOWN WIT' DA NERDS!
STONERS NOT PWNERS!
HEEEY! HOOOO!
CHRIS AND I HAVE IT ALL FIGURED OUT.
TEAM L.A.S.E.R.* WILL BLOW 'EM OUT OF THEIR BONG WATER.
*LET'S ALL STOMP ERRATIC REEFERHEADS
WEREN'T WE ALL MEETING AT THE TRAIN STATION, GWEN? I WAS WAITING THERE.
FORGET THAT. WE'RE AT WAR NOW!
SOUNDS THAT WAY.
WERE THEY DUMB ENOUGH TO PICK A COMPETITION WE'RE GOOD AT?
OH, YES.
HEY, EVE.
WANT ME TO PRINT US SOME TEAM SHIRTS?
DO WHATEVER YOU WANT. I DON'T REALLY CARE.
BEST WE DON'T ADVERTISE OUR GOALS ANY-HOW, GREG.
WAR IS DECEPTION!

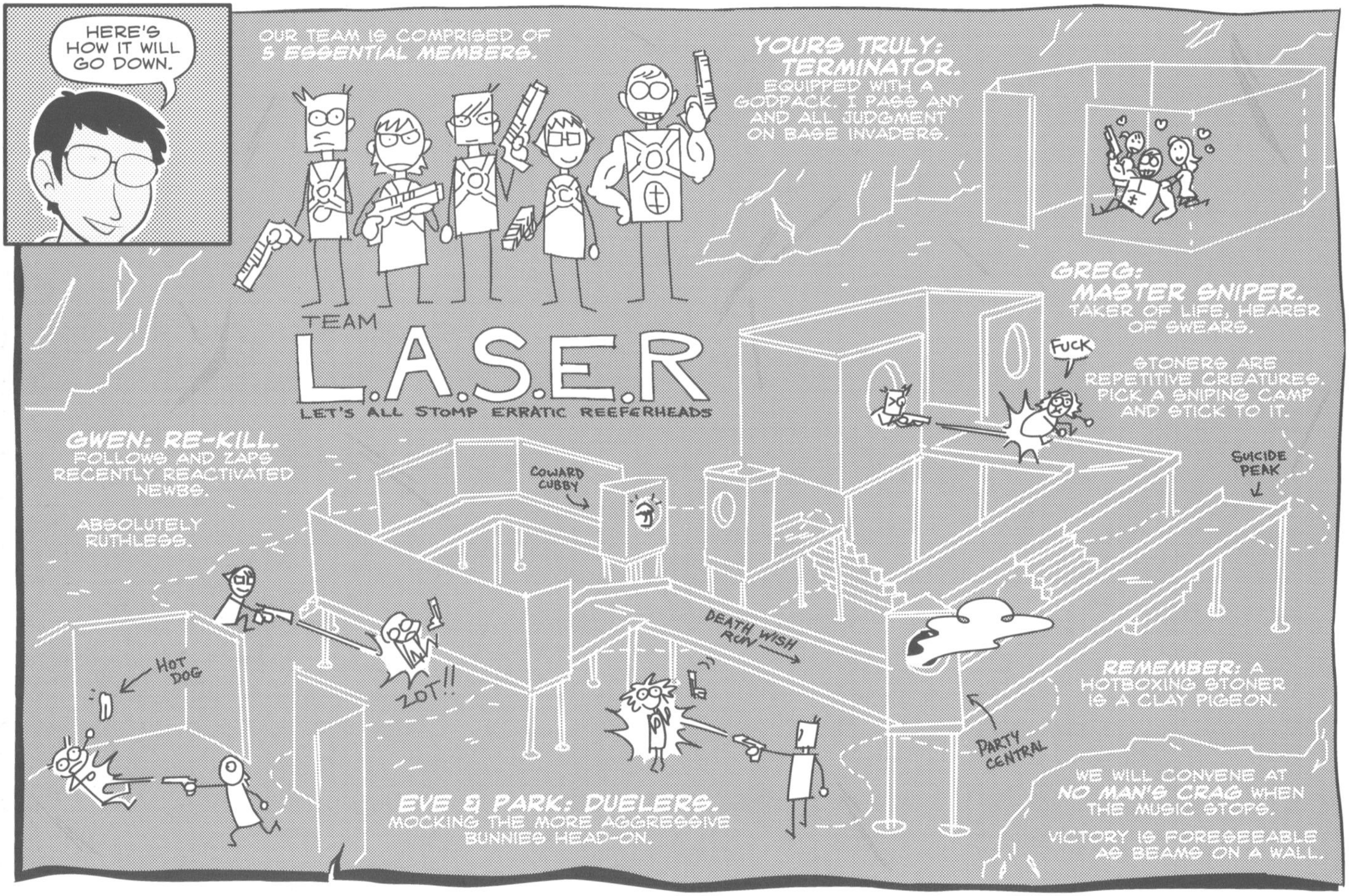
HERE'S HOW IT WILL GO DOWN.
OUR TEAM IS COMPRISED OF 5 ESSENTIAL MEMBERS.
TEAM L.A.S.E.R
LET'S ALL STOMP ERRATIC REEFERHEADS
YOURS TRULY: TERMINATOR.
EQUIPPED WITH A GODPACK, I PASS ANY AND ALL JUDGMENT ON BASE INVADERS.
GREG: MASTER SNIPER.
TAKER OF LIFE, HEARER OF SWEARS.
STONERS ARE REPETITIVE CREATURES. PICK A SNIPING CAMP AND STICK TO IT.
FUCK
GWEN: RE-KILL.
FOLLOWS AND ZAPS RECENTLY REACTIVATED NEWBS.
ABSOLUTELY RUTHLESS.
COWARD CUBBY
SUICIDE PEAK
DEATH WISH RUN
ZOT!!
HOT DOG
REMEMBER: A HOTBOXING STONER IS A CLAY PIGEON.
PARTY CENTRAL
EVE & PARK: DUELERS.
MOCKING THE MORE AGGRESSIVE BUNNIES HEAD-ON.
WE WILL CONVENE AT NO MAN'S CRAG WHEN THE MUSIC STOPS.
VICTORY IS FORESEEABLE AS BEAMS ON A WALL.

GOOD STUFF, EVE. SEE YOU SUNDAY.

YEAH. RIGHT. WHEN I'M NOT SO TIRED.

SIGH.

I THOUGHT THEY'D NEVER LEAVE.

UM... HOLD ON.

LISTEN, I THINK I'M DEALING WITH SOME GROWING PAINS RIGHT NOW.

IS IT YOUR WISDOM TEETH?

NO, I MEAN...!

I'M STRUGGLING TO ADAPT TO CHANGE!

IT'S LIKE EVERYONE ELSE GOT THE MEMO.

AND NOT MUCH ABOUT THE PAST IS A COMFORT, EITHER.

SLUMP

EVEN YOU AND I HAD PROBLEMS.

EVE, WE'RE DIFFERENT PEOPLE NOW. WE KNOW BETTER.

AND WE UNDERSTAND EACH OTHER, RIGHT?

YEAH, BUT...

AND THE OTHERS DON'T MATTER, RIGHT?

YEAH, BUT...

WELL... "IT'S COMPLICATED."

OH. I SEE.

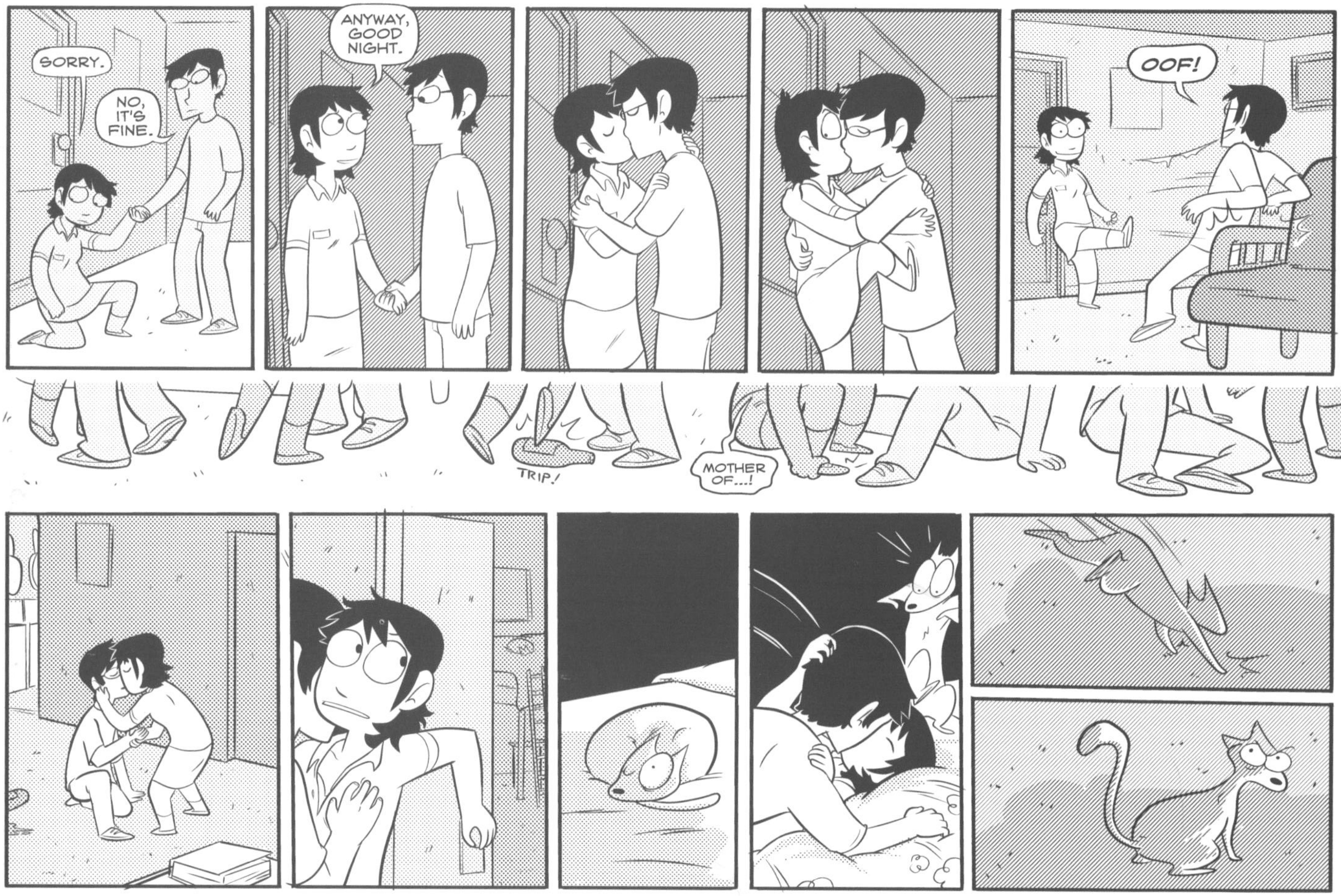
SORRY.
NO, IT'S FINE.
ANYWAY, GOOD NIGHT.
OOF!
TRIP!
MOTHER OF...!

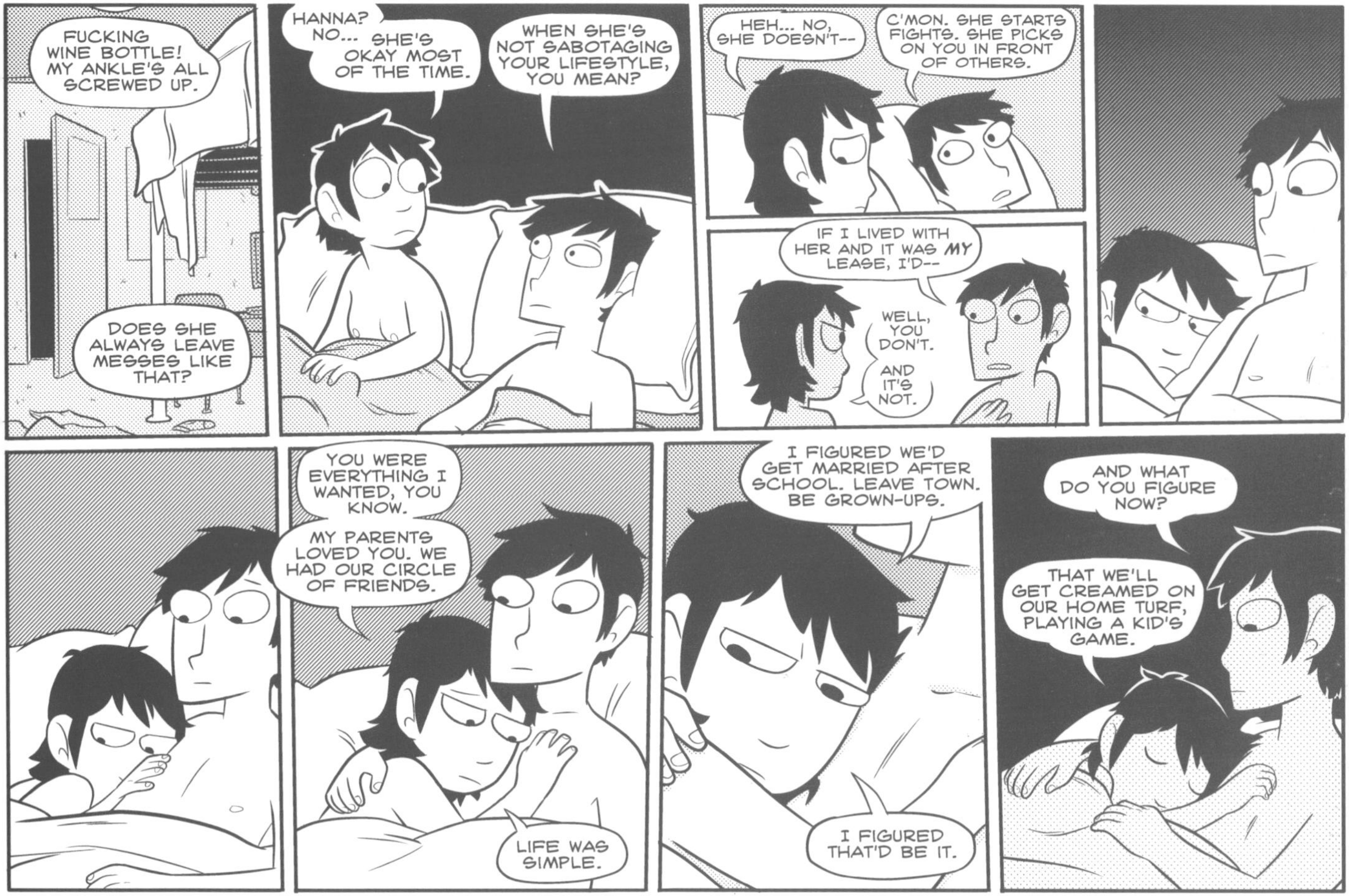
FUCKING WINE BOTTLE! MY ANKLE'S ALL SCREWED UP.
DOES SHE ALWAYS LEAVE MESSES LIKE THAT?
HANNA? NO... SHE'S OKAY MOST OF THE TIME.
WHEN SHE'S NOT SABOTAGING YOUR LIFESTYLE, YOU MEAN?
HEH... NO, SHE DOESN'T--
C'MON. SHE STARTS FIGHTS. SHE PICKS ON YOU IN FRONT OF OTHERS.
IF I LIVED WITH HER AND IT WAS MY LEASE, I'D--
WELL, YOU DON'T.
AND IT'S NOT.
YOU WERE EVERYTHING I WANTED, YOU KNOW.
MY PARENTS LOVED YOU. WE HAD OUR CIRCLE OF FRIENDS.
LIFE WAS SIMPLE.
I FIGURED WE'D GET MARRIED AFTER SCHOOL. LEAVE TOWN. BE GROWN-UPS.
I FIGURED THAT'D BE IT.
AND WHAT DO YOU FIGURE NOW?
THAT WE'LL GET CREAMED ON OUR HOME TURF, PLAYING A KID'S GAME.

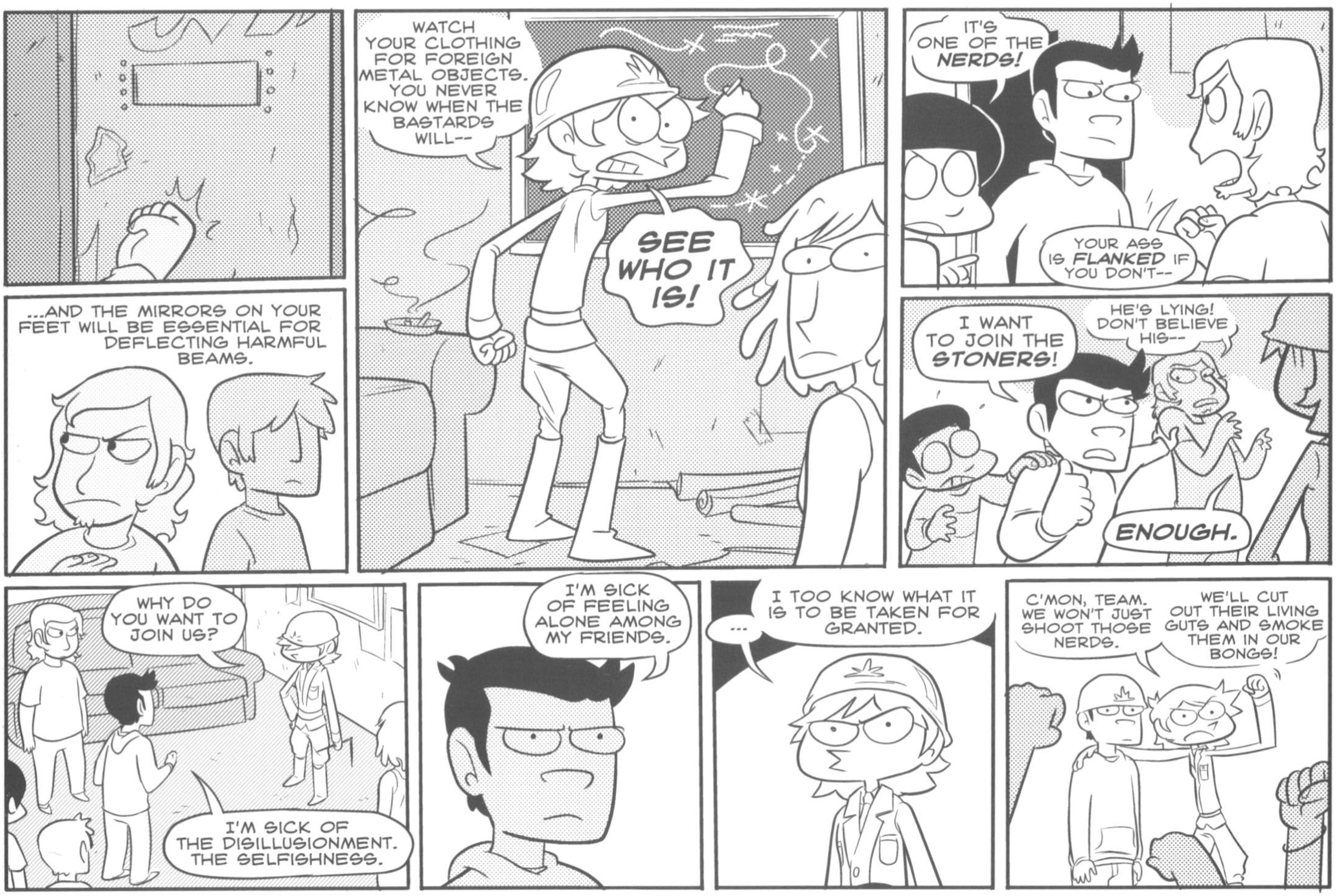
WATCH YOUR CLOTHING FOR FOREIGN METAL OBJECTS. YOU NEVER KNOW WHEN THE BASTARDS WILL--
SEE WHO IT IS!
IT'S ONE OF THE NERDS!
YOUR ASS IS FLANKED IF YOU DON'T--
...AND THE MIRRORS ON YOUR FEET WILL BE ESSENTIAL FOR DEFLECTING HARMFUL BEAMS.
I WANT TO JOIN THE STONERS!
HE'S LYING! DON'T BELIEVE HIS--
ENOUGH.
WHY DO YOU WANT TO JOIN US?
I'M SICK OF THE DISILLUSIONMENT. THE SELFISHNESS.
I'M SICK OF FEELING ALONE AMONG MY FRIENDS.
...
I TOO KNOW WHAT IT IS TO BE TAKEN FOR GRANTED.
C'MON, TEAM. WE WON'T JUST SHOOT THOSE NERDS.
WE'LL CUT OUT THEIR LIVING GUTS AND SMOKE THEM IN OUR BONGS!

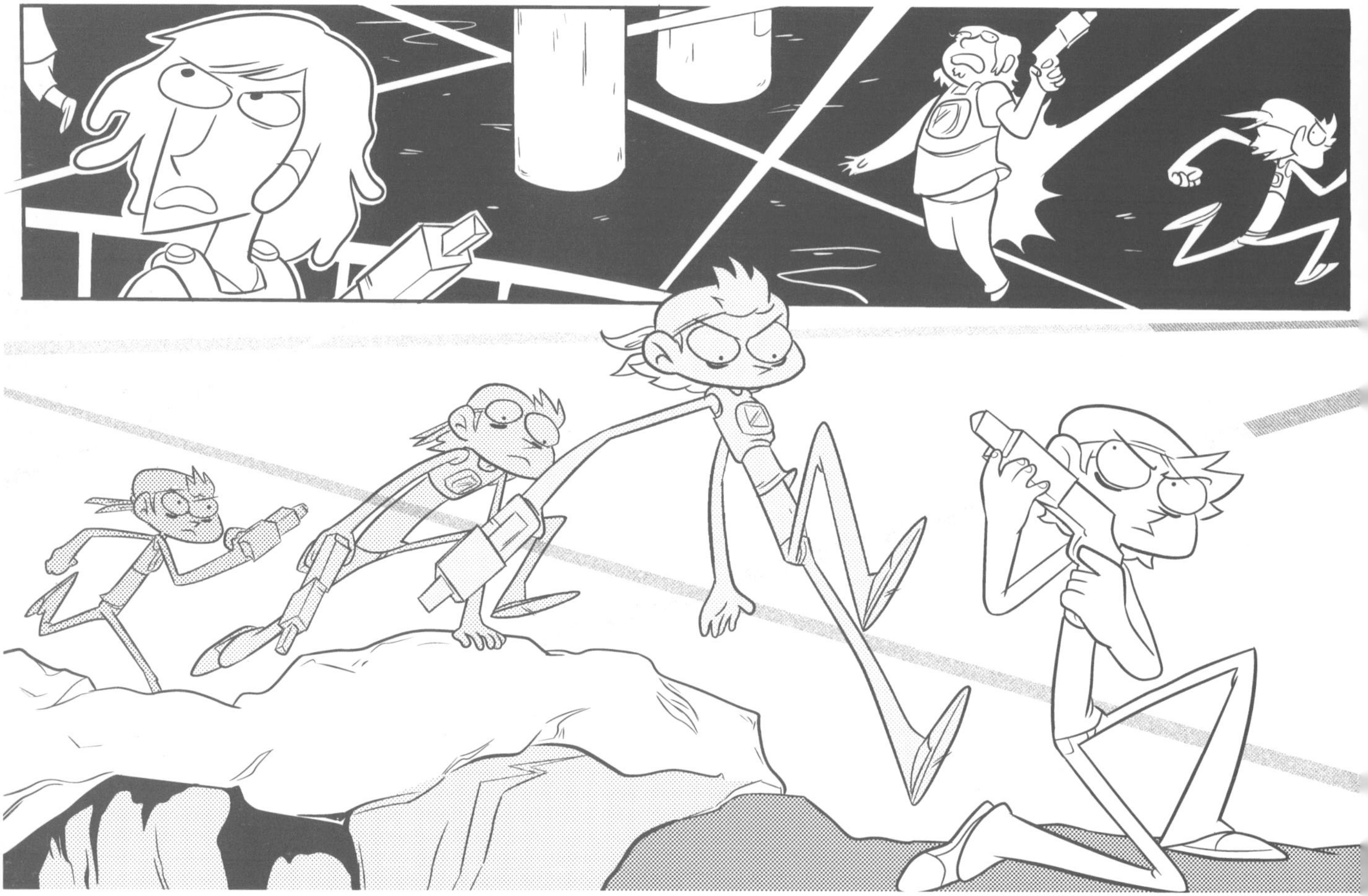

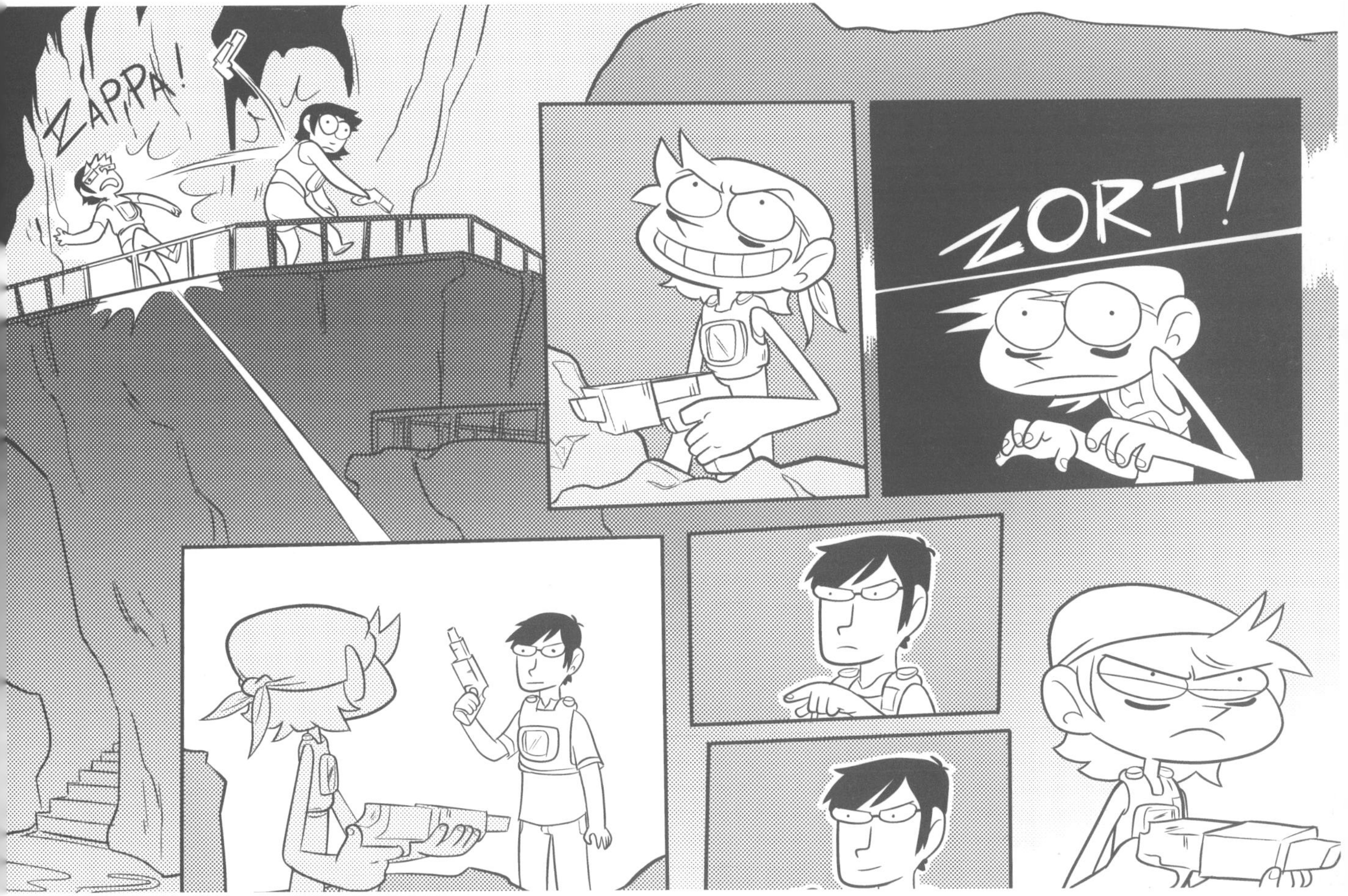
ZAPPA!
ZORT!

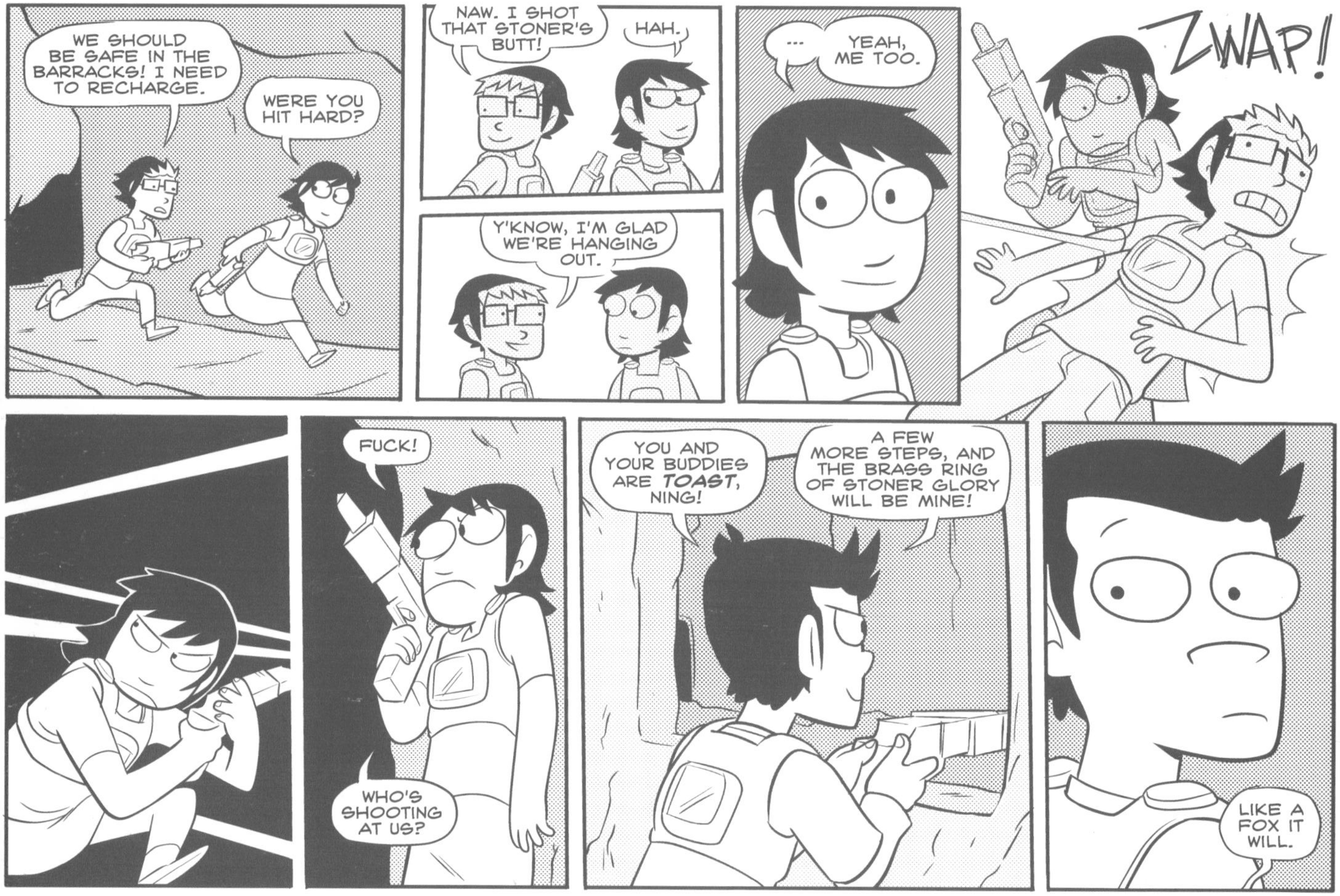
WE SHOULD BE SAFE IN THE BARRACKS! I NEED TO RECHARGE.
WERE YOU HIT HARD?
NAW. I SHOT THAT STONER'S BUTT!
HAH.
Y'KNOW, I'M GLAD WE'RE HANGING OUT.
...
YEAH, ME TOO.
ZWAP!
FUCK!
WHO'S SHOOTING AT US?
YOU AND YOUR BUDDIES ARE TOAST, NING!
A FEW MORE STEPS, AND THE BRASS RING OF STONER GLORY WILL BE MINE!
LIKE A FOX IT WILL.

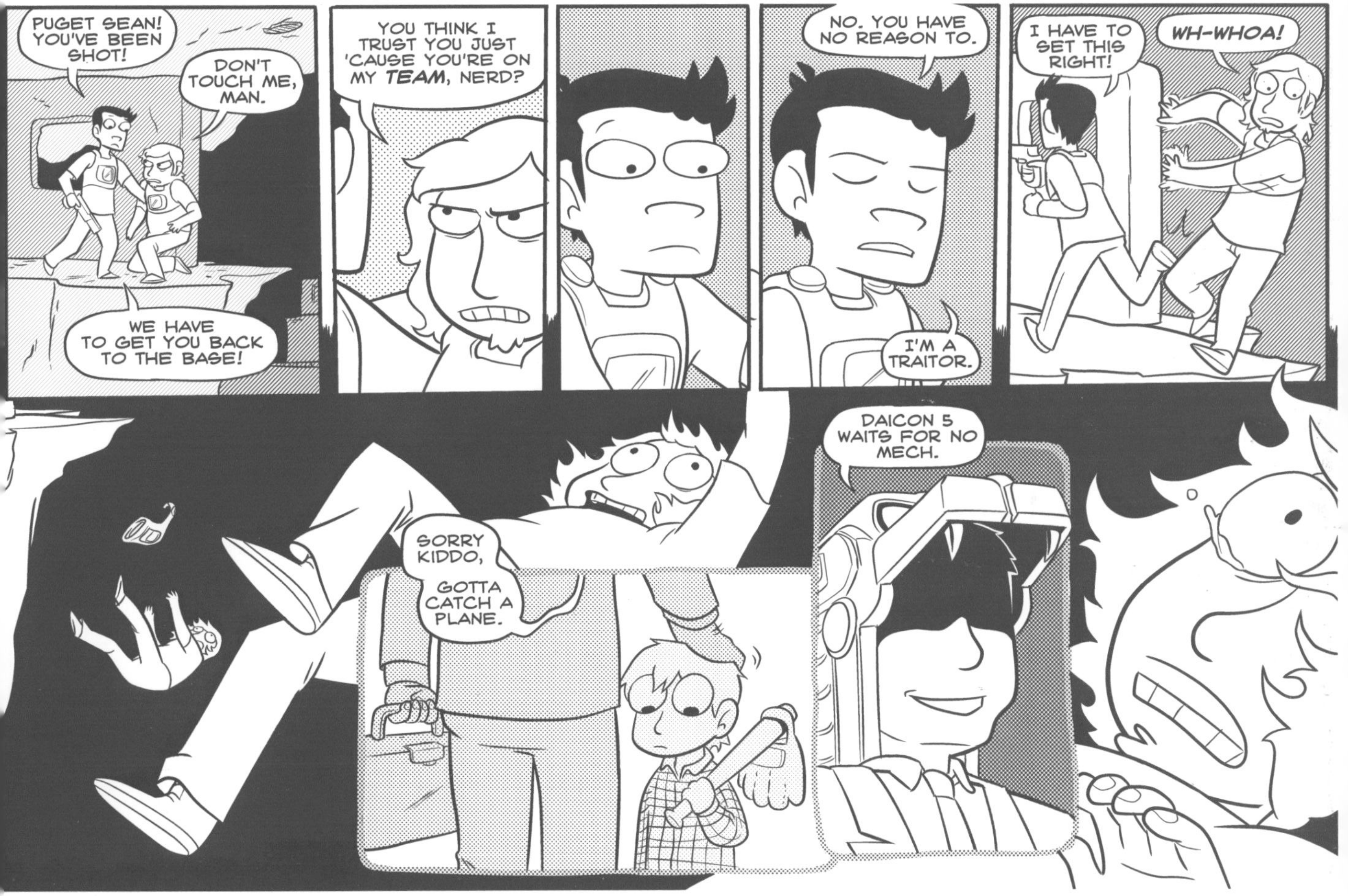
PUGET SEAN! YOU'VE BEEN SHOT!
DON'T TOUCH ME, MAN.
WE HAVE TO GET YOU BACK TO THE BASE!
YOU THINK I TRUST YOU JUST 'CAUSE YOU'RE ON MY *TEAM*, NERD?
NO. YOU HAVE NO REASON TO.
I'M A TRAITOR.
I HAVE TO SET THIS RIGHT!
WH-WHOA!
SORRY KIDDO,
GOTTA CATCH A PLANE.
DAICON 5 WAITS FOR NO MECH.

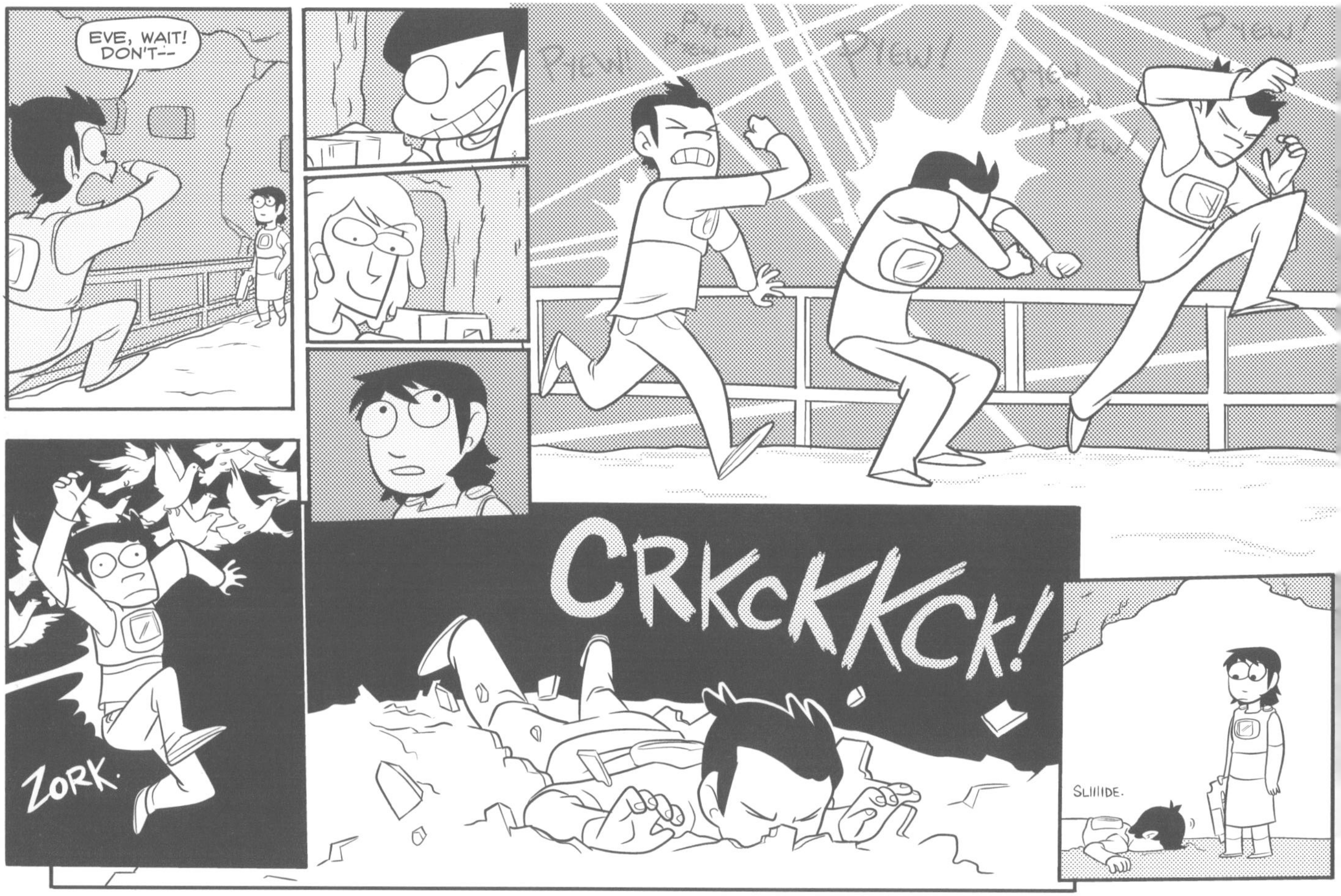
EVE, WAIT! DON'T--
PIEW!
PIEW!
PIEW!
ZORK.
CRKCKKCK!
SLIIIIDE.

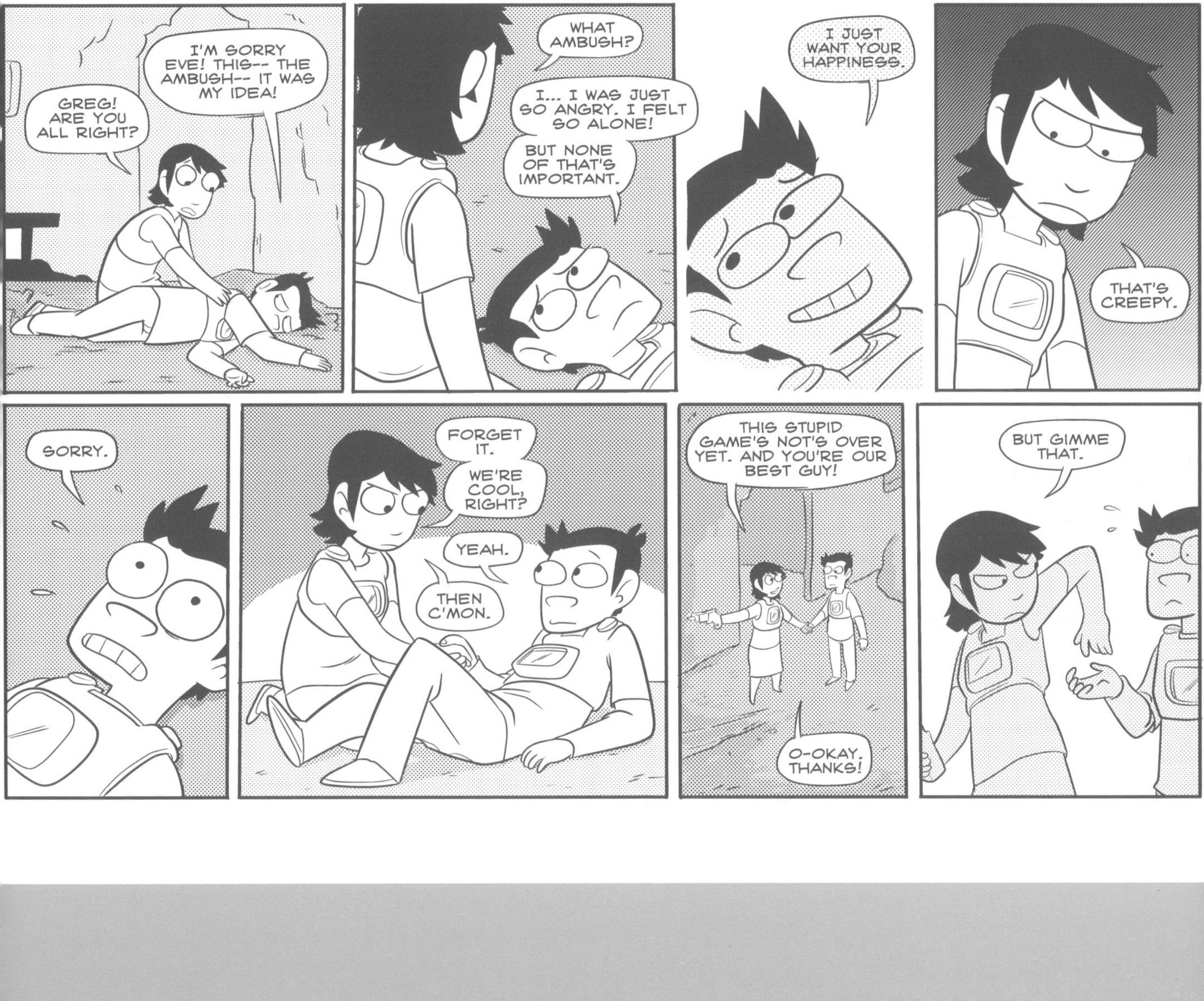
GREG! ARE YOU ALL RIGHT?
I'M SORRY EVE! THIS-- THE AMBUSH-- IT WAS MY IDEA!
WHAT AMBUSH?
I... I WAS JUST SO ANGRY. I FELT SO ALONE!
BUT NONE OF THAT'S IMPORTANT.
I JUST WANT YOUR HAPPINESS.
THAT'S CREEPY.
SORRY.
FORGET IT.
WE'RE COOL, RIGHT?
YEAH.
THEN C'MON.
THIS STUPID GAME'S NOT'S OVER YET. AND YOU'RE OUR BEST GUY!
O-OKAY. THANKS!
BUT GIMME THAT.

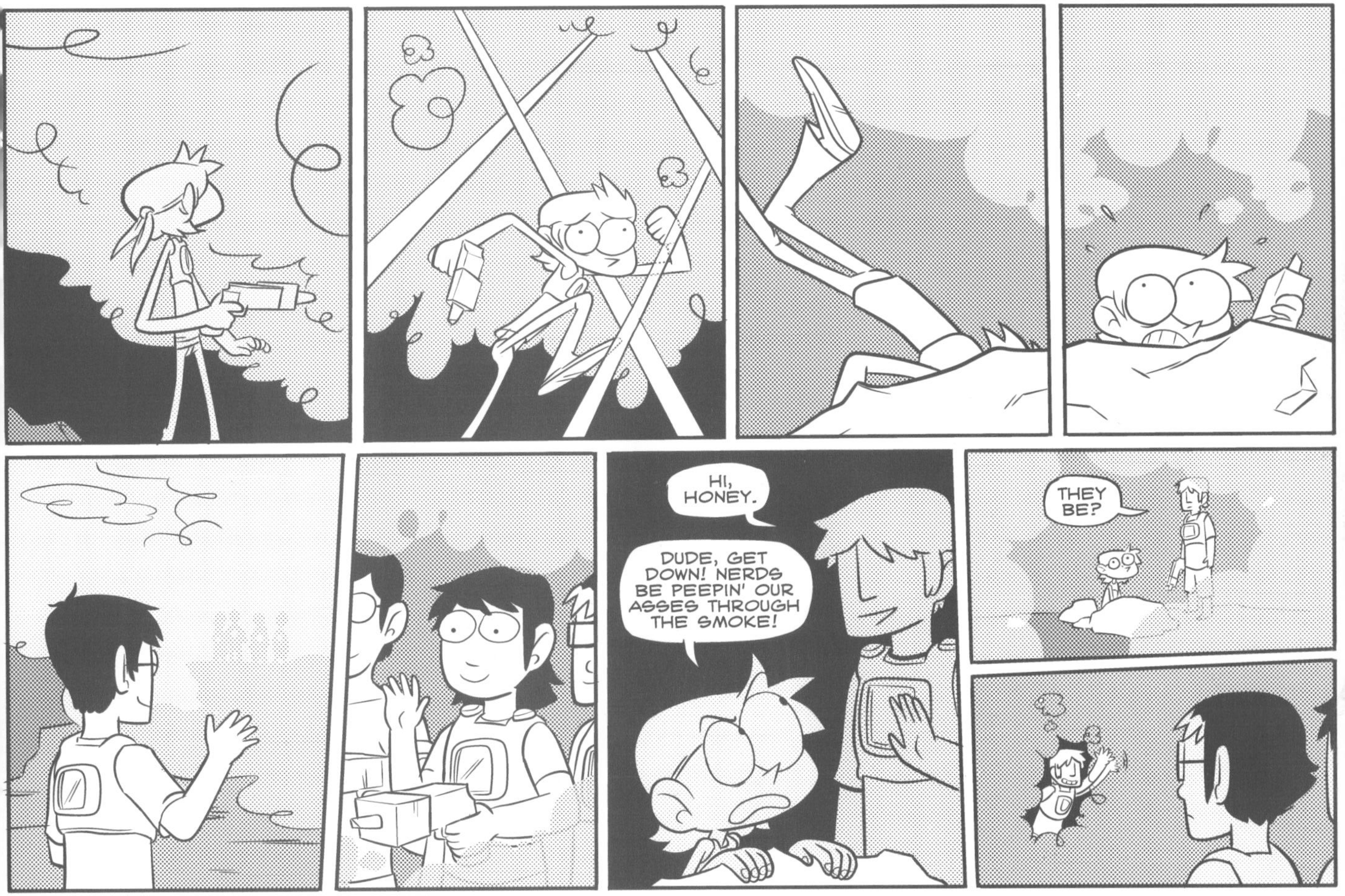
HI, HONEY.
DUDE, GET DOWN! NERDS BE PEEPIN' OUR ASSES THROUGH THE SMOKE!
THEY BE?

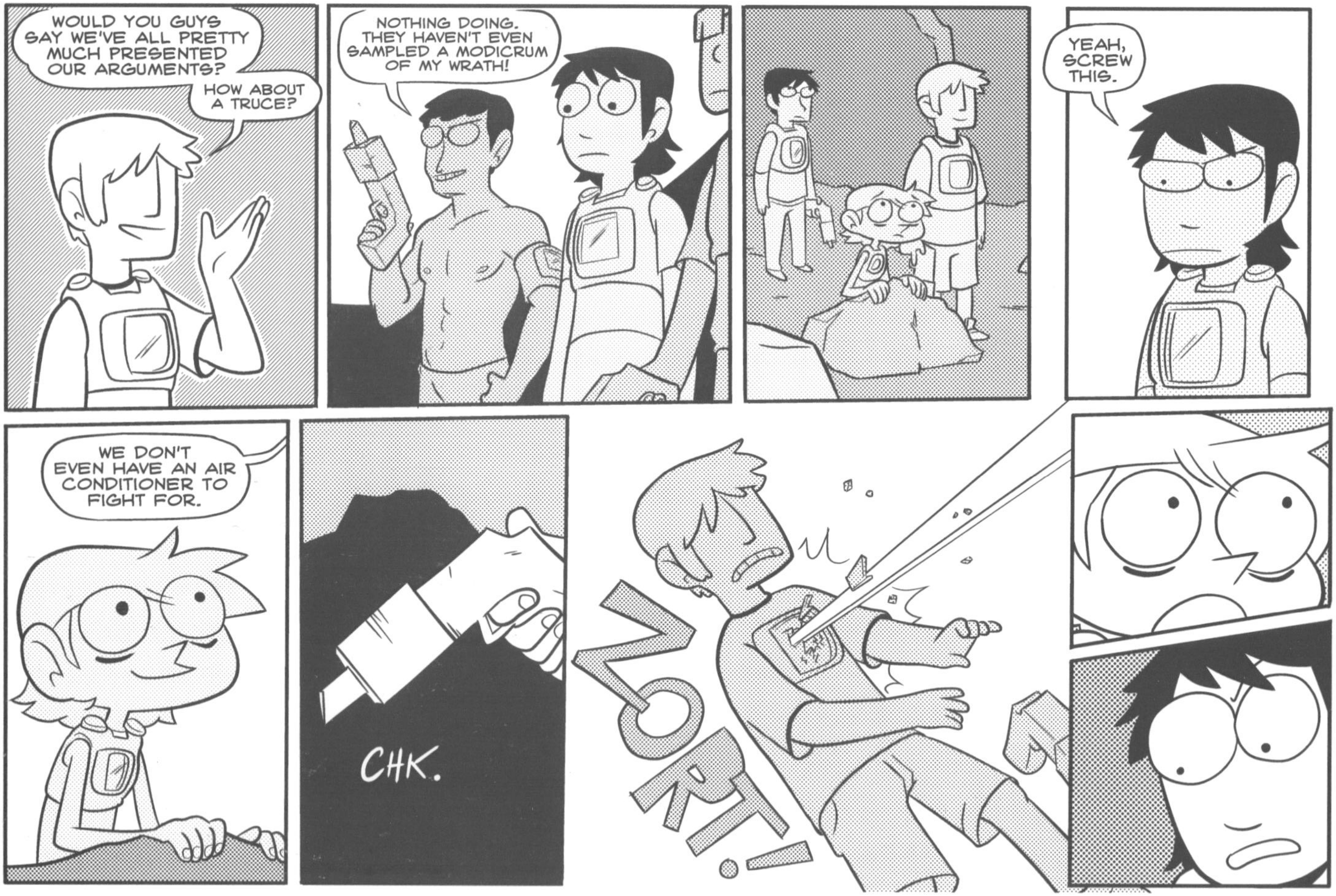
WOULD YOU GUYS SAY WE'VE ALL PRETTY MUCH PRESENTED OUR ARGUMENTS?
HOW ABOUT A TRUCE?
NOTHING DOING. THEY HAVEN'T EVEN SAMPLED A MODICRUM OF MY WRATH!
YEAH, SCREW THIS.
WE DON'T EVEN HAVE AN AIR CONDITIONER TO FIGHT FOR.
CHK.
ZORT!

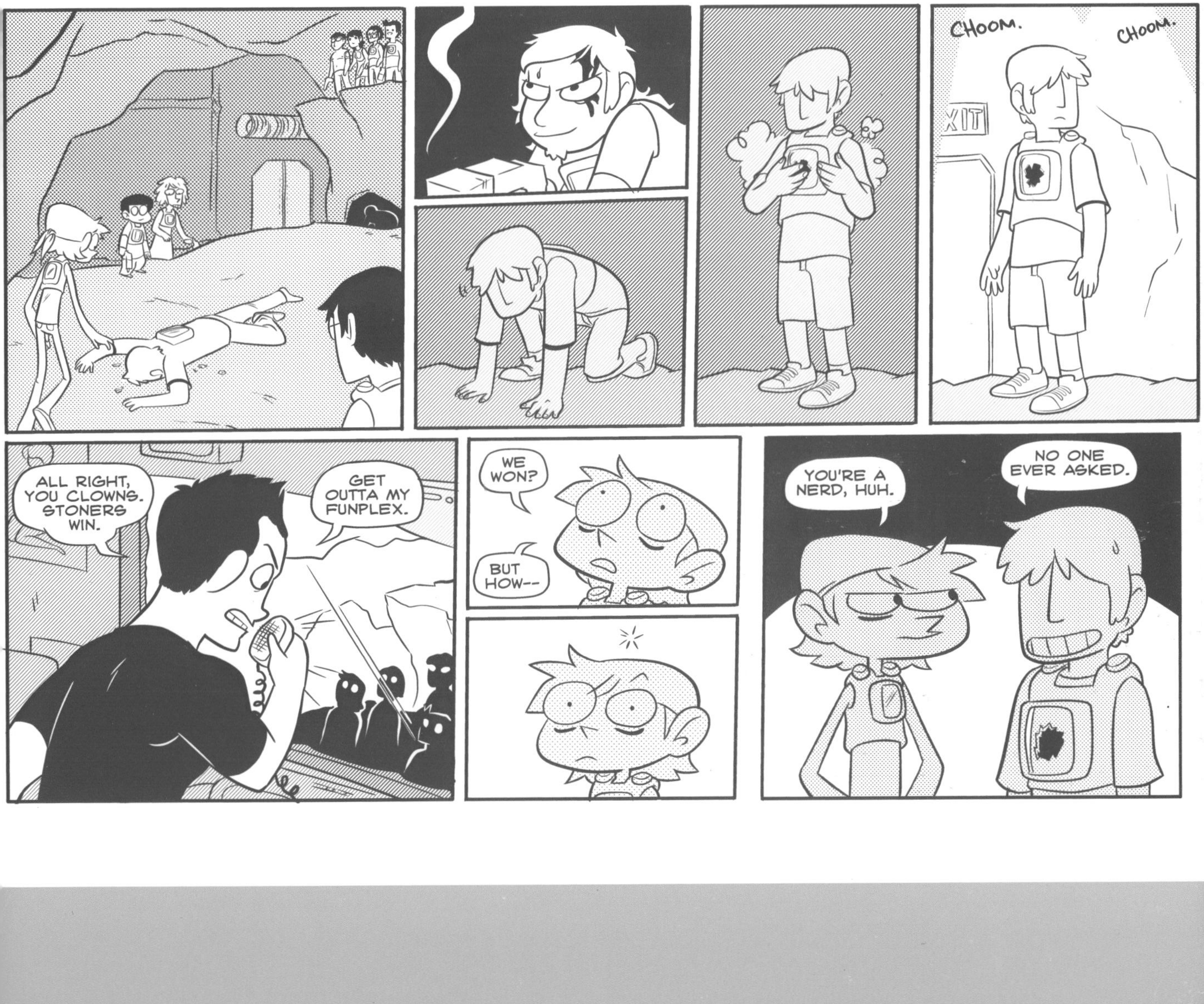
CHOOM.
CHOOM.
XIT
ALL RIGHT, YOU CLOWNS. STONERS WIN.
GET OUTTA MY FUNPLEX.
WE WON?
BUT HOW--
YOU'RE A NERD, HUH.
NO ONE EVER ASKED.

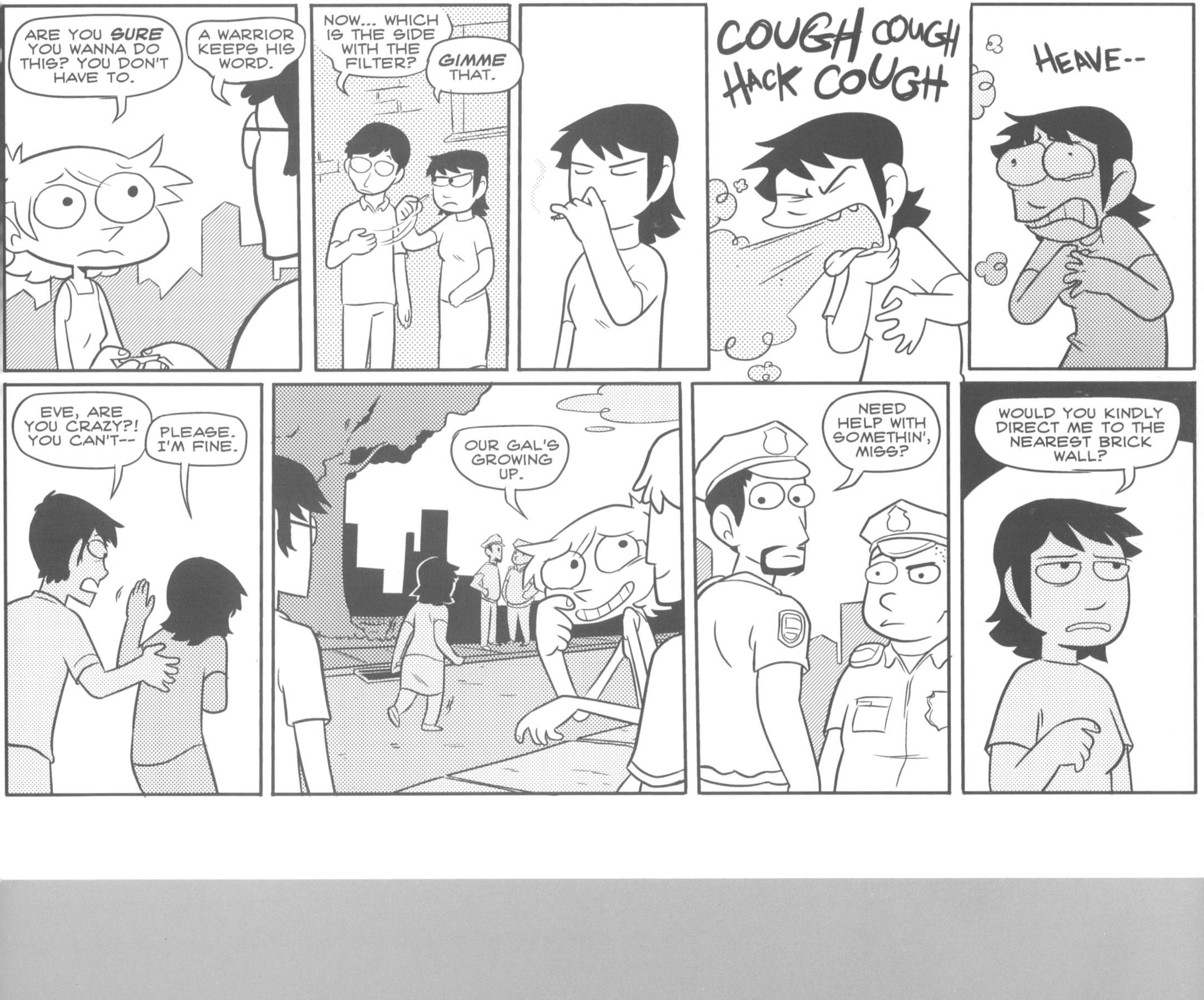
ARE YOU **SURE** YOU WANNA DO THIS? YOU DON'T HAVE TO.
A WARRIOR KEEPS HIS WORD.
NOW... WHICH IS THE SIDE WITH THE FILTER?
GIMME THAT.
COUGH COUGH
HACK COUGH
HEAVE--
EVE, ARE YOU CRAZY?! YOU CAN'T--
PLEASE. I'M FINE.
OUR GAL'S GROWING UP.
NEED HELP WITH SOMETHIN', MISS?
WOULD YOU KINDLY DIRECT ME TO THE NEAREST BRICK WALL?

renaissance unfair

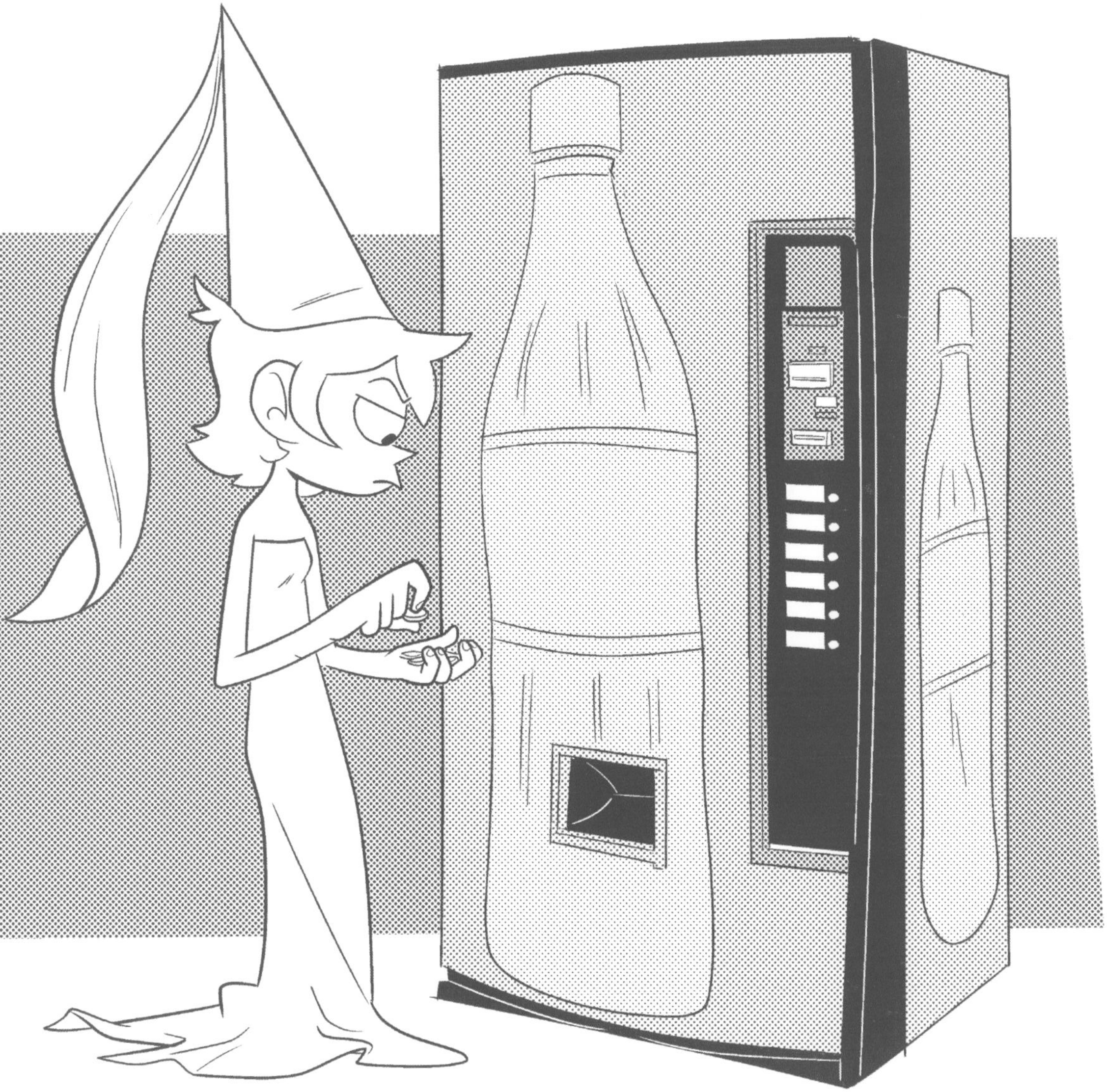

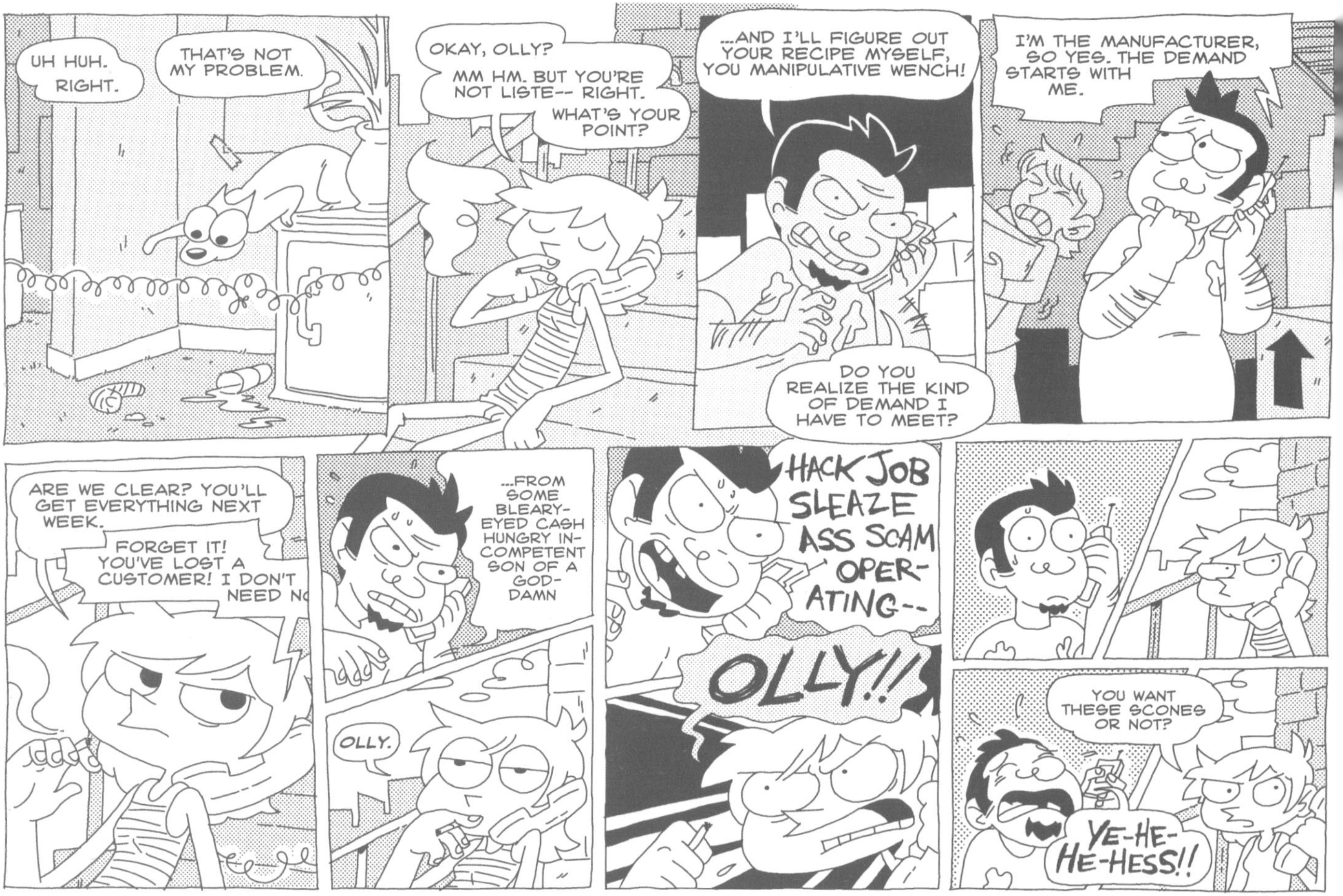
UH HUH.
RIGHT.
THAT'S NOT MY PROBLEM.
OKAY, OLLY?
MM HM. BUT YOU'RE NOT LISTE-- RIGHT.
WHAT'S YOUR POINT?
...AND I'LL FIGURE OUT YOUR RECIPE MYSELF, YOU MANIPULATIVE WENCH!
DO YOU REALIZE THE KIND OF DEMAND I HAVE TO MEET?
I'M THE MANUFACTURER, SO YES. THE DEMAND STARTS WITH ME.
ARE WE CLEAR? YOU'LL GET EVERYTHING NEXT WEEK.
FORGET IT! YOU'VE LOST A CUSTOMER! I DON'T NEED N
...FROM SOME BLEARY-EYED CASH HUNGRY IN-COMPETENT SON OF A GOD-DAMN
OLLY.
HACK JOB SLEAZE ASS SCAM OPER-ATING--
OLLY!!
YOU WANT THESE SCONES OR NOT?
YE-HE-HE-HESS!!

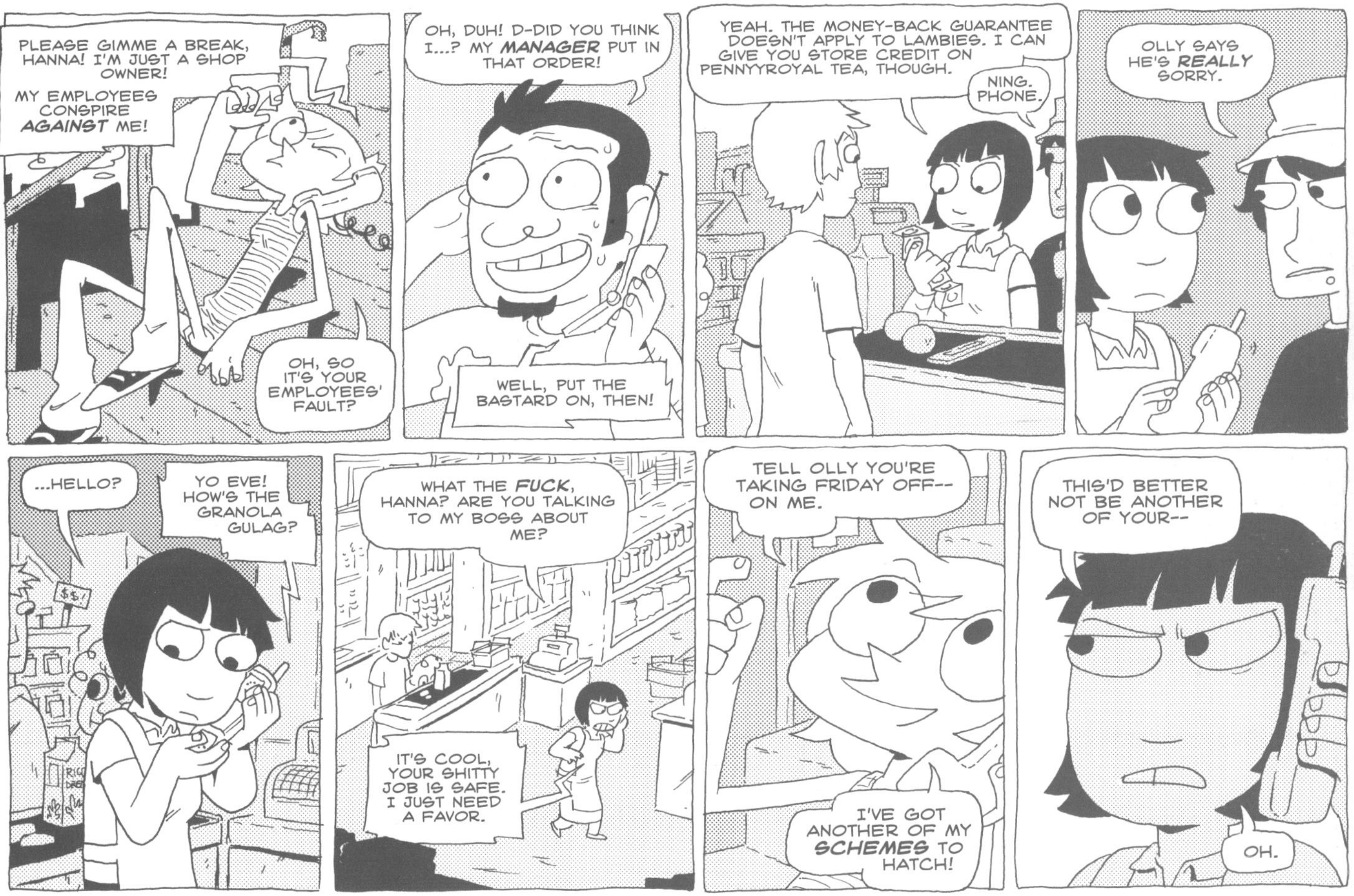
PLEASE GIMME A BREAK, HANNA! I'M JUST A SHOP OWNER!
MY EMPLOYEES CONSPIRE AGAINST ME!
OH, SO IT'S YOUR EMPLOYEES' FAULT?
OH, DUH! D-DID YOU THINK I...? MY MANAGER PUT IN THAT ORDER!
WELL, PUT THE BASTARD ON, THEN!
YEAH. THE MONEY-BACK GUARANTEE DOESN'T APPLY TO LAMBIES. I CAN GIVE YOU STORE CREDIT ON PENNYYROYAL TEA, THOUGH.
NING. PHONE.
OLLY SAYS HE'S REALLY SORRY.
...HELLO?
YO EVE! HOW'S THE GRANOLA GULAG?
WHAT THE FUCK, HANNA? ARE YOU TALKING TO MY BOSS ABOUT ME?
IT'S COOL, YOUR SHITTY JOB IS SAFE. I JUST NEED A FAVOR.
TELL OLLY YOU'RE TAKING FRIDAY OFF-- ON ME.
I'VE GOT ANOTHER OF MY SCHEMES TO HATCH!
THIS'D BETTER NOT BE ANOTHER OF YOUR--
OH.

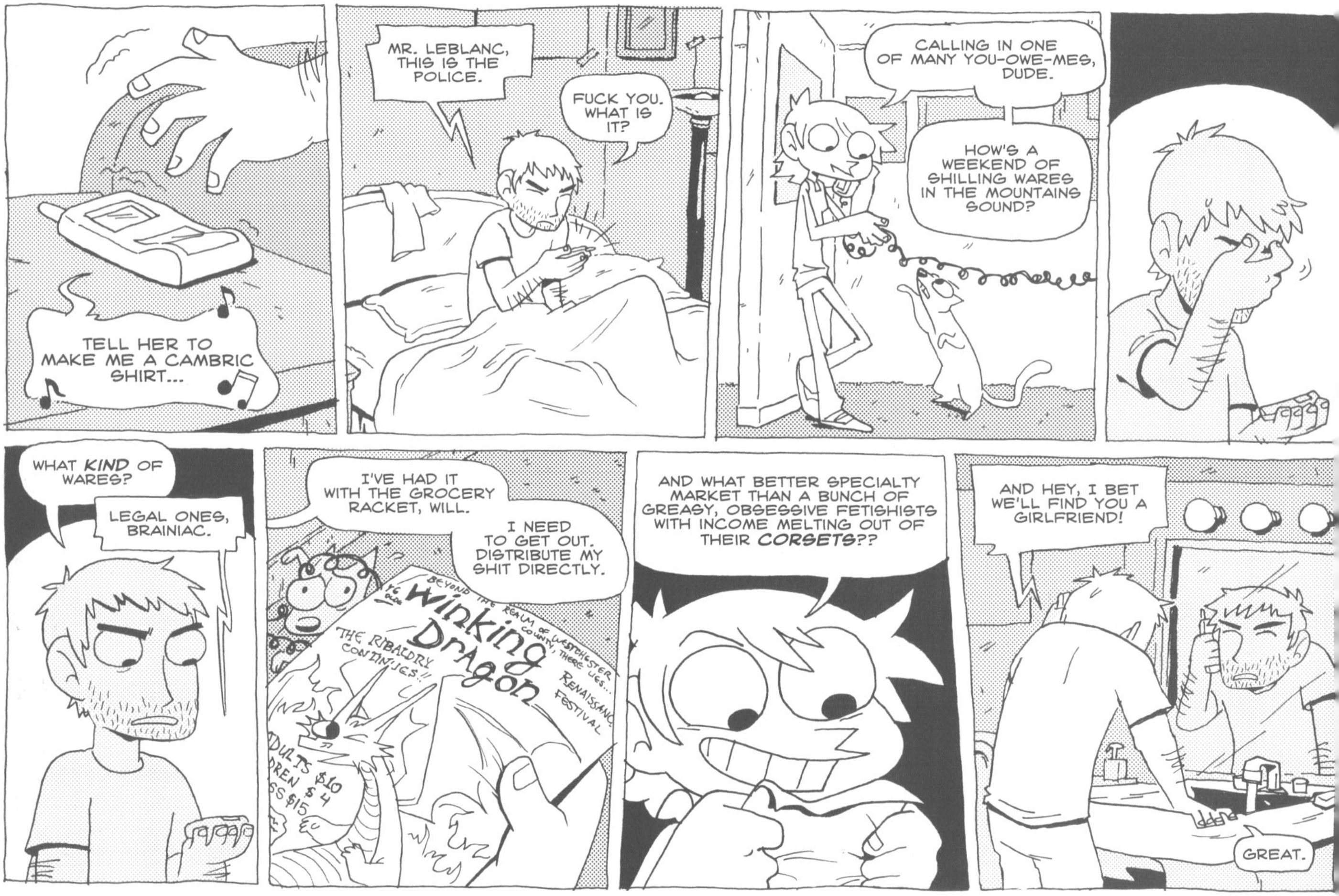
TELL HER TO MAKE ME A CAMBRIC SHIRT...
MR. LEBLANC, THIS IS THE POLICE.
FUCK YOU. WHAT IS IT?
CALLING IN ONE OF MANY YOU-OWE-MES, DUDE.
HOW'S A WEEKEND OF SHILLING WARES IN THE MOUNTAINS SOUND?
WHAT KIND OF WARES?
LEGAL ONES, BRAINIAC.
I'VE HAD IT WITH THE GROCERY RACKET, WILL.
I NEED TO GET OUT. DISTRIBUTE MY SHIT DIRECTLY.
BEYOND THE REALM OF WESTCHESTER COUNTY, THERE LIES...
Winking Dragon
RENAISSANCE FESTIVAL
THE RIBALDRY CONTINUES!!
AND WHAT BETTER SPECIALTY MARKET THAN A BUNCH OF GREASY, OBSESSIVE FETISHISTS WITH INCOME MELTING OUT OF THEIR CORSETS??
AND HEY, I BET WE'LL FIND YOU A GIRLFRIEND!
GREAT.

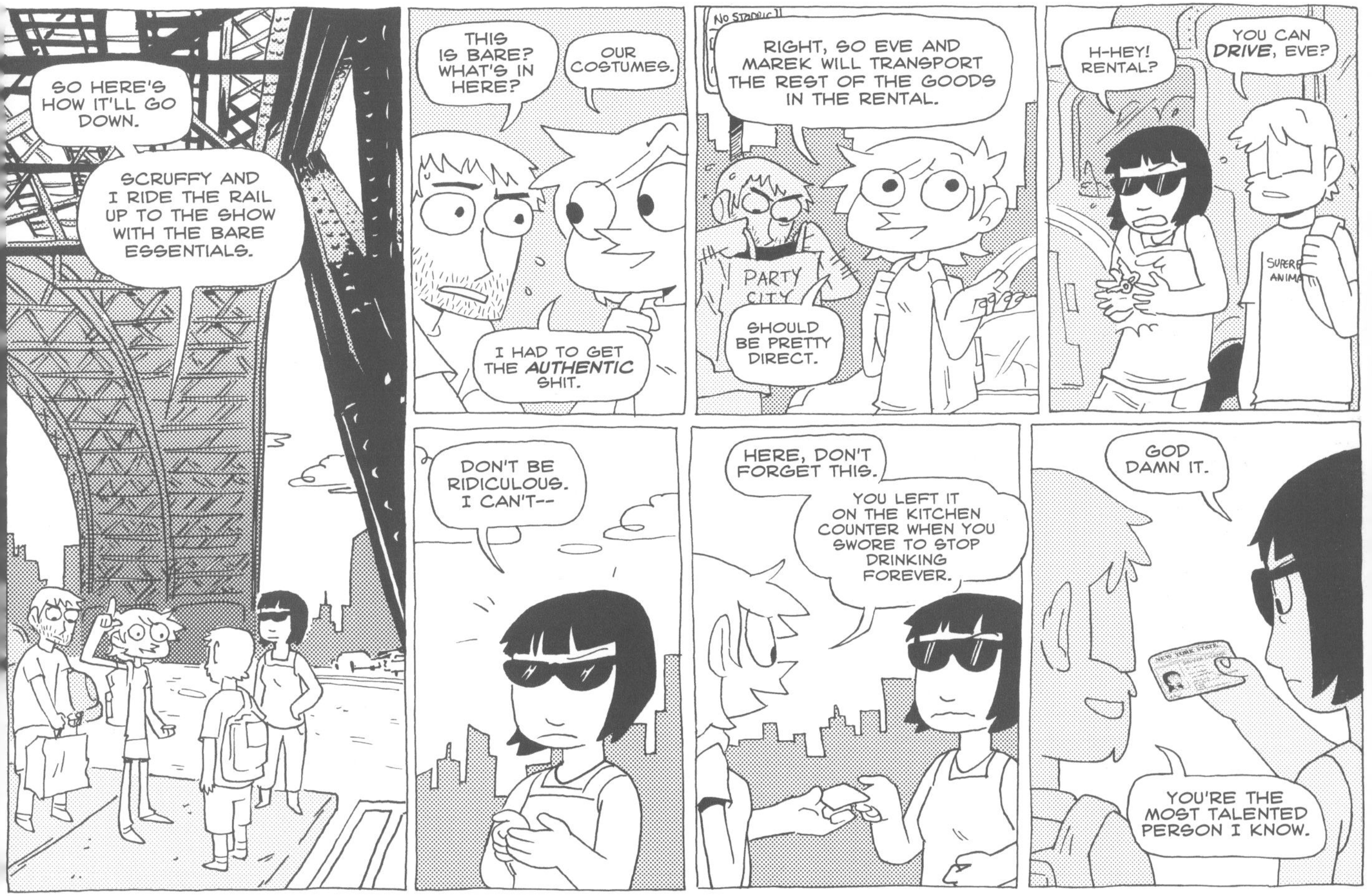
SO HERE'S HOW IT'LL GO DOWN.
SCRUFFY AND I RIDE THE RAIL UP TO THE SHOW WITH THE BARE ESSENTIALS.
THIS IS BARE? WHAT'S IN HERE?
OUR COSTUMES.
I HAD TO GET THE **AUTHENTIC** SHIT.
RIGHT, SO EVE AND MAREK WILL TRANSPORT THE REST OF THE GOODS IN THE RENTAL.
PARTY CITY
SHOULD BE PRETTY DIRECT.
H-HEY! RENTAL?
YOU CAN **DRIVE**, EVE?
DON'T BE RIDICULOUS. I CAN'T--
HERE, DON'T FORGET THIS.
YOU LEFT IT ON THE KITCHEN COUNTER WHEN YOU SWORE TO STOP DRINKING FOREVER.
GOD DAMN IT.
YOU'RE THE MOST TALENTED PERSON I KNOW.

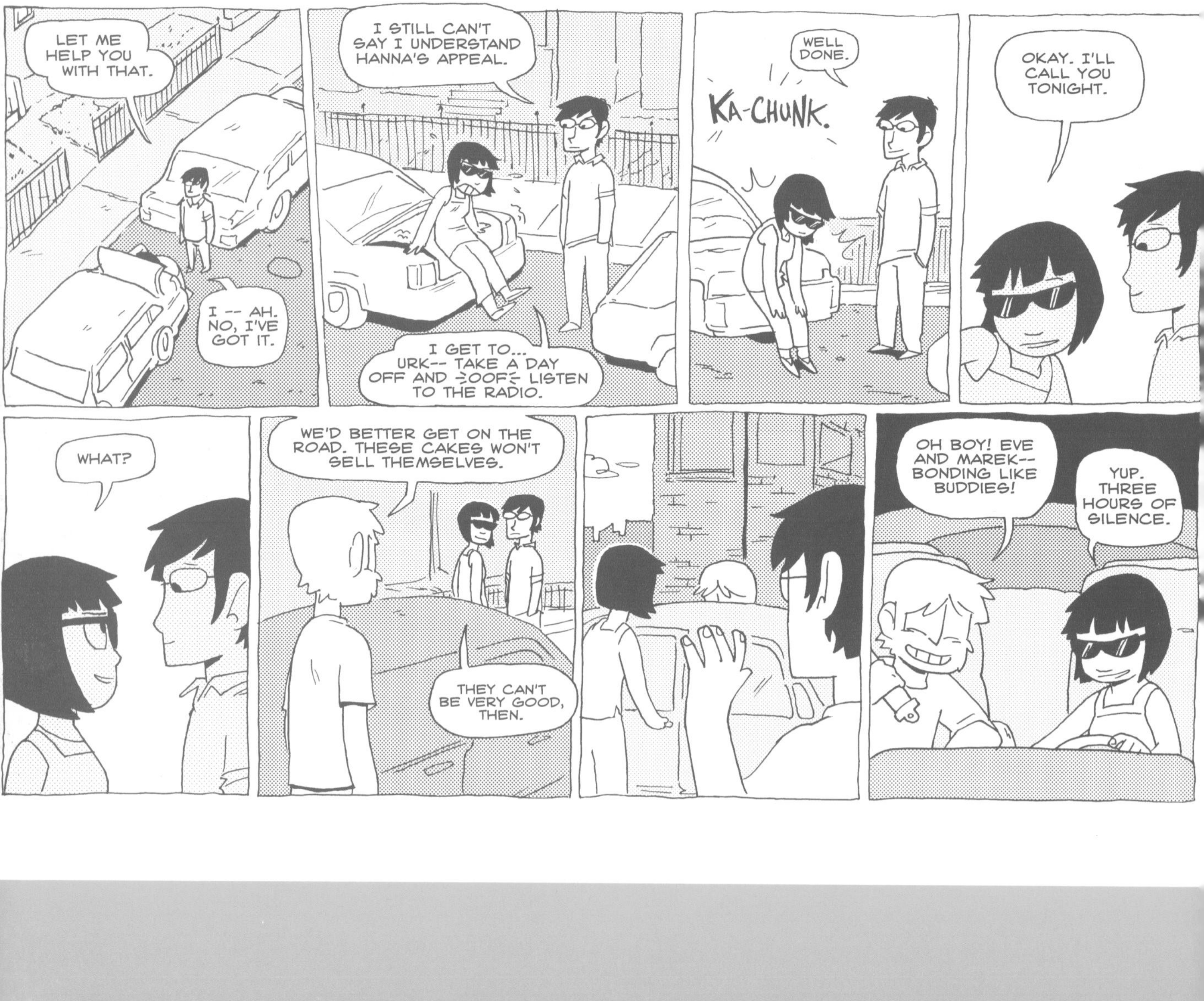
LET ME HELP YOU WITH THAT.
I -- AH. NO, I'VE GOT IT.
I STILL CAN'T SAY I UNDERSTAND HANNA'S APPEAL.
I GET TO... URK-- TAKE A DAY OFF AND =OOF= LISTEN TO THE RADIO.
KA-CHUNK.
WELL DONE.
OKAY. I'LL CALL YOU TONIGHT.
WHAT?
WE'D BETTER GET ON THE ROAD. THESE CAKES WON'T SELL THEMSELVES.
THEY CAN'T BE VERY GOOD, THEN.
OH BOY! EVE AND MAREK-- BONDING LIKE BUDDIES!
YUP. THREE HOURS OF SILENCE.

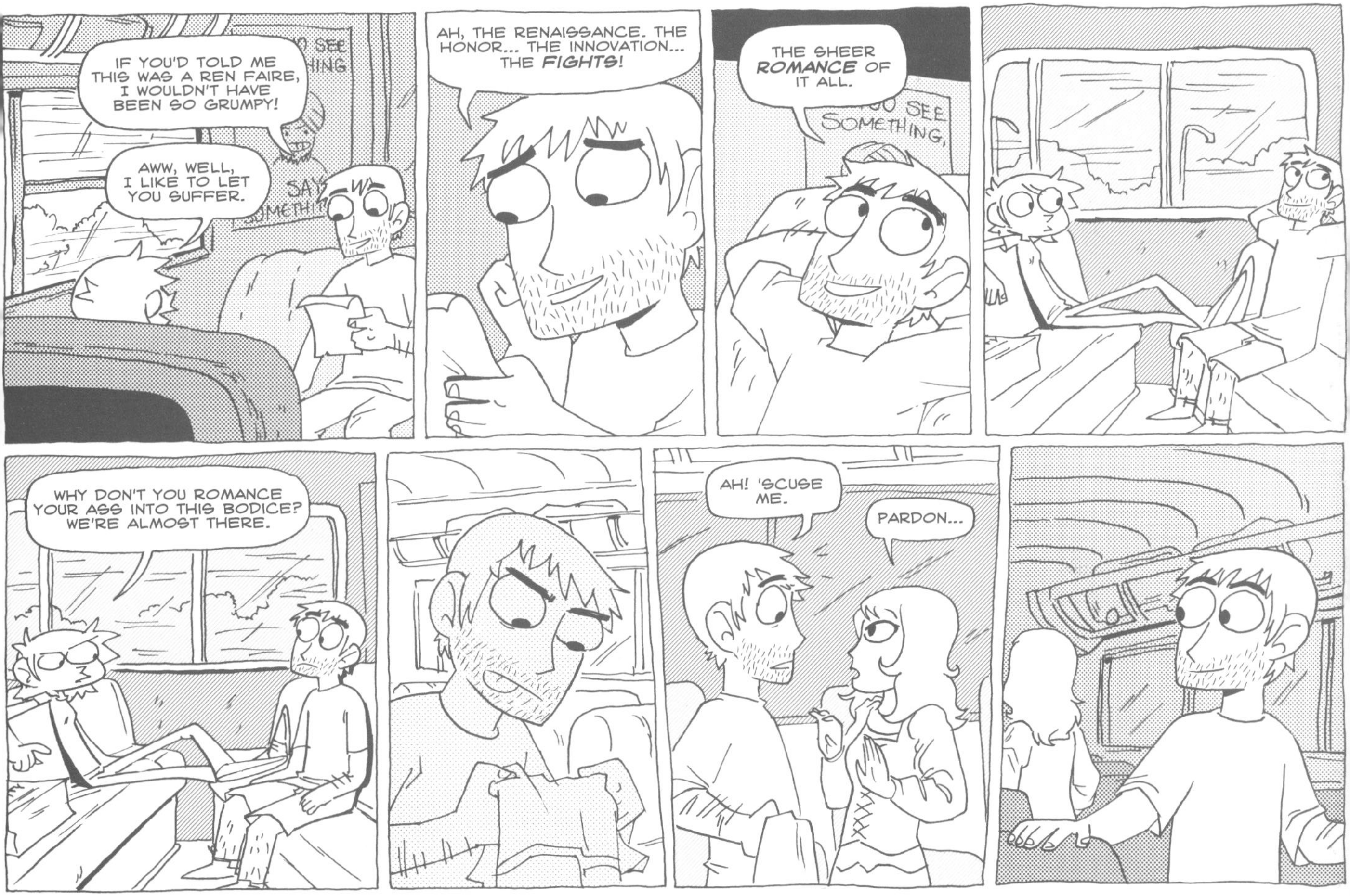
IF YOU'D TOLD ME THIS WAS A REN FAIRE, I WOULDN'T HAVE BEEN SO GRUMPY!
AWW, WELL, I LIKE TO LET YOU SUFFER.
AH, THE RENAISSANCE. THE HONOR... THE INNOVATION... THE *FIGHTS*!
THE SHEER *ROMANCE* OF IT ALL.
SOMETHING,
WHY DON'T YOU ROMANCE YOUR ASS INTO THIS BODICE? WE'RE ALMOST THERE.
AH! 'SCUSE ME.
PARDON...

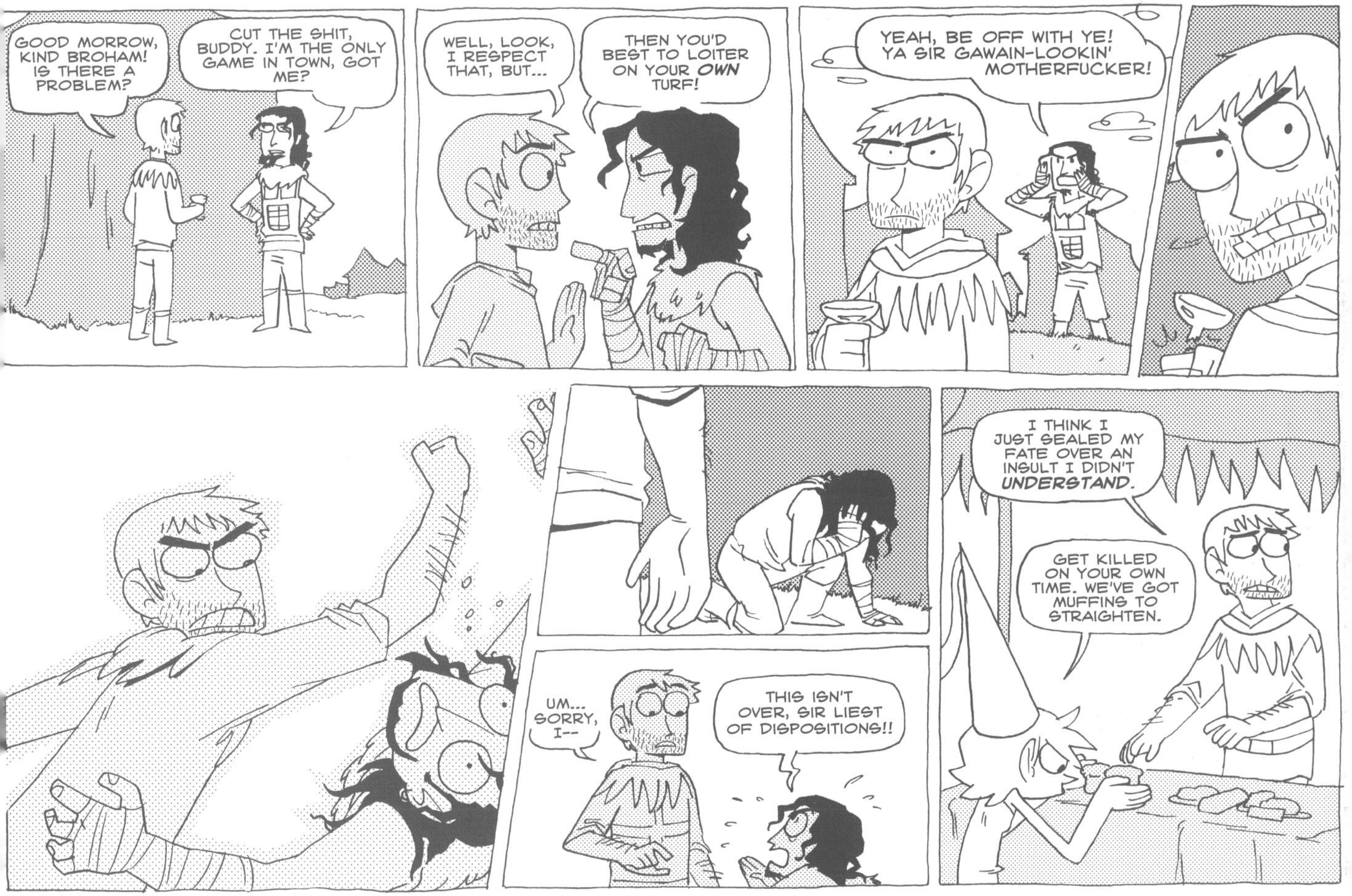
GOOD MORROW, KIND BROHAM! IS THERE A PROBLEM?
CUT THE SHIT, BUDDY. I'M THE ONLY GAME IN TOWN, GOT ME?
WELL, LOOK, I RESPECT THAT, BUT...
THEN YOU'D BEST TO LOITER ON YOUR OWN TURF!
YEAH, BE OFF WITH YE! YA SIR GAWAIN-LOOKIN' MOTHERFUCKER!
UM... SORRY, I--
THIS ISN'T OVER, SIR LIEST OF DISPOSITIONS!!
I THINK I JUST SEALED MY FATE OVER AN INSULT I DIDN'T UNDERSTAND.
GET KILLED ON YOUR OWN TIME. WE'VE GOT MUFFINS TO STRAIGHTEN.

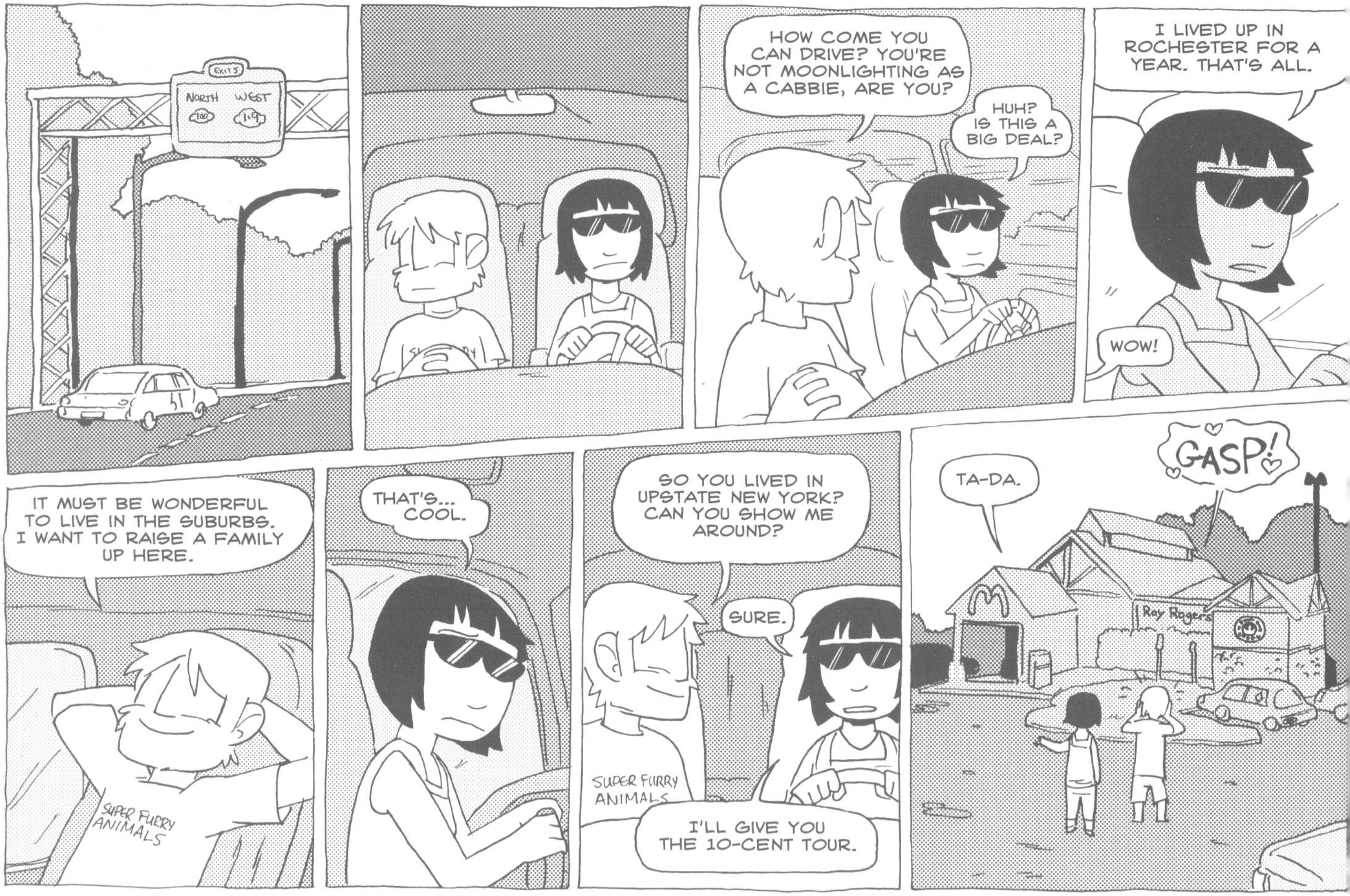
EXITS
NORTH
WEST
HOW COME YOU CAN DRIVE? YOU'RE NOT MOONLIGHTING AS A CABBIE, ARE YOU?
HUH? IS THIS A BIG DEAL?
I LIVED UP IN ROCHESTER FOR A YEAR. THAT'S ALL.
WOW!
IT MUST BE WONDERFUL TO LIVE IN THE SUBURBS. I WANT TO RAISE A FAMILY UP HERE.
SUPER FURRY ANIMALS
THAT'S... COOL.
SO YOU LIVED IN UPSTATE NEW YORK? CAN YOU SHOW ME AROUND?
SURE.
SUPER FURRY ANIMALS
I'LL GIVE YOU THE 10-CENT TOUR.
TA-DA.
GASP!
Ray Rogers

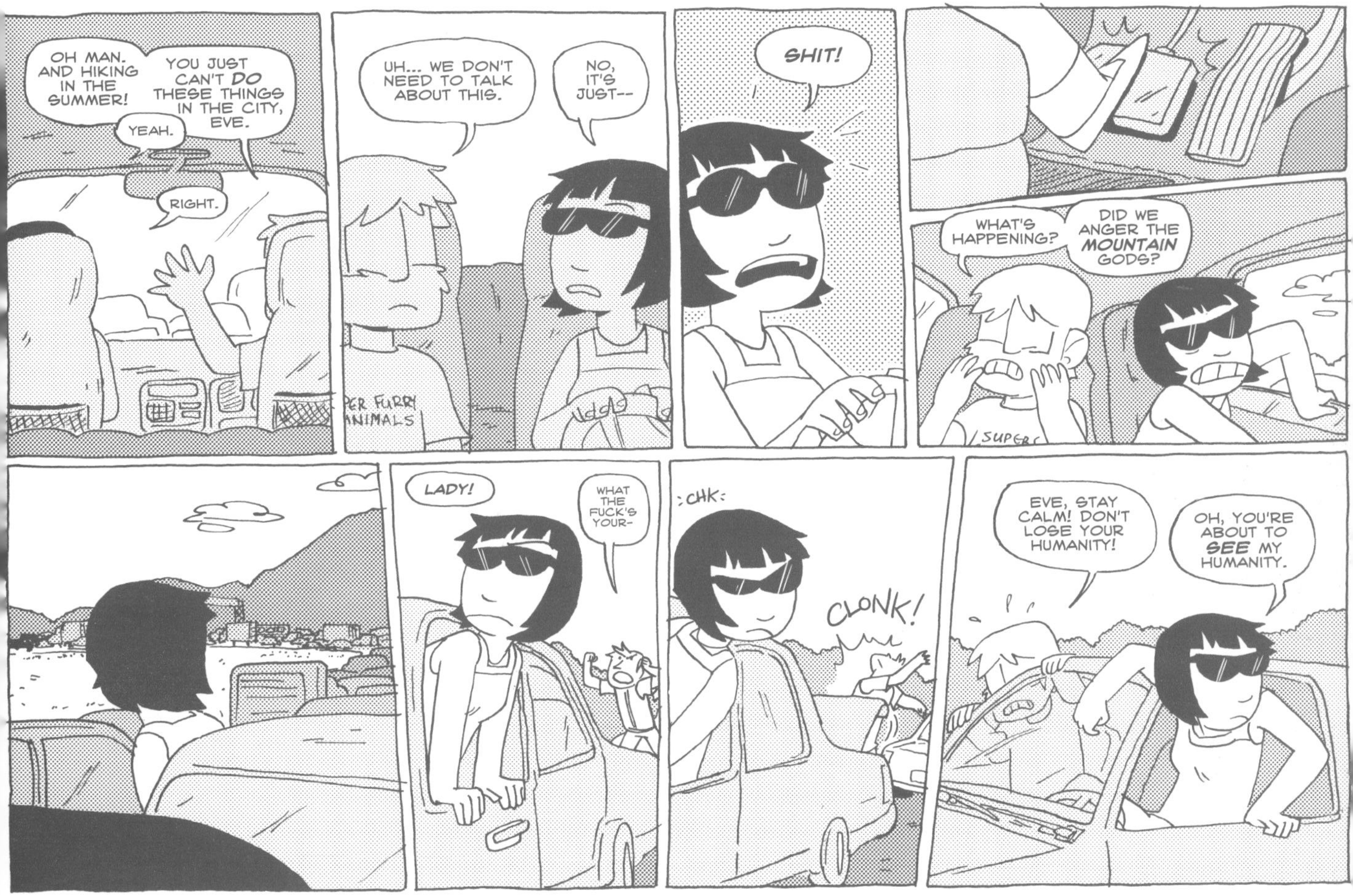
OH MAN. AND HIKING IN THE SUMMER!
YOU JUST CAN'T DO THESE THINGS IN THE CITY, EVE.
YEAH.
RIGHT.
UH... WE DON'T NEED TO TALK ABOUT THIS.
NO, IT'S JUST--
PER FURRY ANIMALS
SHIT!
WHAT'S HAPPENING?
DID WE ANGER THE MOUNTAIN GODS?
LADY!
WHAT THE FUCK'S YOUR-
:CHK:
CLONK!
EVE, STAY CALM! DON'T LOSE YOUR HUMANITY!
OH, YOU'RE ABOUT TO SEE MY HUMANITY.

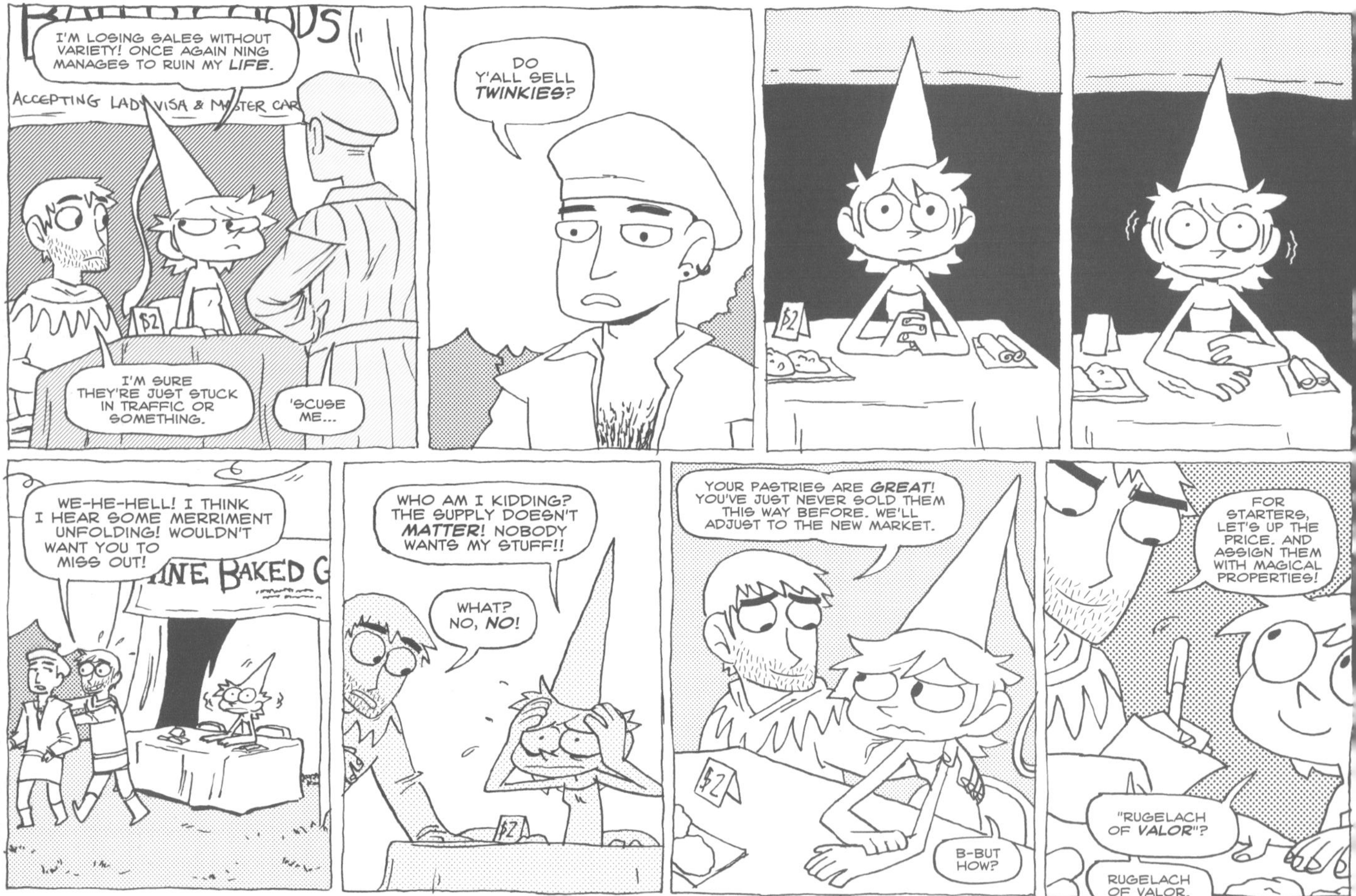
I'M LOSING SALES WITHOUT VARIETY! ONCE AGAIN NING MANAGES TO RUIN MY LIFE.
ACCEPTING LADY VISA & MASTER CAR
$2
I'M SURE THEY'RE JUST STUCK IN TRAFFIC OR SOMETHING.
'SCUSE ME...
DO Y'ALL SELL TWINKIES?
$2
WE-HE-HELL! I THINK I HEAR SOME MERRIMENT UNFOLDING! WOULDN'T WANT YOU TO MISS OUT!
INE BAKED G
WHO AM I KIDDING? THE SUPPLY DOESN'T MATTER! NOBODY WANTS MY STUFF!!
WHAT? NO, NO!
$2
YOUR PASTRIES ARE GREAT! YOU'VE JUST NEVER SOLD THEM THIS WAY BEFORE. WE'LL ADJUST TO THE NEW MARKET.
$2
B-BUT HOW?
FOR STARTERS, LET'S UP THE PRICE. AND ASSIGN THEM WITH MAGICAL PROPERTIES!
"RUGELACH OF VALOR"?
RUGELACH OF VALOR.

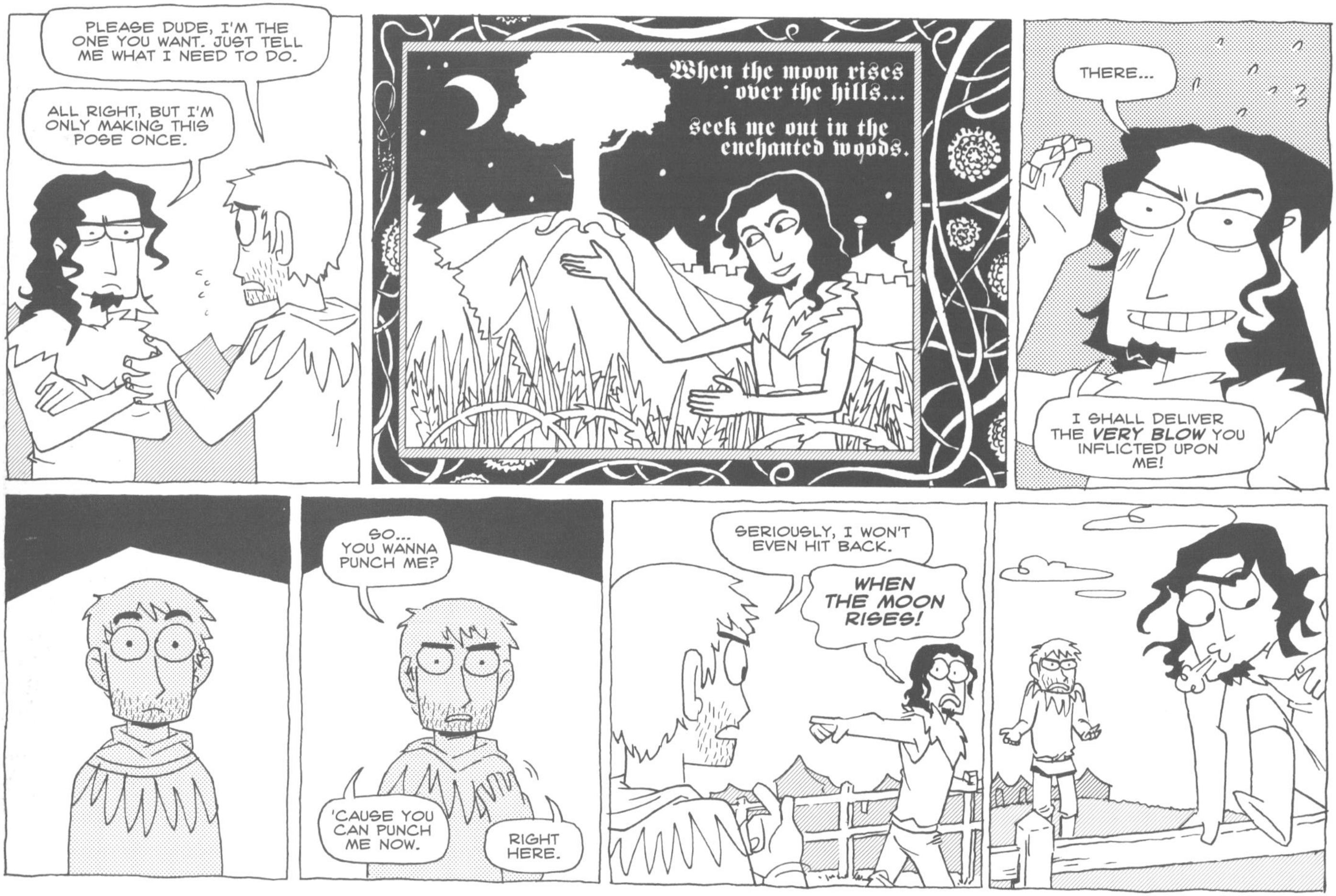
PLEASE DUDE, I'M THE ONE YOU WANT. JUST TELL ME WHAT I NEED TO DO.
ALL RIGHT, BUT I'M ONLY MAKING THIS POSE ONCE.
When the moon rises over the hills...
seek me out in the enchanted woods.
THERE...
I SHALL DELIVER THE VERY BLOW YOU INFLICTED UPON ME!
SO... YOU WANNA PUNCH ME?
'CAUSE YOU CAN PUNCH ME NOW.
RIGHT HERE.
SERIOUSLY, I WON'T EVEN HIT BACK.
WHEN THE MOON RISES!

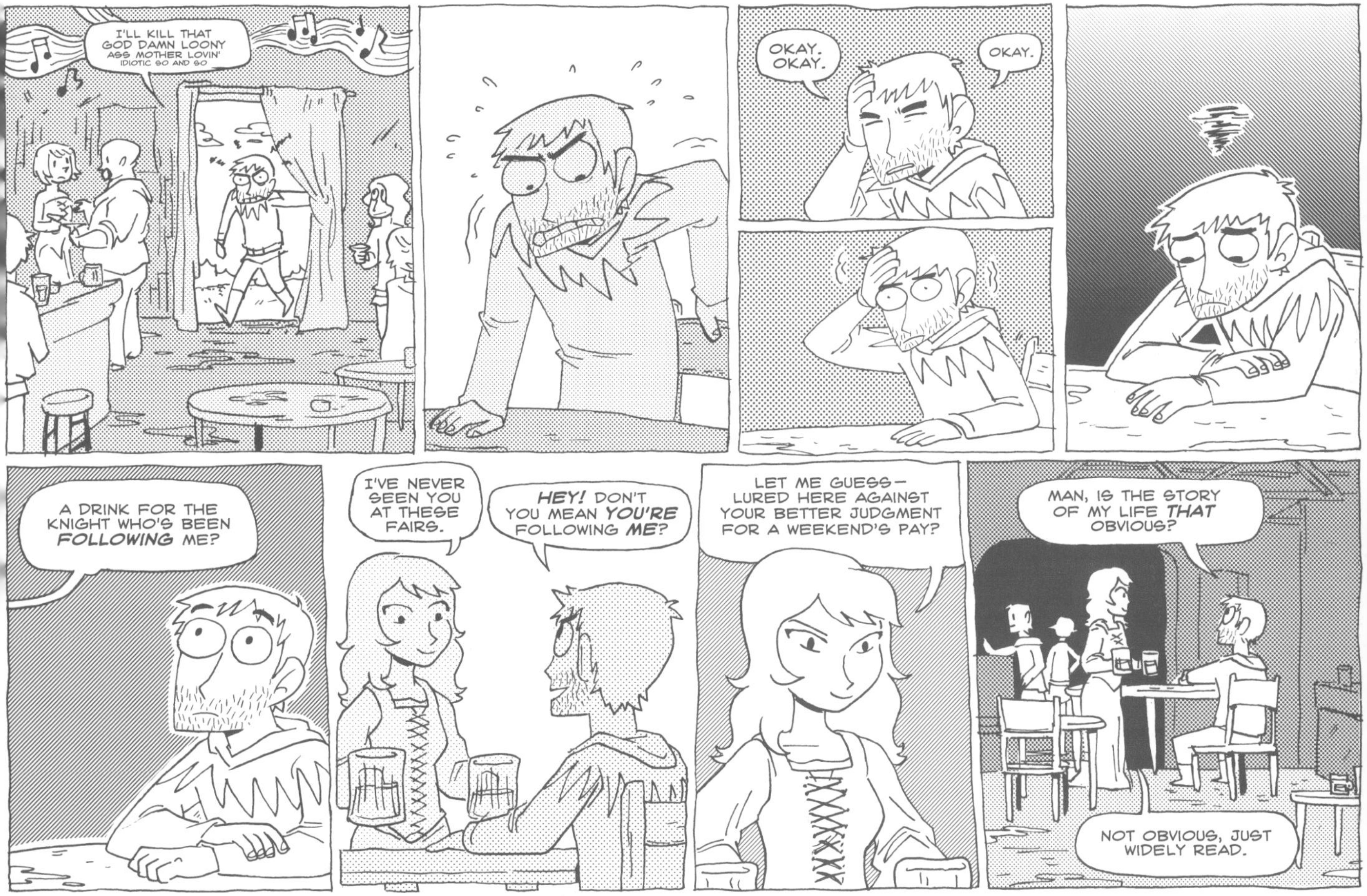
I'LL KILL THAT GOD DAMN LOONY ASS MOTHER LOVIN' IDIOTIC SO AND SO
OKAY. OKAY.
OKAY.
A DRINK FOR THE KNIGHT WHO'S BEEN *FOLLOWING* ME?
I'VE NEVER SEEN YOU AT THESE FAIRS.
HEY! DON'T YOU MEAN *YOU'RE* FOLLOWING *ME*?
LET ME GUESS— LURED HERE AGAINST YOUR BETTER JUDGMENT FOR A WEEKEND'S PAY?
MAN, IS THE STORY OF MY LIFE *THAT* OBVIOUS?
NOT OBVIOUS, JUST WIDELY READ.

I HAVE BEFORE ME THE BOLDEST WARRIORS IN THE LAND.

COURAGEOUS UPHOLDERS OF THE CHIVALRIC CODE AND ALL ITS VALUES!

NOW, I'LL NEED YOU TO LEAN YOUR HEAD ON THE KILTED MAN'S LAP...

WHAT?

BEHOLD, TRUE BELIEVERS -- THE POWER OF *MAGIC!*

WOBBLE WOBBLE

CLAP CLAP CLAP CLAP CLAP CLAP
WOO! YEAH!! CLAP
CLAP CLAP CLAP
CLAP CLAP CLAP CLAP CLAP
CLAP HURRAH! CLAP CLAP CLAP
CLAP YAYY! CLAP
CLAP CLAP

WHUMP.

CLUNK!

NOW DO YOU BELIEVE I'M A SHITTY KNIGHT?

I DUNNO -- YOU *VANQUISHED* THAT GUY'S BALLS.

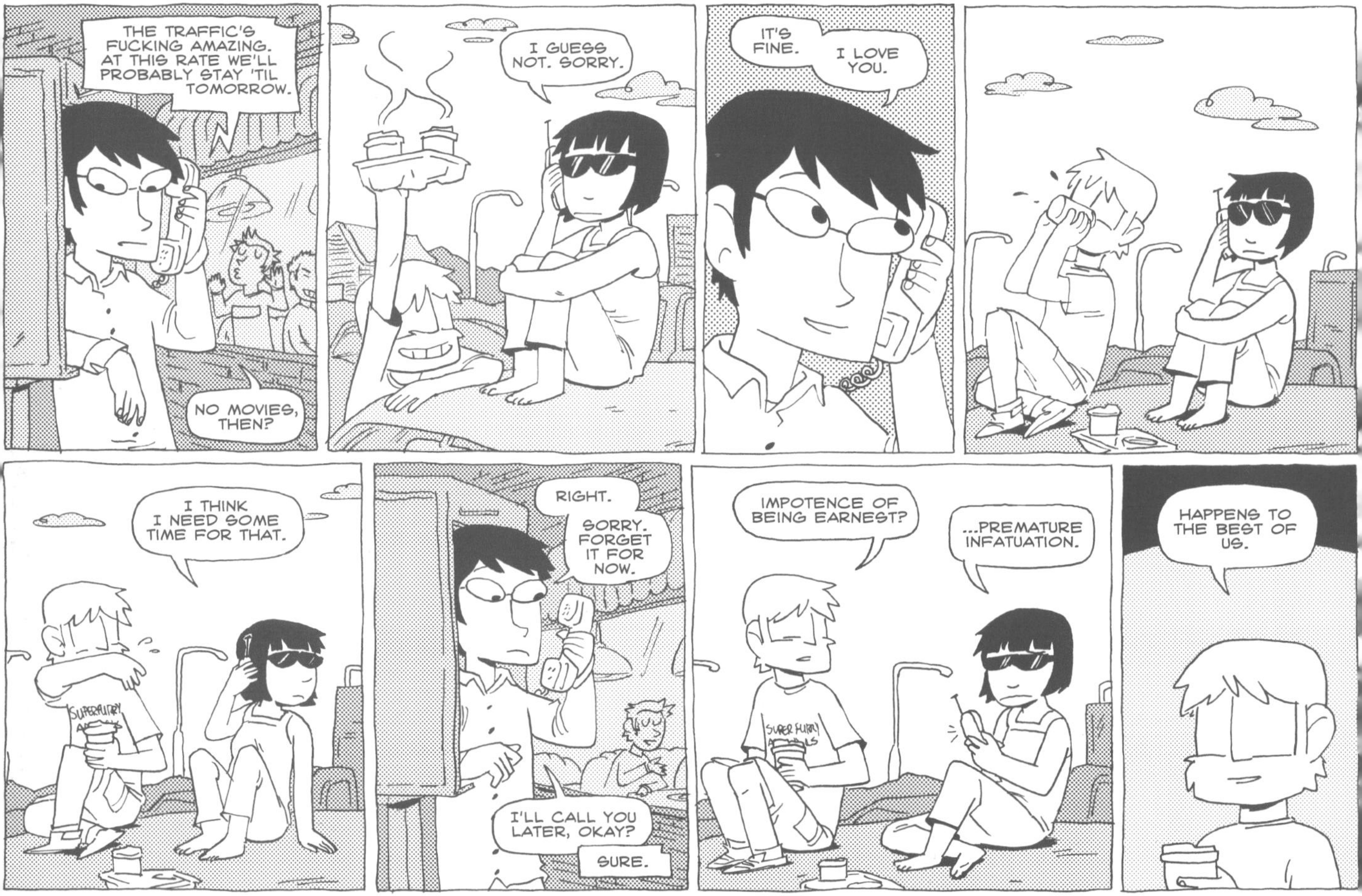
THE TRAFFIC'S FUCKING AMAZING. AT THIS RATE WE'LL PROBABLY STAY 'TIL TOMORROW.
NO MOVIES, THEN?
I GUESS NOT. SORRY.
IT'S FINE.
I LOVE YOU.
I THINK I NEED SOME TIME FOR THAT.
RIGHT.
SORRY. FORGET IT FOR NOW.
I'LL CALL YOU LATER, OKAY?
SURE.
IMPOTENCE OF BEING EARNEST?
...PREMATURE INFATUATION.
HAPPENS TO THE BEST OF US.

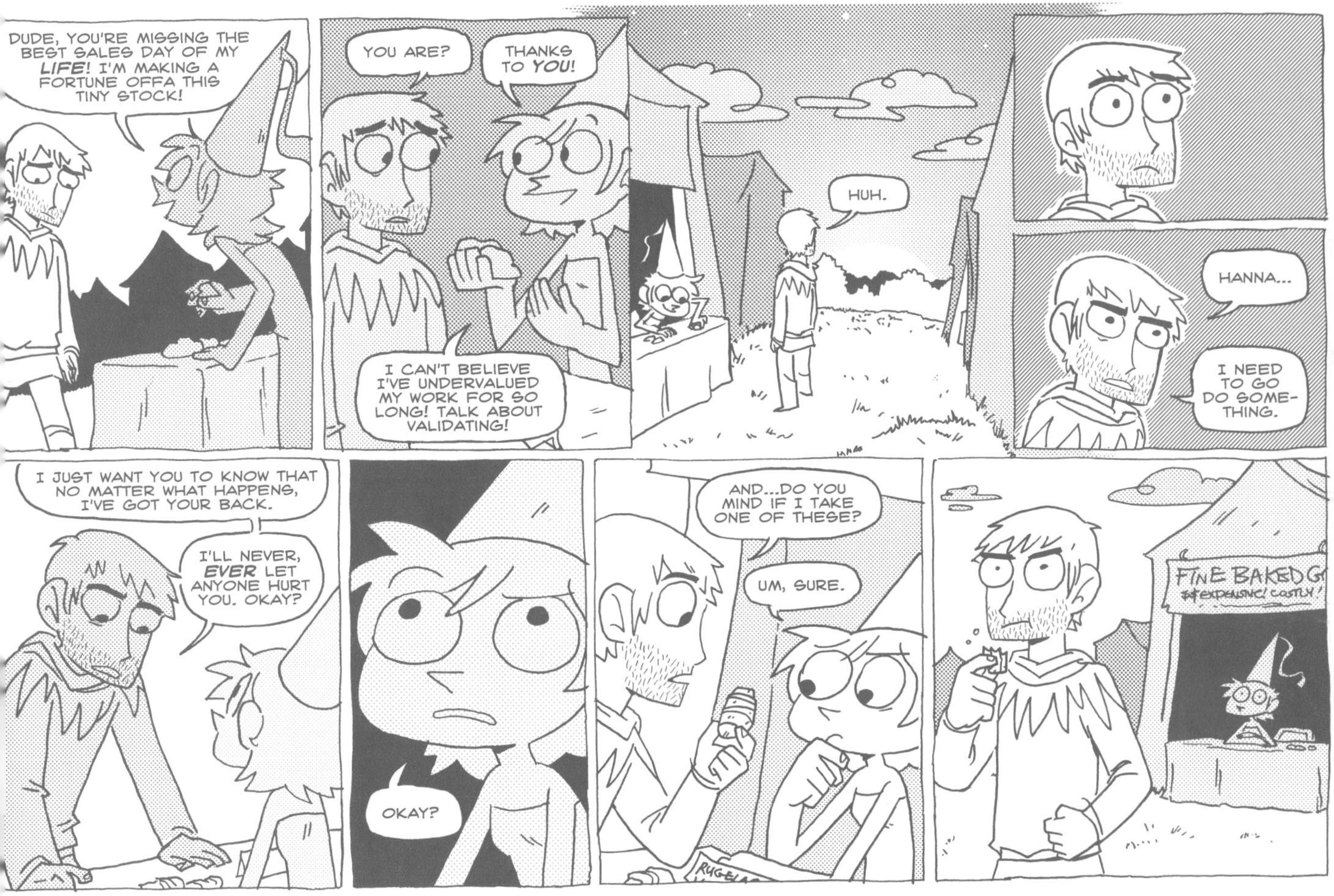
DUDE, YOU'RE MISSING THE BEST SALES DAY OF MY LIFE! I'M MAKING A FORTUNE OFFA THIS TINY STOCK!
YOU ARE?
THANKS TO YOU!
I CAN'T BELIEVE I'VE UNDERVALUED MY WORK FOR SO LONG! TALK ABOUT VALIDATING!
HUH.
HANNA...
I NEED TO GO DO SOME-THING.
I JUST WANT YOU TO KNOW THAT NO MATTER WHAT HAPPENS, I'VE GOT YOUR BACK.
I'LL NEVER, EVER LET ANYONE HURT YOU. OKAY?
OKAY?
AND...DO YOU MIND IF I TAKE ONE OF THESE?
UM, SURE.
FINE BAKED G

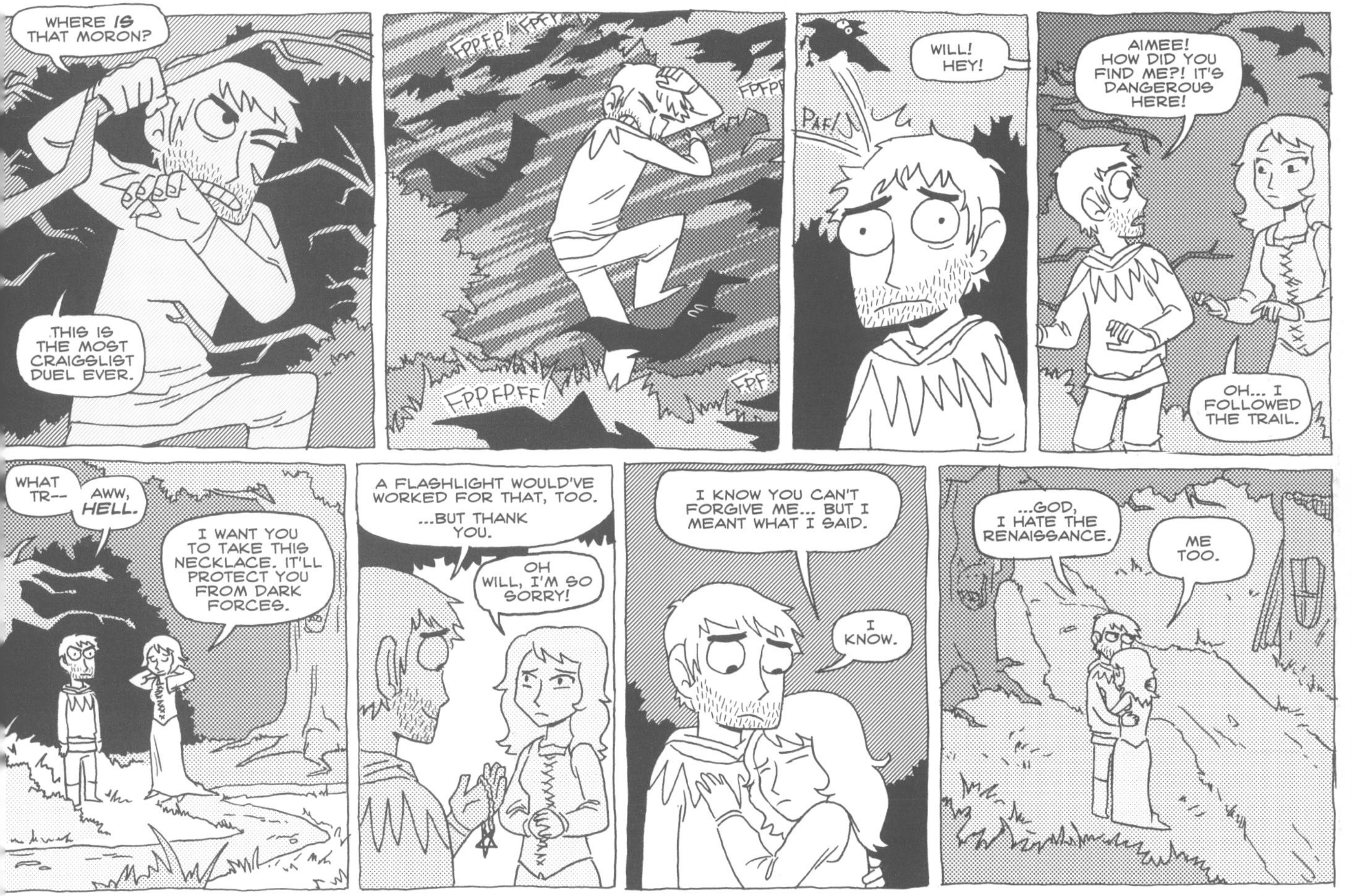
WHERE IS THAT MORON?
THIS IS THE MOST CRAIGSLIST DUEL EVER.
FPPFP! FPF!
FPFP
FPPFPFF!
FPF
PAF!
WILL! HEY!
AIMEE! HOW DID YOU FIND ME?! IT'S DANGEROUS HERE!
OH... I FOLLOWED THE TRAIL.
WHAT TR--
AWW, HELL.
I WANT YOU TO TAKE THIS NECKLACE. IT'LL PROTECT YOU FROM DARK FORCES.
A FLASHLIGHT WOULD'VE WORKED FOR THAT, TOO.
...BUT THANK YOU.
OH WILL, I'M SO SORRY!
I KNOW YOU CAN'T FORGIVE ME... BUT I MEANT WHAT I SAID.
I KNOW.
...GOD, I HATE THE RENAISSANCE.
ME TOO.

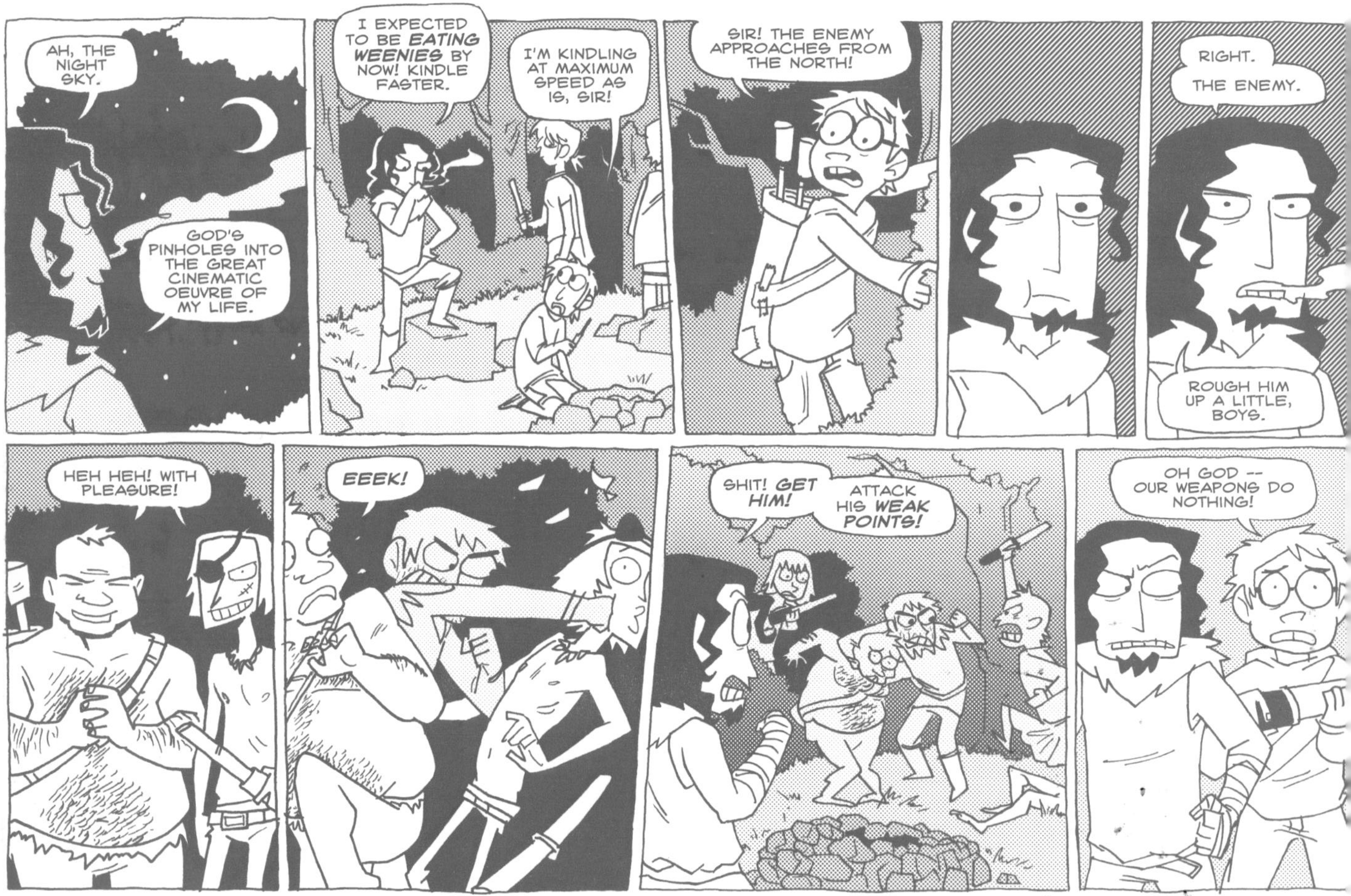
AH, THE NIGHT SKY.
GOD'S PINHOLES INTO THE GREAT CINEMATIC OEUVRE OF MY LIFE.
I EXPECTED TO BE EATING WEENIES BY NOW! KINDLE FASTER.
I'M KINDLING AT MAXIMUM SPEED AS IS, SIR!
SIR! THE ENEMY APPROACHES FROM THE NORTH!
RIGHT.
THE ENEMY.
ROUGH HIM UP A LITTLE, BOYS.
HEH HEH! WITH PLEASURE!
EEEK!
SHIT! GET HIM!
ATTACK HIS WEAK POINTS!
OH GOD -- OUR WEAPONS DO NOTHING!

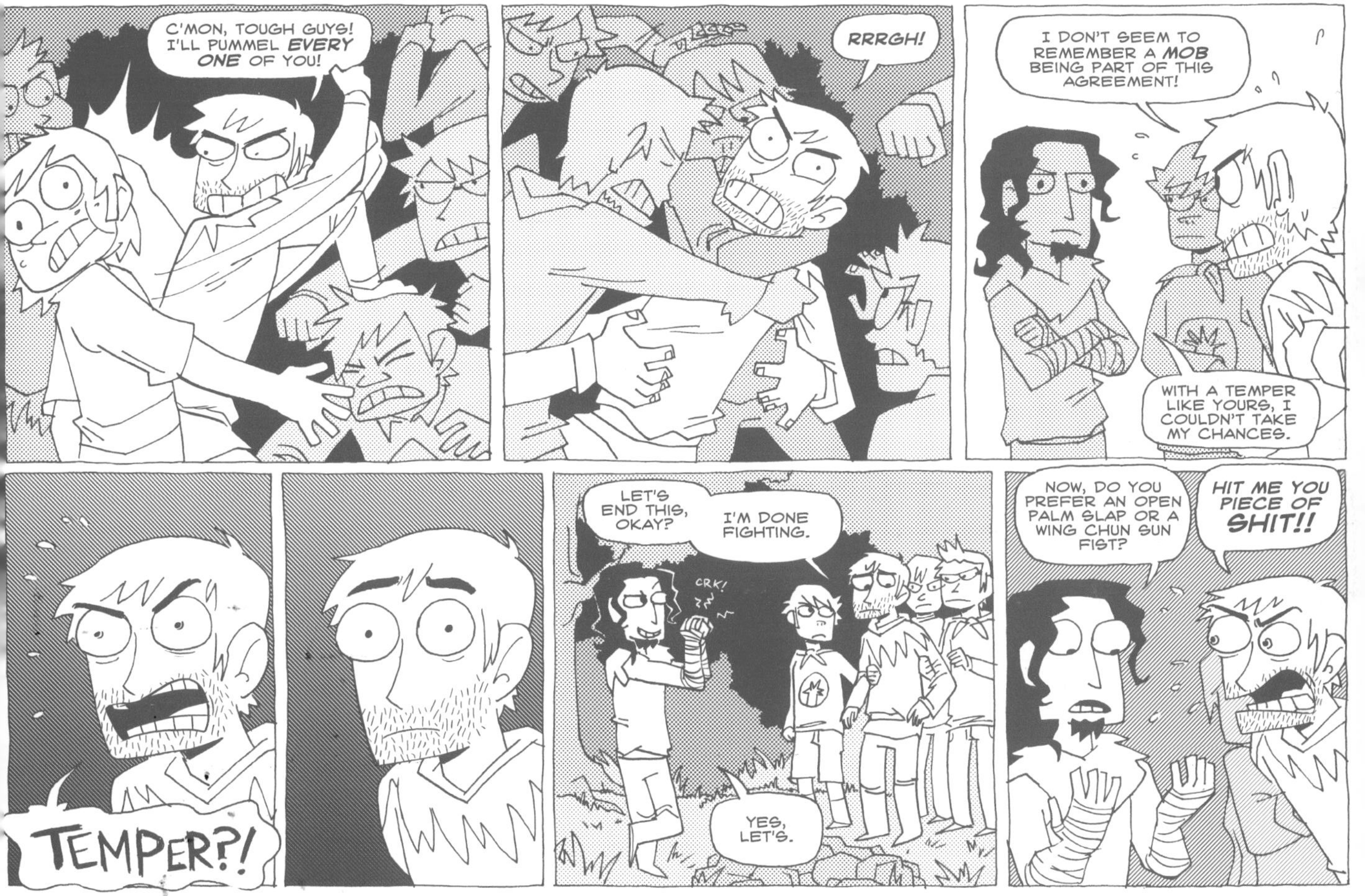
C'MON, TOUGH GUYS! I'LL PUMMEL EVERY ONE OF YOU!
RRRGH!
I DON'T SEEM TO REMEMBER A MOB BEING PART OF THIS AGREEMENT!
WITH A TEMPER LIKE YOURS, I COULDN'T TAKE MY CHANCES.
TEMPER?!
LET'S END THIS, OKAY?
I'M DONE FIGHTING.
CRK!
YES, LET'S.
NOW, DO YOU PREFER AN OPEN PALM SLAP OR A WING CHUN SUN FIST?
HIT ME YOU PIECE OF SHIT!!

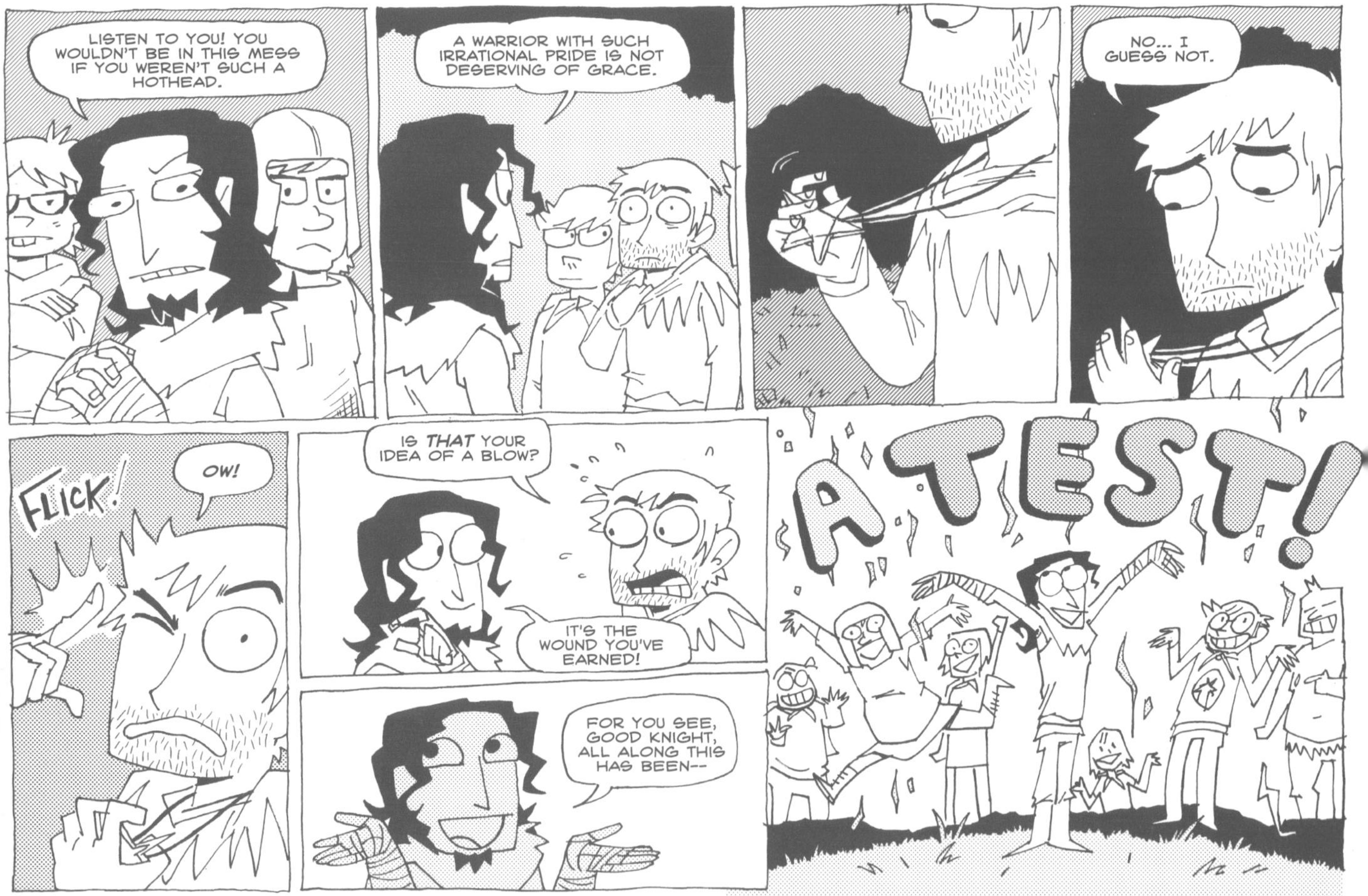
LISTEN TO YOU! YOU WOULDN'T BE IN THIS MESS IF YOU WEREN'T SUCH A HOTHEAD.
A WARRIOR WITH SUCH IRRATIONAL PRIDE IS NOT DESERVING OF GRACE.
NO... I GUESS NOT.
FLICK!
OW!
IS *THAT* YOUR IDEA OF A BLOW?
IT'S THE WOUND YOU'VE EARNED!
FOR YOU SEE, GOOD KNIGHT, ALL ALONG THIS HAS BEEN--
A TEST!

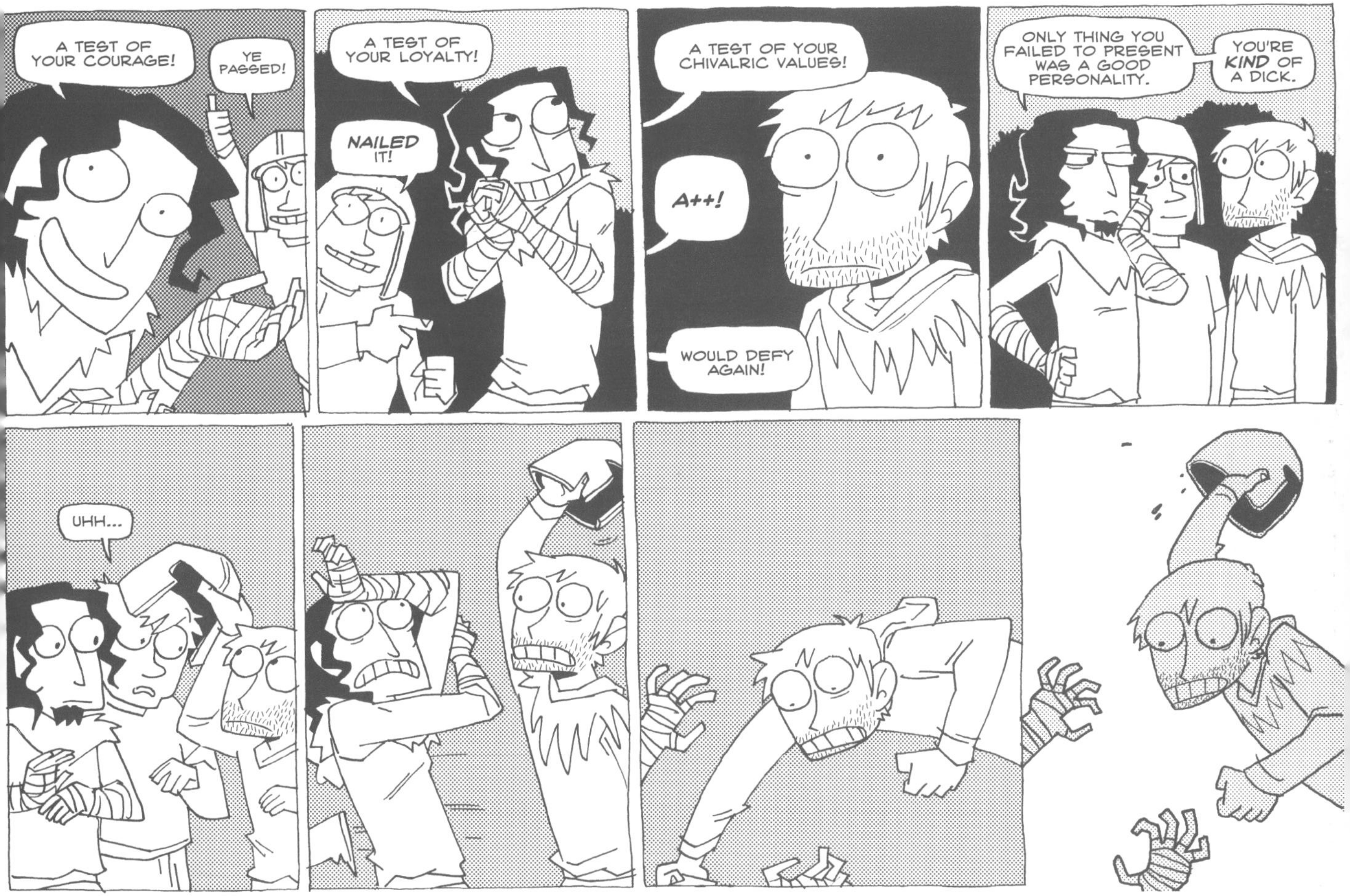
A TEST OF YOUR COURAGE!
YE PASSED!
A TEST OF YOUR LOYALTY!
NAILED IT!
A TEST OF YOUR CHIVALRIC VALUES!
A++!
WOULD DEFY AGAIN!
ONLY THING YOU FAILED TO PRESENT WAS A GOOD PERSONALITY.
YOU'RE KIND OF A DICK.
UHH...

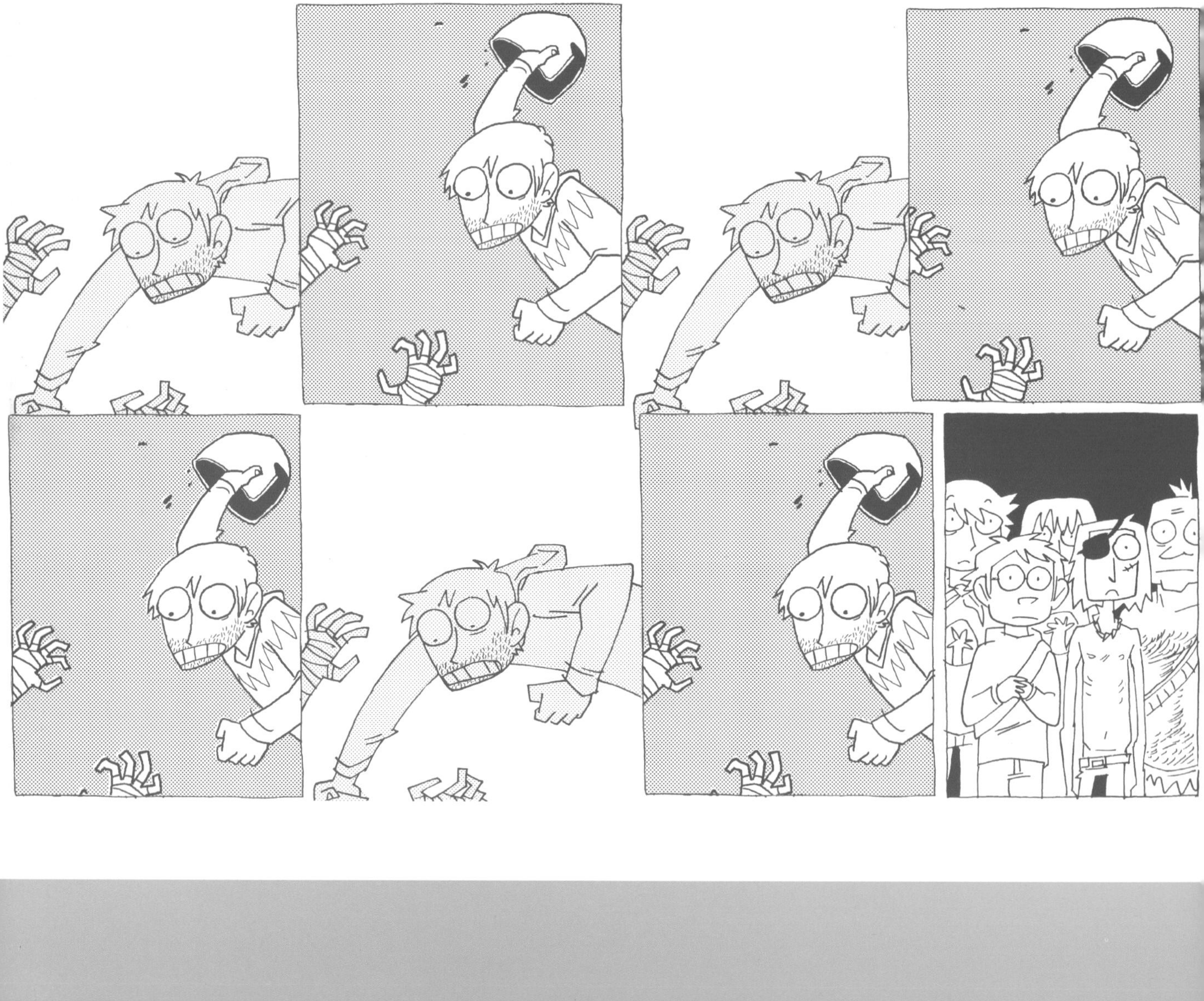

YOU SHOULD'VE SEEN ME, HONEY! I'M LIKE AN ETSY ON WHEELS. AND LOOKIT ALL THE *CASH* I MADE! NOTHING FOR THE MIDDLEMAN.

I *KNEW* YOU COULD DO IT ON YOUR OWN!

YEEAAH, BUT I CAN'T *WAIT* TO HAND IT OFF TO THE GROCERY STORES AGAIN.

HUH?

SUPER FU IMALS

GOD, HAULING MY OWN STOCK AROUND? DEALING DIRECTLY WITH CUSTOMERS AND CRITICS? YEESH. I'D GO INSANE.

SUPER FURRY ANIMALS

SO... YOU'D RATHER SOMEONE ELSE MARKET YOUR WORK AND TAKE ALL YOUR MONEY?

YES.

HOORAY FOR SANITY!

SUPER FURRY ANIMALS

SO, WILL... WHAT HAVE WE LEARNED FROM THIS MONUMENTAL WASTE OF TIME?

THAT COURTLY LOVE IS A *MYTH*. IT WAS BULLSHIT WHEN IT WAS INVENTED. IT'S BULLSHIT TODAY.

OH, *YEAH*. AGREED.

KOBA

NO WAIT. I THOUGHT YOU SAID *COURTNEY* LOVE.

KOBAYAS

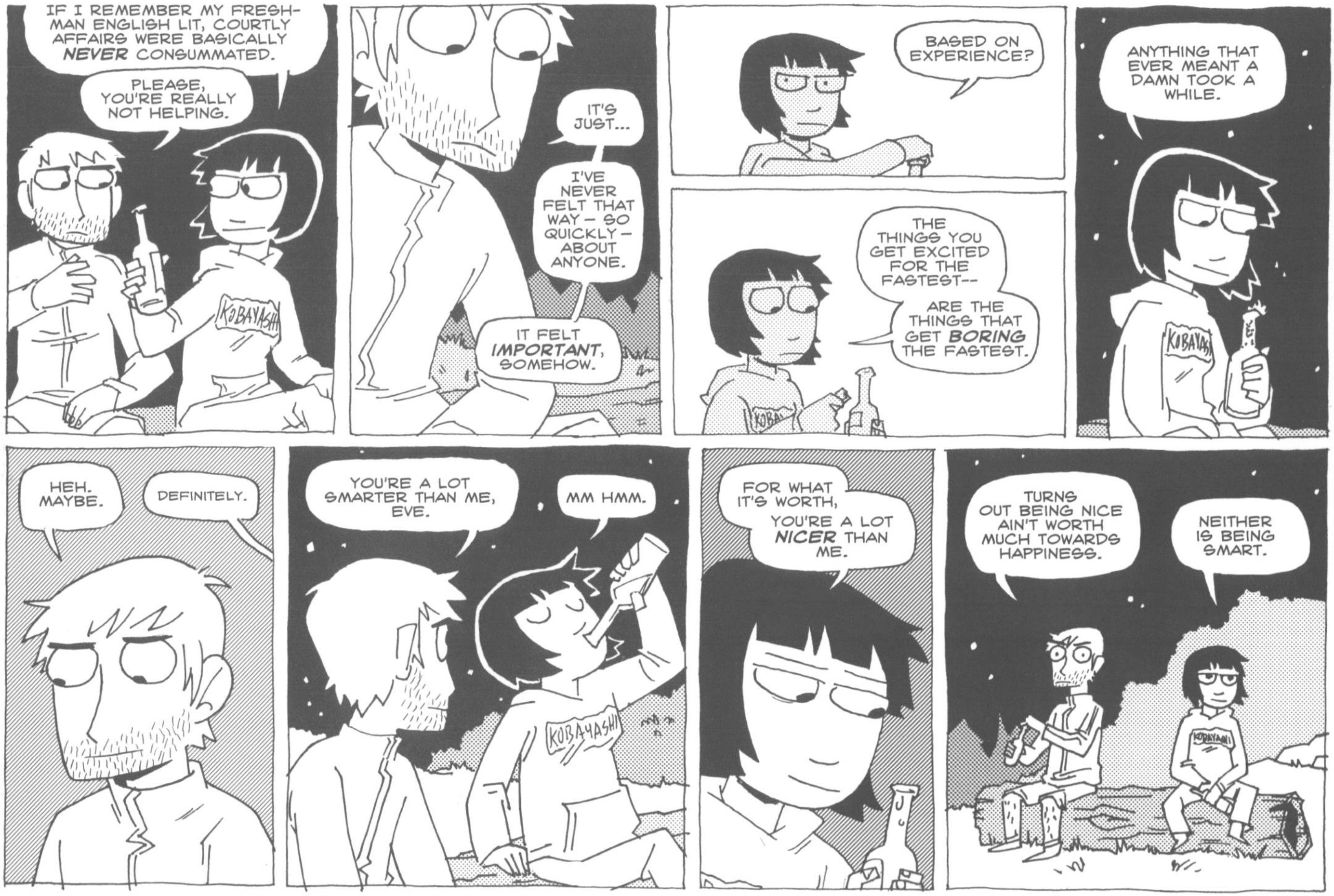
IF I REMEMBER MY FRESHMAN ENGLISH LIT, COURTLY AFFAIRS WERE BASICALLY NEVER CONSUMMATED.
PLEASE, YOU'RE REALLY NOT HELPING.
KOBAYASHI
IT'S JUST...
I'VE NEVER FELT THAT WAY – SO QUICKLY – ABOUT ANYONE.
IT FELT IMPORTANT, SOMEHOW.
BASED ON EXPERIENCE?
THE THINGS YOU GET EXCITED FOR THE FASTEST--
ARE THE THINGS THAT GET BORING THE FASTEST.
ANYTHING THAT EVER MEANT A DAMN TOOK A WHILE.
HEH. MAYBE.
DEFINITELY.
YOU'RE A LOT SMARTER THAN ME, EVE.
MM HMM.
KOBAYASHI
FOR WHAT IT'S WORTH,
YOU'RE A LOT NICER THAN ME.
TURNS OUT BEING NICE AIN'T WORTH MUCH TOWARDS HAPPINESS.
NEITHER IS BEING SMART.
KOBAYASHI

...SO THEN, WOULD YOU SAY I DONE GOOD?

OH, YOU DONE *GOOD.*

YOU SHOULDA SEEN ME, UNCLE OLLY. I MADE FULL USE OF MY THEATER ARTS DEGREE!

I *TOLD* YOUR MOM THAT'D PAY OFF.

NOW LET'S SEE IF THAT TWIGGY LITTLE OPPORTUNIST *THINKS TWICE* ABOUT ABANDONING MY NEEDS AND STEALING MY EMPLOYEES.

HEH. WELL. I WOULDN'T QUITE CALL HIM "TWIGGY."

NOW, ABOUT THOSE XANADU TICKETS...

"HIM"?

HUH? YOU KNOW. THE PASTRY DUDE I WAS PUNKING?

BURLY, HAIRY? KIND OF A PSYCHO?

THAT'S THE GUY, RIGHT?

HELLOO?

OH I WILL KILL YOU YOU GOSH DARN NO GOOD

MOTH FUCKIN SON UNHO FOR

EEE EEE EE

217

dumbo

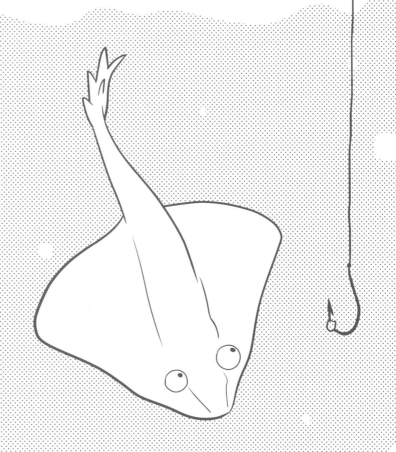

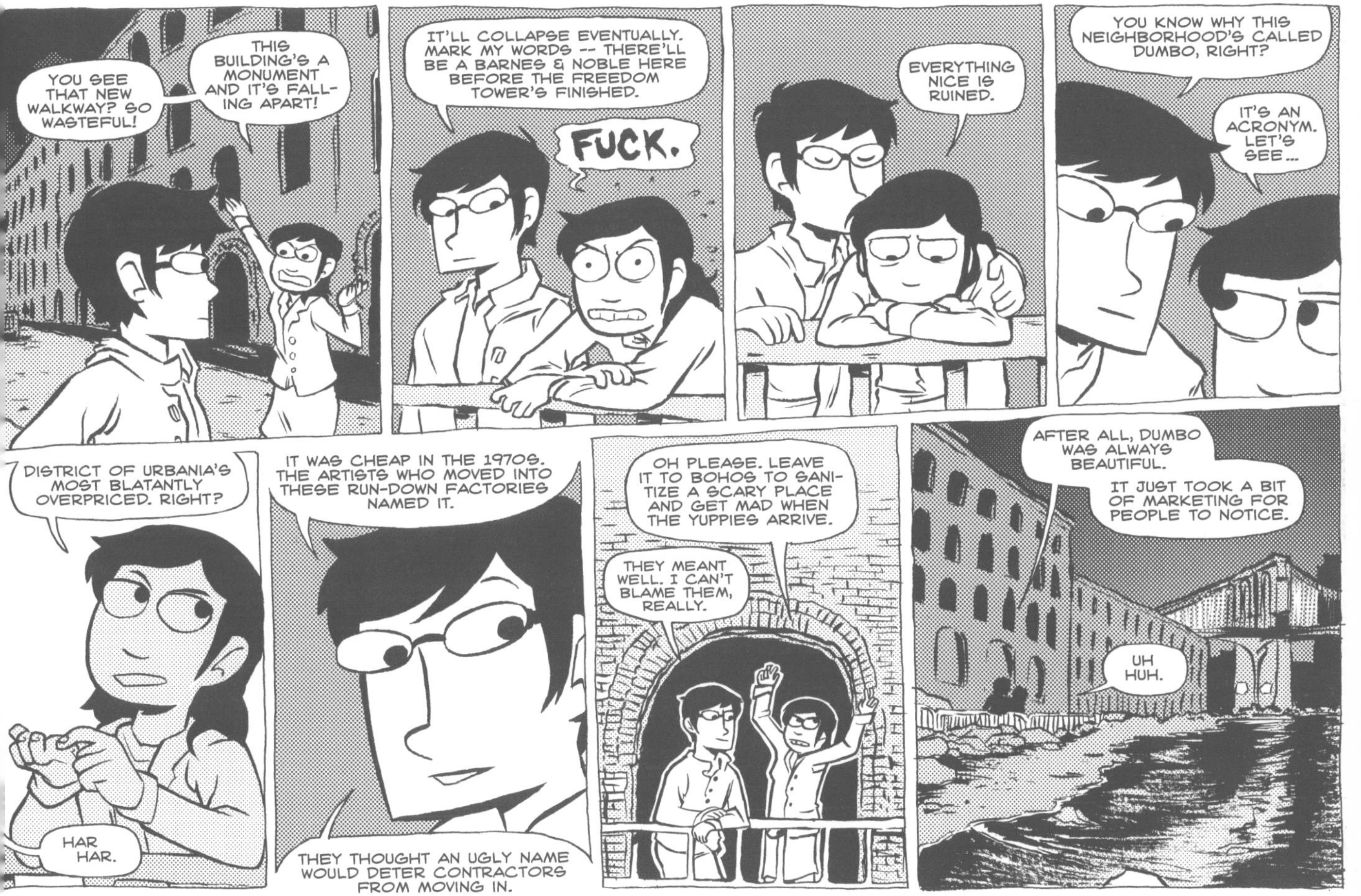
YOU SEE THAT NEW WALKWAY? SO WASTEFUL!
THIS BUILDING'S A MONUMENT AND IT'S FALLING APART!
IT'LL COLLAPSE EVENTUALLY. MARK MY WORDS -- THERE'LL BE A BARNES & NOBLE HERE BEFORE THE FREEDOM TOWER'S FINISHED.
FUCK.
EVERYTHING NICE IS RUINED.
YOU KNOW WHY THIS NEIGHBORHOOD'S CALLED DUMBO, RIGHT?
IT'S AN ACRONYM. LET'S SEE...
DISTRICT OF URBANIA'S MOST BLATANTLY OVERPRICED. RIGHT?
HAR HAR.
IT WAS CHEAP IN THE 1970S. THE ARTISTS WHO MOVED INTO THESE RUN-DOWN FACTORIES NAMED IT.
THEY THOUGHT AN UGLY NAME WOULD DETER CONTRACTORS FROM MOVING IN.
OH PLEASE. LEAVE IT TO BOHOS TO SANITIZE A SCARY PLACE AND GET MAD WHEN THE YUPPIES ARRIVE.
THEY MEANT WELL. I CAN'T BLAME THEM, REALLY.
AFTER ALL, DUMBO WAS ALWAYS BEAUTIFUL.
IT JUST TOOK A BIT OF MARKETING FOR PEOPLE TO NOTICE.
UH HUH.

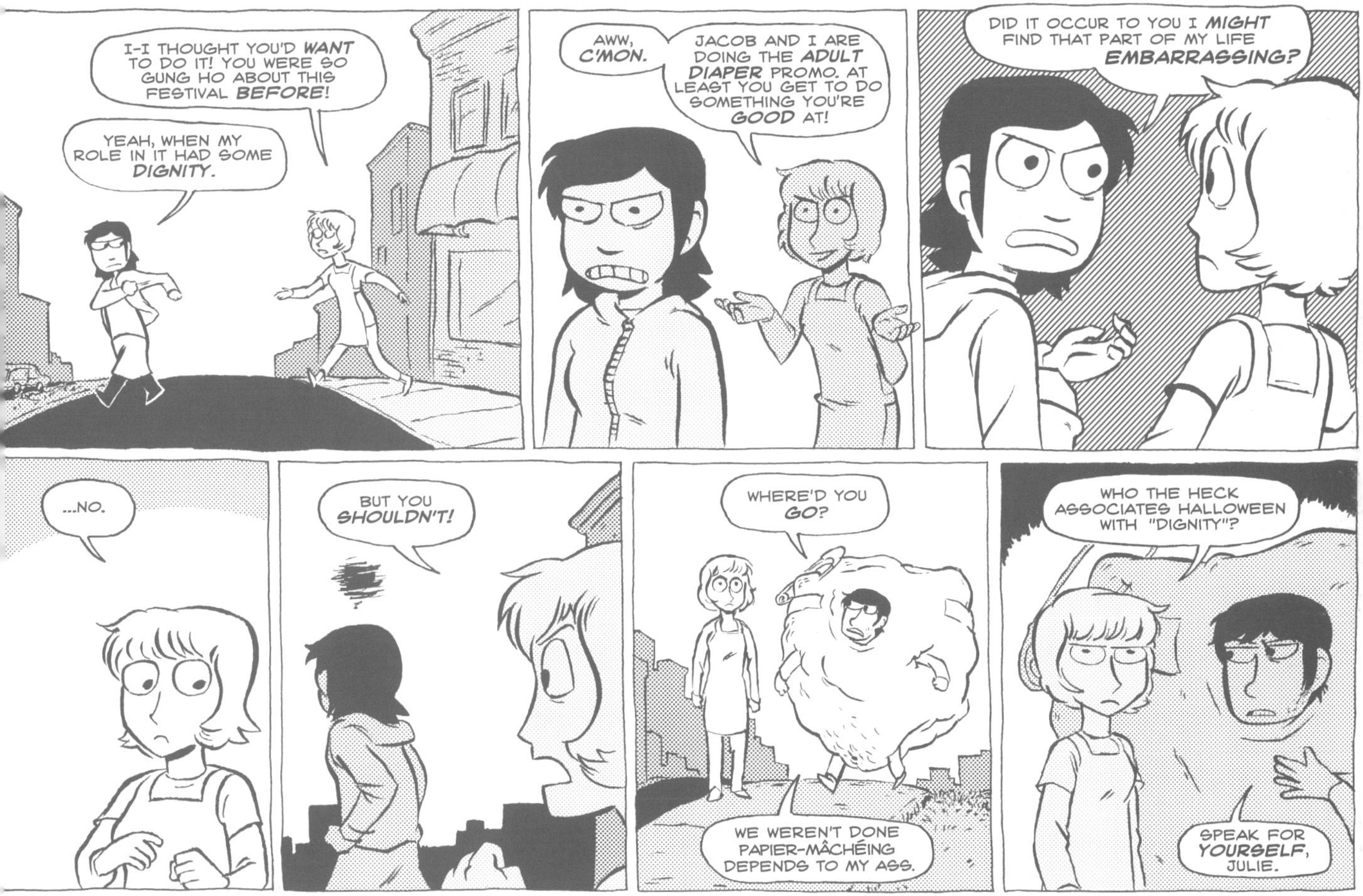
I-I THOUGHT YOU'D WANT TO DO IT! YOU WERE SO GUNG HO ABOUT THIS FESTIVAL BEFORE!
YEAH, WHEN MY ROLE IN IT HAD SOME DIGNITY.
AWW, C'MON.
JACOB AND I ARE DOING THE ADULT DIAPER PROMO. AT LEAST YOU GET TO DO SOMETHING YOU'RE GOOD AT!
DID IT OCCUR TO YOU I MIGHT FIND THAT PART OF MY LIFE EMBARRASSING?
...NO.
BUT YOU SHOULDN'T!
WHERE'D YOU GO?
WE WEREN'T DONE PAPIER-MÂCHÉING DEPENDS TO MY ASS.
WHO THE HECK ASSOCIATES HALLOWEEN WITH "DIGNITY"?
SPEAK FOR YOURSELF, JULIE.

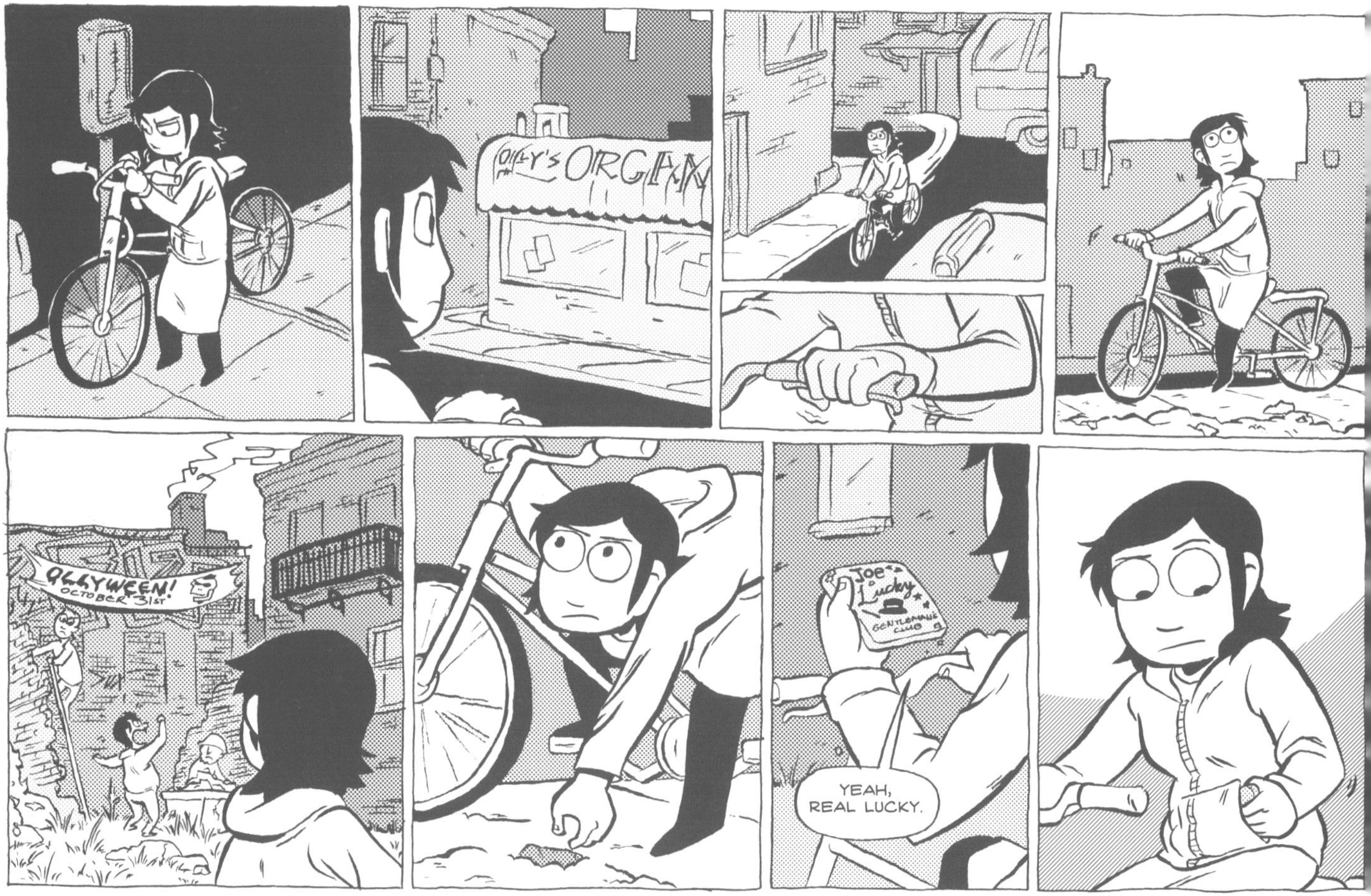
OLLY'S ORGAN
OLLYWEEN!
OCTOBER 31ST
Joe Lucky
GENTLEMAN'S CLUB
YEAH,
REAL LUCKY.

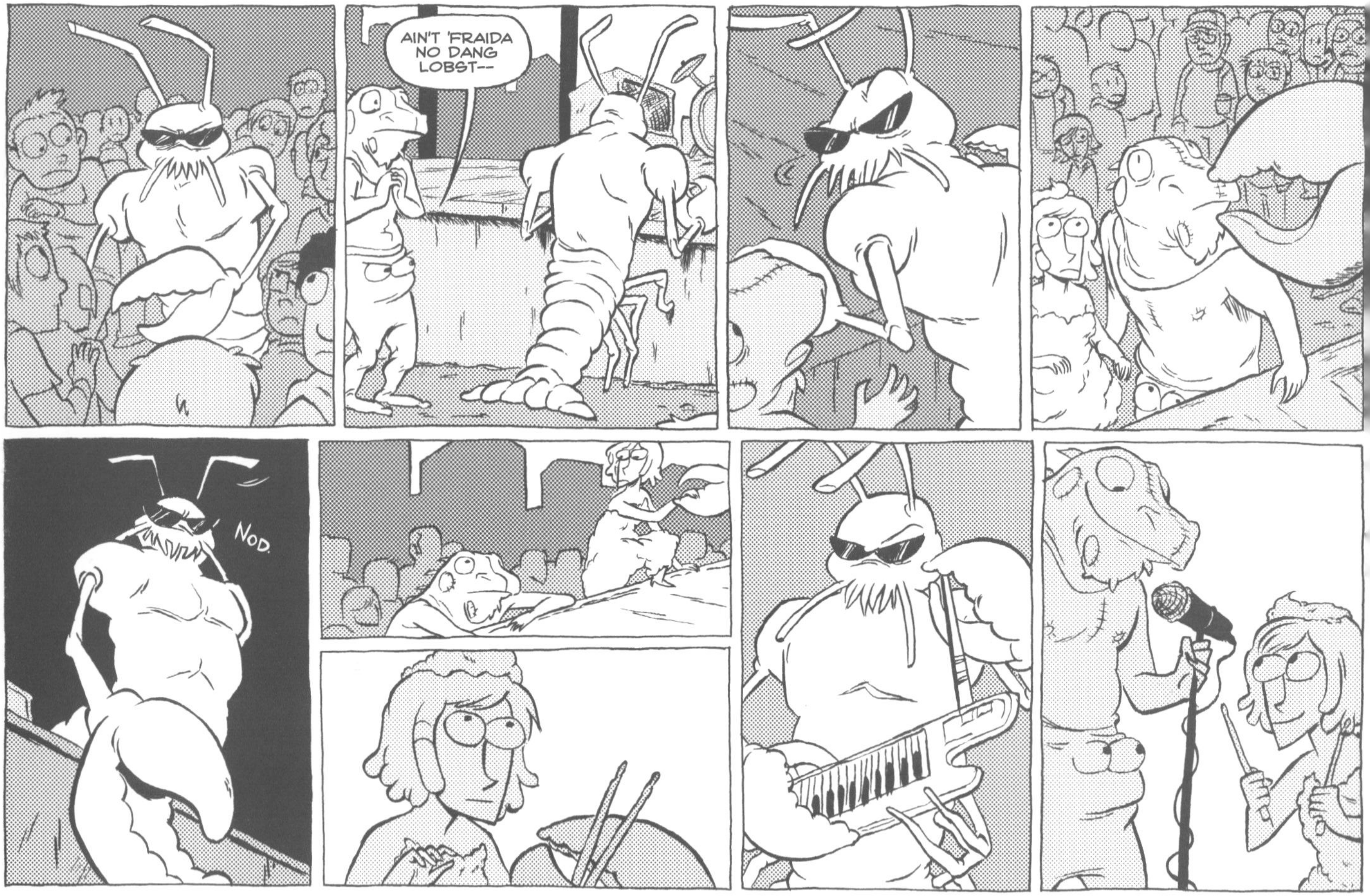
AIN'T 'FRAIDA NO DANG LOBST--
NOD.

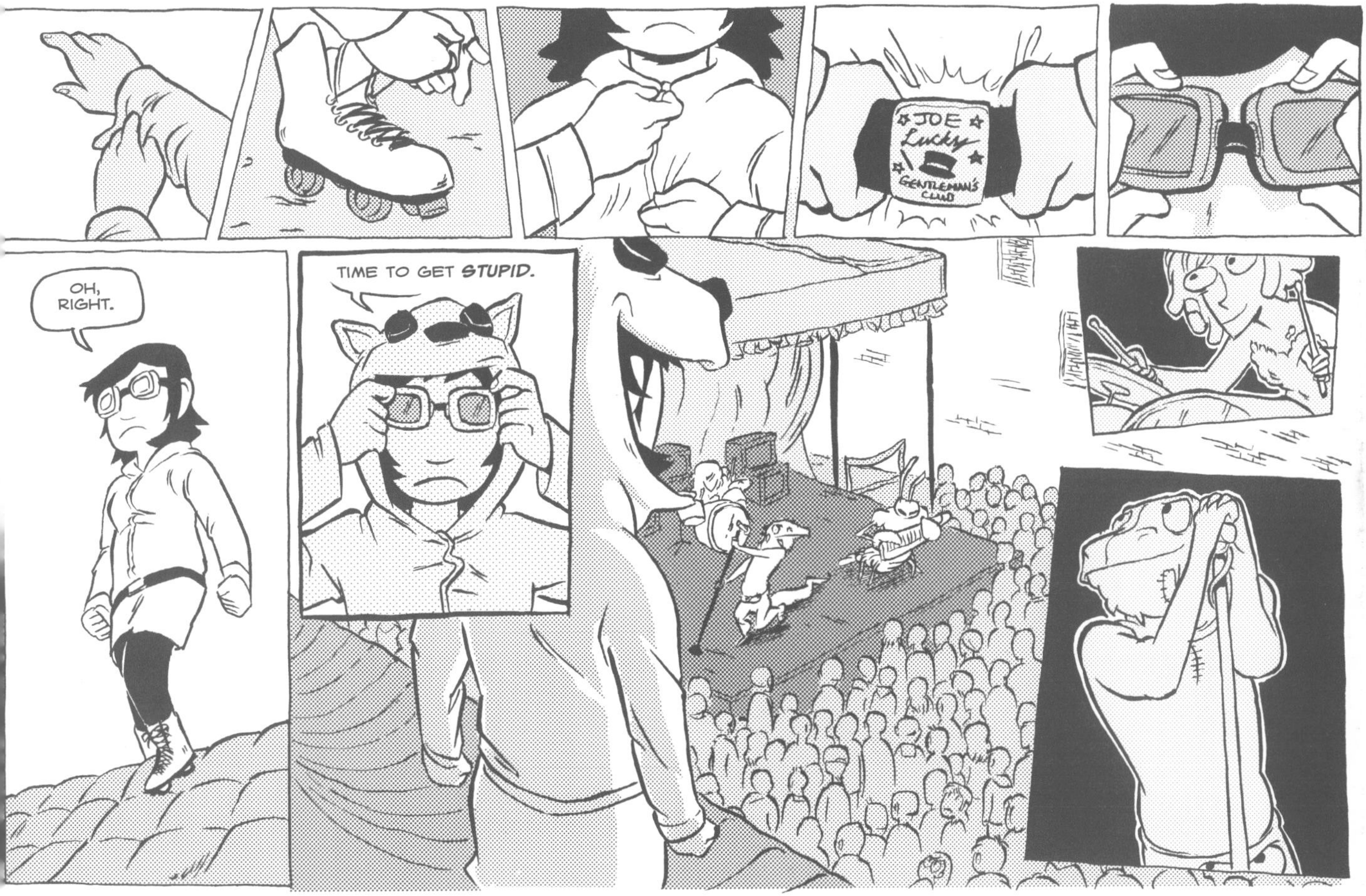
JOE
Lucky
GENTLEMAN'S CLUB
OH, RIGHT.
TIME TO GET STUPID.

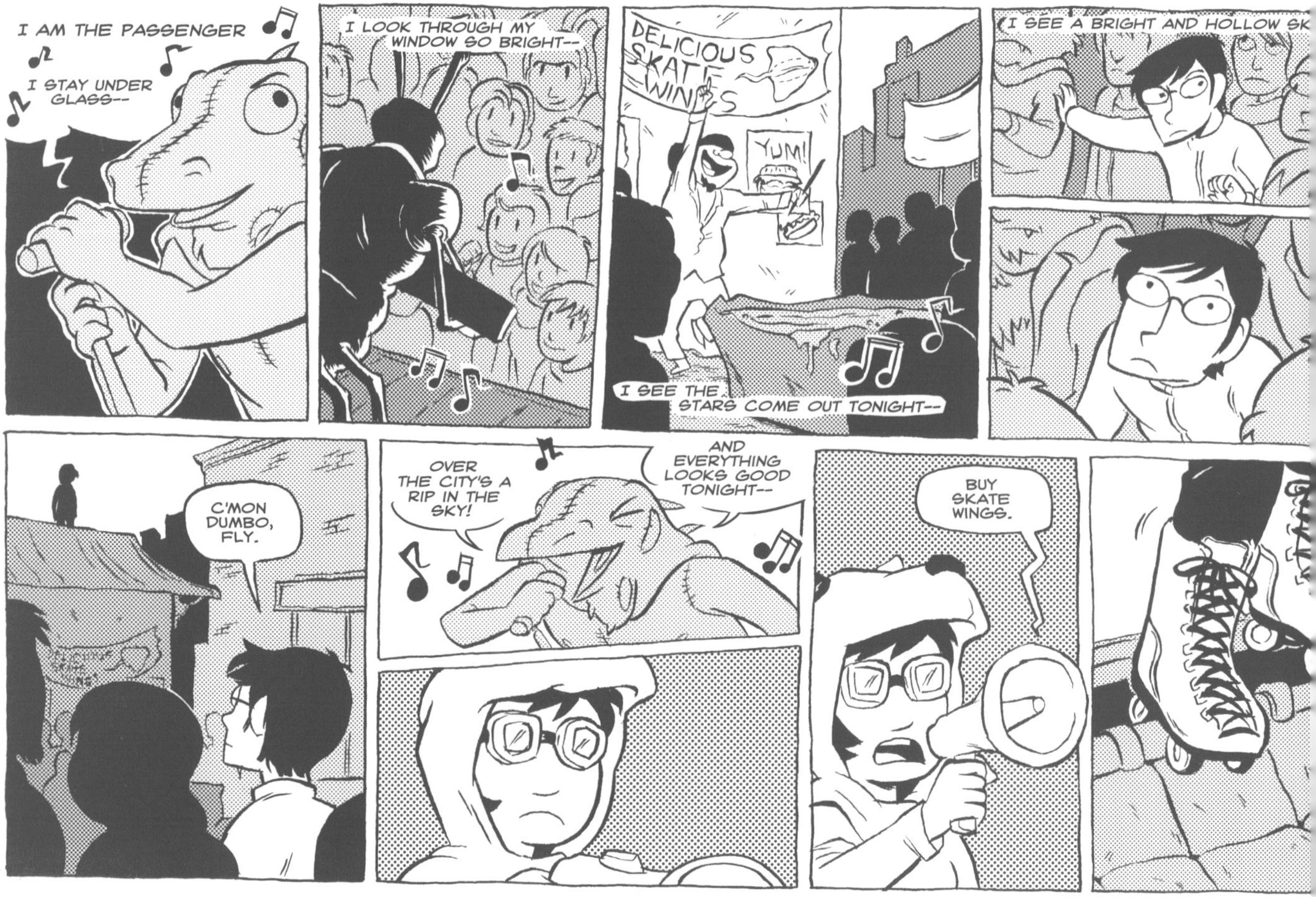
I AM THE PASSENGER
I STAY UNDER GLASS--
I LOOK THROUGH MY WINDOW SO BRIGHT--
DELICIOUS SKATE WINGS
YUM!
I SEE THE STARS COME OUT TONIGHT--
I SEE A BRIGHT AND HOLLOW SK
C'MON DUMBO, FLY.
OVER THE CITY'S A RIP IN THE SKY!
AND EVERYTHING LOOKS GOOD TONIGHT--
BUY SKATE WINGS.

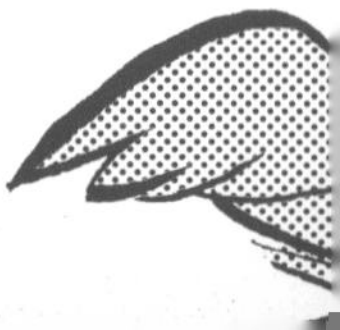

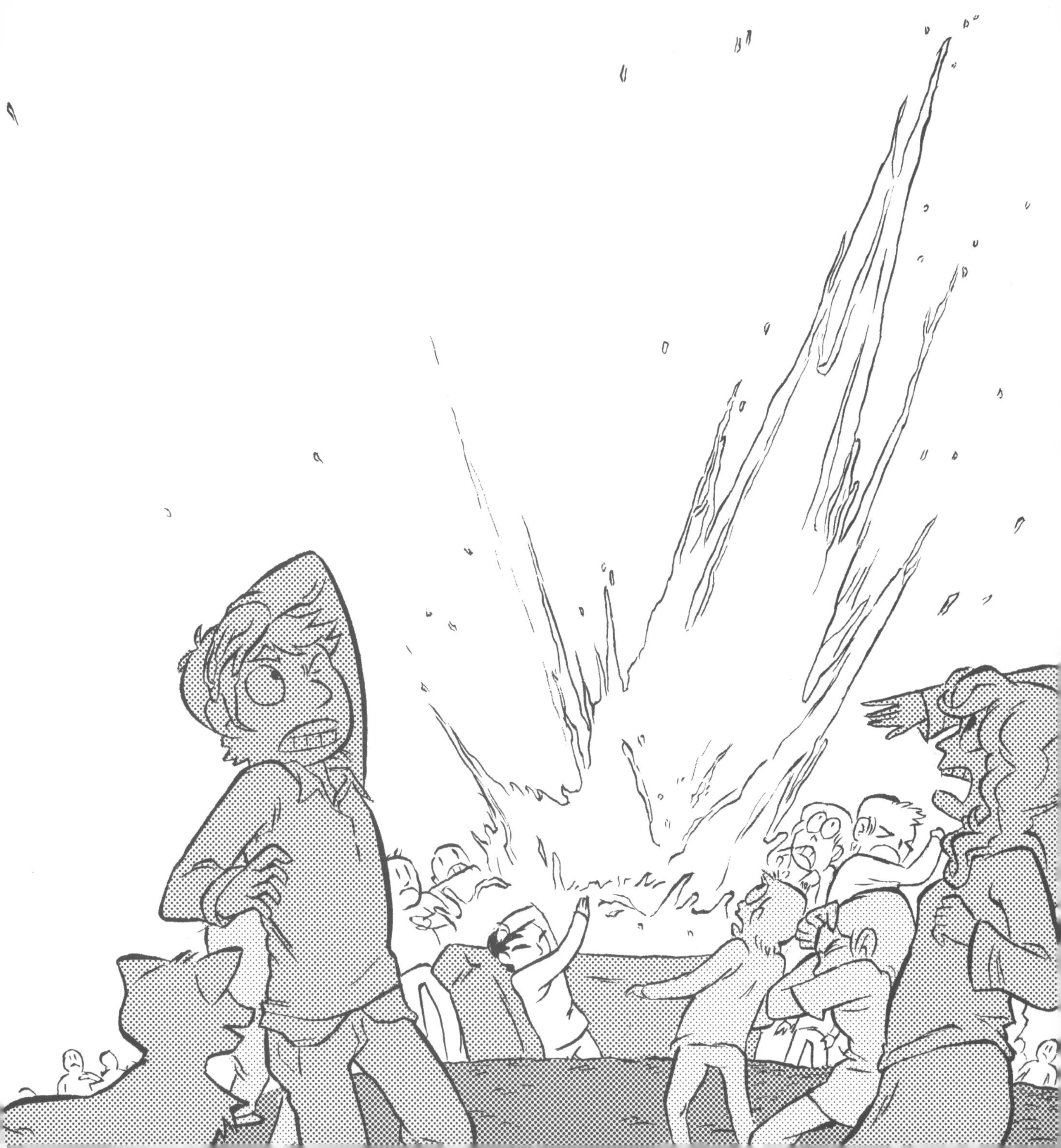

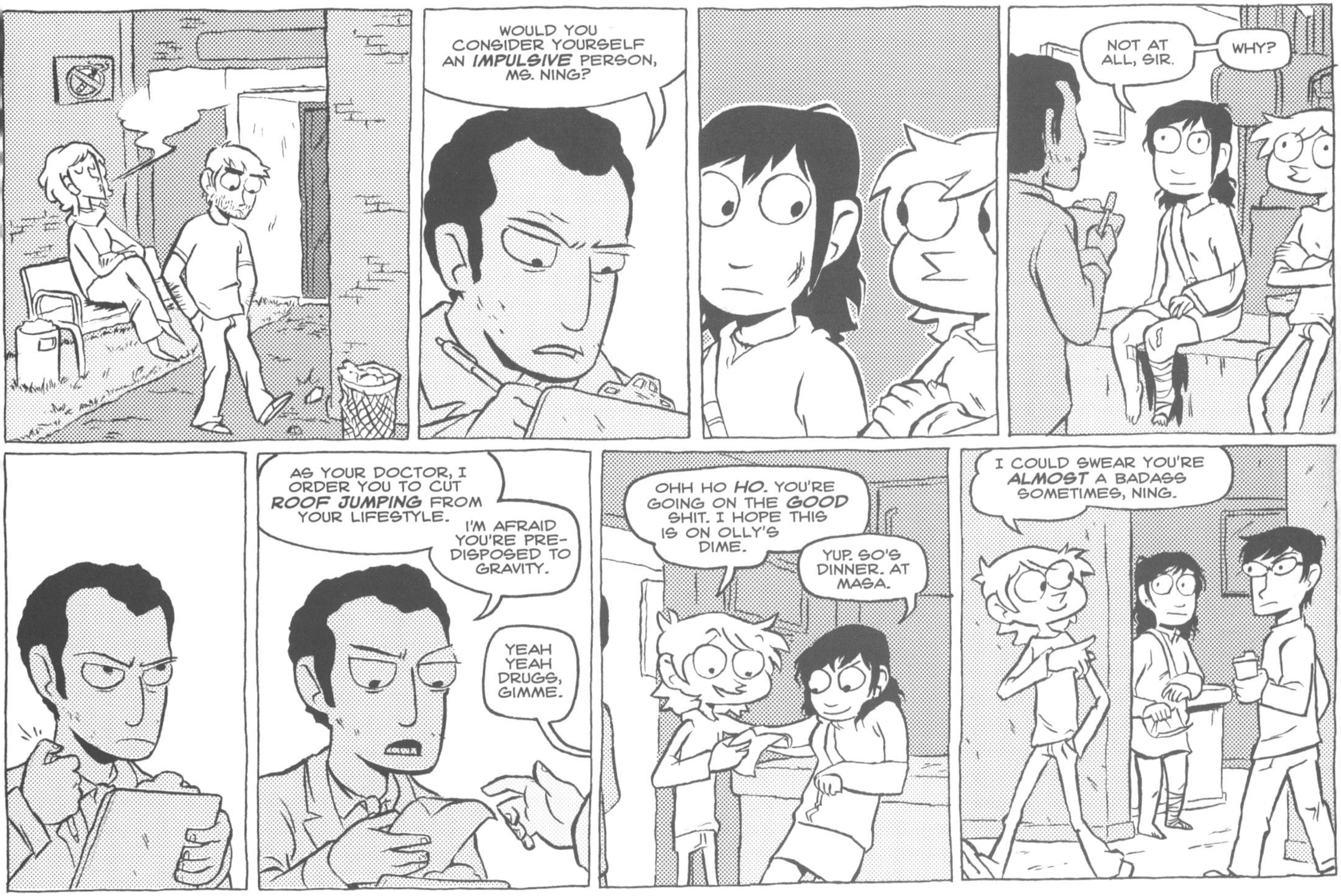
WOULD YOU CONSIDER YOURSELF AN IMPULSIVE PERSON, MS. NING?
NOT AT ALL, SIR.
WHY?
AS YOUR DOCTOR, I ORDER YOU TO CUT ROOF JUMPING FROM YOUR LIFESTYLE.
I'M AFRAID YOU'RE PRE-DISPOSED TO GRAVITY.
YEAH YEAH DRUGS, GIMME.
OHH HO HO. YOU'RE GOING ON THE GOOD SHIT. I HOPE THIS IS ON OLLY'S DIME.
YUP. SO'S DINNER. AT MASA.
I COULD SWEAR YOU'RE ALMOST A BADASS SOMETIMES, NING.

interview

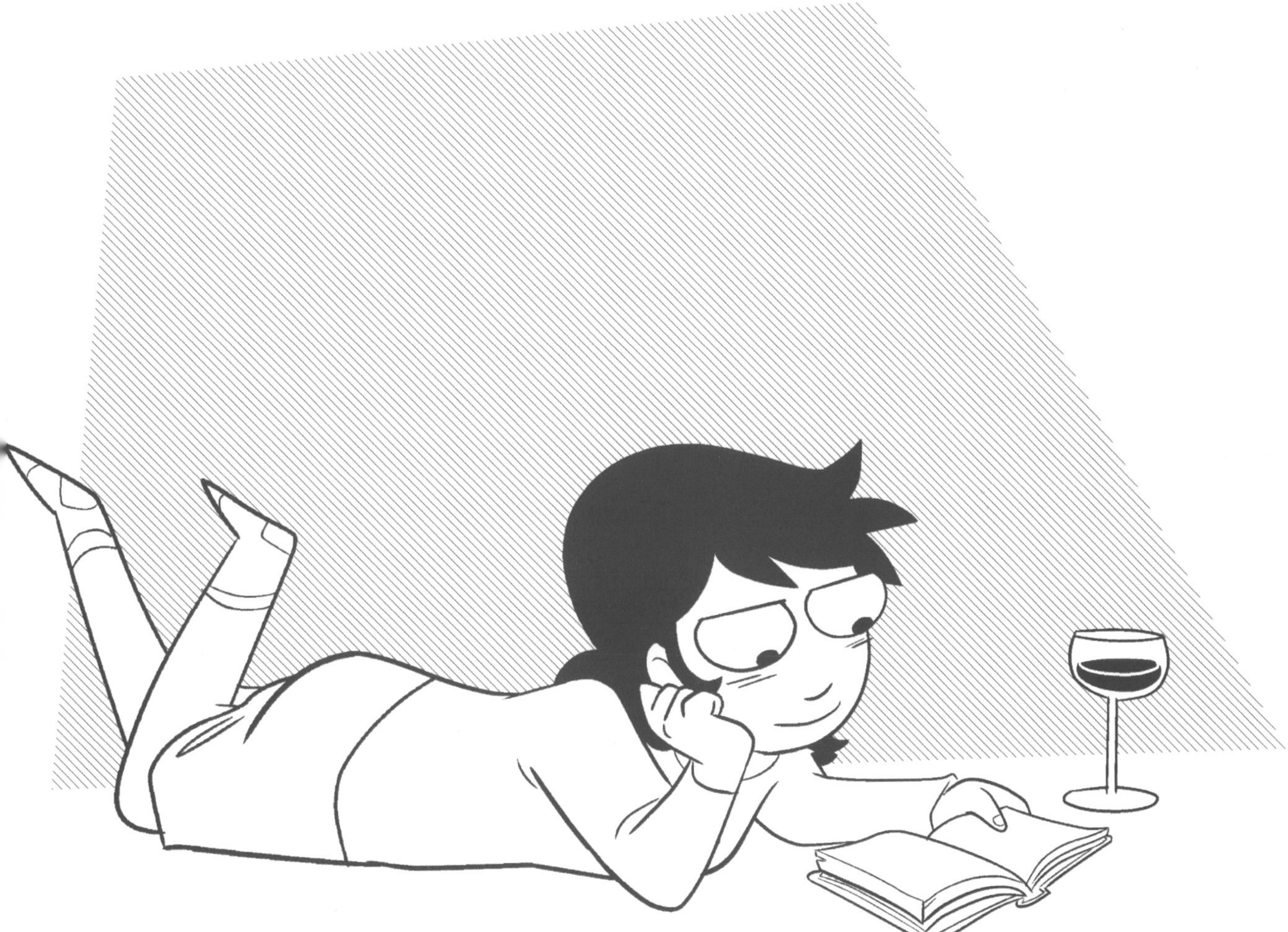

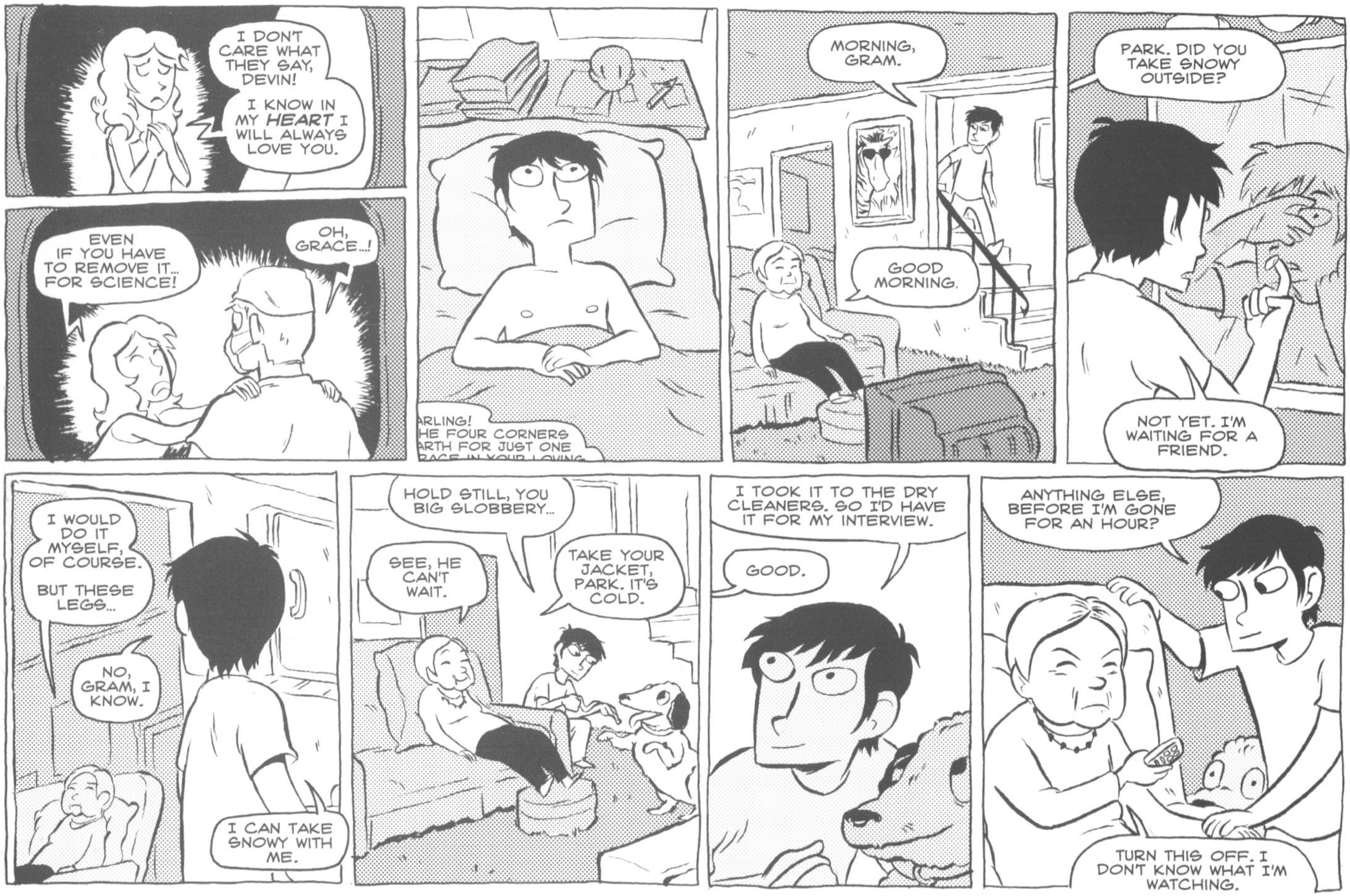
I DON'T CARE WHAT THEY SAY, DEVIN!
I KNOW IN MY HEART I WILL ALWAYS LOVE YOU.
EVEN IF YOU HAVE TO REMOVE IT... FOR SCIENCE!
OH, GRACE...!
ARLING! HE FOUR CORNERS ARTH FOR JUST ONE
MORNING, GRAM.
GOOD MORNING.
PARK. DID YOU TAKE SNOWY OUTSIDE?
NOT YET. I'M WAITING FOR A FRIEND.
I WOULD DO IT MYSELF, OF COURSE.
BUT THESE LEGS...
NO, GRAM, I KNOW.
I CAN TAKE SNOWY WITH ME.
HOLD STILL, YOU BIG SLOBBERY...
SEE, HE CAN'T WAIT.
TAKE YOUR JACKET, PARK. IT'S COLD.
I TOOK IT TO THE DRY CLEANERS. SO I'D HAVE IT FOR MY INTERVIEW.
GOOD.
ANYTHING ELSE, BEFORE I'M GONE FOR AN HOUR?
TURN THIS OFF. I DON'T KNOW WHAT I'M WATCHING.

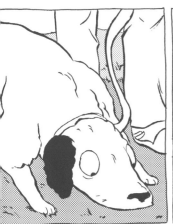

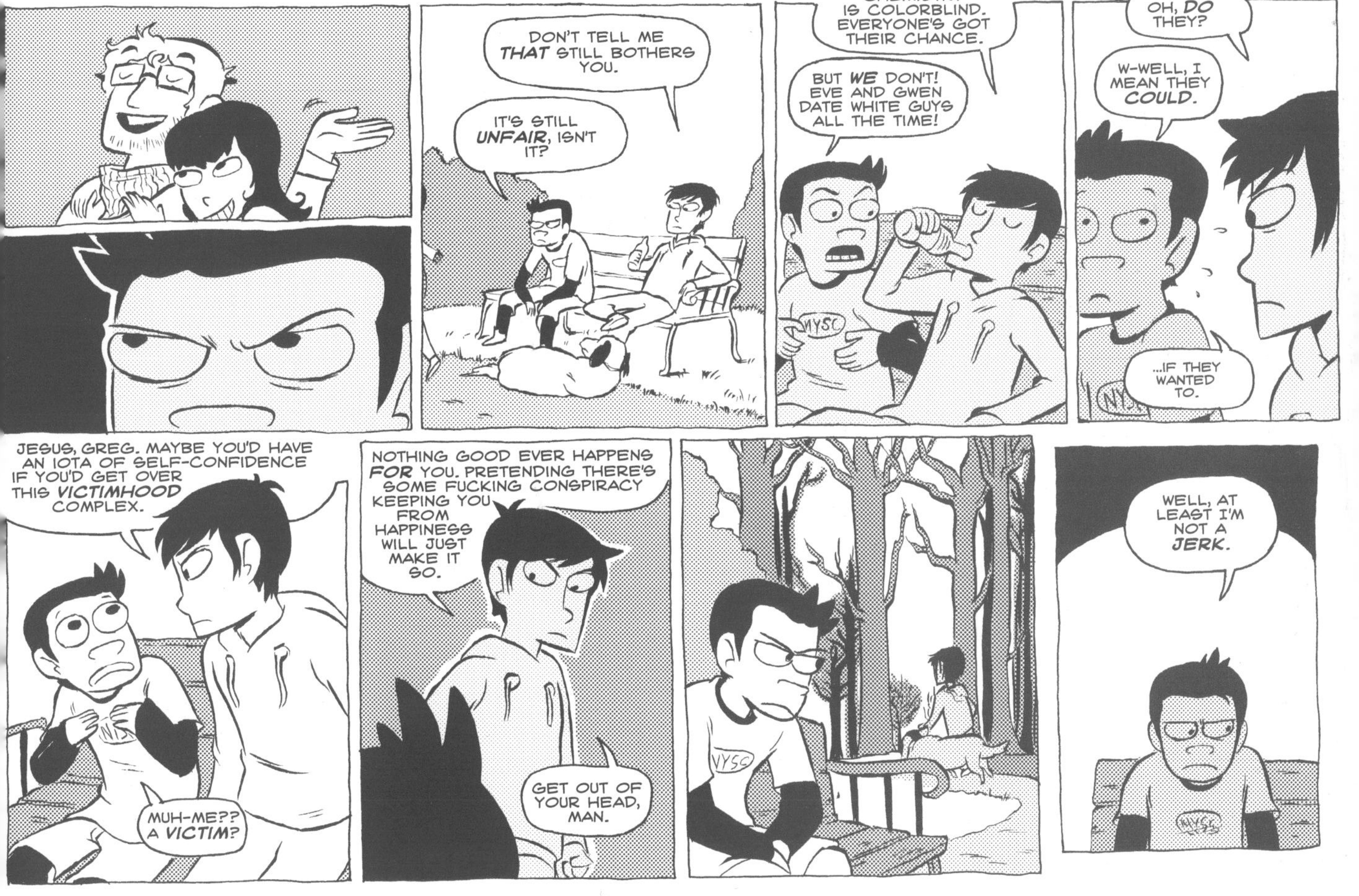
DON'T TELL ME THAT STILL BOTHERS YOU.
IT'S STILL UNFAIR, ISN'T IT?
CHEMISTRY IS COLORBLIND. EVERYONE'S GOT THEIR CHANCE.
BUT WE DON'T! EVE AND GWEN DATE WHITE GUYS ALL THE TIME!
OH, DO THEY?
W-WELL, I MEAN THEY COULD.
...IF THEY WANTED TO.
NYSC
JESUS, GREG. MAYBE YOU'D HAVE AN IOTA OF SELF-CONFIDENCE IF YOU'D GET OVER THIS VICTIMHOOD COMPLEX.
MUH-ME?? A VICTIM?
NOTHING GOOD EVER HAPPENS FOR YOU. PRETENDING THERE'S SOME FUCKING CONSPIRACY KEEPING YOU FROM HAPPINESS WILL JUST MAKE IT SO.
GET OUT OF YOUR HEAD, MAN.
WELL, AT LEAST I'M NOT A JERK.

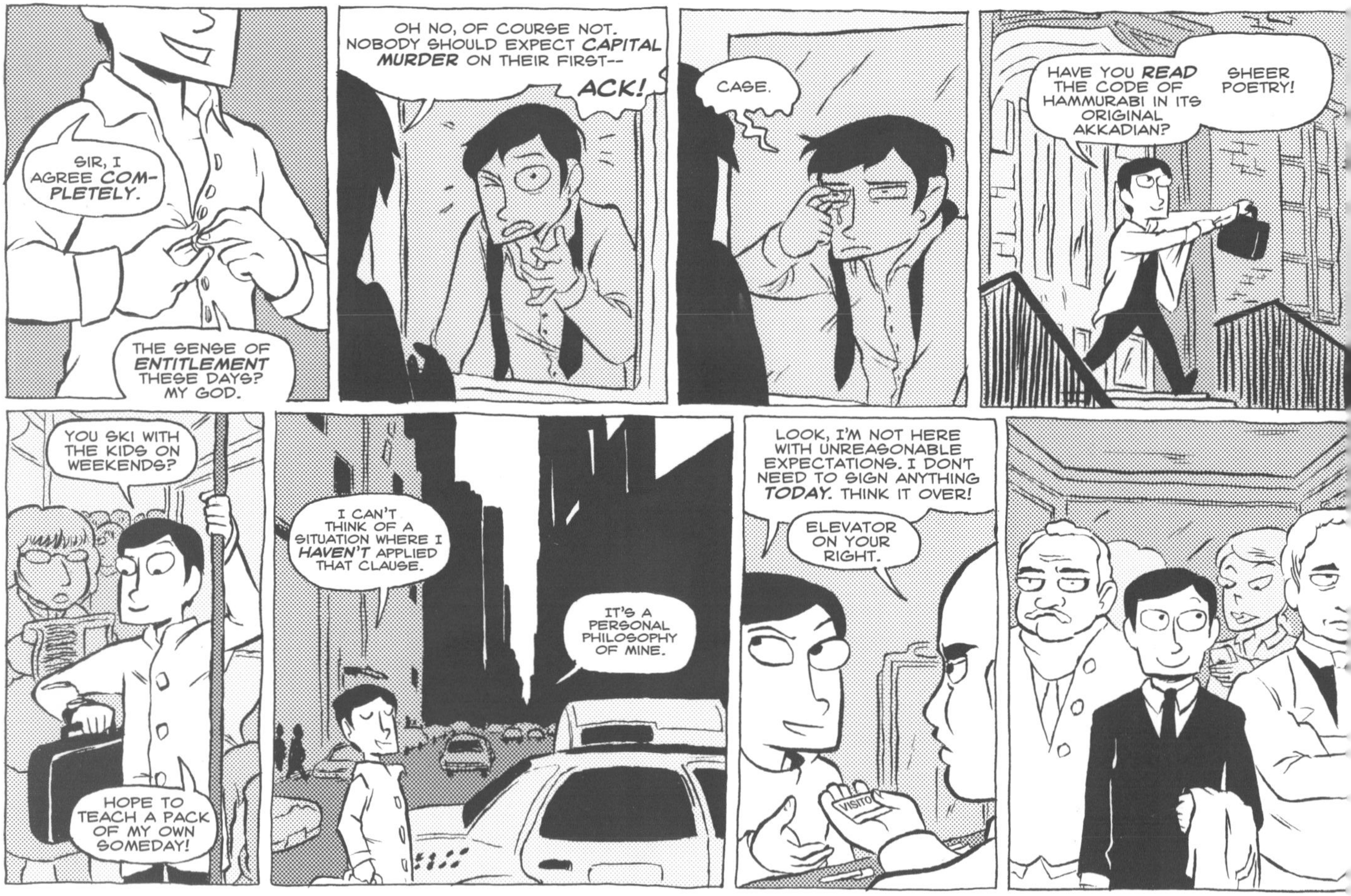
SIR, I AGREE COMPLETELY.
THE SENSE OF ENTITLEMENT THESE DAYS? MY GOD.
OH NO, OF COURSE NOT. NOBODY SHOULD EXPECT CAPITAL MURDER ON THEIR FIRST--
ACK!
CASE.
HAVE YOU READ THE CODE OF HAMMURABI IN ITS ORIGINAL AKKADIAN?
SHEER POETRY!
YOU SKI WITH THE KIDS ON WEEKENDS?
HOPE TO TEACH A PACK OF MY OWN SOMEDAY!
I CAN'T THINK OF A SITUATION WHERE I HAVEN'T APPLIED THAT CLAUSE.
IT'S A PERSONAL PHILOSOPHY OF MINE.
LOOK, I'M NOT HERE WITH UNREASONABLE EXPECTATIONS. I DON'T NEED TO SIGN ANYTHING TODAY. THINK IT OVER!
ELEVATOR ON YOUR RIGHT.
VISITO

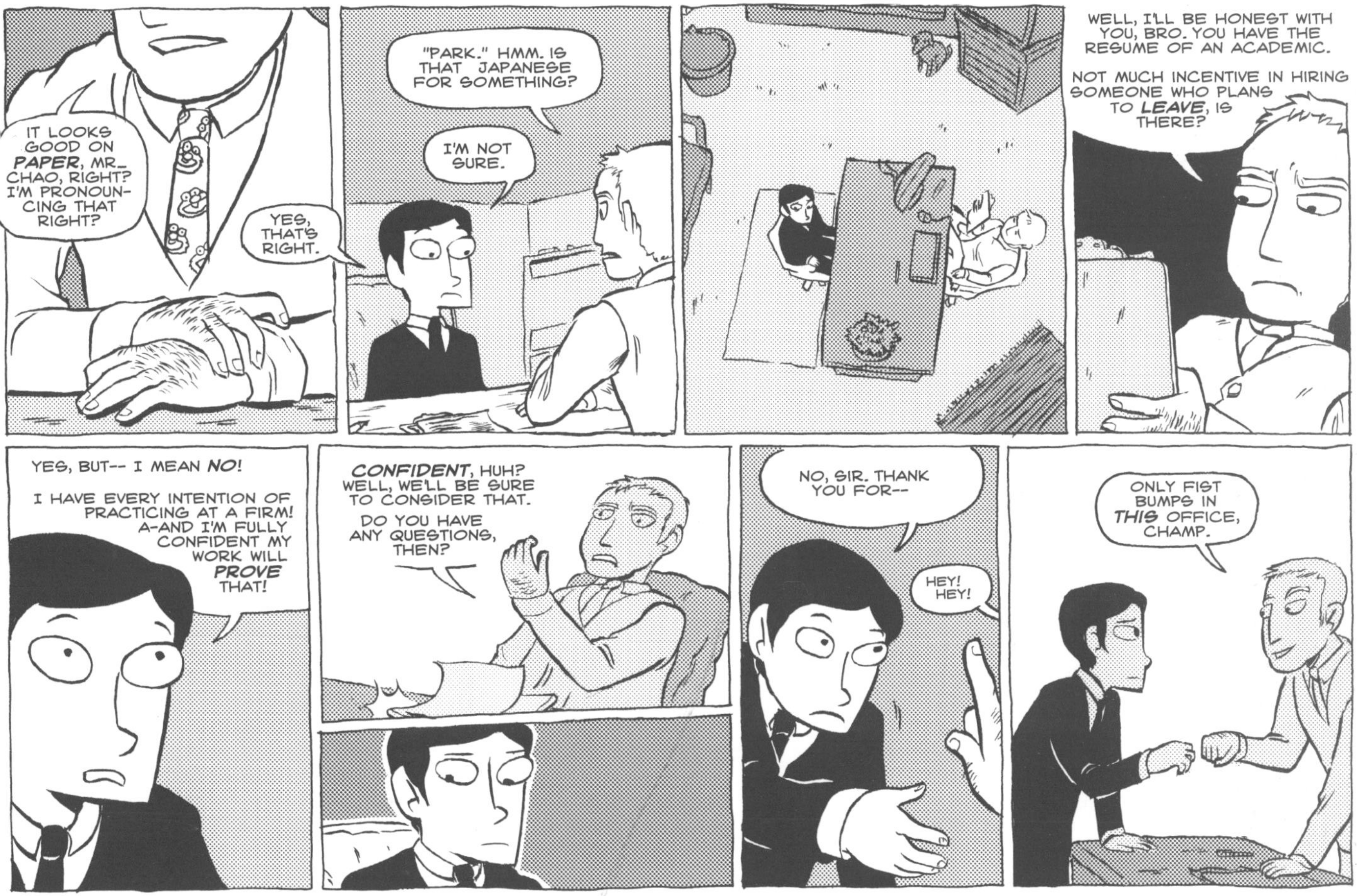
IT LOOKS GOOD ON PAPER, MR. CHAO, RIGHT? I'M PRONOUNCING THAT RIGHT?
YES, THAT'S RIGHT.
"PARK." HMM. IS THAT JAPANESE FOR SOMETHING?
I'M NOT SURE.
WELL, I'LL BE HONEST WITH YOU, BRO. YOU HAVE THE RESUME OF AN ACADEMIC.
NOT MUCH INCENTIVE IN HIRING SOMEONE WHO PLANS TO LEAVE, IS THERE?
YES, BUT-- I MEAN NO!
I HAVE EVERY INTENTION OF PRACTICING AT A FIRM! A-AND I'M FULLY CONFIDENT MY WORK WILL PROVE THAT!
CONFIDENT, HUH? WELL, WE'LL BE SURE TO CONSIDER THAT.
DO YOU HAVE ANY QUESTIONS, THEN?
NO, SIR. THANK YOU FOR--
HEY! HEY!
ONLY FIST BUMPS IN THIS OFFICE, CHAMP.

the end of the world

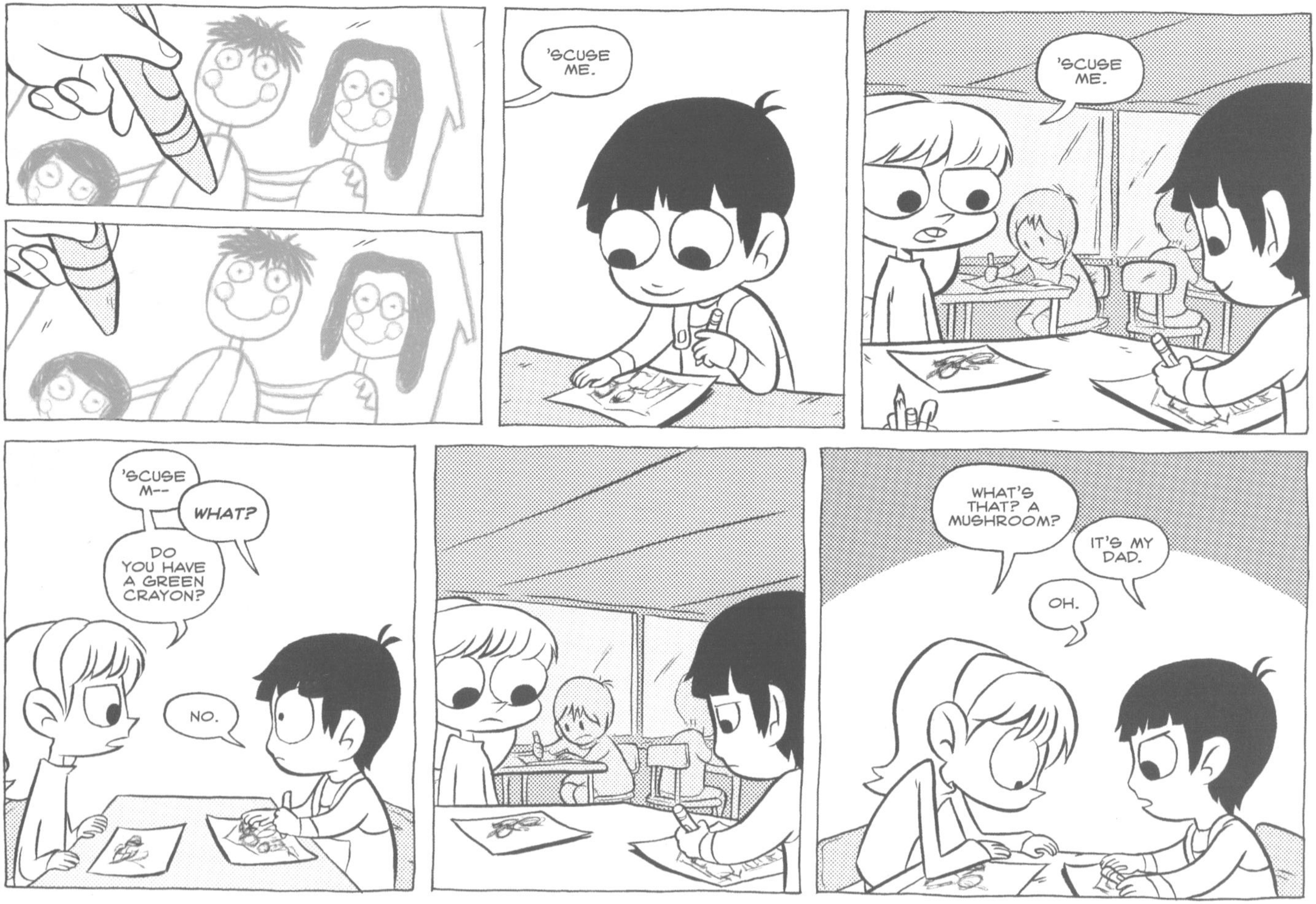
'SCUSE ME.
'SCUSE ME.
'SCUSE M--
WHAT?
DO YOU HAVE A GREEN CRAYON?
NO.
WHAT'S THAT? A MUSHROOM?
IT'S MY DAD.
OH.

WELL, IT LOOKS LIKE A MUSHROOM.

IT'S *NOT!*

DON'T YELL JUST CAUSE YOUR DAD LOOKS LIKE A MUSHROOM.

SHUT UP!!

EVEREST. HANNA. WORK QUIETLY.

AND YOUR MOM LOOKS LIKE A CHICKEN.

WELL *YOUR* PICTURE IS A PIECE OF *POO!* YOU CAN'T EVEN DRAW A CIRCLE!

GIRLS!

IT'S CONCEPTUAL!

DON'T FORGET 2 LEARN!!!

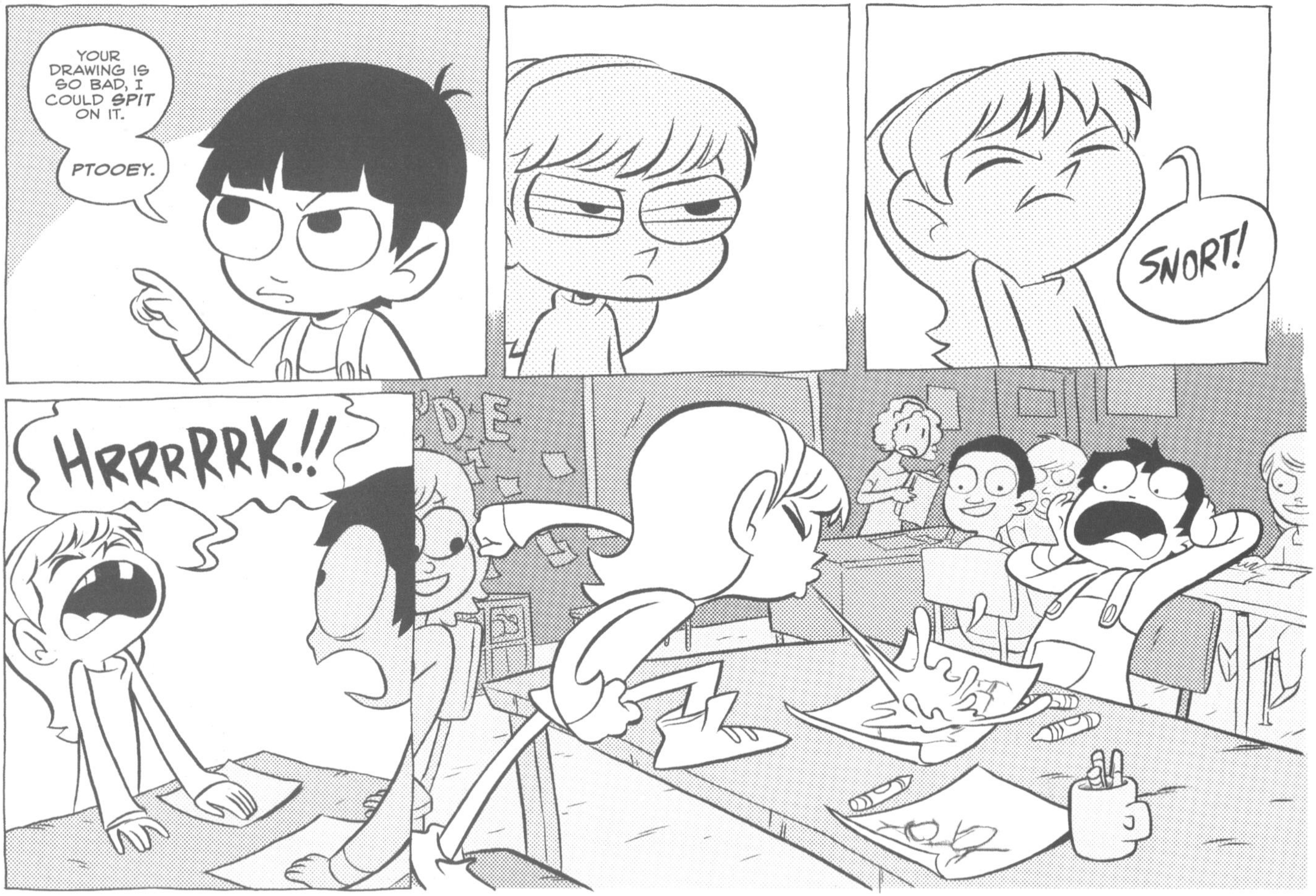
YOUR DRAWING IS SO BAD, I COULD SPIT ON IT.
PTOOEY.
SNORT!
HRRRRRK.!!

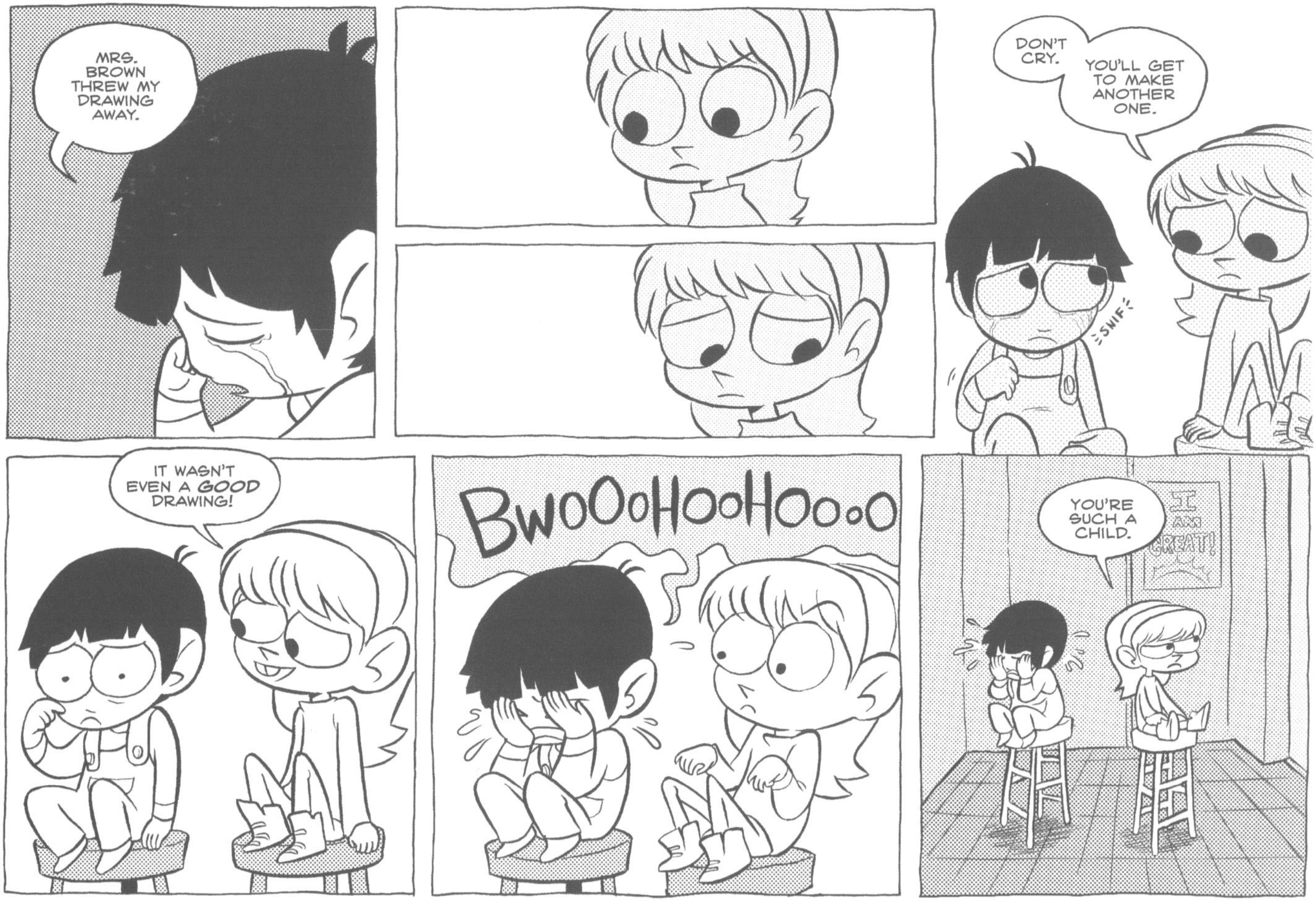
MRS. BROWN THREW MY DRAWING AWAY.
DON'T CRY.
YOU'LL GET TO MAKE ANOTHER ONE.
SWIF
IT WASN'T EVEN A GOOD DRAWING!
BWOOoHOoHOo∘O
YOU'RE SUCH A CHILD.
I AM GREAT!

ABOUT THE AUTHOR

MEREDITH GRAN JUST WON'T LEAVE THAT LIZARD CREATURE
ALONE. SHE WAS BORN IN NEW YORK IN 1984, ATTENDED
THE SCHOOL OF VISUAL ARTS, AND CURRENTLY
RESIDES IN PORTLAND, OREGON, WHERE SHE
DRAWS COMICS ALL DAY LONG.